Advance praise for
AMERICA'S WAR FOR THE GREATER MIDDLE EAST

"[Andrew J.] Bacevich is thought-provoking, profane and fearless. . . . [His] call for Americans to rethink their nation's militarized approach to the Middle East is incisive, urgent and essential."

—*The New York Times Book Review*

"Andrew Bacevich offers the reader an unparalleled historical tour de force in a book that is certain to affect the formation of future U.S. foreign policy and any consequent decisions to employ military force. He presents sobering evidence that for nearly four decades the nation's leaders have demonstrated ineptitude at nearly every turn as they shaped and attempted to implement Middle East policy. Every citizen or military officer aspiring to high office needs not only to read, but also to study and learn from this important book. In more than half a century of public service this is one of the most essential and serious books I have read."

—LIEUTENANT GENERAL PAUL K. VAN RIPER, U.S. Marine Corps (Ret.)

"The book reveals a number of critical truths, exposing deep flaws that have persisted for decades in American strategic thinking. . . . Read Bacevich—not for the solutions he proposes but to be sobered by the challenge. Our long war is just beginning. The least we can do is learn from our mistakes." —*National Review*

"A razor-edged chronicle . . . Bacevich takes his readers through the doleful highlights, from major attacks in Libya and Sudan and Kosovo to full-scale operations like Desert Storm in Iraq, Cyclone in Afghanistan, and the ominously vague open-ended Inherent Resolve. His accounts of these conflicts are filled with immediacy. . . . In these and all other sections of the book, the note of precisely controlled anger is nothing short of mesmerizing." —*The Christian Science Monitor*

"A remarkable book . . . He employs an analytical razor. . . . Andrew J. Bacevich, a military historian and an American patriot who served in the United States military, and who lost his son in the Iraq war, is a no-nonsense no-warmonger. Sober and comprehensive, Bacevich's balance sheet of US wars in the Muslim world is a testimony to Washington's military failures in the Greater Middle East." —Al Jazeera

"*America's War for the Greater Middle East* is Mr. Bacevich's magnum opus. . . . A deft and rhythmic polemic aimed at America's failures in the Middle East from the end of Jimmy Carter's presidency to the present." —Robert Kaplan, *The Wall Street Journal*

"A critical review of American policy and military involvement . . . Those familiar with Bacevich's work will recognize the clarity of expression, the devastating directness and the coruscating wit that characterize the writing of one of the most articulate and incisive living critics of American foreign policy." —*The Washington Post*

"Bacevich's book, in addition to providing a thought-provoking and penetrating account of the evolution of an ultimately futile conflict, is also a passionate plea to a self-absorbed American public to awake from their slumber, reflect seriously on what their leaders are doing in their name in the Islamic world, and force them to bring an end to the project. . . . This is an exceptionally important book" —*The Daily Beast*

"Mr. Bacevich puts our repeated failures—in Afghanistan, Bosnia-Herzegovina, Iraq, Kosovo, Lebanon, Libya, Somalia, Syria and Yemen—down to 'a gap between military muscle and political acuity.' He cites chapter and verse, at length, in each chosen battleground, writing about events and people in a very lively, personal way. He doesn't spare individuals. . . . An irreplaceable backstory to what is more generally known of U.S. and international political developments of the past few decades." —*Pittsburgh Post-Gazette*

"A remarkable book . . . The first book to explain the Middle Eastern wars we have lived with for thirty-six years now as one unbroken conflict with many theaters. And it is scholarship of the best kind—carefully researched and referenced, but written with unscholarly grace—to the put the point bluntly—and perfectly accessible to the intelligent general reader. You put it down thinking, 'I understand a great deal more than I did when I started reading this.'" —*Salon*

"[Bacevich] is more willing than most journalists to question the justice and utility of expanded military operations in the Middle East and to challenge the media-hyped reputations of some of America's favorite generals. . . . This tour de force of a book covers the modern history of American warfare with sharp criticism of political decisions and rigorous analysis of battlefield strategy and tactics. As such, it should be required reading" —*The Intercept*

"[A] monumental new work . . . One of the grim and eerie wonders of his book is the way in which just about every wrongheaded thing Washington did in that region in the fourteen-plus years since 9/11 had its surprising precursor in the two decades of American war there before the World Trade Center towers came down." —*The Huffington Post*

"Americans have been at war in the Greater Middle East for almost forty years. It hasn't gone well—far from it. What have we done to our enemies? What have we done to ourselves? Why? Andrew J. Bacevich lays it all out in this eminently readable account. A scholar, a distinguished combat soldier, and a fearless challenger of conventional wisdom, Bacevich 'goes there' as only an insider can. If you want to know the hard truths behind the parade of jarring headlines from the Middle East, read this book."

—LIEUTENANT GENERAL DANIEL P. BOLGER, U.S. Army (Ret.), author of *Why We Lost: A General's Inside Account of the Iraq and Afghanistan Wars*

"A critical examination of the four-decades-long failed U.S. policy of using military force to solve the ongoing crises in the Middle East. From the disastrous attempt to rescue the U.S. embassy hostages in Tehran in 1980 to the present day, Army veteran and author Bacevich . . . finds few accomplishments in the U.S. military action in the Middle East. . . . An immensely readable, nondidactic study." —*Kirkus Reviews*

"Andrew Bacevich is a warrior academic who understands war and has the great talent to make the complex understandable. And so he has done with our Middle East conflict, which started with Desert One and endures today. A must read for soldiers, politicians and the American citizen." —MAJOR GENERAL PAUL D. EATON, U.S. Army (Ret.)

"Bacevich asks and answers a provocative, inconvenient question: In a multigenerational war in the Middle East, 'Why has the world's mightiest military achieved so little?'"

—GRAHAM ALLISON, director, Belfer Center for Science and International Affairs, and Douglas Dillon Professor of Government at Harvard's John F. Kennedy School of Government

"In one arresting book after another, Bacevich has relentlessly laid bare the failings of American foreign policy since the Cold War. This one is his sad crowning achievement: the story of our long and growing military entanglement in the region of the most tragic, bitter, and intractable of conflicts."

—RICHARD K. BETTS, director, Saltzman Institute of War and Peace Studies, Columbia University

"In this fascinating work, one of America's most provocative thinkers confronts our greatest geopolitical conundrum: the Middle East. No other book shows so clearly how U.S. interventions there have blended into a single long war. This is not just invaluable history, but also a cry of protest against policies that have devastated the Middle East while undermining America's own national security."

—STEPHEN KINZER, senior fellow at the Watson Institute for International and Public Affairs at Brown University

"Andrew Bacevich has done a great service by providing a much-needed continuum in a foreign policy area that remains frustratingly random for too many Americans. He is one of a very few in academia with the credibility to outline dispassionately the shortcomings of responsible civilian and military leaders, on the facts and without histrionics or bitterness. His military background and training as a historian have enabled him to lay out not only the evolution of policy but also the details of the military endeavors themselves."

—JIM WEBB, former U.S. senator

"Andrew Bacevich's thoughtful, persuasive critique of America's crusade for the Greater Middle East should be compulsory reading for anyone charged with making policy for the region. We cannot afford to repeat the past misjudgments on the area, for as Bacevich wisely argues, the stakes are nothing less than the future well-being of the United States."

—ROBERT DALLEK, presidential historian

"*America's War for the Greater Middle East* by Andrew Bacevich lays out in excruciating detail the disasters orchestrated over decades by the architects of the American empire in the Middle East. Blunder after blunder, fed by hubris along with cultural, historical, linguistic and religious illiteracy, has shattered cohesion within the Middle East. The wars we have waged have given birth to a frightening nihilistic violence embodied in radical jihadism. They have engendered an inchoate rage among the dispossessed and left in their wake a series of failed and disintegrating states. These wars have, as Bacevich writes, laid bare the folly of attempting to use military force as a form of political, economic and social control. Bacevich is one of our finest chroniclers of the decline of empire. *America's War for the Greater Middle East* is an essential addition to his remarkable body of work."

—CHRIS HEDGES, former Middle East bureau chief for *The New York Times* and author of *Wages of Rebellion: The Moral Imperative of Revolt*

By Andrew J. Bacevich

AMERICA'S WAR FOR
THE GREATER MIDDLE EAST

America's War
for the Greater
Middle East

A Military History

Andrew J. Bacevich

Random House | New York

2017 Random House Trade Paperback Edition

Copyright © 2016 by Andrew J. Bacevich

All rights reserved.

Published in the United States by Random House,
an imprint and division of Penguin Random House LLC, New York.

RANDOM HOUSE and the HOUSE colophon are registered trademarks
of Penguin Random House LLC.

Originally published in hardcover
in the United States by Random House,
an imprint and division of Penguin Random House LLC, in 2016.

Maps by David Lindroth

LIBRARY OF CONGRESS CATALOGING-IN-PUBLICATION DATA
Names: Bacevich, Andrew J., author.
Title: America's war for the greater Middle East : a military history /
Andrew J. Bacevich.
Description: New York : Random House, [2016] | Includes
bibliographical references and index.
Identifiers: LCCN 2015038868 | ISBN 9780553393958 |
ISBN 9780553393941 (ebook)
Subjects: LCSH: United States—Foreign relations—Middle East. |
Middle East—Foreign relations—United States. | United States—
History, Military—20th century. | United States—History, Military—
21st century.
Classification: LCC DS63.2.U5 B3214 2016 | DDC 956.05/4—dc23
LC record available at lccn.loc.gov/2015038868

Printed in the United States of America on acid-free paper

randomhousebooks.com

2 4 6 8 9 7 5 3

Book design by Virginia Norey

To Nancy

The Lord's anger burned against Israel
and he made them wander in the wilderness forty years.

NUMBERS 32:13

CONTENTS

PART III

MAIN CARD

A NOTE TO READERS

Of Balzac, Henry James wrote, "The way to judge him is to try to walk all round him," undertaking a preliminary survey to reveal "how remarkably far we have to go."[1] The history that follows, an account of U.S. military efforts to determine the fate and future of the Greater Middle East, is itself a preliminary walk around, or through, a comparably large subject. If nothing else, *America's War for the Greater Middle East* seeks to reveal how remarkably far we have to go to understand what those efforts have produced and what they have cost.

Questions raised by this undertaking will preoccupy—and perhaps confound—scholars for decades to come. I have limited myself to four of the most fundamental, the answers to which lay the basis for further inquiry. First, what motivated the United States to act as it has? Second, what have the civilians responsible for formulating policy and soldiers charged with implementing it sought to accomplish? Third, regardless of their intentions, what actually ensued? And fourth, with what consequences? In short, the book links aims to actions to outcomes.

As an American who cares deeply about the fate of his country, I should state plainly my own assessment of this ongoing war, now well into its fourth decade. We have not won it. We are not winning it. Simply trying harder is unlikely to produce a different outcome. Some may consider this history premature. Yet only by remembering and confronting what we have largely chosen to disregard will Americans be able to choose a different course.

Andrew J. Bacevich
Walpole, Massachusetts
December 2015

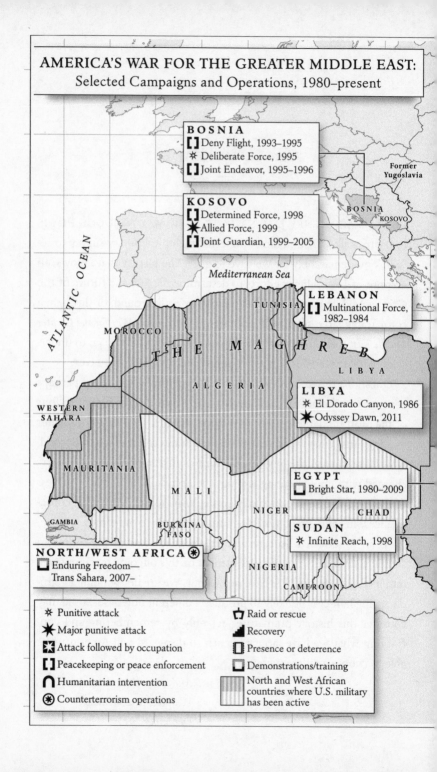

AMERICA'S WAR FOR THE GREATER MIDDLE EAST:
Selected Campaigns and Operations, 1980–present

BOSNIA
[ ] Deny Flight, 1993–1995
✳ Deliberate Force, 1995
[ ] Joint Endeavor, 1995–1996

Former Yugoslavia

KOSOVO
[ ] Determined Force, 1998
✴ Allied Force, 1999
[ ] Joint Guardian, 1999–2005

BOSNIA
KOSOVO

Atlantic Ocean

Mediterranean Sea

LEBANON
[ ] Multinational Force, 1982–1984

TUNISIA

MOROCCO

THE MAGHREB

LIBYA

ALGERIA

LIBYA
✳ El Dorado Canyon, 1986
✴ Odyssey Dawn, 2011

WESTERN SAHARA

MAURITANIA

MALI

EGYPT
□ Bright Star, 1980–2009

NIGER   CHAD

GAMBIA

BURKINA FASO

SUDAN
✳ Infinite Reach, 1998

NORTH/WEST AFRICA ✸
□ Enduring Freedom—
Trans Sahara, 2007–

NIGERIA

CAMEROON

✳ Punitive attack
✴ Major punitive attack
✴✴ Attack followed by occupation
[ ] Peacekeeping or peace enforcement
∩ Humanitarian intervention
✸ Counterterrorism operations

⛊ Raid or rescue
◣ Recovery
◫ Presence or deterrence
□ Demonstrations/training
▨ North and West African countries where U.S. military has been active

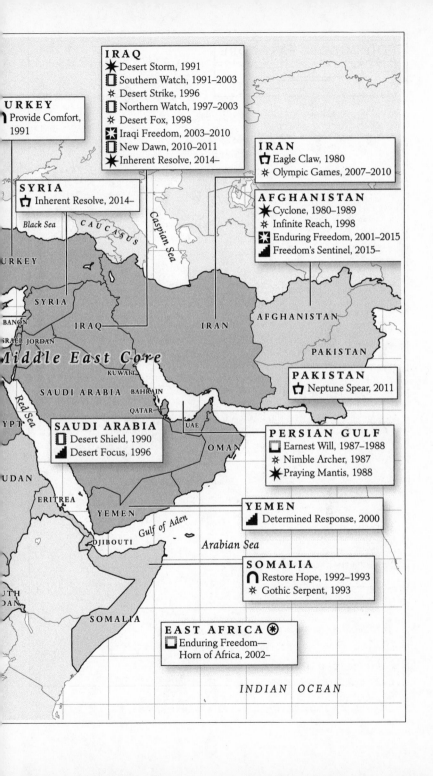

TURKEY
- Provide Comfort, 1991

IRAQ
- Desert Storm, 1991
- Southern Watch, 1991–2003
- Desert Strike, 1996
- Northern Watch, 1997–2003
- Desert Fox, 1998
- Iraqi Freedom, 2003–2010
- New Dawn, 2010–2011
- Inherent Resolve, 2014–

SYRIA
- Inherent Resolve, 2014–

IRAN
- Eagle Claw, 1980
- Olympic Games, 2007–2010

AFGHANISTAN
- Cyclone, 1980–1989
- Infinite Reach, 1998
- Enduring Freedom, 2001–2015
- Freedom's Sentinel, 2015–

PAKISTAN
- Neptune Spear, 2011

SAUDI ARABIA
- Desert Shield, 1990
- Desert Focus, 1996

PERSIAN GULF
- Earnest Will, 1987–1988
- Nimble Archer, 1987
- Praying Mantis, 1988

YEMEN
- Determined Response, 2000

SOMALIA
- Restore Hope, 1992–1993
- Gothic Serpent, 1993

EAST AFRICA
- Enduring Freedom—Horn of Africa, 2002–

Black Sea
CAUCASUS
Caspian Sea
TURKEY
SYRIA
LEBANON
ISRAEL JORDAN
IRAQ
IRAN
AFGHANISTAN
PAKISTAN
Middle East Core
KUWAIT
SAUDI ARABIA
BAHRAIN
QATAR
UAE
OMAN
Red Sea
EGYPT
SUDAN
ERITREA
YEMEN
Gulf of Aden
DJIBOUTI
Arabian Sea
SOUTH SUDAN
SOMALIA
INDIAN OCEAN

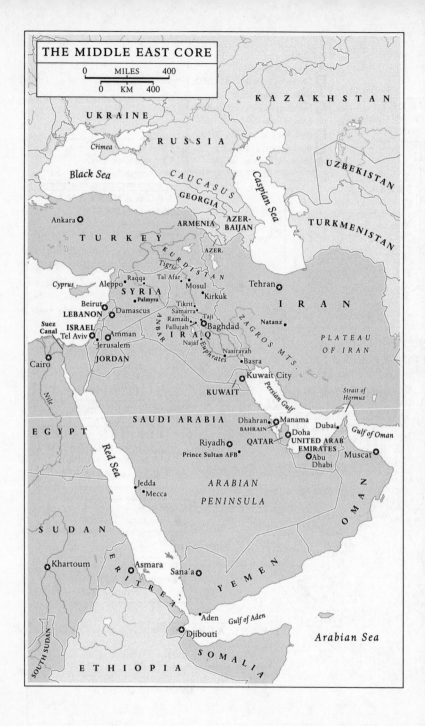

THE MIDDLE EAST CORE

0	MILES	400
0	KM	400

KAZAKHSTAN

UKRAINE

RUSSIA

Crimea

Black Sea

CAUCASUS

GEORGIA

Caspian Sea

UZBEKISTAN

ARMENIA

AZER-
BAIJAN

TURKMENISTAN

Ankara ✪

TURKEY

KURDISTAN

AZER.

Tigris

Cyprus

Aleppo
Raqqa
Tal Afar
Mosul
Kirkuk

Tehran ✪

IRAN

SYRIA
Palmyra

Beirut

Damascus

LEBANON

ANBAR

Tikrit
Samarra
Ramadi Taji
Fallujah Baghdad
IRAQ

ZAGROS MTS.

Natanz

PLATEAU
OF IRAN

Suez
Canal

Tel Aviv

Amman

Jerusalem

ISRAEL

JORDAN

Najaf

Euphrates

Nasirayah

Basra

Cairo

KUWAIT

Kuwait City

Persian Gulf

Strait of
Hormuz

EGYPT

Nile

SAUDI ARABIA

Dhahran Manama

BAHRAIN

Dubai

Gulf of Oman

Red Sea

Riyadh

Prince Sultan AFB

QATAR

Doha UNITED ARAB
EMIRATES

Abu
Dhabi

Muscat

Jedda
Mecca

ARABIAN

PENINSULA

SUDAN

ERITREA

Asmara

Sana'a ✪

OMAN

Khartoum ✪

YEMEN

Aden Gulf of Aden

Arabian Sea

SOUTH SUDAN

Djibouti ✪

SOMALIA

ETHIOPIA

THE FORMER YUGOSLAVIA

	MILES	
0		200
0	KM	200

Danube

Vienna

AUSTRIA

Budapest

HUNGARY

Danube

SLOVENIA

Ljubljana

Zagreb

ROMANIA

CROATIA

KRAJINA

SLAVONIA

Banja Luka

**BOSNIA-
HERZEGOVINA**

DALMATIA

Sarajevo

Belgrade

Srebrenica

Danube

SERBIA

BULGARIA

ADRIATIC SEA

**MONTE-
NEGRO**

Dubrovnik

Podgorica

Battle of
Kosovo

Pristina

KOSOVO

Skopje

ITALY

ALBANIA

**FORMER YUGOSLAV
REPUBLIC OF
MACEDONIA**

GREECE

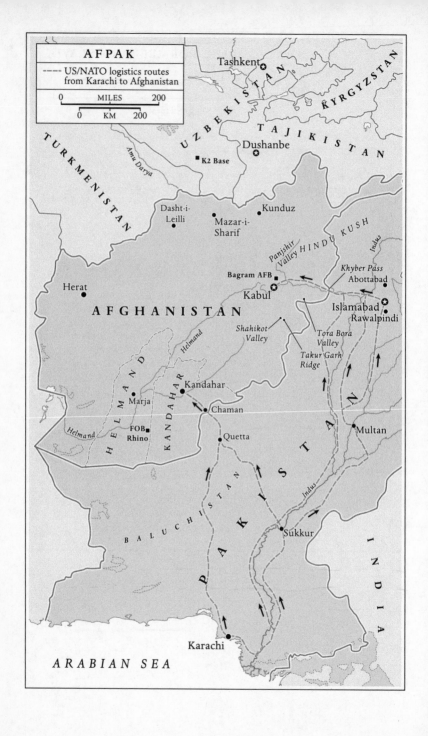

AFPAK

- - - - - US/NATO logistics routes
from Karachi to Afghanistan

0   MILES   200

0   KM   200

Tashkent

UZBEKISTAN

KYRGYZSTAN

TAJIKISTAN

Dushanbe

TURKMENISTAN

Amu Darya

K2 Base

Dasht-i-
Leilli

Mazar-i-
Sharif

Kunduz

Panjshir
Valley   HINDU KUSH

Indus

Khyber Pass

Abottabad

Bagram AFB

Herat

AFGHANISTAN

Kabul

Islamabad

Rawalpindi

Shahikot
Valley

Tora Bora
Valley

Takur Garh
Ridge

HELMAND

Helmand

KANDAHAR

Kandahar

Marja

Chaman

FOB
Rhino

Quetta

Multan

Helmand

PAKISTAN

BALUCHISTAN

Indus

Sukkur

INDIA

Karachi

ARABIAN SEA

PROLOGUE

—

AMERICA'S WAR FOR THE GREATER MIDDLE EAST BEGAN WITH failure in the desert. In no way did this failure compare to the disasters that once befell U.S. forces at Kasserine Pass during World War II or the Chosin Reservoir in Korea. On those earlier battlefields, many hundreds of Americans lost their lives. During Operation Eagle Claw, which began and ended on the night of April 24–25, 1980, U.S. fatalities numbered in the single digits. Even before U.S. troops closed with the enemy, Eagle Claw unraveled—the equivalent of a football team succumbing to defeat even before taking the field.

For those who devised, ordered, and participated in this mission, the resulting humiliation was almost unbearable. Yet humiliation makes for a poor teacher. The lessons that the United States would take from this failure turned out to be the wrong ones. The underlying premise—that the problems facing the United States in the Greater Middle East would yield to a military solution—not only escaped notice but became more deeply entrenched.

Eagle Claw combined modesty of purpose with audacity of design. As America's War for the Greater Middle East evolved over the next several decades, a succession of presidents described U.S. objectives in expansive terms. Through its use of superior military power, they promised, the United States was going to liberate and uplift. U.S. forces would restore peace and spread democracy. They would succor the afflicted and protect the innocent. They would promote the rule of law and advance the cause of human rights.

Yet participants in the abbreviated campaign that initiated the War for the Greater Middle East set out to do none of these things. They sought merely to rescue.

The previous November, a group of young Iranian radicals, fueled by revolutionary fervor, had seized the U.S. embassy in Tehran and taken American diplomats and other officials captive. Efforts to negotiate the hostages' release had proven futile. Now, having apparently exhausted all other alternatives, a frustrated President Jimmy Carter ordered America's warriors to give it a try.

The plan developed by U.S. military officers and ultimately approved by the president himself was nothing if not complex. It allowed little room for chance or error.[1]

Eagle Claw was to begin with a rendezvous in the dead of night, six air force C-130 transports flying out of Masirah Island near Oman linking up with eight heavy-lift helicopters from the carrier USS *Nimitz* sailing nearby. The place chosen for the rendezvous, dubbed Desert One by the Pentagon, was an uninhabited spot in the Iranian outback, as flat as it was remote.

The C-130s carried fuel and a contingent of elite commandos and army rangers. At Desert One, after taking on both, the helicopters would transport the commandos to a staging area near Tehran. A rescue plan as daring as the 1942 Doolittle Raid and several times more intricate would then unfold.

Whether that plan could possibly have succeeded is a moot point. It never got past phase one. Bad luck intervened, its impact magnified by human foibles and frailties.

Desert One turned out to be insufficiently remote and not especially accommodating. As the aircraft began arriving at the site, so too did unwelcome Iranian company. First came a fuel truck, probably involved in smuggling, which U.S. troops hastily engaged and destroyed, although the driver escaped. Then came a bus loaded with civilians. These the Americans detained. The security essential to success was being breached. Meanwhile, as aircraft landed but kept their engines running they stirred up a powdery dust that dangerously compromised visibility.

Worse still were the equipment breakdowns. Although eight helicopters had launched from the *Nimitz,* a cracked rotor blade forced one to land en route. A second experienced navigation problems and turned back. At Desert One, hydraulic failure rendered a third inoperable. The mission required a minimum of six flyable helicopters. With only five remaining, there was no way to proceed other than by seat-of-the-pants changes to the carefully calibrated plan. This the swaggering, irascible commander of the commando task force balked at doing. Instead, with Washington concurring, he scrubbed the mission. As quietly and as quickly as possible, all parties would go back to where they came from. No harm, no foul—so far at least.

Then disaster struck. Prior to departing Desert One, all remaining operable aircraft needed to take on fuel. During the refueling operation, in the dark and dust, the rotor of a hovering helicopter clipped a stationary C-130. The chopper slammed into the cockpit of the cargo plane, and both aircraft burst into flame. Those able to evacuate the burning aircraft did so. But in the ensuing chaos, America's War for the Greater Middle East claimed its first casualties. Eight Americans were killed, with several others badly injured. The survivors climbed aboard the remaining C-130s and hastily departed the scene, abandoning helicopters, documents, classified gear, and the remains of their comrades.

On the morning of April 25, a somber President Carter appeared on national television to inform his countrymen of the rescue attempt and its ignominious conclusion. While attributing Eagle Claw's disappointing outcome to "equipment failure," Carter forthrightly shouldered responsibility for the mission's collapse. "It was my decision to attempt the rescue operation," he told the nation. "It was my decision to cancel it. . . . The responsibility is fully my own."[2]

As a damage control device, the buck-stops-here position that Carter staked out may have been politically expedient. Yet while making a show of accepting responsibility, the president was deflecting attention from questions of far larger importance. Here was obfuscation dressed up as accountability.

Granted, as commander in chief, Carter had signed off on the hostage rescue attempt. Yet when it came to planning and execution, the president had played no direct role. Virtually without exception, the myriad errors in design and execution that doomed the parlous mission fell under the purview of the armed forces. Military professionals had presided over a military failure.[3]

The president's own errors were of a higher order and occurred in the realm of basic policy. To be fair, his predecessors going back to World War II had done him no favors. Across the Greater Middle East, a vast swath of territory stretching from North and West Africa to Central and South Asia, they had forged ill-advised relationships and made foolhardy commitments while misconstruing actual U.S. interests— even while treating the region as a strategic afterthought.[4]

During Jimmy Carter's watch, this ramshackle structure had begun to collapse. First came the Iranian Revolution, then hard on its heels the Soviet invasion of Afghanistan. In response, prompted largely by domestic concerns, this least bellicose of recent U.S. presidents formally added to the list of places for which the United States would fight the oil-rich regions forming the core of the Islamic world. However unwittingly, Carter thereby inaugurated America's War for the Greater Middle East, compounding rather than reversing the errors he had inherited. With no end in sight and little prospect of achieving success, that war continues to the present day.

As the action that initiated that war, Operation Eagle Claw proved an apt harbinger. Here was a portent of things to come: campaigns launched with high hopes but inexplicably going awry. In retrospect, we might see the events at Desert One as a warning from the gods or from God: Do not delude yourself. Do not indulge in fantasies of American arms somehow resolving the contradictions besetting U.S. policy in the Greater Middle East.

At the time, Americans were blind to any such warnings. Or perhaps out of laziness or irresponsibility, they chose not to heed them. We've lived with the consequences ever since.

PART I

PRELIMINARIES

1

WAR OF CHOICE

FROM THE OUTSET, AMERICA'S WAR FOR THE GREATER MIDDLE East was a war to preserve the American way of life, rooted in a specific understanding of freedom and requiring an abundance of cheap energy. In that sense, just as the American Revolution was about independence and the Civil War was about slavery, oil has always defined the raison d'être of the War for the Greater Middle East. Over time, other considerations intruded and complicated the war's conduct, but oil as a prerequisite of freedom was from day one an abiding consideration.

As a young man I required no instruction in that relationship, whose sweetness I had tasted at first hand. In June 1969, a newly commissioned shavetail fresh out of West Point, I was home on leave courting the girl who was to become my wife. She lived on Chicago's South Side. My mother lived in northwest Indiana.

Every evening I drove my brand-new Mustang Mach I—candy-apple red with black piping—into Chicago to see my beloved and then in the early morning hours returned home. Before each trip, I stopped at a service station to top off. Ten gallons at 29.9 cents per gallon usually sufficed. The three bucks weren't trivial—a second lieutenant's pay came to $343 per month before taxes (more importantly, before the monthly car payment)—but the expense took a backseat to romance. I do not recall wondering where the gas came from—Texas? California?—nor about how much more there was. Like most Americans, I took it for granted that the supply was inexhaustible. All I knew for sure was that with four years of West Point behind me and Vietnam just ahead, life behind the wheel of a pony car in the summer of 1969 was pretty good.

It is easy to disparage this version of freedom, as postwar social critics from C. Wright Mills and David Riesman to William Whyte and Vance Packard had already done and others would do. For the ostensibly alienated and apathetic citizens of postwar America, trapped in a soul-deadening "new universe of management and manipulation," as Mills put it, freedom had become little more than "synthetic excitement."[1]

Maybe so. Yet whatever the merit of that critique, it never made much of a dent in the average American's aspirations. The American way of life may have been shallow and materialistic, its foundation a bland conformity. But even for people of modest means, the exercise of American-style freedom did not lack for pleasures and satisfactions.

As with the smell of a new car, those pleasures tended to be transitory. But an unspoken premise underlying that way of life was that there was more still to come, Americans preferring to measure freedom quantitatively. More implied bigger and better. Yet few of those driving (or coveting) the latest made-in-Detroit gas-guzzler appreciated just how precarious such expectations might be.

As I sped off to Chicago each evening, with radio and AC blasting, the gasoline in my tank was increasingly likely to come from somewhere other than a stateside oilfield. In 1969, imports already accounted for 20 percent of the 15 million barrels that Americans consumed daily. The very next year U.S. domestic oil production peaked at nearly 12 million barrels per day, thereafter beginning a decline that continued through the remainder of the century and appeared irreversible. The proportion of oil coming from abroad increased accordingly. Within a decade, imports of foreign oil had reached 8 million barrels per day.[2]

By 1973, even I was obliged to take notice. That fall, in retaliation for the U.S. supporting Israel in the October War, Arabs suspended oil exports to the United States and the West. The impact of the embargo was immediate and severe. The resulting oil shortage all but paralyzed the U.S. economy and produced widespread alarm among Americans suddenly deprived of the mobility that they now considered their birthright. Oil had become a weapon, wielded by foreigners intent on harming Americans. Here, it seemed, coming out of nowhere, was a direct existential threat to the United States.

With the crisis inducing another eyeball-to-eyeball confrontation between the United States and the Soviet Union, Secretary of State Henry Kissinger announced that U.S. forces were on alert, pending their possible deployment to the Middle East. At the time, I was a captain, stationed at Fort Bliss, Texas, alongside El Paso and just across from Mexico. The regiment in which I served had war plans to deploy to West Germany to participate in NATO's defense of Western Europe. If required, we probably could have occupied Juarez. But we had no plans to fight in the Persian Gulf, whether to thwart a threatened Soviet intervention there or to seize Arab oil fields.[3] The very notion seemed preposterous. At the time it was. Not for long, however.

Fortunately, no such deployment occurred, the immediate emergency passed, and oil imports from the Persian Gulf eventually resumed. Yet the availability and price of gasoline had now become and thereafter remained a matter of national concern. Even as Americans were learning to live with nuclear weapons—the prospect of a nuclear exchange with the Soviet Union now appearing more theoretical than real—they were also learning that they could not live without oil. Ever so subtly, the hierarchy of national security priorities was beginning to shift.

As an immediate response to the crisis, the Nixon administration hastily cobbled together a plan that promised, in the president's words, "to insure that by the end of this decade, Americans will not have to rely on any source of energy beyond our own." Project Independence, Nixon called it. The immediate emphasis was on conservation. Details of what the government intended beyond urging Americans to save were vague, Nixon simply vowing that "we will once again have plentiful supplies of energy," with the energy crisis "resolved not only for our time but for all time."[4]

This did not occur, of course, but Nixon's vision persisted. The nation's political agenda now incorporated the goal of energy independence as one of those "must-do" items that somehow never get done, like simplifying the tax code or reducing cost overruns on Pentagon weapons programs.

The idea persisted because it had broad popular appeal. Yet in some quarters, the larger policy implications of pursuing energy independence did not sit well. The very effort implied retrenchment or giving in. This was not the way the world was supposed to work in the latter half of the twentieth century. Rather than the United States accommodating others—in this case, the newly empowered Organization of the Petroleum Exporting Countries (OPEC), with its largely Arab membership—others were expected to accommodate the United States.

As an outgrowth of this dissatisfaction, the notion that American military muscle might provide a suitable corrective began to insinuate itself into the policy debate. Writing in the January 1975 issue of *Commentary*, for example, the noted political scientist Robert W. Tucker bemoaned Washington's apparent unwillingness even to consider the possibility of armed intervention in the Arab world. "If the present situation goes on unaltered," Tucker warned, "a disaster resembling the 1930s" beckoned. To "insist that before using force one must exhaust all other remedies, when the exhaustion of all other remedies is little more than the functional equivalent of accepting chaos" was therefore the height of folly. When it came to something as important as oil, the putative lessons of the recently concluded Vietnam War simply didn't apply. Tucker wanted policymakers to get serious about the possibility of using force in the Middle East.[5]

Two months later, in *Harper's,* the pseudonymous but apparently well-connected Miles Ignotus went a step further, outlining in detail a plan to seize Saudi oil fields outright. Four divisions plus an air force contingent, with Israel generously pitching in to help, would do the trick, he argued. Echoing Tucker, Ignotus categorized spineless American leaders alongside "the craven men of Munich." Allowing OPEC to dictate the price of oil amounted to "a futile policy of appeasement" and would inevitably lead to further disasters.[6] In contrast, forceful military action promised an easy and nearly risk-free solution.

Ignotus was actually Edward Luttwak, well-known national security gadfly and Pentagon consultant. In positing a U.S. attack on Saudi oil fields, he was pursuing an agenda that looked far beyond mere energy security. Luttwak was part of group seeking to "revolutionize warfare." Saudi Arabia, he and his like-minded colleagues believed, offered the prospect of demonstrating the feasibility of using "fast, light forces to penetrate the enemy's vital centers," thereby providing a shortcut to victory. This was an early version of what twenty years later became known as the Revolution in Military Affairs. The invasion of Iraq in 2003, Luttwak would later claim, signified "the accomplishment of that revolution."[7]

Along with a strikingly strident tone, a strong sense of entitlement pervaded both essays. That Americans might submit to "the political blackmail of the kings and dictators of Araby," Ignotus wrote, in order to ensure access to "a product [Arabs] had neither made nor found" represented an affront. Sure, the vast petroleum reserves were located on "their" territory. But for Tucker and Ignotus, that fact qualified as incidental at best. Middle East oil properly belonged to those who had discovered, developed, and actually needed it. By all rights, therefore, it was "ours," a perspective that resonated with many ordinary Americans. All that was required to affirm those rights was the vigorous use of U.S. military power.

Notably absent from this analysis, however, was any appreciation for context. Tucker and Ignotus alike showed no interest in the recent history of the Middle East. They ignored the dubious legacy of previous Western interventionism, especially by Great Britain, until recently the region's imperial overlord. That the United States was willy-nilly supplanting the British as the dominant power in the Arab world and more broadly in the Greater Middle East ought to have given Americans pause. After all, the lessons to be taken from the British experience were almost entirely cautionary ones. That was not a baton that the Americans were grasping but a can of worms.

More astonishingly still, neither Tucker nor Ignotus showed any interest in religion or its political implications. Theirs was a thoroughly secular perspective. Islam, therefore, simply went unmentioned. Once having asserted direct control over Arab oil, Tucker and Ignotus took it for granted that U.S. troops would remain for years to come. Yet they were oblivious to the possibility that a protracted military occupation might encounter unforeseen snags, whether by violating local sensitivities or enmeshing the United States in ancient sectarian or ethnic disputes. In contemplating action, the United States routinely took into account the potential response of powerful adversaries like the Soviet Union. More often than not, it factored in the concerns of valued allies like West Germany or Japan. That a lesser country like Iran or Iraq or Saudi Arabia could obstruct or stymie a superpower was not a proposition that many Americans at this juncture were prepared to entertain. The policy prescriptions offered by Tucker and Ignotus reflected this view—even if the North Vietnamese had only recently exposed it as false.

This first round of proposals to militarize U.S. policy in the Middle East found little favor in the Pentagon. Ever since World War II, apart from the brief intervention in Lebanon that Dwight D. Eisenhower had ordered back in 1958—a virtually bloodless comma inserted between Korea and Vietnam—America's military had by and large steered clear of the region, leaving it in the hands of diplomats and spooks.[8]

Now, in the early 1970s, U.S. forces had their hands full with other concerns. The just-concluded American war in Vietnam had left the armed services, especially the U.S. Army, battered in body and spirit. Recovering from that unhappy ordeal was the order of the day. This meant re-equipping and adjusting to the end of the draft, priorities addressed with the Soviet threat very much in mind. The prospect of intervening in the Persian Gulf figured as exceedingly improbable. The idea of sending U.S. forces elsewhere in the wider Islamic world, to Afghanistan, say, or Somalia, appeared absurd.

So when Secretary of Defense Elliott Richardson released his annual report to Congress in April 1973, he evinced little interest in the Middle

East and only perfunctory concern about energy security. The 126-page document devoted exactly one anodyne paragraph to each.

In the first, Richardson expressed his hope for an end to "the potentially explosive Arab-Israeli conflict." He cited U.S. arms sales and its "limited military presence" as intended "to produce stability" and to encourage negotiations. Yet Richardson also made it clear that the core problem wasn't Washington's to solve: "Peace and stability will be possible only if all the parties involved develop a mutual interest in accommodation and restraint."

In the second paragraph, while noting that the Persian Gulf contained "approximately one-half of the world's proven oil reserves," Richardson emphasized that the United States would look "primarily to the states in the area to maintain peace and stability."[9] Pentagon priorities lay elsewhere.

A year later, in the wake of the October War and with Americans still reeling from the first oil shock, Richardson's successor James R. Schlesinger made it clear that those priorities had not changed. The Pentagon remained fixated on the U.S.-Soviet competition. When the United States evaluated threats to national security, Schlesinger wrote, "We do so primarily with the Soviet Union in mind."

His 237-page report reflected that priority. Apart from a brief reference to the lessons of the most recent Arab-Israeli conflict, which merely "confirmed prior judgments" about war, Schlesinger ignored the Middle East altogether. Under the heading of "planning contingencies," the defense secretary identified Europe, Northeast Asia, and (surprisingly) Southeast Asia as places where U.S. forces could potentially fight. The oil-rich lands touched by the waters of the Persian Gulf didn't make the cut.[10]

The passing of a year brought yet another defense secretary but no real change in perspective. In November 1975 Donald Rumsfeld ascended to the post of Pentagon chief, which he held for only fourteen months, his tenure curtailed when Gerald Ford lost the 1976 presidential election. In January 1977, Rumsfeld's annual report, issued as eight years of Republican rule were coming to an end, claimed credit over the course of more than three hundred pages for vastly improving U.S. military capabilities while simultaneously issuing dire warnings about the ever-increasing Soviet threat. In its competition with the Soviet Union, the United States was getting stronger and stronger while falling further and further behind.

For Rumsfeld too, therefore, the Middle East remained an after-thought. The United States had a "fundamental interest in uninter-rupted access to Middle East oil and gas," he acknowledged. But satisfying that interest was not going to entail the commitment of U.S. forces and was not going to absorb any substantial part of the Penta-gon's budget. The troops and the dollars were needed elsewhere. So Rumsfeld affirmed Washington's preference for outsourcing the prob-lem to "reliable friendly forces (for example Iran, Saudi Arabia, Mo-rocco) capable of contributing to regional order." Arming "friendly, important governments" that were themselves "striving to maintain peace and stability in the region" promised to suffice.[11]

Through the mid-1970s, in other words, Pentagon strategic priorities remained unaffected by developments in and around the Persian Gulf. To hawkish observers like Robert Tucker, growing U.S. energy depen-dence along with the rise of OPEC might signify a "radical shift in power" and therefore require drastic action.[12] Those actually responsi-ble for formulating U.S. national security policy didn't see it that way. They shied away from addressing the implications of any such shift. All that was now about to change as Jimmy Carter became president.

In a world of nation-states, good will and good intentions will not suffice to achieve peace. Simply avoiding war—the minimalist defini-tion of peace—implies a meeting of devious minds. In statecraft, calcu-lation necessarily precedes concurrence.

Jimmy Carter saw himself as a peacemaker. On that score, there is no doubting the sincerity of his aspirations. He meant well—by no means the least among his many admirable qualities. Yet when it came to the exercise of power, Carter was insufficiently devious. He suffered from a want of that instinctive cunning that every successful statesman possesses in great abundance. Carter could be vain, petty, and thin-

skinned—none of these posed a fatal defect. But he lacked guile, a vulnerability that, once discovered, his adversaries at home and abroad did
not hesitate to exploit.

One direct consequence was to trigger a full-scale reordering of U.S.
strategic interests. From a national security perspective, as never before, the Greater Middle East began to matter. From the end of World
War II to 1980, virtually no American soldiers were killed in action
while serving in that region.[13] Within a decade, a great shift occurred.
Since 1990, virtually no American soldiers have been killed in action
anywhere *except* in the Greater Middle East. President Carter neither
intended nor foresaw that transformation—any more than European
statesmen in the summer of 1914 intended or foresaw the horrors they
were unleashing. But he, like they, can hardly be absolved of responsibility for what was to follow.

[handwritten margin note: 1980's shifted Focus to ME]

When Carter moved into the Oval Office in late January 1977, he
inherited a mess. The previous decade and a half, punctuated by assassinations, racial unrest, cultural upheaval, the forced resignation of a
president, and a costly, divisive war, had left Americans in something of
a funk. That the economy was in a shambles didn't help matters. U.S.
power and influence seemed to be waning. The amoral machinations
of Richard Nixon and his chief lieutenant Henry Kissinger—cutting
deals with the Kremlin, toasting Red China's murderous leaders, and
abandoning the South Vietnamese to their fate—mocked the ideals
that America ostensibly represented.

Like every new president, Carter promised to turn things around.
He would be the un-Nixon. On the stump, he had repeatedly assured
Americans, "I'll never lie to you." At a time when Washington seemed
especially thick with liars, cheats, and thieves, this constituted a radical
commitment. Carter took it upon himself to repair the nation's moral
compass. This defined what history had summoned him to do. In foreign policy, that meant aligning actions with words. The United States
would once more stand for freedom. It would promote peace. It would
advance the cause of universal human rights.

Doing these things required first overcoming what Carter called an "inordinate fear of communism" that had for too long found the United States crawling into bed with corrupt, repressive regimes and other unsavory elements. Unreasoned anticommunism had made Americans stupid and distorted U.S. policy. Shedding its self-imposed ideological shackles, Carter believed, would enable the United States to transcend the Cold War and pursue a course "designed to serve mankind." In service to humanity, Carter envisioned a diplomatic agenda that was nothing if not ambitious. It involved alleviating Third World poverty, definitively resolving the Arab-Israeli conflict, and "eliminating nuclear weapons completely from our arsenals of death."[14]

In no way did inaugurating a War for the Greater Middle East figure as part of that agenda. But hardly had the president embarked upon his saving mission than events began getting in the way. The most important of those events was the Iranian Revolution.

In the mid-1970s, Washington assumed that Iran could be counted on to serve as America's steadfast and dependable surrogate in the Persian Gulf.[15] Although eliciting occasional grumbling, the assumption was largely noncontroversial. Yet it was foolish in the extreme, based on expectations that the Shah was politically secure and could be counted on to serve as a reliable proxy. Neither of these, however, turned out to be correct. Carter himself was oblivious to the possibility that the Shah might turn out to be a weak reed.

At a state dinner in Tehran on December 31, 1977, as such occasions require, Carter responded to a toast that the Shah had made in his honor. His effusive remarks, offered with cameras running, were destined for permanent inclusion in the Carter presidency blooper reel. Iran stood as "an island of stability in one of the more troubled areas of the world," Carter declared. "This is a great tribute to you, Your Majesty, and to your leadership and to the respect and the admiration and love which your people give to you."[16]

As events were soon to demonstrate, the president had significantly mischaracterized the relationship between the people of Iran and their monarch. Yet when Carter spoke, he was merely affirming existing U.S.

policy. Washington had a lot riding on the Shah and did not want to see its investment go bad.

That investment dated from 1953, when the CIA helped engineer a coup that returned the young Shah to his throne while overthrowing a democratically elected Iranian government. It continued during the Cold War, with Washington offering the Shah substantial military and economic assistance in return for his strongly anticommunist stance. It culminated in 1969 with the Nixon Doctrine, a Vietnam-induced effort to reduce worldwide U.S. military obligations. Nixon proposed to deputize dependable allies to shoulder responsibility for maintaining regional security, thereby easing the burdens placed on the United States. With proxies recruited to do more, the United States could get by with doing less.

The Persian Gulf seemed the ideal place to put this concept into effect. By selling top-line American weapons to Iran, now flush with cash thanks to booming oil exports, President Richard Nixon was counting on the Shah to ensure stability in the gulf, taking over a role long performed by Great Britain until its 1968 decision to withdraw from "East of Suez." At no time did the promotion of democracy and human rights figure in Washington's Iranian agenda.

On that score at least, the authoritarian Shah certainly concurred. Otherwise, however, his purposes differed somewhat from Washington's. He viewed military modernization as one part of a larger top-down effort to transform Iran into a modern, regionally dominant, but still autocratically governed powerhouse.

Still, if Nixon's aims and the Shah's ambitions did not "dovetail neatly," as one *New York Times* dispatch suggested, they at least intersected.[17] As one immediate consequence, U.S. arms exports to Iran skyrocketed. Between 1950 and 1972, the United States had provided Iran with approximately $1.5 billion of weapons, the costs largely covered by grant aid. By 1973 Tehran had become a paying customer. That year alone, it agreed to *purchase* U.S. arms to the tune of more than $2 billion.[18] Over the next six years, Iran contracted to buy over $19 billion in weapons. Purchases included F-14 fighters, C-130 transport aircraft, and guided missile destroyers, plus helicopters, tanks, and air defense missiles.[19] In 1978, the now-besieged Iranian monarch presented Washington with a shopping list requesting an additional $12 billion in military hardware. The Shah did not get everything he requested—just almost everything. Indeed, after considerable wrangling, the United States even agreed to provide Iran with nuclear reactors, the Shah offering personal—if suspect—assurances that Iran had no intention of acquiring nuclear weapons.[20] This was the precursor to the Iranian nuclear program destined in the twenty-first century to become a source of such controversy and concern.

Skyrocketing arms sales increased the number of Americans living in Iran. By 1978, the U.S. military mission in Tehran, which facilitated arms transfers and coordinated training support for Iranian forces, consisted of 1,122 personnel. In addition, some forty thousand American civilians worked in Iran as employees of U.S.-based defense contractors. The Grumman Corporation kept one thousand engineers and technicians in Iran to maintain Iranian air force F-14s. Northrop provided a similar contingent to support Iran's F-5 squadrons. Bell Helicopter's presence consisted of over 1,500 employees working under the direction of a retired U.S. Army major general.[21] This was not unusual—weapons manufacturers active in Iran and elsewhere in the Persian Gulf offered lucrative opportunities for former military officers.[22] Other high-profile defense firms with a major Iranian presence included General Electric, Hughes, Lockheed, McDonnell-Douglas, Raytheon, Rockwell, and TRW. Although some in Congress expressed concern that the United States—far and away the world's leading weapons exporter—might be fueling a Middle East arms race, most members found little reason to complain about this boon to the American military-industrial complex.[23]

Back in Washington, State and Defense Department officials calculated that the Iranian military's reliance on American expertise and technical assistance translated into leverage. In outsourcing security, the Nixon Doctrine assumed that America's chosen partners could be counted on to act in ways that were consistent with Washington's desires. Should they do otherwise, a threat to suspend U.S. communications, intelligence, and logistics support would bring them to heel.[24] More than likely, Iranian awareness of their dependence would alone suffice.

The Shah himself entertained the opposite view. The Americans sold weapons to Iran, he believed, because Iran was performing a critical security function that the United States was unable or unwilling to perform itself. In the U.S.-Iran relationship, he held the upper hand. Questioned by American reporters at a press conference in 1976, the Shah did not disguise his confidence in that regard. "What will you do if one day Iran will be in danger of collapsing?" he asked rhetorically. "Do you have any choice?" Washington would continue to build up Iranian military power because the only alternatives, the Shah said, were "an all-out nuclear holocaust or other Vietnams."[25]

Enhancing Iranian (and also Saudi) military capacity would obviate the need for direct U.S. military involvement in the region. That was the object of the exercise. On this point senior U.S. officials were explicit. Testifying before a House subcommittee in August 1972, Assistant Secretary of State Joseph J. Sisco stated, "There is no need for the United States to exercise responsibilities for security that the British exercised in the gulf in a different era." Militarily, in other words, the Greater Middle East was a region the United States wished to avoid. "It is not our intention," Sisco emphasized, "to undertake an operational military role in any state in the area."[26]

In fact, however, even as the United States was pouring arms into Iran, the Shah was losing his grip on power. His so-called White Revolution had alienated segments of Iranian society ranging from secularized liberals to religious conservatives. All viewed the Shah as an American lackey. All saw the United States as parasitic, profiting from even while underwriting the regime's corruption. By early 1978, these groups had coalesced into a political force united by a single common aim: a determination to oust the Shah and his henchmen. Beginning barely a week after Carter's New Year's Eve visit to Tehran, protests on an ever-expanding scale rocked major Iranian cities. As opposition mounted, the Shah vacillated between offering concessions and cracking heads, evidence of uncertainty that the protestors read as weakness.

With the Shah's opponents increasingly rallying around an exiled but charismatic and intensely anti-American Shiite cleric known as the Ayatollah Ruhollah Khomeini, Washington dithered. Within the Carter administration, sharp disagreement existed over whether the Shah could be or even should be saved. Mixed signals from the United States further undercut the Shah's dwindling reserves of courage and self-confidence. On January 16, 1979, his position increasingly untenable, he fled into exile. On February 1, Khomeini returned to Iran. With his arrival in Tehran, greeted by millions of ecstatic supporters, the Nixon Doctrine became a dead letter. The U.S. military mission and American arms firms soon thereafter closed up shop.

Within the Pentagon, reassessing U.S. policies in the Greater Middle East became the order of the day. By June 1979, a just-completed study by a then-obscure Defense Department official named Paul Wolfowitz was attracting notice throughout the national security bureaucracy. The United States, Wolfowitz wrote in what became known as the "Limited Contingency Study," had "a vital and growing stake in the Persian Gulf," stemming from "our need for Persian-Gulf oil and because events in the Persian Gulf affect the Arab-Israeli conflict." Wolfowitz adhered to an expansive definition of the Persian Gulf, his paper referring to "the region between Pakistan and Iran in the northeast to the Yemens in the southwest."[27]

Threats to the stability of this region were legion, Wolfowitz citing "ideological rivalries, territorial disputes, the clash between modernizing trends and the forces of tradition, ancient ethnic and religious hatreds, and sheer personal ambition fed by the enormous wealth that is at the disposal of some very weak governments." Even so, two concerns stood out as paramount: first, possible troublemaking by America's rival superpower, the Soviet Union; and second, the ambitions of Ba'athist Iraq, with its pan-Arab, radical nationalist agenda.

The first possibility was arguably the more dangerous; the second

Wolfowitz considered far more probable. "Iraq has become militarily pre-eminent in the Persian Gulf," he asserted. To address "the emerging Iraqi threat" now required the United States to "make manifest our capabilities and commitments to balance Iraqi power."[28] In plain language, Wolfowitz was proposing to throw American military might into that balance, whether in the form of "advisors and counter-insurgency specialists, token combat forces, or a major commitment." Demonstrating a willingness to take on Iraq would enable the United States to maintain the region's precarious stability or at the very least to make other threats more manageable.

Whether Wolfowitz's early preoccupation with Iraq qualifies as prescient or a blatant exercise in fear-mongering may be a matter of taste. While substantially overstating Iraqi military capabilities, Wolfowitz was more right than wrong in his estimate of Iraqi ambitions. No one would mistake Saddam Hussein's Iraq for a status quo power. Yet what matters here is not a personal fixation destined to blossom into an obsession but Wolfowitz's larger argument for making the Persian Gulf a U.S. military priority.

Leading defense intellectuals lent their support to the proposition. In Washington, challenges to entrenched habits seldom go anywhere unless they acquire a critical mass, usually as a result of repetition by the putatively reputable. In this instance, Albert Wohlstetter, Wolfowitz's graduate school mentor and intellectual doppelgänger, weighed in with a series of well-timed op-eds that echoed Wolfowitz's analysis and called for Washington to "prepare for contingencies on the flanks," notably in the Persian Gulf. "For years our eyes have been fixed on a possible massive attack through Germany's Fulda Gap," Wohlstetter pointed out, but now the United States needed to widen its gaze.[29] "Like it or not, the fate of America and its major allies is tied to OPEC," Wohlstetter wrote. Developing the capacity to "cope with violence and instability in regions like the Gulf and the Middle East" had therefore emerged as a strategic imperative.[30]

As we shall see, within a matter of months, such reasoning—however flawed—prevailed. In the interim, however, President Carter himself floated an alternative to militarizing U.S. policy in the Greater Middle East, one that questioned whether America's fate was, in fact, tied to OPEC. Here, in retrospect, was the strategic road not taken.

The Iranian Revolution that overthrew the Shah triggered a second "oil shock." Iranian production fell off sharply. OPEC seized the opportunity to announce a succession of price increases, adversely affecting the already troubled U.S. economy. Although ample supplies of gasoline remained available, Americans panicked. Once again, long lines appeared at gas stations. Jimmy Carter's approval ratings plunged, putting him on par with Richard Nixon on the eve of his resignation. The following year's presidential election now loomed on the political horizon. By the summer of 1979, Carter's prospects for winning a second term did not appear promising.

The moment called for a vigorous demonstration of presidential leadership. The White House duly announced the president's plan to make a major policy speech on energy. But then Carter had second thoughts. Postponing the speech, he sequestered himself at Camp David, in Maryland's Catoctin Mountains. Over the course of ten days, he consulted with Americans of high station and low, hoping to discern what was actually ailing the nation. His conclusion: Oil was not the problem; rather, America's oil addiction signified something far, far more troubling—a people that had lost its moral bearings. Yet within that very addiction lay the prospects of recovery.

When Carter finally came down from the mountain, he shared his findings with the American people. In content if not in delivery, his nationally televised address of July 15, 1979, bears comparison with Abraham Lincoln at his most profound, Woodrow Wilson at his most prophetic, and Franklin Roosevelt at his most farsighted.[31]

Apologetic, confessional, and even self-flagellating, Carter began with a mea culpa and then briskly transitioned from his own shortcomings to the nation's "true problems." The president characterized those problems as "deeper than gasoline lines or energy shortages, deeper even than inflation or recession," that is, deeper than the actual problems Americans had elected him to solve. Surpassing all such concerns was "a fundamental threat to American democracy," which Carter termed "a crisis of confidence." In reality, this crisis stemmed not from an absence of confidence but from a collapse of values. "In a nation that was proud of hard work, strong families, close-knit communities, and our faith in God," the president continued, "too many of us now tend to worship self-indulgence and consumption. Human identity is no longer defined by what one does, but by what one owns. But we've discovered that owning things and consuming things does not satisfy our longing for meaning. We've learned that piling up material goods cannot fill the emptiness of lives which have no confidence or purpose."

Carter warned against expecting government to restore a sense of purpose to empty lives. Officeholders at all levels, he charged, had shown themselves seemingly "incapable of action." Failures of governance had left the country awash with "paralysis and stagnation and drift." Salvation, therefore, lay in the people's hands:

We are at a turning point in our history. There are two paths to choose. One is a path I've warned about tonight, the path that leads to fragmentation and self-interest. Down that road lies a mistaken idea of freedom, the right to grasp for ourselves some advantage over others. That path would be one of constant conflict between narrow interests ending in chaos and immobility. It is a certain route to failure.

All the traditions of our past, all the lessons of our heritage, all the promises of our future point to another path, the path of common purpose and the restoration of American values. That path leads to true freedom for our nation and ourselves.

Then came the punch line: "We can take the first steps down that path as we begin to solve our energy problem."

Energy will be the immediate test of our ability to unite this nation, and it can also be the standard around which we rally. On the battlefield of energy we can win for our nation a new confidence, and we can seize control again of our common destiny.

> *So, the solution of our energy crisis can also help us to conquer the*
> *crisis of the spirit in our country. It can rekindle our sense of unity, our*
> *confidence in the future, and give our nation and all of us individually*
> *a new sense of purpose.*

Ending their addiction to oil would enable Americans to rediscover and to reclaim authentic freedom. At least in the interim, that implied sacrifice and getting by with less.

It was as if, judging the nation to be fat and out of shape, Carter was prescribing a regimen of fresh fruits and vegetables. No more fast food. Instead, daily trips to the gym were the order of the day.

Except that Carter didn't view himself as a lifestyle coach or fitness instructor. He was an agent of the Lord. Hendrik Hertzberg, then a White House speechwriter, subsequently described the "crisis of confidence" speech as "an exercise in national pastorship."[32] Although couching his appeal in nonsectarian language, Carter was calling for a new Great Awakening, which like its predecessors promised to purge and purify and renew. If Americans heeded their pastor, they would cease to worship the Golden Calf and return to the true religion.

Now, the America that Carter so nostalgically described never existed. But this myth of a people defined by faith, community, family, and hard work has always exerted considerable appeal and does so even today. So not all that surprisingly, the "crisis of confidence" speech evoked a largely positive immediate response.[33] Overnight polling showed that many Americans liked what they'd heard. In his diary later that evening, a pleased Carter wrote that Americans "were getting the message."[34] But enthusiasm soon began to fade.

The *idea* of giving up pretzels and potato chips in favor of broccoli and asparagus is one thing. Actually following through tends to be something else again. And so it was with Carter's call to restore American virtue through self-denial and sacrifice. The imagined satisfaction of reconstituting the United States as a sort of Amish community stretching from sea to shining sea had a limited shelf life. As Americans contemplated all that they would be obliged to give up, the prospect became less attractive.

The carping started within days. "Mr. President, we're not out of confidence," *Wall Street Journal* columnist Roger Ricklefs complained, "we're out of gas."[35] Ronald Reagan, positioning himself for another run at the presidency, quickly chimed in, chiding Carter for "shifting the blame to the people."[36] Irving Kristol, godfather of the emergent neoconservative movement, embellished Reagan's theme, lambasting Carter for "scapegoating the American people." According to Kristol, self-interest, not self-sacrifice, formed the "bedrock of our heterogeneous and pluralistic society."[37] *Me* and *mine* took precedence over *us* and *ours*. The columnist George Will concurred. The United States was a "big, muscular nation" consisting of many factions with competing interests. "The politician's task," Will continued, is "to broker them, not to sermonize against them."[38]

But it was Eugene Kennedy, former Catholic priest and a professor of psychology at Chicago's Loyola University, who weighed in with the most devastating appraisal. Kennedy's essay "Carter Agonistes," appearing in *The New York Times Magazine,* insisted that the only one afflicted with a "crisis of confidence" was the president himself. Kennedy likened Carter to "the parson, who having studied hard and said his prayers, is scandalized to discover sin in the congregation." By "blaming others for the house of woe he inhabited," the president had "infected Americans with his own gloom." But Americans weren't buying, Kennedy divined. Carter was making "a moral issue out of a basic economic problem," one that they expected him to address. They were sick of "the played-out thesis" that as Americans they were "all guilty for everything," including "every kind of self-gorging sin, original or not, in the archives of wickedness." They didn't want some "distressed angel, passing judgment" on their failings. They wanted a president who would fix things. When it came to oil, that meant more, not less.

Fair or not, accurate or not, Kennedy's savage critique stuck. In the end, Carter's "crisis of confidence" speech—subsequently enshrined as his "malaise" speech—flopped and became emblematic of his perceived inability to lead.[39]

What had occurred was democracy through informal plebiscite. Carter had taken his case directly to the people, asking them to decide. Reaction to the speech served as a de facto referendum on the correlation between oil and the American way of life. The outcome of that referendum was unambiguous: In the eyes of most Americans, the two remained inextricably linked.

Carter had invited his fellow citizens to think otherwise. Yet doing so would necessarily entail redefining freedom. This Americans refused to do. With that refusal, the Persian Gulf and its environs acquired massively heightened significance. Ensuring regional stability and access to its resources became for the United States a categorical imperative.

So a speech intended to chart an alternative course had the opposite effect. It foreclosed alternatives, reducing Carter's room for maneuver. In short order, two dramatic developments abroad—each of which Washington radically misunderstood—completed his entrapment. By default, the logic of Wolfowitz's Limited Contingency Study prevailed. To ensure American access to oil, Carter, would-be peacemaker and advocate of spiritual renewal, took his country to war.

Even as he was searching for a mechanism to disentangle the United States from the Greater Middle East, President Carter was simultaneously approving an initiative destined to embroil the United States more deeply in that region. On July 3, 1979, the very day the president departed for the ten-day retreat at Camp David that culminated with his "malaise" speech, he signed off on a memo committing the United States to assist Afghan insurgents who were warring against the Soviet-supported regime in Kabul. The amount involved was small—initially, only five hundred thousand dollars. Material provided would be primarily "non-lethal"—medical supplies and communications equipment, for example—with a few crates of obsolete British rifles thrown in for good measure.[40] But the scope of the initial investment belied the magnitude of the mayhem the United States was seeking to promote.

Three months earlier, a mid-level Pentagon official attending a White

House meeting called to consider Afghanistan's growing political insta-bility suggested that the situation there offered the possibility of "suck-ing the Soviets into a Vietnamese quagmire."[41] The idea caught on. Considered in a Cold War context, the prospect of inducing conflict on the scale of Vietnam exerted great appeal. That such a conflict might, however inadvertently, yield adverse consequences for the United States (never mind the Afghan people) simply did not occur.

From our distant vantage point we may wonder how a war compa-rable to Vietnam could prove beneficial for anyone. At the time, such considerations had no purchase. In the dichotomous logic of the Cold War, whatever discomfited the Soviets automatically qualified as desir-able and was presumed to be strategically advantageous.

The Shah's overthrow, wrote Zbigniew Brzezinski, President Cart-er's national security adviser, had shattered the "protected tier shielding the crucial oil-rich region of the Persian Gulf from possible Soviet in-trusion." What better way to prevent the Kremlin from capitalizing on this opportunity than to throw in with the "Afghan freedom fighters" opposed to Soviet meddling in Afghan affairs.[42] Fomenting trouble in Afghanistan would dissuade the Soviets from meddling in the Persian Gulf. Such was the expectation, at least.

So the explicit purpose of aiding Afghan insurgents, Brzezinski sub-sequently acknowledged, was to "induce a Soviet military interven-tion," which the United States intended to exploit for its own purposes.[43]

Meanwhile, the toppling of the Shah and the triumph of the Islamic Revolution had not yet persuaded the United States to give up on Iran. Throughout most of 1979, the Carter administration looked for ways to reach an accommodation with Tehran's new rulers. A formal alli-ance might be out of the question, but oil and a shared antagonism toward the Soviet Union seemed to offer the prospect of fruitful col-laboration. Avoiding outright antipathy still seemed a possibility.

So contacts between senior U.S. and Iranian officials continued. On November 1, for example, Brzezinski met privately in Algiers with Iran's prime minister, offering assurances that "we are prepared for any relationship you want. . . . We have a basic community of interests but we do not know what you want us to do." Brzezinski made it clear that virtually nothing was off limits. "The American government," he emphasized, "is prepared to expand security, economic, political, and intelligence relationships at your pace."[44] The invitation was nothing if not open-ended: Let's make a deal.

Within a handful of days, however, Iran offered the United States ample reason to withdraw that invitation. On October 22, Carter had allowed the Shah to enter the United States for medical treatment. On November 4, outraged Iranian students, interpreting a humane gesture to a dying man as a portent of counterrevolutionary action, expressed their anger by overrunning the U.S. embassy in Tehran and taking members of the embassy staff prisoner.

From the students' perspective, having once mounted a coup on the Shah's behalf, the United States seemed likely to do so once again. Any expression of sympathy for the despised former monarch amounted to a provocation, the equivalent of offering sanctuary to a known war criminal. From Washington's perspective, the embassy seizure was more than an outrageous violation of diplomatic protocol. With the Iranian government assumed to have instigated the attack, it was tantamount to an act of war.

In fact, each party misconstrued the other's actual motives. The Carter administration had no intention of replaying the events of 1953 by mounting another coup on the Shah's behalf. Further, the Ayatollah Khomeini had not ordered the students to seize the U.S. embassy and appears to have had no prior knowledge of their plan. The students had acted of their own volition, with the evidence suggesting that they intended only to "make a statement" rather than to touch off a protracted crisis.[45] Yet Khomeini himself soon endorsed what the students had done. In doing so, he transformed what might have been a difficult, but not insoluble, diplomatic problem into a standoff charged with a symbolism that raised the stakes appreciably.

So began an excruciating ordeal that would continue for 444 days, ending only on the very date that Jimmy Carter left office. From the outset, safely freeing the hostages remained Carter's first priority, a po-

sition that necessarily limited U.S. policy options. Yet efforts to negotiate, reinforced by diplomatic condemnation and economic sanctions,
failed to produce a resolution. As the crisis dragged on, the sense of
mortifying helplessness deepened, affirming already existing impressions that President Carter was weak and inept. That Pakistani students
burned the U.S. embassy in Islamabad to the ground on November 21
while Libyan protestors set fire to the shuttered U.S. embassy in Tripoli
on December 4 served to reinforce this impression.[46]

So too did obsessive media coverage. "The great American television
networks placed their full facilities at the service of the captors," wrote
George Ball, formerly a high official at the State Department, "faith-
fully recording their grunts and gestures, when they assembled each
day at the appointed hour to shout abusive slogans and shake their fists
with contrived ferocity at the camera lens."[47] To report on each day's
developments (or lack thereof), ABC television unveiled a nightly news-
cast called *America Held Hostage,* the very title driving home the magnitude of Carter's failure.

Ball likened the result to "a long-running soap opera." Others took
the matter more seriously. Even the First Lady lost patience, Rosalynn
Carter, by her own account, chiding her husband to "Do something!
Do something!"[48] As an incumbent earnestly hoping for a second term,
the president was looking ever more vulnerable.

Yet behind the scenes, the premises of U.S. policy in the Greater Middle East were already undergoing revision. The argument embedded in
Wolfowitz's Limited Contingency Study—that the United States should
rely on soldiers rather than diplomats to secure its interests in the
region—was gaining traction. Laying the groundwork for direct military action was emerging as an urgent priority.

Just one month into the hostage crisis, at a National Security Council
meeting on December 4, 1979, President Carter directed the Pentagon
to look for bases and other facilities in and around the Persian Gulf.[49]
Ten days later a delegation of State and Defense Department officials
departed Washington for Egypt, Saudi Arabia, Oman, Somalia, and
Kenya. Their mission was to begin conversations about obtaining

U.S. military access to those countries, sweetening those requests with promises of increased U.S. military aid.[50] Much work remained to be done to make large-scale U.S. armed intervention possible. But that work had now begun.

At this juncture, the Carter administration's hopes of covertly instigating further unrest in Afghanistan seemingly bore fruit. On Christmas Eve 1979, Soviet forces entered that country and murdered the president, a communist who had outlived his usefulness. After installing in power a puppet more to the Kremlin's liking, the occupiers set out to pacify a country that time and again had demonstrated intense hostility to foreign occupation. Soviet leaders intervened in Afghanistan because they feared that instability in that country could endanger the larger Soviet empire.[51] In the end, intervention brought about the very outcome they were attempting to avert.

In Washington, a different interpretation of Soviet intentions, one more in keeping with Cold War imperatives, prevailed. Senior U.S. officials and other influential observers attributed Russian behavior not to fear but to ambition. This was certainly Brzezinski's view, expressed in a December 26 memo to President Carter. The Russians were on the march. Absent a firm U.S. response, the national security adviser envisioned a "Soviet presence right down on the edge of the Arabian and Oman Gulfs."[52] The Soviet invasion of Afghanistan—a development he had actively promoted—transformed "that neutral buffer into an offensive wedge." Soviet control of this offensive wedge, he quickly concluded, would encourage the Kremlin to turn next to "dismembering Pakistan and Iran."[53] Carter himself endorsed this view, characterizing Soviet actions in Afghanistan as "an unprecedented act" and "the most serious threat to world peace since the Second World War," thereby ranking it above the Berlin Blockade, the Korean War, and the Cuban Missile Crisis on the roster of Cold War emergencies.[54]

Administration critics advanced an even more fevered interpretation. Here was the ultimate expression of Carter's fecklessness. Soviet forces, warned Theodore L. Eliot, former U.S. ambassador to Afghanistan, were now "within a two-day march from the Persian Gulf." Any further evidence of timorousness on Washington's part would surely "encourage the Soviets to keep moving in the direction of our and our allies' oil supplies."[55] *The Wall Street Journal* spelled out the implications for U.S. policy. It was time to get tough. Washington needed "a resolute and steady plan to oppose Soviet expansion." Essential to that plan was a demonstrated willingness to go to the mat. "The U.S. considers itself the world's strongest nation, but it's clear other countries won't think that unless America shows it's not afraid to use strength."[56]

To have any hope whatsoever of winning election to a second term, Carter needed to rebut the impression that Afghanistan, coming on top of Iran, had created: that he was too dim, too soft, too lacking in vision for the office he held. The occasion of the upcoming State of the Union Address, scheduled for January 23, 1980, offered the chance to do just that. To show that he grasped the seriousness of the situation, Carter seized upon that opportunity to unveil a new policy that nominally addressed the situation in the Persian Gulf but in practice encompassed the core of the entire Islamic world.

Carter began by conceding that simultaneous crises in Iran and Afghanistan—"one of international terrorism and the one of military aggression"—constituted serious "threats to peace." Yet of the two, the Soviet threat posed "a broader and more fundamental challenge" for one very simple reason:

> *The region which is now threatened by Soviet troops in Afghanistan is of great strategic importance: It contains more than two-thirds of the world's exportable oil. The Soviet effort to dominate Afghanistan has brought Soviet military forces to within 300 miles of the Indian Ocean and close to the Straits of Hormuz, a waterway through which most of the world's oil must flow. The Soviet Union is now attempting to consolidate a strategic position, therefore, that poses a grave threat to the free movement of Middle East oil.[57]*

The president who just months before had earnestly sought to persuade Americans to shake their addiction to oil now decried—even as he exaggerated—the possibility of outsiders preventing Americans from getting their daily fix. This he refused to permit. "Let our position be absolutely clear," Carter continued. "An attempt by any outside force to gain control of the Persian Gulf region will be regarded as an assault on the vital interests of the United States of America, and such an assault will be repelled by any means necessary, including military force."

This statement, subsequently enshrined as the Carter Doctrine, inaugurated America's War for the Greater Middle East. The United States was not going to seize Persian Gulf oil directly, as Robert Tucker and Miles Ignotus had once urged. Instead, it was going to prevent a hostile takeover of the Persian Gulf, thereby ensuring that Americans and their allies would not want for oil.

The moment bears comparison with the interval between the fall of 1946 and the spring of 1947 when the United States embarked upon the Cold War. Back then, a series of troubling developments, among them Soviet confrontations with Iran and Turkey and an ongoing civil war in Greece, persuaded President Harry Truman that further cooperation with the Soviet Union had become impossible. The upshot was a policy known as *containment,* which found initial expression in Truman's promise to "support free peoples who are resisting attempted subjugation by armed minorities or by outside pressures"—coded language signifying that the United States would henceforth oppose any prospective increase in communist influence anywhere.

Yet the promulgation of this Truman Doctrine in April 1947 represented not only a decision of profound importance but also a capitulation. Senior members of his administration, their views amplified by influential outsiders, had been urging Truman to take a tougher line with the Kremlin. Those views now prevailed, with Truman abandoning his oft-expressed hope that the end of World War II would give way to an era of peace.

Similarly, the promulgation of the Carter Doctrine in January 1980, issued in response to a series of troubling developments, also represented a capitulation of sorts. In the vain hope of winning a second *caved to pressures*

term, Carter was repudiating the premises—and promises—that had formed the foundation of that presidency.

In his memoirs, Brzezinski wrote, "The Carter Doctrine was modeled on the Truman Doctrine."[58] The comparison is a telling one. The expansive language employed in articulating the Truman Doctrine invited misinterpretation and misuse, with the Vietnam War one example of the consequences.

So too with the articulation of the Carter Doctrine. It represented a broad, open-ended commitment, one that expanded further with time. As subsequent events made clear, the Carter Doctrine applied to areas well beyond the Persian Gulf per se, much as Wolfowitz's Limited Contingency Study had advocated. And along with external threats such as the Soviet Union, it also encompassed local ones, such as Iran, Iraq, and lesser entities generically referred to as "terrorists."

Yet in contrast to the Truman Doctrine, successful implementation of the Carter Doctrine was going to require something more than mere *containment*. Ensuring that Americans and America's allies would not want for oil required that the United States impose order on the Persian Gulf and its environs.

At the time few said so out loud, but implementing the Carter Doctrine implied the conversion of the Persian Gulf into an informal American protectorate. Defending the region meant policing it. While keeping the Soviets out, the United States would assume responsibility for enforcing good behavior on the part of anyone inclined to make mischief. How else could the United States safeguard the uninterrupted flow of oil?

As to the specifics of implementation, Carter's State of the Union Address offered few details. The president spoke of "improving our capability to deploy U.S. military forces rapidly to distant areas" and of "making arrangements for key naval and air facilities to be used by our forces in the region of northeast Africa and the Persian Gulf." He promised to expand the U.S. naval presence and to provide increased military aid to Pakistan, now once again in Washington's good graces as a valued ally

against a common foe. But these amounted to little more than preliminary steps. The real goal, as yet unstated, was to achieve what Brzezinski
referred to as "military preponderance" throughout this quarter of the
globe.[59] Nothing less would suffice in a region of vital importance.

The logic appeared compelling. In a region threatened by external
aggression and internal disorder, the introduction of U.S. military
power would have a stabilizing and reassuring effect.

Not everyone bought this line, of course. The iconoclastic journalist
I. F. Stone, always suspicious of what policymakers were cooking up
behind closed doors, speculated that Carter's vow to defend the Persian
Gulf might be little more than a cover story. Soviet actions in Afghanistan, he suggested, were providing the United States with a pretext "for
moving into place a rapid-deployment force that could someday tempt
us to try to seize the Arab oilfields."[60] However outlandish at the time,
some twenty-three years later this prediction came to pass, at least in
the eyes of some observers, when the United States invaded Iraq.

Less given to conspiracy theories but equally skeptical of militarizing U.S. policy in the Persian Gulf was Hermann Eilts, former U.S. ambassador to Egypt and Saudi Arabia and a key figure in the negotiations
at Camp David that in 1978 had produced the Egypt-Israeli peace agreement. Writing in the journal *International Security*, Eilts warned that
U.S. military action in the Persian Gulf "would be viewed as blatant
imperialism and provide grist for the mill of anti-American elements."
Only the most extreme circumstances, "where the very survival of this
nation is at stake," would justify sending U.S. forces into the region.
Instead of girding for war, Eilts counseled, Washington would be better
served in pursuing "an equitable solution to the Palestinian problem,"
thereby transforming the region's political climate.[61] The situation required not force but creative diplomacy.

As with I. F. Stone, subsequent events would vindicate Eilts. Yet at
the time, they were outliers, their views carrying little weight. For the
most part, those critical of the Carter Doctrine complained not that it
was provocative or unwise but that the president was guilty of doing
too little, too late. It was now an election year and critics hammered

Carter relentlessly for having put the United States in such jeopardy, whether out of apathy or incompetence having stood idly by while adversaries acted.

By entering Afghanistan, wrote columnist Joseph Kraft in *The Washington Post*, "The Soviets have asserted themselves as the dominant power in the vortex of world politics."[62] A *Saturday Review* cover story—the cover itself depicting Soviet leader Leonid Brezhnev decked out in Arab robes and *keffiyeh*—cited "plenty of physical evidence" showing that the Russians were "gearing themselves up for an invasion of Iran." But Iran was merely a way station. For the Kremlin, "the real objective" was "control of the West's largest reservoir of oil in the Gulf." In short, seizing Saudi Arabia was the ultimate goal.[63] The noted Harvard historian Richard Pipes went even further. He described a giant Soviet pincer movement "directed toward the Middle East." Denying the West access to Persian Gulf oil would put the Kremlin in a position to strangle Europe, leaving the United States isolated and alone.[64] A *Boston Globe* columnist concurred, writing that "the Russian move into Afghanistan creates new facts of immense strategic importance." Chief among those facts was the evident Soviet willingness "to use its new brute force frontally," thereby positioning itself "one giant step closer to the biggest strategic prize in the postwar world, the Persian Gulf oil tap."[65]

In the eyes of Ronald Reagan, none of these "facts" qualified as new. According to the former California governor, already in the race for the 1980 Republican presidential nomination, Russia's invasion of Afghanistan simply affirmed that the Soviet Union remained what it had always been: "a hostile, imperial power whose ambitions extend to the ends of the earth."[66] The evidence suggested that the Kremlin was now targeting the world's oil supply as its next objective. The situation called for a far more vigorous response than Carter had outlined in his State of the Union Address. Reagan had a simple solution: Impose a naval blockade on Cuba, which the Soviet Union owned, as he put it, "lock, stock, and barrel." Then send the Kremlin an ultimatum: "Get your troops out of Afghanistan and we give up the blockade."[67]

More tellingly, George Ball, a Democrat who was not running for office, nonetheless joined the stampede, expressing slightly less inflammatory but still similar views. "It goes without saying," he wrote, "that America should promptly establish its military competence to cope with further Soviet penetration in the gulf area." Otherwise, the Russians would have an easy time "picking up the pieces of a disintegrating Iran," while directly threatening "the world's coronary artery"—the Persian Gulf itself.[68]

Lending particular weight to Ball's views was the fact that he was the one member of Lyndon Johnson's inner circle said to have gotten Vietnam right. In Ball's judgment, Southeast Asia hadn't been worth fighting for. The Persian Gulf was.[69]

Yet what now went without saying, at least in Ball's estimation, represented a remarkable turnabout from what had gone without saying just a year earlier. Then, outsourcing the security of the Persian Gulf had seemed a reasonable proposition. By early 1980, according to the new consensus, it represented the height of folly. A series of unwelcome surprises coming in rapid succession—along with the (erroneous) interpretation that Americans assigned to each in turn—now made it imperative for the United States itself to guarantee regional stability and access to oil.

In the summer of 1979, Jimmy Carter had invited Americans to consider changing the American way of life, trading a shallow freedom for true freedom and dependence for autonomy. They had rejected the invitation. The existing American way of life remained sacrosanct. If its preservation meant fighting, Americans welcomed the fight, even without knowing what fighting might entail. So in January 1980, they embarked upon a war for oil, which was in its way a war to preserve the American way of life, but which was destined by fits and starts to become a War for the Greater Middle East. Even at the outset, no one thought that the challenges ahead would be easy. But at least they appeared straightforward and unambiguous. They would prove to be neither.

2

GEARING UP

IN TERMS OF IMMEDIATE IMPACT, THE CARTER DOCTRINE HIT America's military establishment with something less than dramatic effect. Adding the Persian Gulf to the list of U.S. strategic priorities in no way lessened the emphasis placed on defending Western Europe or Northeast Asia. If anything, in an atmosphere of heightened tension, preexisting priorities acquired additional emphasis. So the day-to-day existence of most U.S. soldiers, sailors, airmen, and Marines went on much as before.

The Soviet invasion of Afghanistan and the election of Ronald Reagan to succeed Jimmy Carter combined to revive the Cold War. The Nixon-era conception of détente joined the Nixon Doctrine on the scrapheap of discarded ideas. That the Soviet-American rivalry would within a decade pass out of existence seemed about as likely as Washington reconciling with Fidel Castro's Cuba or North and South Korea agreeing to peaceful reunification. In international relations, some facts were, or at least appeared to be, simply permanent.

Whether the furious preparations to defend the Fulda Gap that Albert Wohlstetter had disparaged helped avert World War III, increased the possibility of its occurrence, or were largely irrelevant to the issue is impossible to say with certainty. Yet in retrospect, this much seems abundantly clear: Even as U.S. forces in Europe during the 1980s were manning what Americans liked to call the "Frontier of Freedom," a profound shift was already underway. In almost imperceptible increments, the actual center of America's military universe was in the process of moving thousands of miles to the south and east.

Jimmy Carter's declaration that the United States would henceforth defend the Persian Gulf elicited this response: Okay, how? Presidential Directive 63, issued as Carter was preparing to leave office, provided a preliminary answer, detailing the "Persian Gulf Security Framework" that his administration had begun to put in place. Although PD 63 expressed the hope that allies and friendly local nations might lend a hand, it placed primary emphasis on "building up our own capabilities to project force into the region while maintaining a credible presence there." That the United States should shoulder primary responsibility for securing the planet's principal oil storehouse was no longer a proposition to be debated. It had been decided.[1]

As a first step toward fulfilling that responsibility, Carter in March 1980 created the Rapid Deployment Joint Task Force (RDJTF).[2] To stand up this new headquarters, Carter selected a Marine, Lieutenant General P. X. Kelley. Despite its imposing name, the RDJTF did not qualify as an actual fighting force. As an organization, it existed largely on paper.

Minimally potent as a combat force, the RDJTF primarily served symbolic purposes, as Kelley himself admitted. Yet even in its infancy, he insisted, the RDJTF sent a "strong and powerful signal" to the Soviet Union that "we will not tolerate military adventurism" and to other countries that "we are indeed a nation to be reckoned with."[3] The general was talking through his hat.

Granted, when it came to providing the RDJTF with a modicum of muscle, Kelley confronted very large practical constraints. Deploying U.S. forces across great distances into the theater of operations and then sustaining them when they got there posed major challenges. Existing transportation assets—ships and planes capable of moving military equipment over long distances—came nowhere near to satisfying projected requirements. Within the region, port facilities, airfields, and roads were limited. And in contrast to the Soviets, Kelley wrote, "we do not have—nor do we seek—a permanent base structure near the Middle East." Yet however daunting the mission, the United States really had no choice in the matter. To an even greater extent than the United States itself, America's allies needed Persian Gulf oil. "As long as they are dependent," Kelley concluded, "so are we."[4]

A series of unspoken and largely unexamined assumptions provided the foundation for this commitment. The first was that the Soviet Union coveted the Persian Gulf and possessed both the will and the capacity to seize it. In other words, the most worrisome threat came from *outside* the region. A second assumption was that America's friends and allies were incapable of fending for themselves, even when their own most vital interests were at risk. They needed help that only the United States could provide—a conviction destined to remain intact for the next several decades. A third assumption, stemming from the first two, was that there existed only one sure way to guarantee access to the stores of energy that Americans and America's allies required to sustain their economies and their lifestyles, namely the military might of the United States. Danger and dependence combined to dictate a military response.

Within a year, Lieutenant General Robert Kingston, an army officer, succeeded Kelley. Announcing with admirable candor that his job was "to ensure the unimpeded flow of oil from the Arabian Gulf," Kingston set out to transform his command from an embryonic stopgap into a force able to mount a plausible defense against a Soviet offensive headed toward the Straits of Hormuz.[5]

During Kingston's tenure, his command gained both a measure of permanence and enhanced standing when the RDJTF was rechristened United States Central Command, more commonly known as CENT-COM. The three-star Kingston thereby picked up a promotion.

CENTCOM's creation qualified as an important but not surprising development. The Pentagon had previously divided the planet into four vast territorial entities, one focused each on Europe, the Atlantic, the Pacific, and Latin America. CENTCOM now became a fifth such "unified command" assigned its own geographic "area of responsibility" or AOR.

As employed in this context, the term *responsibility* carries with it quasi-imperial connotations. It is a euphemism. No senior U.S. military officer, whether in the 1980s or today, would dream of claiming to rule or govern another people or nation. Yet the "responsibility" accorded to regional commanders endows them with the contemporary equivalent of viceregal authority.[6] From CENTCOM's inception, General Kingston and his successors have wielded that authority over an AOR including not only countries immediately adjacent to the Persian Gulf but others considerably further afield, such as Egypt, Ethiopia, Somalia, Kenya, and Pakistan. At CENTCOM's founding in January 1983, its AOR encompassed nineteen countries in all.[7] Although the Pentagon created the command in response to very specific crises, in other words, right from the outset its charter reflected expectations of—or provided a pretext for—more wide-ranging action.

Yet with CENTCOM's creation came some less obvious implications. The RDJTF had represented the Pentagon's hastily improvised response to events in Iran and Afghanistan. It was a quick fix. By comparison, as a four-star headquarters, CENTCOM conveyed an enduring commitment—the equivalent of a government creating a new ministry or a university creating a new college. It signified that the United States was getting serious about the Greater Middle East.

"Getting serious" also implied a preference for uniforms over suits as the principal agents of U.S. policy. Henceforth, rather than military power serving as the handmaiden of diplomacy, the reverse would be true: Across the CENTCOM AOR, diplomacy now took a backseat to military imperatives.[8]

Furthermore, there was no turning back. Once made, such an arrangement becomes irreversible and open-ended. This, at least, describes the American experience throughout the postwar era.

At the conclusion of the war against Nazi Germany, from his headquarters in Reims, France, Dwight D. Eisenhower had sent this admirably succinct cable to the War Department: "The mission of this Allied Force was fulfilled at 02:41, local time, May 7th, 1945." In the seven decades since, no U.S. regional commander has replicated Eisenhower's achievement. Not one has ever fulfilled his mission. That is, at no time have conditions within the command's assigned AOR ever reached the point where the officer in charge has felt able to report the job finished.

CENTCOM would prove no exception. In that regard, it has not disappointed.

In addition to presiding over this reshuffling of organizational furniture, General Kingston faced the immediate challenge of discerning exactly what his assigned task was likely to entail. The questions he faced were fundamental. If the principal aim was to defend Persian Gulf oil, where was the prospective battlefield? What forces would the mission require? How would they get to the theater of operations? Once there, how could they be provided with the wherewithal to survive, much less to fight?

Kingston's answer to the first question both clarified and complicated his task. Shielding the Gulf from external threat meant positioning that shield well forward of the Gulf itself. Accepting the view that Soviet entry into Afghanistan presaged a further lunge through Iran toward Iraq and Saudi Arabia, Kingston's planners identified the Zagros Mountains—traversing western Iran along a northwest-southeast axis—as the place on which to anchor that defense. To hold the Zagros against an attack coming from the east or north was to safeguard the bulk of Persian Gulf oil reserves along with the maritime lines of communication needed to move that oil to market. Much as they had the Fulda Gap, U.S. military planners designated the Zagros as key terrain.

There were several differences, of course. Whereas the United States maintained substantial combat forces in proximity to Fulda, it had none within thousands of miles of the Zagros, save a few token naval forces stationed at Bahrain. Whereas the Federal Republic of Germany, a close NATO ally, welcomed U.S. efforts to defend its territory, Iran was unlikely to view with favor the presence of troops from a country it routinely denounced as the Great Satan. A contingent dispatched into the CENTCOM AOR, Kingston remarked, "would start from almost zero in terms of combat power and support structure in the region."[9]

Above all, there was the matter of already existing large-scale hostilities. In September 1980, Iraqi forces had invaded the Islamic Republic. Envisioned by Saddam Hussein as a quick land grab, the ensuing Iran-Iraq War turned out to be an inconclusive slugfest, destined to last for eight bloody years. In short, as Kingston considered how to thwart a Soviet offensive into Iran, that country was already under assault by an altogether different adversary coming from the opposite direction. It was the equivalent of U.S. forces trying to defend the Fulda Gap while the Federal Republic of Germany was simultaneously fending off a French attack from the west.

Even so, Kingston persisted in attempting to adapt the standard Cold War template for organizing a defense of this just-discovered frontier of freedom. Doing so entailed simply ignoring inconvenient cultural, religious, and sectarian complexities. So in a presentation on his command's "new challenges" delivered to his British counterparts in London, for example, Kingston pointedly cited five occasions over the previous three hundred years when Russia had invaded Persia and proceeded to rattle off the army divisions, tactical fighter wings, and carrier battle groups for which he'd received planning authority in the event of incursion number six.

Notably, Islam did not qualify for mention anywhere in Kingston's presentation, suggesting that the CENTCOM commander's checklist of factors affecting developments in his AOR did not include matters of faith.[10] The prevailing CENTCOM worldview allowed no room for God, even in a region where God was still very much alive. Nor did Kingston even acknowledge the fault lines—Arab vs. Israel, Arab vs. Persian, Arab vs. Arab—that posed more enduring threats to regional stability than anything the Soviets were likely to introduce.

It was like giving a talk about American politics and ignoring the influence of lobbies or special-interest groups or Mammon. Do it if you like, but you will come across as naïve or simply disingenuous.

This see-what-you-want-to-see-and-ignore-the-rest perspective found expression in a document known as OPLAN 1002, formally known as "Defense of the Arabian Peninsula." This was CENTCOM's blueprint for war, shaped by a Cold War mindset and therefore fixated with the prospect of Soviet leaders, their forces struggling unsuccessfully to pacify Afghanistan, nonetheless launching a major offensive to conquer Iran.

OPLAN 1002 spelled out the intended U.S. response. From bases in the United States, five army and two Marine Corps divisions would deploy to Iran. Upon arrival, they would move overland to take up positions along the Zagros. To provide supporting firepower, American naval and air assets would also converge on the region. Given sufficient advanced warning, CENTCOM planners counted on these forces to deter any prospective attack or, if need be, to inflict on the Soviets the sort of crushing defeat they themselves had inflicted on the Wehrmacht at Stalingrad back in 1943.[11]

Of course, during the few years remaining in the USSR's existence, no such attack materialized. As to whether the Soviet offensive postulated by Central Command was ever remotely in the cards (or even operationally feasible), opinions may differ. Even at the time, Kingston himself expressed doubts. With their ongoing troubles in Eastern Europe and Afghanistan, he thought the Soviets had "a pretty full plate." He believed the Kremlin unlikely to invite a direct military confrontation with the United States.[12]

Yet for our purposes, what did *not* occur matters less than what *did*. A panoply of Pentagon initiatives undertaken to avert Soviet armed intervention subsequently facilitated U.S. armed intervention not only in the Persian Gulf but also throughout the entire CENTCOM AOR. In that regard, the putative Soviet threat of the 1980s served as a placeholder, providing a handy rationale for developing capabilities subsequently put to other purposes. The upshot: A posture justified by the need to defend the Persian Gulf from outside intrusion positioned the United States itself to intrude. As the Soviet Union faded from the scene, Washington began entertaining visions of policing the entirety of the Greater Middle East.

Those Pentagon initiatives sought chiefly to reduce the impact of distance, thereby removing impediments to the projection of U.S. military power. The number repeatedly cited by American officials and echoed by obliging American journalists was 7,000. That number represented the approximate distance in miles that U.S. forces stationed in the United States needed to traverse in order to reach the Persian Gulf.

In late 1979, the Carter administration had begun tackling this distance problem when it dispatched envoys to persuade "friendly" nations in and around the Gulf to allow U.S. access to ports and airfields in the event of an emergency. During the Reagan administration, such efforts continued and intensified.[13]

Even at the time, this did not qualify as some deep secret. It occurred in the American equivalent of broad daylight, courtesy of mainstream media outlets, which kept readers and viewers abreast of the expanding U.S. military footprint in the region.

Consider, for example, the puff piece that Richard Halloran contributed to *The New York Times Magazine* in April 1984.[14] If Halloran's essay had a theme, it was this: Americans could rest easy in the knowledge that CENTCOM was hard at work and becoming more capable day by day.

Halloran brought *Times* readers up to date on Pentagon efforts to upgrade ports and airfields to which the U.S. had been promised access in Egypt, Kenya, Morocco, Oman, and Somalia. Meanwhile, he noted, Saudi Arabia was "building a complex of bases far beyond its needs or its ability to operate." President Ronald Reagan had already vowed publicly that the United States would defend the existing Saudi political order against any threat.[15] In such an eventuality, it was tacitly understood that the Saudis would make their ports and airfields available to U.S. forces.

Halloran also reported on the flotilla of fifteen cargo ships, already loaded with military equipment, that the United States had positioned at Diego Garcia, an island in the Indian Ocean that had become "vital to the Central Command's logistic, naval and air support." He detailed efforts to improve various facilities there and to lengthen Diego Garcia's runway, permitting it to accommodate long-range bombers. In 1983, Congress had earmarked nearly $60 million for these improvements, with another $90 million for the following fiscal year.[16]

Back in Tampa, CENTCOM headquarters was by no means sitting on its hands. "General Kingston has begun to build a relationship with each nation in his command's operating region," Halloran reported. Along with building relationships, Kingston had programmed a series of training exercises to cycle U.S. forces through his AOR. The aim was both to acclimate U.S. troops to conditions in the region and to promote within the region "an increasing tolerance" for the presence of American military forces.[17]

Just the year before, for something called Operation Bright Star, over twenty-five thousand U.S. troops had deployed to Egypt, Sudan, Somalia, and Oman. "B-52 bombers flew from bases in the United States to make bombing runs, [American] paratroopers jumped with Egyptian paratroopers, and Marine tanks churned ashore through heavy surf in Somalia." Fostering this atmosphere of cooperation was the $7.7 billion in security assistance—mostly in the form of arms—that the United States had poured into the CENTCOM AOR in 1983. That figure had increased to $9.1 billion in 1984 and was scheduled to hit $11 billion the year following.

When the RDJTF had formed just four years earlier, critics had "scoffed that it was not rapid, had little to deploy, and was not much of a force." Although work remained to be done, Halloran noted that such critics "have been less vocal recently, as the Central Command has started to make progress." The title of his essay made the point explicitly: CENTCOM now stood "Poised for the Persian Gulf."

Halloran's upbeat interpretation was broadly representative of mainstream opinion.[18] To the extent that U.S. military commitments pursuant to the Carter Doctrine generated debate, that debate centered on whether or not Central Command could move sufficient combat forces fast enough and far enough to make a difference.[19] In effect, it was a dispute over timetables and scheduling rather than policy.

So as Halloran assessed CENTCOM's progress and prospects, he confined himself to narrowly military considerations. History prior to the Shah's overthrow possessed little relevance. The upheavals that had done so much to shape the region—the dismantling of the Ottoman

Empire after World War I, the creation of Israel in 1948, the Suez Crisis of 1956, the Arab-Israeli Wars of 1967 and 1973—escaped notice. References to countries like Oman and Somalia implied that they were more or less interchangeable with Norway or the Netherlands. Religion went unmentioned. How might a very hot and very dry climate affect the operations of combat forces? Need to think about that. The cleavage between Sunni and Shia? Someone else's problem.

Even when U.S. officials acknowledged local sensitivities, they did so in order to dismiss them. In an interview recorded subsequent to his retirement, for example, Kingston recalled that his military counterparts within the CENTCOM AOR had been "very chary of getting too close to us." He thought he knew why: They resented powerful outsiders treating them like "second class citizens" even on their own turf, as, for example, the British had done for decades. Even so, Kingston expressed confidence that events would obviate any such reservations about welcoming a U.S. presence. "There will come a point," he remarked, "where they'll say, 'we see the threat as much as you do and we invite you in.'"[20] Kingston took it for granted that "they" and "we" would share a common understanding of threats and, by extension, of actions needed to deflect those threats.

Fulfilling these expectations required de facto Soviet collaboration. U.S. military planners were counting on Kremlin leaders to play their assigned role as bogeymen. Quite unexpectedly, the Soviets refused to cooperate. In so doing they induced a radical change in CENTCOM's orientation.

By the time General George Crist, a Marine, replaced Kingston to become CENTCOM's second commander on November 27, 1985, a considerably more important succession in leadership had already occurred in Moscow. Earlier that year, Mikhail Gorbachev had become general secretary of the Communist Party of the Soviet Union and soon thereafter embarked upon a doomed effort to reform and thereby save the USSR. Doing so, he believed, required first calling off the Cold War.

Initially, the United States military responded to this disconcerting news by attempting to downplay or deny it. Abetted by the more militant members of the Reagan administration and of the American political elite, the Pentagon strove mightily to ignore or discredit Gorbachev's attempt to ease Soviet-American tensions. As late as 1987, in releasing the Pentagon's annual assessment of Soviet military power, Secretary of Defense Caspar Weinberger was still warning about what he called "a dynamic, and an expanding, Soviet threat." Weinberger refused to be taken in by stunts and promises. "No matter who is general secretary, no matter what proposals are made, no matter what public relations activities are undertaken," he insisted, the Soviet danger persisted and, if anything, was growing worse.[21]

Concrete steps taken at Gorbachev's initiative made it difficult to sustain that view. In 1987, he accepted U.S. terms for a treaty eliminating intermediate-range nuclear missiles from Europe. He also announced plans to end the Soviet occupation of Afghanistan, a tacit admission of defeat. The following year brought a commitment to withdraw five hundred thousand Soviet troops from Eastern Europe, no Western quid pro quo required. In February 1989, as promised, the final contingent of Soviet forces left Afghanistan for good. In the meantime, summit meetings between Gorbachev and his U.S. counterpart, first Reagan and then George H. W. Bush, took on an atmosphere of cheerful conviviality and good fellowship.

By November 1988, when General H. Norman Schwarzkopf, Jr., of the U.S. Army succeeded Crist, the jig was up, with Schwarzkopf astute enough to notice. In the things-got-better-on-my-watch perspective to which virtually all U.S. military commanders are prone, Crist boasted of guiding CENTCOM from "adolescence to young adulthood." Even so, Crist had remained gripped by the prospect of massive Soviet intervention—several dozen divisions with thousands of tanks—aimed at seizing "some sort of hegemony over the oil."[22] Schwarzkopf knew better. The likelihood of Soviet armored formations making a mad dash across Iran to seize the Straits of Hormuz was nil.

So once installed in Tampa, Schwarzkopf took one look at OPLAN 1002 and recognized it for the dubious proposition it had always been.

"We'd used the operating plan for years," he later wrote, "but most generals knew it made no sense and would eventually be junked." Schwarzkopf spelled out the plan's deficiencies. "For one thing, it was suicidal. It called for Central Command to rush forces to the Zagros Mountains . . . [where] we would be seriously outnumbered, seven thousand miles from home, and destined to run out of supplies and troops in a matter of weeks." Even so, the plan had not been without redeeming value, Schwarzkopf noting that "Central Command [had] used it for years to justify spending millions of dollars of taxpayers' money."[23]

The disappearance of the (largely fictive) Russian threat to the Persian Gulf removed that justification, leaving CENTCOM without a compelling argument for spending more taxpayer money. An operationally defective war plan that had at least offered some budgetary leverage now became something worse: an operationally defective war plan devoid of bureaucratic utility.

The solution to this problem was obvious: To stay in business, U.S. Central Command needed to identify a new threat. Conveniently, such a threat was even then presenting itself. With impeccable timing, Iraq, the adversary that Paul Wolfowitz had identified a decade earlier as a looming concern, was now finally coming into its own.

In the bitter conflict between Iran and Iraq, Washington had feigned neutrality while actually playing a nontrivial role. As we will see in a subsequent chapter, that role combined incoherence with self-deception, both to become abiding hallmarks of America's evolving War for the Greater Middle East. Suffice it to say here that as the Cold War was winding down, so too was the Iran-Iraq War—good news, in a way, for CENTCOM.

The conflict that began with a naked act of Iraqi aggression reached its conclusion in August 1988 with that country on the ropes. Believing that the Islamic Revolution had left Iran militarily vulnerable, Saddam Hussein had expected an easy win. Not for the last time, he miscalculated. While sustaining huge losses, his army had not distinguished itself in battle. Even with the benefit of extensive outside financial and material support, Iraq had managed only with difficulty to avoid outright defeat.

Saddam insisted otherwise, of course. Yet his claim of victory involved considerable misdirection. Much as a series of U.S. presidents would do when their forays into the Islamic world met with less than the promised success, he quietly modified his originally declared objectives.

Even so, in a nearly seamless transition, Saddam Hussein's Iraq now replaced the once-mighty USSR as the chief threat to CENTCOM's AOR. Making the case that Iraq posed an imminent danger required placing greater weight on Saddam's record of brutality and reckless adventurism than on his army's record of demonstrated performance. U.S. estimates of Iraqi military power glossed over Iraq's manifest failure to defeat Iran, emphasizing instead its substantial array of relatively modern tanks, missiles, and fighter planes. Quantity ostensibly implied quality. At Senate committee hearings in January 1990, Schwarzkopf himself pronounced judgment, reviving the view first articulated by Paul Wolfowitz a decade earlier. "Iraq is now the preeminent military power in the Gulf," he testified, possessing the wherewithal "to militarily coerce its neighboring states."[24]

By that time, down at CENTCOM headquarters in Tampa, Schwarzkopf's staff was already hard at work hammering out a revision of OPLAN 1002. In one sense, the result narrowed the scope of CENTCOM's primary mission. Rather than purporting to defend the entire Persian Gulf from an outside attack, the updated plan focused on countering "an intraregional threat" to "critical ports and oil facilities on the ARABIAN PENINSULA."[25] What this meant, in plain language, was that defending the Kingdom of Saudi Arabia from a prospective Iraqi invasion had become priority number one.

Unlike the largely fanciful Zagros Mountains contingency, here was a scenario that possessed a semblance of plausibility. It was, furthermore, the sort of problem with which the American officers were intellectually comfortable—suiting up against a sort of junior varsity version of the Red Army that U.S. forces in Europe had energetically been preparing to fight. Better still, for an officer corps perplexed by the implications of Hiroshima while still haunted by Vietnam, the outcome of any actual conflict with Iraq would be decided by the clash of arms on a conventional battlefield—no nuclear weapons and no guerrillas.

CENTCOM planners had no difficulty incorporating into their new scenario the various preparations made for war against the Russians. The "overbuilt" Saudi facilities, the ongoing work at Diego Garcia, the stockpiles of military stores, the agreements providing access to ports and airfield: All of these retained their utility for staff officers formulating ways of dealing with the newly discovered Iraqi threat.

The demise of the Warsaw Pact and the announced withdrawal of Soviet troops from Eastern Europe even provided a bonus of sorts. The possibility of repurposing U.S. forces now presented itself. Units once earmarked for plugging the Fulda Gap were now becoming available for reassignment. War games evaluating preliminary versions of the revised OPLAN 1002 had revealed a shortage of available mechanized forces to counter the large number of Iraqi tanks.[26] By the end of 1989, the U.S. Army found itself awash with more tanks and tank crews than it knew what to do with, all made redundant by the Cold War's sudden end. Here was a reservoir of combat power on which CENTCOM could draw.

For those paid to think about potential wars in the Middle East, in other words, the fading danger of World War III meant opportunity. What some at the time were calling a "peace dividend" offered CENTCOM a way of expanding its portfolio of assets.

The alacrity with which the United States fingered Saddam Hussein's Iraq as its next Public Enemy Number One—a judgment seemingly validated by Saddam's subsequent actions—offers one important explanation for why the hoped-for peace dividend never materialized.[27] Rather than ushering in a debate about first-order questions related to national security, the end of the Cold War—commonly described as an event of seismic significance—produced remarkably little change in the makeup and posture of America's armed forces. To the extent that

change did occur, it involved little more than making an about-face—
a reorientation toward a new foe.

Yet if designating Iraq as successor to the USSR solved some
problems—enabling the Pentagon to avert unwelcome change—it also
planted the seeds of complications to which U.S. military leaders at the
time appeared oblivious.

With something akin to unanimity, civilian policymakers and their
military advisers at this juncture took it for granted that the principal
threats to Persian Gulf stability *came from states*. The key to maintaining
access to the region's oil reserves, therefore, was to *make states behave*.
And when it came to keeping unruly or recalcitrant states in line, they
were counting on military power to do the trick.

In later years, among senior U.S. military officers, it became fashion-
able to say of some particular problem in the Greater Middle East that
there existed "no military solution." At this juncture, just the opposite
judgment applied. When it came to Persian Gulf security, alternatives
to a military solution appeared inconceivable. It was guns or give up.

During the Cold War, in places like the Fulda Gap, the reliance on
military power to make states behave had produced more or less satisfactory results. For the most part, when facing the prospect of a determined U.S. response, the Soviets and others in the Communist orbit
had backed off. Rather than mounting a direct challenge to the United
States, they had opted for prudence as the better part of valor. There
had been exceptions, of course—in 1948, the Berlin Blockade; in 1950,
the Korean War; in 1962, the Cuban Missile Crisis—but Washington
generally saw these as proving the rule. In each instance, standing firm
had limited the scope of a problem that could have gotten much worse.

Overall, containment had worked. The Cold War mostly stayed
cold. World War III never happened. Some observers described the result as a "Long Peace," attributed to American vigilance backed by
armed might. Here, in a nutshell, was the unspoken justification for
postwar U.S. national security policy with its very large, heavily armed,
and globally deployed military establishment.

Yet however valid this formula when applied to Western Europe or East Asia, it did not translate easily to the Greater Middle East. The problem was not that Iraq differed from the Soviet Union, although it did in myriad ways. Instead, the problem was that the most fundamental threats to the stability of the Greater Middle East did not come from states that the United States chose to put on its enemies list, whether the Soviet Union in 1980 or Iraq by 1990. Rather, the real threats arose from factors that CENTCOM planners were inclined to ignore or to categorize as beyond their purview.

One such factor was history, above all the pernicious legacy of Western imperialism to which the United States, willingly or not, had become the principal heir. Whether in drawing borders, installing compliant rulers, or abruptly abandoning colonies, protectorates, and mandates no longer deemed worth the bother, Europeans, above all the British, had fostered dysfunction across much of the Greater Middle East, thereby creating the basis for an endless stream of intraregional conflicts. In this regard, Iraq, created by arbitrarily cobbling together disparate bits of the Ottoman Empire after World War I, ranked as Exhibit A. Trailing not far behind were Israel-Palestine and Pakistan.

A second factor was religion, which mattered in two respects. On the one hand, it created fault lines that became in turn the basis for conflict within and beyond the CENTCOM AOR. The division between Sunni and Shia Muslims offers the best-known but hardly the sole example. More broadly, religion posed obstacles to the reconciliation with modernity that may hold the best prospect of peoples across the Greater Middle East finding an antidote to the troubles afflicting the region.

But among those paid to think about strategy, soldiers and civilians alike, history and religion counted for little. In the wake of World War II, in large part due to the primacy assigned to nuclear issues, economists, mathematicians, political scientists, and specialists in game theory had come to exercise an outsized influence in framing the debate over basic national security policy. On matters where so little history existed, historians seemingly had little to offer and could therefore safely be ignored. As for theologians, with rare exceptions, they were excluded altogether. National security policy was a thoroughly secular enterprise.[28]

For Generals Kingston, Crist, or Schwarzkopf to incorporate history or religion into their thinking alongside geography or the prospective enemy's order of battle would have required an enormous leap of creative imagination. At CENTCOM headquarters, such imagination was—and would remain—in short supply.

3

ARSENAL OF THEOCRACY

DURING THE 1980S, WHILE CENTCOM FOUND ITS FOOTING
and responded to the loss of one would-be enemy by identifying another, the Reagan administration was simultaneously engaging in a variety of military and paramilitary operations on several fronts across
the Greater Middle East. These preliminary campaigns accustomed
Americans to the idea of the United States playing a more forward-
leaning role in managing developments in the Islamic world.

Yet apart from conditioning domestic opinion, the several probes
undertaken on Reagan's watch had little in common. In terms of locale, they were scattered from Libya in the west to Pakistan in the east.
In terms of character, they differed markedly from one another. One
involved supporting insurgents waging jihad against hated occupiers.
Another was an inopportune venture into "peacekeeping" that ended
in disaster. Employing, in effect, an updated version of gunboat diplomacy, a third attempted to cow or intimidate one particularly annoying
two-bit antagonist. A fourth found Washington becoming party to a
bitter conflict and offering assistance to both sides before ultimately
coming down in favor of the aggressor.

If any overarching theme connected these episodes, it was this: activism to convey the image of a nation that had gotten its moxie back.
Jimmy Carter's perceived weakness and passivity had cost him his presidency and ruined his reputation. Ronald Reagan was not going to repeat that error. Yet apart from projecting renewed pugnacity, the thread
tying together Reagan's various forays into the Islamic world was all

but invisible. Assertiveness absent any appreciation for what might be lurking just around the next corner makes a poor basis for strategy.

Near the beginning of his first term as president, Reagan had explained to an aide his approach to the Cold War. "My idea of American policy toward the Soviet Union is simple," he remarked. "It is this: We win and they lose."[1] To simplify was to clarify, stripping down to essentials as a basis for understanding.

Reagan's ability to do just that numbered as not least among the qualities that endeared him to many Americans. Here was language— direct, unvarnished, even manly—they could grasp and appreciate. Us against them. Red Sox vs. Yankees. Notre Dame vs. USC. Here too was the formula that ostensibly served as Reagan's azimuth—at least until he discovered in Mikhail Gorbachev a communist with whom he could do business. Yet however mightily Reagan strove to employ a similarly Manichaean approach when dealing with the Greater Middle East, the realities there refused to cooperate.

So while Reagan certainly stepped up the level of U.S. military activity in that region, he achieved little by way of lasting benefit. Implicitly endorsing the premises of the Carter Doctrine, Reagan never quite figured out a coherent approach to implementing that doctrine. So his piece of America's War for the Greater Middle East was confused, slapdash, and inconsistent. In sum, it was a dog's breakfast.

In retrospect, this appears readily apparent. At the time, the Reagan administration claimed that it had more wins than losses to its credit. Yet while Reagan meted out punishment to parties that arguably deserved what they got, doing so produced consequences both unforeseen and undesired. Notably, in each case where the administration claimed victory—over the Soviets in Afghanistan, over Moamar Gaddafi in Libya, and over Iran in the Persian Gulf—the outcome proved at best inconclusive and at worst plain bad. Meanwhile, in the one instance where the administration inarguably failed—inserting U.S. Marines into Israeli-occupied Lebanon—sacralizing that failure took precedence over learning from it, thereby making future failures on a larger scale that much more likely.

On this roster of campaigns, Afghanistan stands out as the ostensibly big win that over time gave way to an even bigger mess. This signature initiative of the Reagan era, undertaken to wound the Soviet Union, eventually became a wound inflicted by the United States on itself.

In the years since the Carter administration had first begun providing a trickle of assistance to the Afghan resistance, that program had grown dramatically. Neither CENTCOM nor the Pentagon directed that program, which belonged entirely to the Central Intelligence Agency.

Yet Operation Cyclone, as the Agency dubbed it, deserves inclusion in a military history of America's War for the Greater Middle East for at least two reasons. First, the CIA's nominally covert activities in Afghanistan during the 1980s laid the basis for the very overt conflict involving U.S. forces that began in 2001. On the day that the last Soviet soldier departed from Afghanistan in February 1989, the CIA operative charged with running Cyclone famously cabled headquarters in Langley, "We won."[2] Superficially correct, this judgment proved to be both premature and misleading. Having made the USSR pay dearly for foolishly flinging itself into the "graveyard of empires," the United States proceeded to repeat the Soviet mistake without achieving an appreciably better outcome. Put simply, this First Afghanistan War paved the way for a second, even longer iteration.

Second, Operation Cyclone illustrates one of the central ironies of America's War for the Greater Middle East—the unwitting tendency, while intently focusing on solving one problem, to exacerbate a second and plant the seeds of a third. In Afghanistan, this meant fostering the rise of Islamic radicalism and underwriting Pakistan's transformation into a nuclear-armed quasi-rogue state while attempting to subvert the Soviet Union.

Washington did not act unilaterally in Afghanistan. Rather, it drew on the assistance of a very substantial "coalition of the willing"—or perhaps, more accurately, a coalition of the dissimilar—that included not only Pakistan but also Egypt, Saudi Arabia, China, the United Kingdom, and Israel. Beyond a shared hostility toward the Soviet Union, motives for participation differed, as did perceptions of the stakes involved.

This is hardly unusual, of course. History is replete with examples of opportunistic alliances forged in the face of a common enemy. When the absolutist King of France threw in with antimonarchical American revolutionaries in 1778, he was not aiming to advance the inalienable rights enumerated in the Declaration of Independence. And when Winston Churchill made common cause with Joseph Stalin in 1941, he did so without amending his decidedly negative view of Bolshevism.

Yet two things distinguished this particular conglomeration of strange bedfellows. First, none of the participants cared a lick for the Afghan people. Second, apart from Pakistan, none attributed any intrinsic value to Afghanistan itself. What lent that impoverished, landlocked country its fleeting political significance was the Soviet presence there. End that presence and Afghanistan would command as much international attention as Fiji. As a result, policymakers intent on making Afghanistan a staging ground for a "Vietnamese quagmire" paid scant attention to exactly what that might imply once the agents of mayhem left the scene. "We expected post-Soviet Afghanistan to be ugly," Robert Gates, then a CIA official, later confessed, "but never considered that it would become a haven for terrorists operating worldwide."[3]

Sticking it to the Russians took precedence over all other considerations. That instigating large-scale war in Afghanistan might entail long-term hazards for the United States exceeded the imaginative capacity of U.S. policymakers. After all, as far as Washington was concerned, this was a strictly proxy contest. Money, weapons, ammunition, and training support funneled through Pakistan (which took a generous cut) would sustain members of the Afghan resistance actually doing the fighting and dying.[4] Intent on turning Afghanistan into a Soviet equivalent of Vietnam, Washington was equally intent on avoiding its own direct involvement in anything remotely resembling another Vietnam.

In the age-old manner of Russian armies, the Soviets employed brute force to suppress the insurgents. In the age-old manner of Afghan warriors, the mujahedin relied on stamina and persistence. The U.S.-led coalition leveled the playing field by providing the poorly armed insurgents with additional firepower.

From the outset, the basic facts of this nominally covert operation were widely reported. As early as July 1981, writing in *The New Republic*, Carl Bernstein of Watergate fame reported on the CIA's "complex, far-flung program, involving five countries and more than $100 million, to provide the Afghan resistance with the weaponry of modern guerrilla warfare."[5] An article in *Time* by the journalist (and future senior State Department official) Strobe Talbott enthused that the United States was "turning the tables on Moscow" by "aiding the mujahedin rebels to the tune of many millions of dollars per year."[6] Another *Time* dispatch reported that by 1985 support for Afghan insurgents from the United States alone had reached $470 million per year, albeit with some "seepage" going to Pakistan.[7]

In the self-aggrandizing American narrative of the war, the turning point came the following year when Reagan made the gutsy decision to provide the Afghan resistance with Stinger anti-aircraft missiles. By reducing the threat posed by Soviet attack helicopters, the Stingers gave the mujahedin a decisive edge. All of this was supposedly hush-hush and top secret—although readers of *The Washington Post* quickly learned about it over their morning coffee.[8]

Notably, the entire enterprise enjoyed broad bipartisan support on Capitol Hill. Democrats might bridle at the Reagan administration's efforts to undermine the leftist Sandinistas governing Nicaragua, but they had no objection whatsoever to arming Afghan insurgents.[9]

During the 1980s, U.S. assistance to the mujahedin increased from one year to the next, totaling in all between $4 billion and $5 billion. Although pursuing a different agenda, the Kingdom of Saudi Arabia matched this support dollar for dollar.[10] All of this money provided a basis for flooding Afghanistan with arms and ammunition, mostly old, mostly manufactured within the communist bloc, drawn from stocks held by China, Egypt, Israel, Turkey, and other nations.

Who were the recipients of this largesse? The Reagan administration regarded the insurgents as "noble savages in some sort of a state of purity fighting for an abstract idea of freedom."[11] It added Afghanistan Day to the official state calendar, annually observed as an occasion to offer support to the "freedom fighters" who were "defending principles of independence and freedom that form the basis of global security and stability," those principles including "the right to practice religion according to the dictates of conscience."[12] In 1982, Reagan dedicated an upcoming flight of the space shuttle *Columbia* to the people of Afghanistan, whose resistance to Soviet occupation represented "man's highest aspirations for freedom."[13] The following year, as a further expression of solidarity, the president entertained a mujahedin delegation in the Oval Office.

Reagan's characterization of the Afghan resistance was, to put it mildly, misleading. In fact, those opposing the Soviet occupation consisted of disparate and mutually antagonistic tribes, many of them deeply anti-American in their outlook.[14] Willingness to accept U.S. assistance did not imply that xenophobic Afghan leaders shared Washington's outlook on anything other than a desire to oust the Soviets. In practice, supporting the mujahedin meant promoting a hidebound and intolerant brand of Islamism that viewed non-Muslims with suspicion if not outright contempt. Among many Saudis and Pakistanis, such attitudes resonated with their own. For their part, U.S. leaders appeared oblivious to the actual nature of the struggle, insisting that Afghan jihadists were fighting in pursuit of universal values. We and they were on the same side—so, at least, U.S. policymakers professed to believe.

In his bestselling account of CIA involvement in 1980s Afghanistan, George Crile describes the mujahedin as "in effect, America's surrogate soldiers."[15] By implication, the Afghan fighters served America's cause, becoming, in Crile's telling of the tale, little more than extras in a feature film that cast Americans in the starring roles. Indeed, his book yielded just such a film, which depicted the Afghanistan War of the 1980s—"the biggest and most successful CIA campaign in history"—as an epic victory credited to the United States.[16]

Hollywood has long since mastered the art of interpreting history in ways that express the popular mood of the moment. Especially when it comes to war, the packaging typically involves putting the United States at center stage, while marginalizing or distorting the role of others and ignoring details that don't fit into an America-centric narrative. In this case, the Afghanistan War became "Charlie Wilson's War," its outcome determined by the actions of a sybaritic but otherwise undistinguished member of Congress in league with a maverick CIA operative.

Advanced American weaponry in particular had made all the difference. Explaining in a *Washington Post* op-ed "how the good guys won," Zalmay Khalilzad, a Reagan-era official destined to be the first post-9/11 U.S. ambassador to Afghanistan, noted that in early 1986 the war had been going badly for the mujahedin. Then the Stingers arrived, and in short order those "adverse trends were reversed dramatically."[17]

There was a flip side to this interpretation of the war's outcome. If the mujahedin had won thanks to U.S. assistance, the Soviets had lost because they had not availed themselves of the opportunity to learn from the American experience in Vietnam. "Soviet failure to learn from the U.S. and other applicable COIN [counterinsurgency] experiences," the authors of a 1989 U.S. Army study observed, "caused them to make many of the same errors."[18]

The significance attached to the roughly simultaneous end of the Cold War reinforced this self-congratulatory interpretation. Triumphalism and narcissism fed one another. What ostensibly made Afghanistan a great American (as opposed to Islamist) victory was the conviction that here the United States had inflicted a decisive defeat on the Soviet Union, thereby bringing to a satisfactory conclusion the ideological competition said to define the twentieth century. *We*—not the mujahedin—had prevailed.

So instead of seeing the failure of the Soviet project in Afghanistan for what it was—religious traditionalists emphatically rejecting secular modernity—Washington chose to interpret it as a sign of vindication. If collectivism had lost, democratic capitalism had won. With all the big questions of political economy—the only questions deemed worthy of serious attention—thus settled, the "end of history" itself was thereby at hand.[19]

This was by no means the first occasion on which Americans had succumbed to such delusions of finality. In 1865, they had interpreted Robert E. Lee's surrender at Appomattox as having conclusively resolved fundamental questions of individual freedom. Instead, even with the destruction of slavery, those questions took new form. In 1945, Americans saw in the Axis defeat the prospects of one world united in peace. Instead, competition between rival powers, each seeing the other as bent on achieving global supremacy, resumed.

Similarly, until obliterated by events, belief that the Cold War's passing constituted not simply a turning point but an end point enjoyed wide sway, especially in Washington. Only in the wake of 9/11 did it become apparent that communism's collapse notwithstanding, history had all along remorselessly ground onward, not least of all in poor, benighted Afghanistan itself.

From our present vantage point, all of this appears self-evident, just as it now seems obvious that banishing slavery wasn't of itself going to produce racial harmony and destroying fascism was not going to kindle world peace. Yet the equivalent naïveté that swept post–Cold War Washington is worth recalling because it helps explain why U.S. policymakers were blindsided by what their putative success in Afghanistan actually wrought. A raging bout of victory disease had made them stupid.

Meanwhile, even with outsiders kicking in money and hardware, the Afghans found themselves stuck paying the greater part of the bill. During the Soviet occupation, out of a population totaling approximately 15 million, an estimated 1 to 1.5 million Afghans were killed outright. A comparable number suffered war-related injuries. An additional 6 million Afghans fled to refugee camps in Pakistan and Iran.[20]

Massive violence combined with crude Soviet nation-building initiatives to shatter traditional Afghan society. Offering at least some sanctuary, cities mushroomed in size. In depopulated rural areas, agriculture collapsed, with food production falling by up to 50 percent. Educational and medical systems, never robust in the first place, also fell into disarray, unable to cope with the added strain of protracted war. Corruption and criminality flourished. Smuggling and opium production emerged as the mainstays of a devastated economy.[21] In the countryside, gun-toting warlords displaced traditional elites as local powerbrokers. In this environment, a radical strain of Islamism spread like a virus. According to Thomas Barfield, a leading scholar of Afghanistan, proponents of revolutionary Islamism saw in the Afghan mujahedin "the vanguard of a transnational jihad."[22]

Peering through their Cold War–tinted glasses, Americans saw something else: a landmark achievement. So it appeared, at least, when Soviet leader Mikhail Gorbachev decided to throw in the towel and pull out of Afghanistan. "From a taxpayer's perspective," one such Cold Warrior has boasted, "there may be no other federal program in history that produced so much historic change in world politics at such a small price"—a judgment that requires ignoring both the price already exacted of Afghans and the downstream costs awaiting the United States. That "the Afghans got little or nothing from the victory in 1989," Bruce Riedel continued, rates as "a tragedy," but not one for which Washington felt the least responsibility.[23] Indeed, victory left Afghanistan bereft of further value to the United States.

On February 16, 1989, as the last Soviet troops left Afghanistan, President George H. W. Bush, who had succeeded Ronald Reagan just the month before, released a statement hailing the "extraordinary triumph of spirit and will by the Afghan people" and promising continued U.S. assistance "to remove mines, resettle refugees, and reconstruct Afghanistan's war-torn economy."[24]

Whether Bush actually meant what he said is difficult to say. What ensued, however, was something quite different. "We have to be realistic," a senior U.S. official told *The New York Times*. "Afghanistan is not Iran. It has no oil reserves and isn't located on the Persian Gulf. It's not a particular strategic prize that has to be guarded at all costs."[25] However warmly President Bush might express his personal regard for the Afghan people, their substantive value to the United States was nil.

Losing interest in Afghanistan—and also in Pakistan, an ally now once more deemed expendable—Washington wasted little time in turning its attention to quarters of the Greater Middle East deemed more important. As Barfield put it, "The United States wished no further involvement in a resourceless country on the verge of collapse that had become strategically irrelevant."[26]

Events in Afghanistan provided a convenient excuse to disengage. Although the Soviet-installed regime in Kabul surprised observers by hanging on longer than expected, it finally gave way in the spring of 1992. A civil war immediately ensued, with mujahedin factions now turning on one another with astonishing ferocity. Professing horror, the United States called for an end to the fighting but used the internecine struggle as a pretext to wash its hands of Afghanistan.[27] That civil war continued until 1996, when the Taliban gained precarious control of the country and imposed an order of draconian severity.

Imagine a physician intent on reducing a malignant growth subjecting a patient to an arduous regime of chemotherapy, only to abandon the weakened and vulnerable patient as soon as the growth disappeared. Tumor excised, responsibility fulfilled. Dealing with any lingering aftereffects was someone else's problem. This, in essence, describes U.S. policy toward Afghanistan following the Soviet withdrawal.

Close observers quickly glimpsed the potential implications. Already in March 1989, a correspondent with the Minneapolis *Star-Tribune* suggested that while celebrating the triumph of the mujahedin, "Americans might also contemplate the possibility that other Islamic 'holy warriors' may soon be perched near airports around the world, targeting civilian planes with the deadly U.S. missiles we sent to the 'freedom fighters.'"[28] Another American journalist reported on widespread worries that "the international warriors" who had joined the holy war in Afghanistan might provide the basis of "a dedicated and devout army of fundamentalist Muslim revolutionaries, trained in the art of guerrilla war and prepared to move on to the next jihad."[29] By "encouraging a rebellion based on religious zealotry without stopping to analyze what would happen if the zealots triumphed," had the United States "created a monster"?[30] Long before most Americans had ever heard of Al Qaeda or Osama bin Laden, that possibility had begun to present itself.

An ironic de facto collaboration between Washington and Moscow had transformed Afghanistan from a failing state into a failed one. The nine-year U.S.-led effort to prevent the Soviets from pacifying Afghanistan succeeded without the loss of a single American life. From the experience, the United States took away two lessons destined to shape Washington's response to other crises in the Greater Middle East. The first lesson discredited timidity, with Operation Cyclone seemingly proving that fortune favors the bold. After all, the outcome had vindicated those who had advocated perilous steps such as providing the mujahedin with arms traceable to the United States. The second lesson suggested that sophisticated weapons could have game-changing implications, with Stingers offering seemingly irrefutable proof. Put to further test, both of these lessons would prove wildly misleading.

In fact, by reducing that country to a shambles, Operation Cyclone set in motion a train of events that soon enough produced an even longer pacification campaign, this one led by the United States itself and destined to consume considerable American blood and treasure. In the end, Washington's success in luring the USSR into an Afghan quagmire transformed Afghanistan into an incubator of terrorism and drew the United States back into what became a quagmire of its own.

What judgment to render on all this is a matter of perspective. Asked in 1998 if he had any regrets about having helped instigate Soviet intervention in Afghanistan, Zbigniew Brzezinski, in many respects the godfather of Operation Cyclone, reacted with astonishment. "Regret what?" he replied. "That secret operation was an excellent idea. It had the effect of drawing the Russians into the Afghan trap and you want me to regret it?"

The interviewer pressed the point. Hadn't the subsequent rise of radical Islamism tarnished that victory? Not in Brzezinski's view. "What is most important to the history of the world? The Taliban or the collapse of the Soviet empire? Some stirred-up Moslems or the liberation of Central Europe and the end of the cold war?"[31]

With the passage of time, the answers to rhetorical questions that Brzezinski deemed self-evident became decidedly less so. As U.S. military involvement in the Greater Middle East deepened, dismissing "stirred-up Moslems" as inconsequential came to seem a trifle glib. In the eyes of successive presidential administrations, they represented something akin to a threat of sufficient danger to justify war on an ever-widening scale.

All of this lay in the future, of course. For the moment, Washington fancied that it had finished its work in Afghanistan. Unfortunately, Afghanistan was not yet finished with the United States.

4

SILVER SCREEN SIX

IS CALLING

EVEN AS EVENTS IN AFGHANISTAN WERE UNFOLDING, RONALD Reagan had ordered a contingent of U.S. Marines to Beirut, Lebanon, of all places. There they suffered grievous losses and soon thereafter departed the premises, their mission ending in abject failure. Like a dimwitted cop armed only with a billy club, the United States had wandered into the middle of a gang war. By the time it ended, radical Islamists had "inflicted the largest tactical defeat on the U.S. military since the Korean War."[1]

The contrast between the U.S. interventions in Afghanistan and Lebanon could hardly be greater. Afghanistan was covert and protracted and seemed for a time to have ended successfully. By comparison, the U.S. intervention in Lebanon was overt and comparatively brief and yielded a catastrophic outcome. In Afghanistan, working through intermediaries, the CIA actively promoted violence. In Lebanon, with the stars and stripes prominently displayed, the Marines sought to curb it. Whereas no American policymaker believed that gestures and symbols were going to affect Soviet behavior in Afghanistan, more than a few somehow concluded that a symbolic military presence, accompanied by professions of benign intent, was going to affect the behavior of the various powers vying to control Lebanon. In sum, whereas the architects of U.S. policy in Afghanistan at least had a clear sense of purpose, those who ordered Marines to Beirut had next to none.

As an episode in America's War for the Greater Middle East, the U.S. intervention in Lebanon, lasting from August 1982 to July 1984, surely ranks as one of the most bizarre, leaving the historian to wonder: What exactly possessed policymakers to think this was a good idea? Answering that question requires first reconstructing the circumstances that prompted Reagan to send in the Marines.

An Israeli invasion of Lebanon, which began on June 6, 1982, along with the consequences that ensued, triggered that decision. The political scientist Samuel Huntington once created a stir by writing that "Islam has bloody borders."[2] Much the same can be said about Israel during the first several decades of its existence.

Throughout the preceding decade, the Israeli-Lebanese border had been notably bloody. Expelled from Jordan in 1970, thousands of Palestinians had transformed southern Lebanon into a state-within-a-state controlled by Yasser Arafat's Palestine Liberation Organization. A seemingly endless series of raids and reprisals ensued, reviving among Israeli leaders a long-nurtured ambition to fix Lebanon once and for all, eliminating any further threats from that quarter.

The recently signed peace treaty with Egypt along with the presence of an avid supporter of the Jewish state in the White House made such an attempt appear plausible. A secure southern flank and Ronald Reagan's assurances of undying friendship enhanced Israel's freedom of action.[3] Meanwhile, the ongoing disintegration of Lebanon, wracked since 1975 by a civil war pitting Maronite Christians, Shiite Muslims, Sunni Muslims, and Palestinian refugees against one another, made such an attempt imperative. For the right-wing government of Israeli prime minister Menachem Begin, the prospect of a failed state and haven for terrorists as an immediate neighbor was intolerable.

Yet fixing Lebanon, its territory occupied not only by the PLO but also by the Syrian army, posed immense challenges. Begin's minister of defense, the fiercely hawkish Ariel Sharon, thought otherwise. He resolved to end "the Lebanese problem in one great sweep of Israeli armor" that would destroy the PLO and send the Syrians packing. Israel would then install in Beirut a Maronite government. The two nations would become friends and allies. "In one stroke, Lebanon would move from an Israeli liability to an asset."[4]

Operation Peace for Galilee did not live up to Sharon's expectations, however, either militarily or politically. Begin lied to Reagan in describing Israeli aims as modest, merely a brief push into southern Lebanon to disrupt PLO artillery and rocket attacks. As the actual scope of the Israeli offensive exposed those lies for what they were, Washington reacted with outrage. Although given to tough talk, the Reagan administration was hardly in the mood to have fighting in Lebanon provoke a major East-West showdown. As Israeli mechanized formations clobbered the Syrians and closed in on Beirut (and as the Soviets prepared to make good Syrian equipment losses), U.S. demands for Israel to accept a United Nations–mandated ceasefire became more insistent. At noon on June 11, Israel acceded to (without fully honoring) those demands.[5]

Although Israel Defense Forces had taken up positions in West Beirut, they had neither destroyed the PLO nor ousted the Syrians. And while the Israelis had linked up with Maronite militia fighters led by the erratic quasi-fascist Bashir Gemayel, their dream of installing in power a friendly Christian government remained well beyond reach. Yet Begin and Sharon refused to admit failure. So under the cover of the ceasefire, the IDF laid siege to Beirut itself, indiscriminately pummeling the city with artillery, air strikes, and gunboats operating offshore, cutting off electricity and water supplies, all in an effort to flush Arafat's forces.[6]

Having caught the PLO in a vise, Israel squeezed hard. Yet as the IDF ratcheted up its punishment of Beirut from one week to the next, the Reagan administration ratcheted up its pressure on Israel to lift the siege. Demanding "an end to the unnecessary bloodshed," Reagan warned Begin that "the relationship between our two nations is at stake."[7] On August 12, after an especially harsh series of IDF attacks, the president denounced Israeli actions as "unfathomable and senseless."[8] So Israel too found itself caught in a vise, one of its own making. With the PLO and the government of Israel each under extreme duress and sharing an urgent need to escape, the makings of a deal were at hand. To survive, the PLO agreed to leave Lebanon. To placate Washington, Israel agreed to permit that departure to occur, with the Reagan administration expecting a withdrawal of Israeli forces to follow soon thereafter.

Here was a scenario not envisioned by the Carter Doctrine. Yet reticence about intervening in the Islamic world was already waning. Carter's declaration had signaled greater activism on Washington's part. Enter the United States Marine Corps.

For the previous six weeks, the possibility of Reagan dispatching peacekeepers to Lebanon had been a hot topic on the nation's op-ed pages. In general, the prospect had attracted support, albeit without much enthusiasm. Still, there were dissenters. Among the most prescient was Rear Admiral Robert J. Hanks, a retired naval officer with experience in the Middle East, who argued that sending Marines into Lebanon would provide the "ultimate proof" in Arab eyes that the United States was doing Israel's bidding. U.S. support for Israel had already "engendered widespread antagonism, indeed hatred" throughout much of the Islamic world, Hanks wrote. Troops deployed in the guise of peacekeepers would provide Arabs an ideal target "against which to vent their wrath." It was "wholly unrealistic," Hanks insisted, "to expect any outcome other than American Marines . . . falling casualty to the rage and vengeance of frustrated Palestinians, whether operating under the banner of the PLO or some new and more desperate organization."[9] Hanks erred in one regard only: His timing was off by a year.

In the event, such warnings were easily ignored. So in Beirut, on August 25, 1982, a task force consisting of eight hundred U.S. Marines came ashore, charged by President Reagan "to be once again what Marines have been for more than 200 years—peace-makers." On hand to greet the Americans as they landed were diplomats, local dignitaries, and members of the press. Although the Marines were entering a combat zone, the atmospherics did not suggest expectations of imminent hostilities. Indeed, Reagan himself and Secretary of State George P. Shultz repeatedly emphasized that the mission was not going to involve fighting.[10] So while armed, the Marines did not load their weapons, a "deliberate decision" intended to "demonstrate that the Americans were on a peace-keeping mission."[11]

With the port secured, the evacuation of PLO fighters and some family members commenced almost immediately. Within a matter of days, under watchful American eyes, a total of 6,436 Palestinians had boarded ships bound for Sudan, Syria, Tunisia, and other countries that had agreed to accept the exiles. One of the last to go, on August 30, was Arafat himself, cheered by well-wishers and accompanied by a platoon-sized bodyguard.[12]

Apart from mild obstructionism by Israeli forces and some grand-standing (as the Americans saw it) by French legionnaires also dispatched to the scene, the entire operation went off without a serious hitch. The Marines fired no shots and sustained no casualties. Instead, to pass the time, they "played cards and volleyball," according to *The New York Times*.[13] Things went so well that by September 3 luminaries such as Secretary of Defense Caspar Weinberger, trailed by members of Congress, began arriving to pose for photographs while lunching on C-rations. Their work apparently finished, the Marines themselves soon began packing up to leave. On September 10, the last to depart clambered aboard a landing craft that displayed a large banner proclaiming "Mission Accomplished."[14]

Not for the last time, the claim proved to be illusory. While the Marines had performed admirably, they had accomplished next to nothing. Certainly, they had not fulfilled President Reagan's naïve expectations of making peace.

This became evident just four days later, on September 14, when a bomb planted by a Syrian agent killed Bashir Gemayel along with twenty-six other senior members of his Phalange party. The Lebanese parliament had only recently elected Gemayel as his country's next president—he was the sole candidate—an outcome that Israel and the United States strongly supported.[15] In the eyes of Begin and Sharon, Gemayel's ascendancy kept alive their vision of an Israeli-Lebanese condominium. For its part, the Reagan administration saw Gemayel as the key to restoring some semblance of Lebanese stability. Now the object of these improbable hopes was dead.

Sharon reflexively blamed stay-behind PLO fighters for Gemayel's assassination. Yet if the loss of Israel's would-be Lebanese partner was a setback, it also offered an opportunity to purge Beirut of its Palestinian presence once and for all. The day after Gemayel's murder, IDF units occupied the Palestinian precincts of West Beirut in force. There they facilitated the entry into the Sabra and Shatila refugee camps of Phalangist militiamen bent on liquidating the inhabitants. A massacre ensued. Before it was over, the Phalangists had murdered in cold blood at least 700 and perhaps as many as 3,500 Palestinians.[16]

An international outcry erupted, as belated as it was predictable. A *Time* cover story decried "butchery the mind cannot comprehend." When the killing finally ended more than thirty hours after it began, *Time* reported,

> There were only the sounds of mourning and the bodies, sprawling heaps of corpses: men, women and children. Some had been shot in the head at pointblank range. Others had had their throats cut. Some had their hands tied behind their backs; one young man had been castrated. Middle-aged women and girls as young as three, their arms and legs grotesquely splayed, were draped across piles of rubble. Portions of their heads were blown away.[17]

President Reagan wasted no time declaring his "outrage and revulsion over the murders," offering his condolences to the "broader Palestinian community" and fingering Israel as responsible. He all but ordered the Israeli government to withdraw its forces from Beirut forthwith.[18]

Within days, he also decided to reinsert U.S. Marines into that city. As part of a multinational peacekeeping force, they were to establish "a presence in Beirut, that would in turn help establish the stability necessary for the Lebanese government to regain control of their capital."[19] How exactly the Marines were to accomplish such an ambitious task, even if assisted by other small allied contingents, was not at all clear.

Still, Reagan himself expressed confidence that it could be done. Conditions were ripe, he insisted, for the United States to take "bold and timely initiatives" to free Lebanon of foreign forces and undertake a "systematic program to rebuild Lebanese security forces."[20]

Demonstrating that U.S. forces by their very presence could bring order out of anarchy would establish a valuable precedent, with potential application elsewhere in the Greater Middle East. "For an administration so dedicated to the accumulation of military power," the historian Ronald Steel observed at the time, "how irresistible to have the chance to actually use it—even in the most limited way. What is the point of being a global superpower if one is unable to project that power?"[21] *The Washington Post* surmised that projecting American power into the Lebanese morass would "dramatize the U.S. role as the region's only potential peacemaker." The stakes went beyond Lebanon itself. "If things go well," the *Post* reporter speculated, the United States stood to "regain credibility in the eyes of the Arab world."[22] For his part, Leslie Gelb of *The New York Times* saw the reentry of U.S. forces as evidence that the United States had "assumed the role of Middle East policeman."[23]

Yet the contrast with the brief, just-completed U.S. intervention was striking. In that case, Marines had focused on completing a concrete and narrowly defined mission: Implement an agreed-upon evacuation of PLO fighters. By comparison, this new mission was broad and slippery. Nothing had been agreed upon. The United States was projecting power into a void, vaguely hoping that an agreement of some kind would magically emerge. With unknowns outnumbering knowns by a generous margin, Beirut was about to become a place where Marines strolling around with unloaded weapons did so at their peril.

Nonetheless, on September 29, a somewhat larger task force—approximately 1,200 Marines in all—arrived back in Beirut and took up defensive positions in the city's battered international airport, littered with refuse from years of fighting. That same day, the task force suffered its first casualties, with one Marine killed and three wounded while attempting to clear the airfield of unexploded ordnance. Even so, the mission began in an atmosphere of relative calm, which persisted through the fall and into the winter.

The Americans settled in for what promised to be a long haul. Tours of duty were relatively brief, as every hundred days or so, a new unit rotated in, allowing its predecessor to depart. But the overall mission was open-ended. Marines stayed busy mounting show-the-flag patrols beyond their defensive perimeter while hosting an endless stream of VIPs. Starting in November, they also undertook small-scale training efforts in support of the Lebanese army.[24]

"Presence" was supposed to buy time, allowing Lebanon's ostensibly nonsectarian army to reassert responsibility for maintaining internal security. Such an outcome, of course, was contingent upon Israel and Syria agreeing to withdraw their own forces, a prerequisite to restoring Lebanese sovereignty. Only then would the Marines be able to resurrect their "Mission Accomplished" banner.

Marine relations with the IDF remained contentious. According to Weinberger, the Israelis repeatedly "harassed our forces."[25] Claiming to take fire from areas under U.S. control, IDF units responded vigorously, either by returning fire or dispatching armored reaction forces that intruded into turf under Marine jurisdiction. The Marines responded with equal vigor. In the most dramatic such incident, on February 2, 1983, Captain Charles B. Johnson confronted a column of Israeli tanks advancing toward a Marine checkpoint and ordered them to halt. When the commander of the lead vehicle announced his intention to proceed, Johnson, dismounted with sidearm drawn, replied that he would do so "over my dead body." With that, the Israeli column attempted to bypass Johnson, at which time the young Marine officer leaped aboard the lead tank and angrily ordered the Israeli commander to halt. A nonviolent disengagement ensued, with Johnson thereby earning a place of honor in service lore.[26]

Here, in microcosm, was a validation of what U.S. military presence could achieve not only in Lebanon but elsewhere in the Greater Middle East as well. Because they commanded respect, U.S. forces could persuade the unruly or the mischief-minded to behave, even without having to fire a shot. To stand firm sufficed to make the point. So it appeared, at least.

Far more significant than Captain Johnson's commendable heroics was the intensifying violence between opposing Lebanese sects, which the availability of nearby Western peacekeepers did nothing to avert. Indeed, U.S. support for the Lebanese army, itself increasingly aligned with the Phalangists in opposition to Palestinian, Druze, and Shia militias, had the effect of making the Marines a party to Lebanon's resurgent civil war. The Marines manned checkpoints and conducted joint patrols with Lebanese army forces while also providing them with stocks of ammunition.[27] An ostensibly neutral presence was morphing into active engagement.

Soon enough, the peacekeepers themselves became targets, as did Western interests more generally. On March 16, unknown assailants ambushed a Marine patrol, wounding five. Other small attacks followed, with both Marines and allied forces targeted. Then on April 18, a major escalation occurred. A suicide bomber, driving a van packed with explosives, detonated his vehicle at the entrance of the U.S. embassy, tearing the face off of that seven-story building and killing sixty-three, including seventeen Americans. Marines rushed to secure the site and minister to the injured. The following month, Druze artillery began shelling Marine positions at the airport. During the summer, these attacks, now including mortars and rockets, intensified and became more frequent. Marine helicopters also came under fire. The posture of the Marine force changed. Patrolling ended. Vulnerable outposts were abandoned. No one used terms like *permissive* to describe the situation.[28]

By now tanks and a battery of 155mm howitzers had arrived to reinforce the Marines. Additional assets from the U.S. Sixth Fleet were also gathering off the Lebanese coast. These included a carrier battle group augmented by the USS *New Jersey*, a mothballed World War II battleship that the Reagan administration had recently refurbished. At least the hunkered-down peacekeepers did not lack for firepower.

As the futility of U.S.-led efforts to negotiate a mutual withdrawal of all Syrian and Israeli forces became apparent, the government of Israel took matters into its own hands. On the night of September 3–4, without advance notification to Washington, Israeli forces pulled out of Beirut to a "security zone" in southern Lebanon. This "uncoordinated withdrawal," wrote Colonel Timothy Geraghty, the Marine commander, "put the multi-national peacekeeping force, and especially the U.S. contingent, directly in the crosshairs of the Muslim militias."[29]

The implications became immediately apparent as a hail of rockets and artillery rounds struck the Marine compound on September 5 and 6. U.S. casualties mounted, with several killed and some two dozen wounded. As the Americans endured "incessant pounding," Marine artillerymen returned fire, furthering the transformation of peacekeepers into combatants.[30]

The escalation moved Reagan—call sign "Silver Screen Six"—to phone Geraghty directly.[31] The president vowed to provide "whatever support it takes to stop the attacks." As if reading from a movie script, Geraghty promised the commander in chief that his Marines would "hang tough and carry out our mission."[32]

Reagan himself felt certain that a bit of muscle-flexing could put things right. To his diary on September 7, he confided that "I can't get the idea out of my head that some F-14s . . . coming in at about 200 ft. over the Marines & blowing hell out of a couple of artillery emplacements would be a tonic for the Marines & at the same time would deliver a message to those gun happy middle east terrorists."[33] Within days, he signed off on a classified directive authorizing "naval gunfire support and, if deemed necessary, tactical air strikes" to support the Lebanese army.[34]

Indeed, U.S. forces were already upping the ante. On September 8, navy warships entered the fray, engaging suspected antigovernment militias with 5-inch cannon fire. During subsequent days, shelling continued. On September 19, for example, U.S. warships supporting the Lebanese army fired 350 rounds over a five-hour period, while Navy fighter jets conducted reconnaissance overhead. As the Marine official history noted, "this specific instance of combat support evidently ended the perception of the Marines as neutral in the eyes of anti-government factions."[35] Whether intentionally or out of sheer ignorance, the United States had effectively enlisted as a full-fledged co-belligerent in Lebanon's civil war.

To their credit, the Marines remained steadfast. They neither flinched nor budged, magnificently unaware of the fate awaiting them, despite the flashing-red warning signs. It was as if during the weeks prior to December 7, 1941, the Japanese navy had conducted a series of small-scale preliminary raids on Pearl Harbor while the pride of the Pacific Fleet remained stubbornly tied up two-by-two on Battleship Row.

Of course, the Pearl Harbor disaster stemmed as much from myopia in Washington as from laxness on the part of local commanders. This was true of Beirut as well. There, with the security environment obviously eroding, the Marine presence qualified as either irrelevant or counterproductive. Geraghty understood that and said so to his immediate superiors.[36] Yet the parade of generals, admirals, and high-ranking officials, both elected and appointed, who helicoptered in and out of Beirut to visit weren't listening.

Preoccupied with disorder in Lebanon, U.S. policymakers mistook symptom for disease. The disorder afflicting this one country manifested problems far too large for the entire U.S. Marine Corps to handle, much less Colonel Geraghty's beleaguered 24th Marine Amphibious Unit. In essence, the crisis of the moment had induced a bout of strategic inanity—senior officials talking themselves into believing that by helping Lebanon's army prevail over its adversaries, a reinforced battalion could pave the way for Middle East peace. The imperative of the moment, Secretary of State Shultz insisted, was "to stand firm, showing strength that was purposeful and steady."[37] How having a few hundred Marines holed up at Beirut International Airport communicated a sense of purposefulness was not at all clear. Inevitably, it is ordinary GIs who pay for such folly—a phenomenon destined to recur from one episode to the next during America's evolving War for the Greater Middle East.

In late October, this particular episode came to a head. In a *New York*

Times dispatch published on October 23, dateline Beirut, Thomas Friedman reported what had now become obvious: "Without anyone really noticing it at first, the Marines here have been transformed during the last month of fighting [into] just one more faction in the internal Lebanese conflict."[38]

The period of hardly anyone noticing ended abruptly. The very day that Friedman's article appeared in the *Times,* a suicide bomber, driving a yellow Mercedes truck loaded with explosives, crashed through the main gate of the Marine compound and drove into the four-story building the Marines had converted into a makeshift barracks. The resulting detonation killed 241 U.S. military personnel and wounded another hundred. A near-simultaneous attack on the nearby French compound killed fifty-eight French peacekeepers. A group calling itself Islamic Jihad, subsequently better known as Hezbollah, claimed responsibility.

Rudely awakened from their slumber, the American people wondered what the hell was going on. The prompt, efficient evacuation of those wounded and killed stood in stark contrast with the languid, let's-see-what-tomorrow-brings attitude that had put the Marines in jeopardy in the first place. Why had no one in authority anticipated this catastrophe? By no means would this be the last time during America's War for the Greater Middle East that a U.S. military expedition gone awry would elicit such a public reaction. Seldom would Americans receive a satisfactory answer.

This devastating assault on U.S. troops obviously required a forceful response, if only to distract attention from the ineptitude that had placed the Marines in such jeopardy. Yet formulating that response produced weeks of dithering and indecision that finally culminated in ignominious retreat.

For public consumption, the president projected a stiffly Reaganesque upper lip. "Let no terrorist question our will," he declared at a memorial service held for those killed, "or no tyrant doubt our resolve." Citing the "courage and determination" that formed enduring parts of the American character, Reagan declared that "we must not and will not be intimidated by anyone, anywhere."[39]

Although on-the-ground realities mocked such platitudes, the president remained weirdly upbeat. Within days of the Beirut bombing, he issued a top-secret policy directive in which he cheerfully affirmed that creating "an independent, sovereign Lebanon, free of all foreign forces is an achievable goal." The key to fulfilling that goal and much else besides was for the United States to "continue to be seen as a fair arbiter of justice in the Middle East." With that in mind, notwithstanding the debacle in Beirut, Reagan vowed to "reassert American leadership" and "regain the initiative." The U.S. presidential election looming in the year ahead offered reason enough to press on: "For if we appear to be hunkering down to a more passive policy as we approach an election year, we will not make progress but will slide into a morass of confusion and doubt which will give rise to strong domestic criticism."[40]

Yet almost immediately, confusion and doubt all but paralyzed his administration. Reagan's directive called for retaliating against those who had perpetrated the October 23 Beirut bombing, "subject to reasonable confirmation of the locations of suitable targets." The caveat provided an opening for opponents of further military escalation—notably Secretary of Defense Weinberger and General John Vessey, who chaired the Joint Chiefs of Staff—to block retaliatory action. Instead, they sought to terminate the Marine presence altogether.[41]

Meanwhile, the conflict in Lebanon ground on, belying Reagan's expectations of that country regaining its independence and sovereignty. U.S. military involvement in that conflict mirrored the dithering that consumed Washington. Despite the continued material support and firepower provided by the United States, the Lebanese army was failing—not the last time that American efforts to "build" an army in the Islamic world would fall short.

When Syrian air defenses east of Beirut engaged a U.S. reconnaissance aircraft on December 3, the Reagan administration finally roused itself to respond. The result was a poorly planned, half-hearted air strike that ended with two U.S. Navy fighter jets shot down and one American airman, Lieutenant Robert Goodman, who happened to be black, captured. From the sidelines, Israeli generals jeered. A delegation of African-American clergy, led by Democratic presidential hopeful Reverend Jesse Jackson but also including Jeremiah Wright and Louis Farrakhan, traveled to Damascus and successfully negotiated Goodman's release.[42]

The Marines remaining at Beirut International Airport were still at risk, with several more killed that same day by Syrian artillery fire. With commanders averse to losing any more combat aircraft, surface warships such as the battleship *New Jersey* now became the preferred instrument for registering American unhappiness. Yet if by hurling 1900-pound shells up to twenty miles the *New Jersey*'s 16-inch guns represented military might, they also signified political impotence. No amount of naval bombardment was going to salvage a peacekeeping enterprise that had irredeemably failed.

By the end of January 1984, Reagan himself was ready to throw in the towel, directing the Pentagon to plan for withdrawing the Marines, although allowing for the possibility of a "continuing U.S. military presence offshore." Although Reagan wanted efforts to prop up the Lebanese army to continue, the United States was opting out of the fight.[43] "We're not bugging out," the president insisted. "We're just going to a little more defensible position."[44] Few found the claim persuasive.

On February 26, 1984, the last Marines departed Beirut International Airport. In a fit of pique, the *New Jersey* and other warships, under the pretense of providing covering fire, blasted away at targets ashore.[45] This time, the "Mission Accomplished" banner was nowhere to be seen. Summing things up in *The New York Times*, Thomas Friedman wrote that the Marines had "accomplished virtually nothing."[46] The judgment remains difficult to dispute.

Policy failures typically produce some sort of inquiry, if only for purposes of damage control, and that was the case here. A commission consisting of several senior military officers and a former Pentagon official investigated the events of October 23, carefully steering clear of the policies that had launched the Marines on their exercise in futility in the first place. The resulting report was nothing if not circumspect. Focusing on operational shortcomings, it studiously avoided any more fundamental questions. So the commission concluded, for example, that the attack on the Marine barracks "was tantamount to an act of war using the medium of terrorism." Verily. But what exactly was the nature of this "war"? Who were the belligerents? What were the stakes? What would winning entail? Was the war even winnable? On these questions, the report had little to say. Instead it offered anodyne comments such as "State sponsored terrorism poses a serious threat to U.S. policy . . . and thus merits the attention of military planners."

The commission's report described Lebanon as containing "a veritable jungle of threats." Yet it did not ask why it made sense for U.S. forces to wade into that jungle. To what end? Members of the commission evinced no interest in that question. Instead, they concluded that Colonel Geraghty and his subordinates should have known better and done better, while largely giving a pass to those at higher levels—fairly standard procedure, as these matters go.[47]

What becomes clear in retrospect is this: Among U.S. policymakers, Beirut ought to have set off alarm bells. Failure there might have suggested that dabbling with the use of U.S. forces to "fix" the Greater Middle East was to collide with complexities that even Miles Ignotus could not wish away. Presence, especially by token forces occupying stationary positions, amounted to an incitement. Rather than contributing to stability, it did just the opposite.

The sad fact is that those who sent the Marines into Lebanon had no real idea what they were doing or what they were getting into. For the most part, the resulting failure there served to broadcast American ignorance, ineptitude, and lack of staying power. As for those expectations of dramatizing America's role as peacemaker, enhancing U.S. credibility in Arab eyes, and demonstrating a capacity to police the region: None of it happened.

Near Camp Lejeune, North Carolina, a memorial erected to honor the Americans killed in Beirut bears this inscription: "They came in peace." However inadvertently, the text captures the cardinal error that doomed the enterprise: a fundamental misapprehension of actually existing realities.

To keep peace implies its existence. In Lebanon, peace did not exist before, during, or after the Marine intervention. Nor would it for years to come. Instead, in the wake of the U.S. departure, Lebanon remained a battleground, with the civil war there dragging on for years. Syrian and Israeli forces continued to occupy parts of Lebanese territory. The PLO may have left the scene. Yet as a direct consequence of the Israeli invasion, Hezbollah soon emerged to form another state-within-a-state.[48] Its leaders could reasonably claim to have inflicted a decisive defeat on the world's preeminent superpower, a conclusion not lost on other opponents of the United States.

5

MAD DOG, KICKED,
BITES BACK

LEBANON WAS BY NO MEANS THE ONLY INSTANCE IN WHICH
Ronald Reagan committed U.S. forces into the Islamic sphere. Libya
also attracted intermittent attention during the preliminary phases of
America's War for the Greater Middle East. Here too, as in Lebanon,
Washington experimented with how best to translate military power,
always assumed to be superior, into politically purposeful outcomes.
Here too, the results fell well short of satisfactory.

Apart from sitting on top of considerable oil deposits, Libya as such
possessed little strategic significance to the United States in the 1980s.
Libya's ruler made himself difficult for U.S. policymakers to ignore,
however. Colonel Moamar Gaddafi was an erratic, megalomaniacal
buffoon, less a serious menace than a perennial pain in the behind. The
danger posed by Gaddafi stemmed less from his grandiose ambitions
than from his tendency to act on impulse, without regard for consequences. He was a teenager handed a wad of cash along with keys to a
sports car.

After seizing power in a 1969 military coup, Gaddafi nationalized
Libyan oil, declared himself an ardent pan-Arabist, and began accumulating an arsenal of advanced weapons, mostly purchased from the
Soviet Union. Stridently anti-Western and anti-Israeli, he used Libyan
oil wealth to finance an omnium-gatherum of foreign revolutionaries

variously committed to overthrowing the capitalist order, rooting out the vestiges of colonialism, and, above all, liberating Palestine.[1]

By 1979, these activities had earned Libya a place on the State Department's roster of state sponsors of terrorism. Soon after becoming president, Reagan concluded that Gaddafi needed to be taught a lesson. Bringing Libya's blustering "Brother Leader and Guide of the Revolution" down a peg or two thereby found a spot on the administration's to-do list.

An existing dispute over the Gulf of Sidra provided the United States the opportunity to do just that. In 1973, Gaddafi had claimed ownership of the gulf, a wide U-shaped indentation carved out of the Libyan coastline between Misrata and Benghazi. More specifically, he asserted that anyone entering the gulf—crossing what he called the "line of death"—would be violating Libyan territorial waters and airspace and therefore courting trouble.

The United States had rejected Gaddafi's claim without pressing the issue.[2] Under President Reagan, that changed. In August 1981, invoking what it called "freedom of navigation," the U.S. Sixth Fleet initiated a "stair step" exercise using "progressively more assertive military actions" to challenge Gaddafi.[3] This involved dispatching the carriers *Forrestal* and *Nimitz* across the "line of death" to elicit a response.

Gaddafi rose to the bait, scrambling jet fighters to confront the intruders. Although more than a little shadowboxing ensued, the outcome was never in doubt: On August 19, a pair of U.S. Navy F-14 Tomcats shot down two Libyan Su-22s engaging in aggressive maneuvers.[4] For the White House, it was the perfect outcome: We win, they lose. Here was tangible evidence that with Silver Screen Six in the Oval Office, America wasn't taking any more guff. To commemorate the achievement, as a trophy of sorts, the Reagan Library in Simi Valley, California, has on permanent display an F-14 similar to those that participated in the mission.[5]

Yet as so often in America's War for the Greater Middle East, the victory proved considerably less than advertised. Without actually confiscating cash or car keys, the point of the exercise was to make the delinquent teenager toe the line. In that regard, it fell short. In point of fact, the confrontation settled nothing. Gaddafi refused to behave or even to shut up.

Incidents of anti-Western terrorism, some specifically directed at U.S. targets, others only incidentally involving Americans, continued to accumulate.[6] In December 1983, just two months after the deadly attack on the Marine compound in Beirut, terrorists blew up the U.S. embassy annex in Kuwait, killing five. The kidnappings of American intelligence agents, journalists, and clergymen working in Lebanon became commonplace. In September 1984, a truck bomb destroyed the U.S. embassy annex there. Among the dead were two Americans.

By this time, in a directive called "Combating Terrorism," Reagan had ordered the Pentagon to "develop a military strategy that is supportive of an active, preventive program to combat state-sponsored terrorism," including "a full range of military options."[7] This top-secret policy decision moved the United States incrementally closer toward a fully militarized response to the problems posed by terrorism. Here was a de facto first draft of the Bush Doctrine of preventive war that reached maturity after 9/11.

Itself engaged in a massive military buildup, the Reagan administration did not harbor an aversion to the threat or use of violence. It merely subscribed to a convenient double standard that classified terrorism as illegitimate violence employed pursuant to illegitimate objectives. Under certain circumstances nuking cities might be permissible, but terrorism never. In Washington, the gripes, grievances, and political motives of those perpetrating acts of terrorism had no standing. It was, therefore, unnecessary to take them into consideration.[8] With quite literally nothing to talk about—the very idea of talk implied appeasement—the logic of resorting to military action to counter this evil phenomenon appeared unassailable.

Reagan's directive on combating terrorism did not mention Libya specifically. Even though Gaddafi offered moral encouragement and financial rewards to those who perpetrated acts of anti-Western terrorism, establishing unequivocal Libyan complicity in specific attacks did not come easily. Yet Gaddafi's brazenness combined with Libya's relative puniness made that country the ideal venue to demonstrate the fate that awaited any state tempted to defy Washington's prohibition on terrorism. Striking effectively at organizations such as Hezbollah, Islamic Jihad, or the Palestine Liberation Front posed sizable challenges. By comparison, Tripoli presented a fixed, visible, and even inviting target—just the place to test the viability of a counterterrorism strategy based on "active prevention, preemption, and retaliation."[9]

As terrorist attacks mounted—episodes in 1985 alone included Hezbollah and Islamic Jihad hijacking a TWA jetliner bound from Athens to Rome, the seizure of the cruise ship *Achille Lauro* by members of the Palestine Liberation Front, and murderous airport assaults in Rome and Vienna attributed to the Abu Nidal organization—the administration's exasperation with the Libyan dictator festered. Not for the last time in America's War for the Greater Middle East, U.S. policymakers concluded that eliminating a single bad actor held the key to solving a much larger problem.

By January 1986, the Reagan administration had concluded that taking out Gaddafi had become imperative. That month the president issued another policy directive on Libya, ratcheting up economic sanctions and ordering the Sixth Fleet back into the Gulf of Sidra to "demonstrate U.S. resolve and capability."[10] In his diary, Reagan wrote that should "Libya's top clown" engage in further terrorist activity, "we will have targets in mind & instantly respond with a h—l of a punch."[11] As far as the president was concerned, time was running out for the Gaddafi regime.

The moment bears comparison to late 2002, when the George W. Bush administration persuaded itself that it needed to take out Iraq's Saddam Hussein. The sense of urgency, the rejection of alternatives to military action, the absence of attention to what might ensue after the United States had eliminated its prey: All were present on both occasions. In calculating what effecting regime change was likely to require, however, the two administrations differed. To topple the subject of his ire, Bush was willing to commit more than a few chips. By comparison, in going after Gaddafi, Reagan took a miserly approach. The ensuing campaign violated this fundamental maxim: If you will the end, you must will the means.

In late March 1986, hoping to goad Gaddafi into a showdown, the Sixth Fleet, under the command of Vice Admiral Frank Kelso, once again ventured south of the "line of death." This time three U.S. carriers, accompanied by a panoply of supporting warships, took up the ostensible task of keeping the Gulf of Sidra accessible to all the world's mariners. Libyan forces duly responded by launching SA-5 air defense missiles at F-14s flying combat air patrols. Although the missiles missed their target, the Americans seized the opportunity to sink two Libyan patrol boats and destroy a land-based radar site. Kelso's armada was stoked for a big fight. Rather than escalating hostilities further, however, the clearly overmatched Libyan forces broke contact. As before, the outcome appeared plain: We win, they lose.[12]

By all rights, Gaddafi ought to have conceded defeat. So at least Washington expected. "The Libyans have learned something from us," Admiral William Crowe, chairman of the Joint Chiefs of Staff, stated with satisfaction.[13] Much to the Reagan administration's annoyance, however, the lessons didn't sink in. Gaddafi remained defiant.

Then, on April 5, a bomb detonated in a West Berlin disco frequented by GIs, killing two Americans and wounding dozens more. Citing radio intercepts indicating prior Libyan knowledge of the attack, the United States blamed Gaddafi. Here, finally, was the elusive smoking gun. Just days later, at a press conference, Reagan lambasted Gaddafi as "this mad dog of the Middle East" and denounced his goal of "Moslem fundamentalist revolution."[14] He also ordered the Pentagon to retaliate. The result was Operation El Dorado Canyon.

Planning for just such a contingency had been under way for months. Yet very formidable obstacles stood in the way of implementing Reagan's order. For starters, NATO allies, Great Britain alone excepted, withheld cooperation. Western Europeans were not about to sign up for Reagan's undeclared war on Gaddafi. Countries hosting U.S. air bases such as Spain and Italy refused to permit the attackers to use those facilities. Other allies such as France rejected requests to allow participating U.S. aircraft to overfly their territory.[15]

Coordinating the simultaneous arrival of participating units—F-111 bombers from RAF Lakenheath in England and carrier-based aircraft launched from the USS *Coral Sea* and the USS *America* afloat in the Mediterranean—posed a further complication. For the F-111s, the trip south from England, down the coast of France and Portugal, through the Strait of Gibraltar and east over the Mediterranean would require multiple in-flight refuelings, all conducted at night in radio silence. This round-trip of over six thousand miles was certain to tax the capabilities of the F-111, an airplane never known for its reliability. Although the navy A-6s would have an easier time reaching the target area, they could expect to face worrisome air defenses.

Far and away the biggest hurdle facing the operation was a conceptual one: the assumption that a small-scale, one-and-done bout of bombing would somehow put things right. Reagan wanted El Dorado Canyon to deliver a pointed message that Gaddafi could neither ignore nor misinterpret. Yet when it came to translating presidential intention into specific targets, military commanders struggled. The commander in chief had made his wishes clear: Punish the guilty while sparing the innocent. In practice, reconciling the two was no easy matter.

The plan that emerged after considerable internal wrangling identified five targets for destruction: two airfields, one in Tripoli and the other near Benghazi; one military training camp; a storage and assembly facility for military aircraft; and, most important, the Bab al-Aziziyah Barracks, where Gaddafi maintained his headquarters and principal residence.

Bab al-Aziziyah would bear the weight of the U.S. effort.[16] At this point in America's War for the Greater Middle East, the United States had not yet embraced assassination as a standard practice. That came later. For the moment, U.S. law prohibited political assassination. So killing Gaddafi outright did not figure as one of El Dorado Canyon's stated objectives. If raining bombs on the places where the Libyan dictator lived and worked resulted in his death, the United States would treat that happy outcome as merely incidental rather than intended. But the quantity of ordnance earmarked for Bab al-Aziziyah did not qualify as incidental.[17]

On the afternoon of April 14, with preparations complete and President Reagan having given the order to proceed, El Dorado Canyon commenced. Eighteen air force F-111s, bound for Tripoli and accompanied by tankers and other supporting aircraft, departed their bases in Great Britain and began their six-and-a-half-hour flight.[18] Shortly after midnight on April 15, aircraft comprising the navy's strike force began launching from *Coral Sea* and *America*. Once airborne, they headed for Benghazi. The aim was for both forces to begin attacking their targets at 2:00 A.M. local time.

Without question, no other military establishment, with the possible exception of Israel's, could have undertaken such a complex and demanding operation. That said, as Operation El Dorado Canyon unfolded, things did not go well. In-flight problems forced two of the eighteen F-111s to turn back while en route. Due to last-minute equipment failures, four others aborted while on the approach to their targets. A seventh missed its assigned target altogether, dropping its bombs among houses and apartment buildings and doing considerable damage to the French embassy. An eighth was shot down, with both crewmen killed.

The fifteen navy A-6 Intruders sent to strike Benghazi fared somewhat better, hammering the airfield there while destroying or damaging a number of parked aircraft. In barely ten minutes, it was over and the Americans had departed Libyan airspace.[19]

Overall, apart from rousting the residents of Tripoli and Benghazi out of bed, the attackers had achieved at best so-so success. All that they had destroyed, with the exceptions of several dozen Libyans killed, could be replaced. Most of what they had damaged could be repaired. As for Gaddafi himself, apparently warned of the attack in advance, he had escaped unharmed.

Soon thereafter, a somber President Reagan appeared on television to inform the American people of what had occurred. The president announced that U.S. forces had "succeeded in their mission," thereby avenging the West Berlin disco bombing. "Today we have done what we had to do," Reagan continued. "If necessary, we shall do it again." He expressed hope that "this preemptive action" might provide Gaddafi "with incentives and reasons to alter his criminal behavior." Yet in describing the significance of the just completed action, Reagan looked beyond Gaddafi. El Dorado Canyon stood as a warning for terrorists everywhere to heed. The Libyan dictator had "counted on America to be passive," Reagan concluded. "He counted wrong. I warned that there should be no place on Earth where terrorists can rest and train and practice their deadly skills. I meant it. I said that we would act with others, if possible, and alone if necessary to ensure that terrorists have no sanctuary anywhere. Tonight, we have."[20]

Gaddafi was an Arab nationalist, a radical Islamist, an anti-Semite, a proponent of violent revolution, and something of a nutcase. But it was Gaddafi's support for terrorism that had drawn U.S. attention. As Washington saw it, terrorism was the real enemy, with Gaddafi merely one manifestation of this much larger problem. With Operation El Dorado Canyon, the United States inaugurated what was to become an extended and ultimately futile experiment in employing military might to defeat that enemy.

Even so, surveying the experiment's preliminary results, the Reagan administration pronounced itself pleased. The Defense Department's principal spokesman described El Dorado Canyon as "an absolutely flawless professional performance."[21] Defense Secretary Caspar Weinberger told reporters that the raid would "send an unmistakable signal," predicting that "it will go far toward deterring future acts" of terrorism.[22] Secretary of State George Shultz later wrote that "after twitching feverishly with a flurry of vengeful responses," Gaddafi himself "quieted down and retreated into the desert."[23] The United States had put the Libyan dictator "back in his box, where he belongs."[24]

If so, he did not remain there for long. Less than two years later, the State Department spokesperson admitted that the United States had seen "no evidence that Libya has abandoned support of international terrorism, subversion, and aggression."[25] Soon enough, events affirmed the truth of that statement. On December 21, 1988, as Reagan was preparing to hand the presidency over to George H. W. Bush, a device planted by Libyan agents blew up Pan Am flight 103 over Lockerbie, Scotland, killing all 259 passengers and crew, 189 Americans among them, along with eleven others on the ground.[26] The United States did not retaliate against Gaddafi for engineering this atrocity. If U.S. policymakers intended their response to the Berlin disco bombing to demonstrate that terrorists were no longer going to get away with murdering Americans, the non-response to the destruction of Pan Am 103 showed that they still could.

Clearly, as an exercise in behavior modification through bombing, Operation El Dorado Canyon had a transitory impact at best. Even so, U.S. policymakers clung to their belief that armed might could somehow provide the ultimate solution to terrorism. Here was an illusion destined to last for decades to come.

6

RESCUING EVIL

ON THE LONG LIST OF HITLERS WITH WHOM THE UNITED STATES has contended since the demise of the genuine article back in 1945, Saddam Hussein certainly ranks at or near the very top. Yet in contrast to the real Hitler, who never enjoyed American sympathy or support, Washington once threw in with Saddam-as-Hitler prior to concluding that it needed to throw him over.

This coming to Saddam's aid—indeed, to his rescue—also forms part of America's War for the Greater Middle East during its preliminary stages. Here, more than any other Reagan-era episode, the confusion and incoherence that permeated U.S. policy in the Islamic world during the 1980s become blindingly apparent. Those who revere Reagan remember him as the embodiment of constancy and moral purpose. When it comes to Iraq, little of either quality was evident. Instead, shortsighted opportunism prevailed.

Americans rarely attend to or remember military conflicts not directly involving the United States. There are exceptions, of course, such as the Six-Day War of 1967 and the October War of 1973. Yet the Iran-Iraq War of 1980–1988, although far larger, longer, and more destructive than all of the Arab-Israeli wars combined, does not number among those exceptions. Never having gained more than a toehold on the nation's collective consciousness, this Muslim-on-Muslim conflict has today almost entirely vanished from memory, for the average American retaining about as much salience as the Boxer Rebellion. This is unfortunate since, not unlike the events of 9/11, the Iran-Iraq War thrust the United States more deeply into its War for the Greater Middle East.

Ultimately at stake in this conflict was regional primacy, neighbors vying with one another to determine who would dominate the neighborhood. In that sense, rather than *Iran-Iraq War,* the term *Persian Gulf War* more accurately captures the essential issue. More accurately still, the contest of 1980–1988 deserves to be called the First Gulf War, since it inaugurated a series of armed conflicts, still ongoing even today, to determine who will exercise dominion over the core of the Islamic world.

The United States intervened in this First Gulf War, both directly and indirectly, and thereby helped determine its outcome. Yet in so doing, the U.S. all but ensured that a second Gulf war would follow in 1990 and then a third in 2003. As this succession of conflicts unfolded, U.S. policymakers became ever more insistent that it was incumbent upon the United States itself, employing its superior military power, to determine the region's fate. In short, the First Gulf War marked an important way station propelling the United States toward a fateful attempt to implement a strategy of regional hegemony.

Much as the Sino-Japanese conflict of 1931–1941 served as a precursor of the Pacific War of 1941–1945, the Iran-Iraq War of 1980–1988 served as a precursor to an American war in Iraq destined in its various phases to continue for over a quarter-century. The parallels between these two sets of events are imprecise, of course. Among other things, whereas Washington condemned warmongering in the 1930s, it tacitly abetted warmongering in the 1980s. And while the Pacific War culminated in the enemy's unconditional surrender, the same cannot be said of the American military involvement in Iraq.

The First Gulf War began with an act of unprovoked aggression. Assuming that the Islamic Revolution had left Iran militarily weak and therefore vulnerable, Saddam Hussein spied a chance to help himself to some easy pickings. Although the Iraqi dictator possessed boundless ambition, in this instance narrow objectives prompted his decision for war. He sought not to conquer Iran, nor even to topple its government, but to acquire territory—more or less, the same motive that had once inspired the United States to invade Mexico. Back in 1846, President James K. Polk had coveted the great prize of California. In 1980, Saddam coveted the lesser but still significant prize of Iran's oil-rich Khuzestan Province, just across Iraq's eastern border. He also wanted to assert unquestioned Iraqi control of the Shatt al-Arab waterway, formed by the confluence of the Tigris and Euphrates Rivers.[1]

Put simply, when Saddam sent his Soviet-equipped army plunging into Iran on September 22 of that year, he envisioned a brief, satisfying land grab. What he got was something altogether different. We may wonder how it could have been otherwise. A war pitting Arabs against Persians, secular Ba'athists against Islamist revolutionaries, a Sunni-dominated regime against one controlled by Shiites involved too many grudges to stay limited—especially when Iranians in large numbers evinced an unexpected willingness to fight and die for their country. In short order, a brief campaign launched for small stakes became a long war with both parties shoving more and more chips onto the table. On each side, the contest took on life-or-death implications.

At the war's outset, with Jimmy Carter still in the White House, the United States had declared itself neutral. At a press briefing on the afternoon of September 24, Carter stated categorically that "we have not been and we will not become involved in the conflict between Iran and Iraq." That said, Carter didn't want anyone else nosing in either. "There should be absolutely no interference by any other nation," he continued. Yet the president also warned the two belligerents not to infringe on the "freedom of passage of ships to and from the Persian Gulf region."[2] Access to oil was still of paramount importance.

As a practical matter, with the hostage crisis still ongoing and few Americans predisposed to sympathize with Iran, Washington was not unduly troubled by the prospect of Saddam Hussein subjecting that country to a drubbing. True, the United States did not want to see the Islamic Republic dismembered either.[3] But subjected to a bit of punishment? That possessed a certain appeal. Only when events on the battle-field took an unexpected turn did that hands-off attitude begin to change.

Although Iraqi forces quickly secured their assigned objectives, Teh-ran rejected Saddam's offer to negotiate—on his terms—an end to hos-tilities. Instead, in January 1981, rejuvenated Iranian regulars employing U.S. arms acquired by the Shah and reinforced by highly motivated mi-litias launched the first in a series of counteroffensives. As the hostage crisis that had fixated American attention finally came to an end, the Ayatollah's forces were on the march.

Over the course of the next year, involving months of bitter fighting, Iran succeeded in ejecting the invader from its territory. With the tables now turned and his own survival at risk, a panicked Saddam declared a unilateral ceasefire. This Iran rejected. The clerics who determined Ira-nian policy were intent on pressing their hard-won advantage.[4]

Contemplating the unwelcome prospect of an Iranian victory that could vault the Islamic Republic to a position of regional preeminence, the Reagan administration now committed itself to propping up Iraq as its preferred counterweight. This meant forging a marriage of conve-nience with the very regime that Paul Wolfowitz had identified as the chief emerging threat to U.S. interests in the Persian Gulf. Simply put, by 1982 ensuring Saddam's survival had become an American priority.

For an administration not shy about advertising its moral superiority, assisting a government that claimed charter membership on the State Department's list of state sponsors of terrorism entailed some fancy footwork.[5] Complicating matters further was the absence of a diplo-matic relationship. To protest Washington's support of Israel, Baghdad had severed relations with the United States back in 1967. There things had stood ever since.

Now change was in the wind. In February 1982, the State Depart-ment quietly "de-designated" Iraq as a sponsor of terrorism. Fence-mending U.S. envoys began visiting Baghdad. Friendly messages from Secretary of State Shultz to his Iraqi counterpart emphasized the "very important common interests" shared by the two countries.[6] Although the full restoration of diplomatic relations did not occur until November 1984, that qualified as mere window dressing. A visit to Baghdad the previous December by former (and future) defense secretary Donald Rumsfeld, acting as Ronald Reagan's personal representative, had sealed the deal. Rumsfeld's ceremonial handshake with Saddam, videotaped for posterity, signaled that the United States had joined the ranks of the anti-Persian (and therefore anti-Shiite) axis. The prior U.S. policy of neutrality with regard to the Iran-Iraq War was now defunct.

During his visit to Baghdad, Rumsfeld assured Saddam that any resolution of the ongoing war "which weakens Iraq's role or enhances [the] interests and ambitions of Iran" was not going to find favor in Washington. Along those lines, the United States was "encouraging others not to sell weapons to Iran" and would continue to do so.[7] Rumsfeld was alluding to Operation Staunch, a State Department initiative launched earlier in 1983 to prevent Iran from acquiring arms and particularly the spare parts needed to maintain weapons of U.S. origin.

Needless to say, Staunch exempted Saddam. True, Washington was not going to provide Iraq with U.S.-manufactured Abrams tanks or F-16 fighter jets. Yet the Reagan administration looked the other way as the world's arms merchants—France and the Soviet Union at the forefront—lined up to sell Baghdad armored vehicles, combat aircraft, and other weaponry needed to replace its battlefield losses.[8] ("Looking the other way" also describes the U.S. response when Israel began secretly selling Iran large quantities of U.S. arms and spare parts to sustain the Ayatollah Khomeini's war machine. Ostensible allies, Israel and the United States thus found themselves supporting opposite sides in a war in which *both* warring parties were stridently anti-Israel *and* anti-American.)

Its population only a third of Iran's, Iraq had to fight outnumbered. Enjoying an edge in hardware was, therefore, crucial to Saddam's prospects. Here, indeed, was the essence of his approach to waging war: Rely on a plentiful supply of cannon to compensate for an insufficiency of cannon fodder.

Having at hand an immense and continually replenished arsenal did not improve Saddam's aptitude for generalship, however. Seemingly viewing war as scaled-up terrorism, he used force profligately and indiscriminately, the more so as events on the battlefield tilted in Iran's favor. If there was a method to Saddam's madness, it was to strike out in all directions, vaguely hoping that some maximal threshold of violence would eventually induce his foes to relent.

So, using inaccurate 1950s vintage Soviet missiles, Saddam initiated random attacks against Iranian cities. Iran replied in kind. He employed chemical weapons first against Iranian troops—again, Iran replied in kind—and then against certain restive elements of his own population. And relying on an air force that enjoyed relative superiority, he struck at Iranian oil facilities alongside and within the Persian Gulf and at any ships, regardless of nationality, suspected of aiding the Iranian war effort. Iran responded by targeting tankers belonging to Arab nations that were bankrolling Iraq, lending Saddam billions so that he could continue to procure arms.

Was there a comparable logic to the Reagan's administration's madness in supporting Saddam Hussein? If so, it involved nudging Saddam toward a more focused and less haphazard approach to waging war. Although Arab oil money had bought Iraq a big army, more than money was required to employ that army to good effect.

For Reagan and his advisers, this defined the nub of the problem. Whether Iraqi actions satisfied some legal or moral standard did not trouble U.S. policymakers. That lofting volleys of SCUDs in the general direction of Tehran or blanketing enemy trenches with clouds of mustard gas seemed unlikely to forestall an ultimate Iranian victory did.

Especially egregious Iraqi misbehavior—chemical weapons use against noncombatants, for example—might elicit a pro forma American reproach.[9] Once having gone through the motions of upholding moral principle, however, U.S. officials returned to the task at hand, which was to find ways of enhancing Iraqi military effectiveness.

At intervals during the decades that followed, the urge to build up Iraq's army alternated with an equally emphatic U.S. determination to degrade or destroy it. At podiums in the White House and State

Department, meanwhile, a reciprocal phenomenon occurred: When bolstering Iraqi military capabilities was the order of the day, U.S. government representatives soft-pedaled any criticism of Baghdad; when making the case that Iraq possessed altogether *too much* military power, they portrayed that country's behavior as utterly unconscionable.

Throughout the 1980s, U.S. policy emphasized building up Iraq. Toward that end, the CIA in July 1982 had opened up a secret channel to provide Baghdad with sensitive intelligence, including satellite imagery. The aim was to give Saddam's generals a clearer picture of the battlefield (even if doing so also revealed U.S. intelligence capabilities). In addition, the administration agreed to technology transfers intended to improve Iraqi communications and logistics. Waging war requires more than weapons. By allowing Iraq to purchase nominally nonmilitary equipment possessing direct military utility—examples included computers, helicopters, transport aircraft, and heavy trucks—the Reagan administration was contributing directly to the Iraqi war effort. The administration also approved generous loan guarantees to facilitate Iraqi purchases of U.S. commodities and manufactures, a boon to American farmers and to the U.S. economy more generally.[10]

The support afforded Saddam by the United States and other Western nations (plus the Soviet Union) enabled Iraq to avoid outright defeat. Yet it did not suffice to end the fighting. From one year to the next, the war ground on, Iran refusing to call it quits despite suffering and inflicting enormous casualties.[11] Not unlike the Great War of 1914–1918, both sides demonstrated a remarkable capacity to persist.

Americans like to believe that it took Yanks under the command of General John J. Pershing—the American Expeditionary Forces—to end the bloodletting of 1914–1918. In the Persian Gulf War of 1980–1988, something similar occurred. The commitment of U.S. expeditionary forces under the command of CENTCOM's General George Crist finally brought things to a conclusion—so at least Reagan administration officials persuaded themselves, even if that conclusion quickly came undone.

Back in 1917, the resumption of U-boat attacks on U.S. shipping had brought the United States into the war against Germany and alongside the Allies. In 1987, a devastating aerial attack on a single American ship accomplished something comparable, drawing the United States into a direct confrontation with Iran and on the side of Iraq. The comparison breaks down in one important respect: Iran did not perpetrate that attack. Iraq did.

An apparent paradox: A and B are at war; A attacks C; C holds B responsible and exacts punishment.

Explaining this paradox requires the following admission: While the foregoing account of the Reagan administration's arms-length intervention in the Persian Gulf War on behalf of Iraq is true, the version of truth it offers is incomplete. Even as it was aiding Saddam Hussein, the United States was simultaneously engaged in a second arms-length intervention, this one engineered by the White House on behalf of Saddam's sworn enemies in Tehran.

In what became known as the Iran-Contra affair, the Reagan administration was secretly and illegally diverting U.S. weapons to Iran, with the government of Israel serving as obliging middleman.[12] The motives behind this initiative, initially hatched in 1981 but fully implemented only in 1985, were twofold. First, members of the administration, very much including the president himself, hoped that weapons transfers might purchase Tehran's assistance in negotiating the release of several Americans kidnapped in Lebanon and presumed to be held hostage in the wake of the failed U.S. intervention there.[13] Further, fancying that a small deal might lead to something much bigger, they hoped thereby to establish contact with Iranian "moderates" who might welcome the prospect of ending the U.S.-Iranian estrangement and thereby restoring relations to some approximation of what had existed under the Shah.

Virtually nothing positive resulted from this bizarre episode. In November 1986, a bombshell article appearing in a Beirut-based periodical revealed that the Reagan administration had been surreptitiously arming—and providing battlefield intelligence to—a country whose leaders routinely denounced the United States as the "Great Satan." A president who, in public, was adamantly opposed to negotiating with terrorists had secretly approved doing that very thing. Back home, a huge controversy erupted. Although Reagan managed to avoid impeachment, the ensuing scandal tarnished his reputation and resulted in the firing of several senior U.S. officials and the indictment of others.

The immediate relevance of Iran-Contra to America's War for the Greater Middle East is simply this: By the end of 1986, if not earlier, Saddam Hussein had become fully aware that Washington had been playing a double game at his expense. In his world, double-dealing demanded retribution. Saddam proceeded to exact that retribution in a way that enabled him finally to regain the upper hand over Iran.

While the events of Iran-Contra were unfolding behind the scenes, Saddam had initiated what became known as the "Tanker War"— attacks on merchant ships transiting the Persian Gulf. This war within a war had a specific objective: to prevent Iran from exporting oil while interdicting materials useful in sustaining the Iranian war effort. Between 1984 and 1987, Iraq's air force attacked 240 ships that ventured into an Iraqi-declared "exclusion zone." Predictably, Iran struck back. During that same interval, relying primarily on mines and on small but agile patrol boats known as boghammers, it attacked some 168 ships, notably including tankers belonging to Kuwait and Saudi Arabia.[14]

At least initially, neither side possessed the weapons actually needed to sink a large ship. Causing minor damage and inflicting small numbers of casualties, the attacks drove up insurance rates and reduced profits but were annoying rather than decisive.[15] Oil supplies remained plentiful. Indeed, during the Tanker War, oil prices actually fell appreciably.[16]

The handful of U.S. Navy ships operating in the Gulf did nothing to interfere, even though Iran and Iraq were both violating Jimmy Carter's warning against any disruption of "freedom of passage of ships to and from the Persian Gulf." Meanwhile, the Reagan administration had begun to contemplate the possibility of direct U.S. military action. In April 1984, the president ordered the Pentagon to "review possible escalation scenarios" and to enhance the military's "near-term readiness to respond to sudden attacks on U.S. interests in the region." Reagan wanted to know what additional forces might be required.[17] For the moment, however, planning did not translate into action.

Yet even if the Tanker War hardly amounted to more than harassment, the harassed viewed it as unacceptable, none more so than oil-rich Kuwait. In December 1986, the government of that unloved and unlovely nation approached the United States and the Soviet Union, asking if either might consider volunteering to protect its fleet of very large tankers. Unwilling to allow the Kremlin, in Caspar Weinberger's words, "to supplant us, thereby positioning themselves to become protector of the Gulf," the Reagan administration accepted the invitation in April 1987.[18] Yet along with Cold War–related calculations, a second factor also came into play: Assisting Kuwait might help repair the damage Iran-Contra had done to America's standing among Arabs— implicitly apologizing for Washington's misguided dalliance with Tehran.[19] Here was a chance to demonstrate that the United States was not as feckless and untrustworthy as it had appeared. Arrangements to reflag eleven Kuwaiti tankers, making them eligible for U.S. Navy protection, began shortly thereafter.

While these preparations were underway, disaster struck—a maritime counterpart to 1983's Beirut bombing. On the evening of May 17, the 4,100-ton frigate USS *Stark*, Captain Glenn R. Brindel commanding, was underway in the Persian Gulf, part of a small American flotilla intended to signal U.S. interests in the region. The ship was not engaged in any activity relevant to the ongoing hostilities between Iran and Iraq; it was, in fact, subjecting its main engines to a routine stress test.

At approximately 9:00 P.M., a French-made fighter jet purchased by the Iraqi air force fired two French-manufactured Exocet missiles at the American vessel. As the *Stark* did not react to this unprovoked and unexpected attack in sufficient time to mount an effective defense, both Exocets found their target. Although the first failed to detonate, the second "hit like God picked up the ship and slammed it into the sea," punching a ten-by-fifteen-foot hole in the portside hull and causing massive damage.[20]

Rapidly taking on water and with fires burning out of control, the crippled ship filled with smoke. Emergency systems failed. Over the course of that night, heroic efforts kept the *Stark* from sinking. Two other destroyers, the *Conyngham* and the *Waddell*, rushed to the scene, bringing desperately needed medical and firefighting supplies and searching for crewmen from the *Stark* that the blast had thrown overboard. But by the time the crippled ship was towed to safety, thirty-seven American sailors were dead with twenty-one injured.[21]

Saddam Hussein immediately acknowledged Iraqi involvement. Yet he characterized the incident as a lamentable but honest mistake. The *Stark* had ventured into the Iraqi "exclusion zone," Saddam claimed, which made it fair game. The pilot of the attacking aircraft had erroneously thought he was engaging a large oil tanker, the sort of misidentification that occurs when the fog of war thickens. To make amends, Saddam wrote President Reagan a personal letter of apology and even ordered a floral arrangement sent to the memorial service conducted for the deceased back in Florida.[22]

The Reagan administration found Saddam's explanation fully persuasive and wasted no time in identifying the actual culprit. At a press conference held the day after the incident, the president announced that "the villain in the piece really is Iran."[23] Secretary Shultz agreed, attributing the assault on the *Stark* to a "basic Iranian threat to the free flow of oil and to the principle of freedom of navigation."[24] As Washington saw it, Saddam and his henchmen, who had launched both the Persian Gulf War *and* the Tanker War, were innocent parties; the mullahs in Tehran were to blame.

A subsequent U.S. Navy inquiry complicated matters ever so slightly. It rejected Saddam's assertion that at the time of the attack the *Stark* had intruded into the Iraqi-declared exclusion zone, placing the ship in international waters some twenty miles outside of the exclusion zone. Even so, in assigning responsibility, the navy gave Iraq a pass, fingering the *Stark*'s captain as the fall guy.[25] Cited for failing to defend his ship, Captain Brindel managed to avoid court martial but soon thereafter retired at a reduced rank.[26]

In retrospect, two aspects of this episode are striking. The first is Washington's credulous acceptance of Saddam's version of events. The second is the advantage that accrued to Iraq as a direct result. (The resemblance to the June 1967 Israeli attack on the USS *Liberty*, another lethal assault quickly deemed accidental and benefiting the perpetrators, is difficult to miss.) Rather than inducing second thoughts about the direction of U.S. policy, the *Stark* incident reinforced the Reagan administration's pro-Iraq tilt. Whether truly accidental or, as skeptics believed, undertaken with malice aforethought, Iraq's killing of thirty-seven Americans drew the United States into the First Gulf War as a full-fledged, if still undeclared, belligerent—with Saddam himself the principal beneficiary.[27]

The Reagan administration had seemingly learned its lesson. Gone were the too-clever-by-half expectations that the United States could play both sides and get away with it. With the arms-for-hostages ploy blown sky high, Saddam's fight had now tacitly become America's fight. Valiant damage control efforts onboard the *Stark* had kept that vessel afloat. So Reagan administration efforts to limit the self-inflicted wound caused by its foolish dealings with Iran helped keep Saddam afloat, while effectively allowing him to get away with murdering American sailors.[28]

After the *Stark* episode, preparations to bring the Kuwaiti tanker fleet under U.S. protection continued apace. On July 21, thanks to paperwork and paintbrushes, the first reflagging occurred. The mammoth *Al-Rekkah*, longer than three football fields and displacing 413,000 tons when fully loaded, now became the *Bridgeton*. Flying the stars and stripes from its stern, with Philadelphia its supposed homeport, the *Bridgeton* thereby qualified for U.S. taxpayer–funded security.

One day later, escort operations, carrying the codename Earnest Will, commenced. With U.S. Navy warships fore and aft and air cover above, the *Bridgeton* weighed anchor and departed Oman, heading toward Kuwait some 750 miles distant. Initially, all went well. Then on July 24, the *Bridgeton* struck a mine, assumed to be of Iranian origin. The mission to protect had gotten off to a rocky start. Although the ship itself sustained only minor damage, the navy suffered acute embarrassment.

Here, in spades, was a demonstration of what purveyors of military jargon subsequently dubbed "asymmetric warfare"—relatively primitive weapons giving the technologically superior U.S. military fits. This too emerged as an ongoing theme in America's War for the Greater Middle East. In this instance, the weapon in question derived from a 1908 design attributed to Czarist Russia. Although not especially sophisticated, it more than sufficed against an adversary given to treating mine warfare as an afterthought.[29] Meanwhile, the irrepressible Moamar Gaddafi, sensing an opportunity and apparently having forgotten whatever lesson El Dorado Canyon was supposed to have taught him, was soon offering to provide Iran with mines from his own stockpiles.[30]

The navy put Earnest Will temporarily on hold while it assessed the problem and made the necessary adjustments. Henceforth, whenever mines posed a threat, the relatively unsinkable tankers would lead, with the much smaller and more vulnerable warships trailing behind. Yet even as convoying resumed without further incident, CENTCOM headquarters concluded that a strictly defensive posture was not going to suffice. Rather than allowing Iran to exercise the initiative, CENTCOM adopted a more proactive response—preventing the enemy from sowing mines in the first place.

To create the potential for offensive operations, the Pentagon quietly began assembling additional combat assets in the Gulf. Among the first to arrive were Navy SEALs, to include Special Boat Unit 20 with four 65-foot Mark III patrol boats. From Fort Campbell, Kentucky, came elements of the army's highly classified Task Force 160, its MH-6 and AH-6 "Little Bird" choppers especially adept at night operations. CENTCOM also acquired and refurbished a sizable barge to serve as a floating base for these forces. The number of American warships operating in the Gulf itself more than doubled. Beyond the Straits of Hormuz, one and sometimes two carrier battle groups, augmented by yet another refurbished World War II battleship, stood ready to provide support.[31]

After nightfall on September 21, the American counteroffensive commenced. A team of "Little Birds" ambushed the *Iran Ajr,* a small, lightly armed rust-bucket caught in the act of laying mines. Rocket and machine gun fire cut down some of the Iranian crewmembers and forced the rest to flee. SEALs swept in and scrambled aboard to claim their prize and take into custody the surviving crew. After American sailors subjected the *Iran Ajr* to a thorough scrubbing, Washington notables came calling to inspect the trophy, among them Caspar Weinberger. Declaring that "here was not only a smoking gun but a blazing gun," the defense secretary ordered the *Iran Ajr* sunk.[32] On September 26, well-placed explosive charges consigned it to the deep.[33]

As a milestone in America's evolving War for the Greater Middle East, the seizure of the *Iran Ajr* ranks as a very modest occurrence with very large implications. Here the Reagan administration was crossing an important threshold. Unlike in Soviet-occupied Afghanistan, the United States was no longer content to work through proxies. In contrast to its efforts in Lebanon, it no longer styled its purposes as "peacekeeping." Unlike in Libya, it no longer expected a single gesture to settle the issue. "We're very hopeful that this one episode will be a sufficient warning so that they will stop it," Weinberger remarked, "but we are not going to go on the basis of hopes."[34] When they—the Iranians—did not stop, neither did the Americans.

Instead, the capture of the *Iran Ajr* initiated a sequence of escalating events. Taken together, those events constituted a distinct military campaign. The campaign's immediate purpose, of course, was to "protect the oil." But in a broader sense, its purpose was to dictate the First Gulf War's outcome. Denying victory to Iran would establish the United States as the region's ultimate arbiter, asserting a mandate heretofore implicit within the Carter Doctrine. This was the unstated mission of the U.S. forces now gathering in the Persian Gulf in ever greater numbers.

On October 8, again at night, Little Birds from Task Force 160 ambushed a boghammer and two smaller boats, sinking one and damaging the others. SEALs dispatched to the scene captured six members of the Iranian Revolutionary Guard, two of whom died of wounds while being evacuated. They also recovered a component from a Stinger missile with a serial number matching one that the United States had provided to the Afghan mujahedin.[35] As with Gaddafi's offer of mines, the various threads of America's War for the Greater Middle East were already beginning to converge.

For the moment at least, Tehran remained undeterred. One week later, on October 15, a Chinese Silkworm, an antiship missile recently added to the Iranian arsenal, struck the *Sungari,* an American-owned, Liberian-flagged tanker at anchor off Kuwait. A formidable weapon mounting a thousand-pound warhead, the Silkworm was capable of inflicting serious damage. It did just that. A day later, another Silkworm plowed into the *Sea Isle City,* previously known as the *Umm al Maradem* but now proudly displaying Old Glory.[36] Iran was upping the ante. The United States could either call or fold.

Taking out the Silkworms, whose launch sites were located on the Faw Peninsula, seemed the logical and appropriate response. But this was easier said than done. In early 1986, Iran had captured this key bit of territory, which had provided Iraq with its sole outlet to the sea. Intent on keeping what they had taken, Iranian commanders poured in reinforcements. These included some of the same Hawk air defense missiles that the Reagan administration had secretly sold to Iran.[37] Attacking the Silkworm sites therefore risked the possibility of U.S. aircraft being shot down by U.S.-manufactured missiles. Unwilling to accept that risk, CENTCOM passed, opting instead for an easier target—two largely undefended Iranian oil platforms in the middle of the Persian Gulf.

In appearance, these ungainly structures, both located in international waters, looked like something built from a giant Erector Set. Having been previously targeted by Iraq, they were no longer pumping oil. Yet U.S. commanders believed that Iran was using them as observation posts and tactical bases to support its anti-shipping campaign. The purpose of CENTCOM's Operation Nimble Archer was to put an end to that activity.

Early on the afternoon of October 19, four navy destroyers, *Hoel,*

Kidd, Leftwich, and *John Young,* converged on the larger of the two platforms, known as Rashadt. After radioing orders to evacuate and paus-
ing for a suitable interval, the warships opened fire. Over the course of
the next eighty-five minutes, they bombarded the Rashadt with over a
thousand rounds of unanswered cannon fire. When the shelling ended
and the Rashadt had been reduced to a burning hulk, SEALs boarded
the second, as yet untouched platform. Finding it unoccupied, they
searched it and then set it ablaze. Their work finished and having sustained no casualties, the Americans left the scene. This was asymmetric
warfare inverted: using weapons superiority to hit an enemy lacking
the capacity to hit back. Yet soon thereafter, as if in response, Iran let
loose another Silkworm aimed at Kuwait.[38]

Although these small actions may have appeared cut-and-dried, they
were not. While U.S. forces enjoyed very considerable advantages—
operating virtually unseen or beyond enemy reach—each encounter
occurred in an operational environment of unnerving complexity, with
alarms, false alarms, close calls, and near misses occurring daily. Then
as now, the Persian Gulf was nothing if not crowded. On any given day,
as many as four hundred oceangoing ships, along with even larger numbers of lesser craft, crisscrossed this confined space. Overhead flew
scores of commercial and military aircraft, making it one of the world's
busiest airspaces. Indeed, the onset of the Tanker War had the perverse
effect of adding to the congestion and therefore the uncertainties confronting U.S. commanders on the scene. The fate of the *Stark* (and its
captain) served as a constant reminder of the perils that even a momen-
tary lapse in alertness could entail.[39]

In the unlikely event of U.S. commanders needing a further reminder, the frigate *Samuel B. Roberts* provided it. One of some two
dozen American warships now patrolling the Persian Gulf, the *Roberts,*
on April 14, 1988, inadvertently wandered into a field of floating mines.
A vigilant crewman spotted the problem. Commander Paul X. Rinn
brought his ship to a halt and gingerly attempted to back out to safety.
The attempt failed when the ship brushed up against a mine. The resulting detonation lifted the *Roberts* out of the water and split open the

hull just above the main engine room, which quickly filled with sea-water. With helicopters arriving to evacuate the wounded, sailors fran-tically worked through the night to put out fires and prevent their ship from sinking. Amazingly, they succeeded. More amazing still, no one was killed in the attack, although the damage sustained by the *Roberts* kept it out of action for over a year, with repairs running to almost $90 million.[40]

By happenstance, this incident—the first time Iranian action had harmed a U.S. military asset—occurred just as the First Gulf War was reaching a critical turning point. Intensifying Iraqi missile strikes target-ing Tehran and other cities were taking a toll on Iranian morale. The last in a series of Iranian offensives aimed at seizing the Iraqi city of Basra had failed miserably. Iran was approaching exhaustion, its will and capacity to continue the struggle all but spent. Then, just days after the near-sinking of the *Roberts,* Iraqi forces launched a massive ground attack aimed at "liberating" the Faw Peninsula. It succeeded with aston-ishing ease. For the first time since the war's earliest stages, Saddam was back on top.[41]

While these dramatic events were unfolding, more immediate con-cerns absorbed American attention: determining how to respond to the punishment that the *Roberts* had absorbed. That the United States would act was a given; the only question was how. As message traffic flew back and forth among Washington, CENTCOM headquarters in Tampa, and U.S. forces in the Gulf, a range of punitive options received consideration. In the end, Reagan opted for the least provocative. To diminish Iran's ability to conduct further seaborne attacks, he approved a modest escalation of hostilities. While ports, airfields, and military installations would remain off-limits, U.S. forces set out to cripple Iran's already weak naval forces. The result was Operation Praying Mantis.

The smallest fighting ship in the United States Navy easily outgunned the largest ship in Iran's navy. The plan for Praying Mantis aimed to capitalize on this differential in firepower. At 8:00 A.M. on April 18, near the Straits of Hormuz, a flotilla consisting of eight American warships opened fire on a pair of Iranian gas-oil separation platforms. Although

Iranians onboard responded, their light weapons could not range the American ships. When the shelling ceased, CH-46 helicopters carrying Marine assault teams, flanked by AH-1 Cobra gunships, swooped in to occupy the larger platform, now severely damaged and abandoned. The Americans raised the national and Marine Corps colors, thoroughly searched their objective, and blew it up upon departing.[42]

Iran reacted—as U.S. commanders had hoped—by committing its modest surface fleet to the fight. The Iranians arrived piecemeal, further dissipating their limited strength. The result was a turkey shoot.

The 265-ton gunboat *Joshan* charged in first. While managing to unleash a U.S.-made Harpoon missile at the cruiser USS *Wainwright*—it missed—the *Joshan* paid a steep price for its audacity. Employing an overwhelming combination of missiles and gunfire, the U.S. Navy sank it. Next on the scene came the *Sahand*, a small British-built frigate dating from the Shah's era. Attack aircraft from the carrier *Enterprise* disabled the *Sahand* as well. The destroyer *Joseph Strauss* piled on, leaving the Iranian vessel, according to one American pilot, "a smoking piece of junk."[43] It too soon sank.

Last to arrive was the *Sabalan*, flagship of the Iranian fleet and notorious scourge of neutral shipping in the Gulf. JCS chairman Admiral William Crowe had issued very explicit instructions regarding the *Sabalan*'s fate: "Put her on the bottom."[44] Aviators from the *Enterprise* sought to comply. After sustaining numerous hits, the enemy ship was soon aflame and dead in the water.

Monitoring the fight from the Pentagon's War Room, Crowe relented, deciding that "We've shed enough blood for the day."[45] With the concurrence of Frank Carlucci, Weinberger's successor as defense secretary, he ordered U.S. forces to break contact. Defying American expectations, the *Sabalan* stayed afloat and was towed back to port. For Iran, this provided small consolation. Having suffered an estimated sixty killed in action and another hundred wounded, its navy had all but ceased to exist as even a minimally capable fighting force.[46] U.S. casualties during Praying Mantis totaled two killed—the pilots of a Marine Cobra helicopter that crashed at sea due to undetermined causes.

In an action that had lasted all of eight hours, the forces under General Crist's overall command had won a clear-cut tactical victory. That said, the event more closely resembled 1898's Battle of Manila Bay than 1942's Battle of Midway. So although Praying Mantis was subsequently celebrated as "the largest surface action since the Second World War," this was akin to designating the no-name palooka reigning as today's heavyweight champ the greatest fighter since Muhammad Ali.[47] Even if accurate, such a claim serves chiefly as a reminder of how long it's been since a real champion has graced the world of boxing.

Still, Praying Mantis did mark a turning point in the U.S. military's involvement in the First Gulf War. Old inhibitions fell away in favor of a more assertive stance. On April 29, Carlucci signaled the change by declaring that henceforth, U.S. forces would protect *all* neutral shipping transiting the Gulf, not simply the reflagged Kuwait fleet.[48] Then on July 3, as if to drive home the point that U.S. forces were done playing nice, the cruiser USS *Vincennes,* one of the navy's most advanced ships, shot down Iran Air flight 655, an Airbus A300 with 290 passengers and crew aboard. None survived.

For authorities in Washington the downing of a commercial airliner did not come as welcome news. Yet much as Saddam Hussein had done after the *Stark* episode, they promptly consigned the incident to the category of regrettable mistake. As had Saddam, they attributed the outcome to the victim's own actions. While "operating in international waters" and chasing down a swarm of small Iranian gunboats, the *Vincennes* had detected an unidentified aircraft flying outside of the corridor allocated for commercial air traffic and descending in what appeared to be an "attack profile."[49] Identifying the plane as an Iranian F-14, Captain Will Rogers III took measures necessary to protect his ship from harm. In doing so, he acted in accordance with what President Reagan called "our inherent right to self-defense."[50]

In point of fact, however, the American version of events consisted mostly of untruths. The *Vincennes* was actually sailing inside Iranian territorial waters, thereby violating international law. Transiting the Gulf from Bandar Abbas, Iran, to Dubai on a regularly scheduled flight, the Airbus was flying well within its assigned flight path. Most important, rather than descending, the aircraft was gaining altitude. In short, the assertion that Iran Air 655 had been closing on the *Vincennes* and thereby posing a threat was flat-out wrong. If mistakes had contributed to the downing of the airliner, Captain Rogers and members of his crew had committed the bulk of them.

Even so, the Reagan administration suppressed any inclination to admit wrongdoing. What had occurred was an unfortunate mishap, not a crime, U.S. officials insisted. Running hard for the White House and with elections just months away, Vice President George H. W. Bush made his own position clear: He wasn't about to send flowers to any Iranian memorial service. "I will never apologize for the United States—I don't care what the facts are," he remarked. "I'm not an apologize-for-America kind of guy."[51] Enlightened opinion largely agreed with the vice president: Rather than wallowing in remorse, the United States needed to finish the job. As *The New York Times* editorialized, in order to thwart the Islamic Republic's revolutionary aspirations, the U.S. Navy had been providing "a shield behind which Iraq attacks Iranian oil tankers" without fear of retaliation. "The Airbus tragedy does not alter the validity of that strategy."[52] As the *Times* saw it, "the onus for avoiding such accidents in the future rests on civilian aircraft."[53] It was their job to steer clear of the U.S. military. Opinion polls suggested that the public shared this view.[54]

Not surprisingly, so too did the United States Navy. Upon investigating the incident, it concluded that "Iran must bear principal responsibility for the tragedy."[55]

By extension, the captain of the *Vincennes* had acted appropriately—indeed, according to Admiral Crowe, had "conducted himself with circumspection."[56] In contrast to his counterpart on the *Stark*, Rogers evaded disciplinary action, finished his command tour, and even received a handsome decoration for duties well performed.[57] Certainly, there was no blaming him for failing to defend *his* ship.

For his part, General Crist fully expected Iran to strike back. "It's the old 'Rambo' thing—first blood," he told a reporter. "The Iranians have paid for their attempts to interfere with our ships, and I think they would like to get back at us."[58] Instead, when less than three weeks after the shootdown the Ayatollah Khomeini agreed to accept a ceasefire with Iraq, American observers were quick to detect a causal relationship: Rather than eliciting retaliation, CENTCOM's more confrontational stance had persuaded Iran at long last to concede. Here was a welcome demonstration of what American military power could achieve in the Islamic world. On this point, Weinberger himself was emphatic: "We had now clearly won," he wrote in his memoirs. The United States had prevailed. Iran had conceded defeat. "We had accomplished everything we set out to do," Weinberger bragged, with a momentous foreign policy success the direct result.[59]

Journalistic opinion concurred in this self-congratulatory verdict. "By blocking Iran's move to intimidate Iraq's allies in the Persian Gulf," an approving *New York Times* editorial observed, U.S. forces had "played a critical role in ending the Iran-Iraq War."[60] The hawkishly liberal *New Republic* came to a similar conclusion. "In the name of free passage through the oil straits that Iraq had been the first to impede, the United States [had] intervened decisively, if not massively, against Iran." Iran's agreement to end hostilities amounted to "an admission that the Islamic revolution is finally spent."[61] According to the conservative *National Review*, "Iraq [had] won the war" thanks "to the firmness of the Reagan Administration's resolve." While Operation Praying Mantis had "virtually wiped out the Iranian navy," shooting down Iran Air 655 had provided "the straw that broke the Ayatollah's back."[62] This much was certain: "Without our tilt toward Iraq, the Ayatollah might have won the war and destabilized the entire region."[63] Far-sighted action by Ronald Reagan had averted that prospect.

More than a quarter-century later, such judgments appear either naïve or obtuse. What lingers today from America's undeclared war against Iran is the disconcerting symmetry of the twin incidents bookending the campaign. In using terms like *accident* or *tragedy* to describe the deaths suffered by the *Stark* and inflicted by the *Vincennes*, U.S. civilian and military officials at the time had sought to drain each event of moral or political significance. They were either oblivious to or simply chose to ignore the implications of writing off the American sailors killed by Saddam Hussein's air force or the Iranian civilians killed by American sailors.

Yet these two episodes imparted to Washington's preferred victory narrative a stain that the passage of time has done little to eradicate. U.S. military participation in this first of several Gulf Wars began with a mix of cynicism and betrayal. It ended with an atrocity. Long after Earnest Will, Nimble Archer, and Praying Mantis have disappeared down the memory hole, these discomfiting facts merit reflection.

In the event, the suspension of hostilities between Iran and Iraq offered Americans little reason to celebrate. Winning paid few dividends. If the United States intervened on Saddam's behalf in hopes of promoting regional stability, then that intervention rates as an abject failure. If anything, U.S. military action produced the opposite effect, fostering new sources of instability destined to draw the United States more deeply into a costly and ultimately bootless military enterprise.

Back in 1917, Woodrow Wilson had promised Americans that sending Pershing's troops to Europe would settle things. It didn't. Wilson had erred. Soon enough, a second world war ensued. This entailed U.S. intervention on an even larger scale and cast a shadow over the epic victory said to have been won just two decades earlier.

Something of the same thing occurred with the First Gulf War. American claims that the forces under General Crist's command had settled things proved sadly premature. Within a mere two years another war to determine the fate of the Persian Gulf erupted, Washington's designation of Saddam-as-Hitler entailing U.S. intervention on a substantially larger scale. With the onset of the Persian Gulf War's second phase, Americans simply chose to forget their involvement in the first. In forgetting, they learned nothing.

7

No Clean Ending

THROUGH THE FIRST DECADE OF AMERICA'S WAR FOR THE Greater Middle East, a certain gingerly quality had characterized Washington's approach to the problem at hand. The United States was in, but not all in. Indeed, through the Reagan era, the very nature of the problem that the U.S. military was expected to solve remained ill-defined. Commitments, therefore, tended to be both modest in scope and revocable.

Along with the CIA, the air force, navy, and Marine Corps had taken turns as Washington's preferred instrument of policy. The United States Army, the largest of the services, had remained on the sidelines, preoccupied with commitments in Europe and Northeast Asia that dated back to the 1940s.

In 1990, that began to change, with the larger role now assigned to the army symbolizing that change. Wherever the American army shows up, it tends to stay awhile. In the wake of long-term commitments come enlarged ambitions.

Decades before, during the initial stages of the Cold War, the great moral theologian Reinhold Niebuhr had chided Americans about entertaining "dreams of managing history," a temptation to which he deemed his countrymen peculiarly susceptible. "The recalcitrant forces in the historical drama," he warned, "have a power and persistence beyond our reckoning."[1] Now as the Cold War was winding down, Americans regarded themselves as exempt from such warnings. In

Washington, managing history looked like job one, with military power the means of doing just that.

Yet history itself was on the move, complicating the task of its would-be managers. For decades, the nexus of world politics had been the divided city of Berlin. With reunification, however, Berlin lost its centrality. Among the places that policymakers in Washington eyed as a potential successor, Baghdad almost immediately emerged as a leading contender.

In this elevation of the Iraqi capital to the status of historical epicenter, the campaign known as Operation Desert Storm marked a notable point of inflection. Understanding that campaign—what it did and did not signify—is crucial to our understanding of the much larger undertaking within which Desert Storm once seemingly formed such an important part. At the time, dazzled observers compared it to the German conquest of France in 1940—evidence of unrivaled military mastery. Today, if the comparison still pertains, it does so only in this ironic sense: As with Germany following the Battle of France, victory served to foster illusions and underwrite folly.

Appreciating this outcome requires distinguishing between what actually happened on the battlefield and the interpretation that Americans assigned to what they believed had happened. Arguably, in all wars a gap exists between perception and reality, but in this instance, that gap turned out to be especially wide.

The Second Gulf War began on August 2, 1990, when Iraq remorselessly invaded, occupied, and soon thereafter annexed neighboring Kuwait. Sandwiched between Saudi Arabia and Iraq, this speck of a country occupies a perch along the Persian Gulf that has been both blessing and curse. Even before Saddam Hussein rose to power, Iraq had coveted the Emirate of Kuwait, much as Americans in the late nineteenth century had coveted the Kingdom of Hawaii—both small monarchies that ambitious republics deemed unworthy of independent existence.

Yet the complaints that inspired Saddam Hussein to act derived from

more proximate considerations. During the Gulf War's previous iteration, the al-Sabah family that runs Kuwait like a personal fiefdom had
loaned Saddam billions to fund his fight against Iran. As with the Reagan administration, antipathy toward Iran rather than affection for Saddam had inspired Kuwaiti generosity. Even so, since Iraq had been
fighting on Kuwait's behalf (and by extension on behalf of all Arabs
and all Sunni Muslims), Saddam thought it only appropriate that the
al-Sabahs should forgive Iraq its debt and even provide an additional
line of credit to help Iraq's recovery from its exertions.[2] The Kuwaiti
government begged to differ and even persisted in other annoying behavior. Saddam charged Kuwait with violating OPEC production quo-
tas, which drove down world oil prices, and with extracting crude oil
from a field to which Baghdad laid claim. Both had the effect of hurting
the already-ailing Iraqi economy. Fed up, Saddam took matters into his
own hands and simply seized what he deemed rightfully his.[3] Here
come to life was the contingency that Paul Wolfowitz had foreseen and
that CENTCOM had discovered once the putative Soviet threat had
gone away.

Back in 1898, when the United States annexed Hawaii, no great
power had cared enough about the fate of the islands to restore Queen
Liliuokalani to her throne. This was not the case in 1990 when Iraqi
tanks rolled into Kuwait City. In Washington, the administration of
George H. W. Bush expressed outrage and vowed to act. Gulf War 2.0
was at hand.

Until that moment, U.S. policymakers had been hoping to moderate
Iraqi behavior and "increase our influence" by offering Baghdad "economic and political incentives." An Iraq devastated by years of war,
after all, had needs that the United States could help fill. Cultivating
"normal relations," the Bush administration calculated, would "serve
our longer-term interests and promote stability in both the Gulf and
the Middle East."[4] Now, in a single stroke, Saddam had rendered that
policy inoperative. What would replace it? On August 5, dismounting
from his helicopter on the White House lawn, President Bush made his

own position clear: "This will not stand, this aggression against Kuwait."[5] This time around, in contrast to the First Gulf War, the United States was siding with the victim, not the victimizer.

From a military perspective, the immediate task was to deter Saddam from further aggression. The Iraqi troops who had sent Kuwaiti royals scurrying into exile now threatened the Kingdom of Saudi Arabia, which every U.S. president since Franklin D. Roosevelt had vowed to protect. The time to make good on that commitment had now arrived.

On a hastily arranged visit to Jeddah, Secretary of Defense Dick Cheney, accompanied by CENTCOM commander General H. Norman Schwarzkopf, Jr., briefed King Fahd on CENTCOM's plans for defending the kingdom. Using a series of charts, Schwarzkopf described in detail the proposed buildup of U.S. forces. His "main message was the scale of the operation, to make sure the king understood that we were talking about flooding his airfields, harbors, and military bases with tens of thousands" of American troops. The scale of the proposed commitment showed that Washington meant business. Speaking for President Bush, Cheney assured Fahd that defending Saudi Arabia from possible Iraqi attack defined the limit of U.S. aims. "We will seek no permanent bases," he said. "And when you ask us to go home, we will leave."[6]

Setting aside religious and other sensitivities—hosting a large number of non-Muslim foreign troops in the Land of the Two Holy Places was likely to rile up the devout—the king gave his assent to the American proposal. On August 7, the implementation of OPLAN 1002-90, Defense of the Arabian Peninsula, commenced. In reality, Cheney's promises notwithstanding, U.S. troops were never going to "go home." From this point forward, U.S. military engagement in the Greater Middle East became permanent and sustained, rather than occasional and episodic.

Among those unhappy with King Fahd's decision was a young Saudi veteran just back home from the successfully concluded Afghanistan War. Osama bin Laden strenuously objected to relying on infidels to solve a dispute among Arabs. To liberate Kuwait, he offered to raise an army of mujahedin. Rejecting his offer and his protest, Saudi authorities sought to silence the impertinent bin Laden. Not long thereafter, he fled into exile, determined to lead a holy war that would overthrow the corrupt Saudi royals. Even before the Second Gulf War was fully underway, conditions leading to a third were forming.[7]

In the meantime, U.S. forces began deploying to Saudi Arabia. Among the first to arrive was a brigade from the army's 82nd Airborne Division along with squadrons of F-15 fighter-bombers from Langley Air Force Base in Virginia. The cargo ships pre-positioned in the Indian Ocean at Diego Garcia, filled with weapons, munitions, and other equipment, set sail. As Schwarzkopf had promised, a flood of troops and equipment to support the operation now known as Desert Shield followed. On they came, the United States demonstrating its matchless capacity to move people and things across long distances. In the first sixty days alone, 107,000 personnel and 520,000 tons of cargo arrived in Saudi Arabia. A decade of work by CENTCOM planners was now paying off.[8]

While the initial commitment of U.S. forces made an important political statement, those forces possessed limited combat capabilities. As cargo ships delivered tanks and heavy artillery and as additional naval and air assets closed on the region, however, that soon changed. By early October, a combined arms force numbering several divisions had formed, backed by squadrons of attack aircraft operating from twenty-one separate bases and a huge naval armada that included four carriers. Coalition combat aircraft already outnumbered Saddam's air force by a comfortable margin. Schwarzkopf now expressed confidence that he could defeat any Iraqi push into Saudi Arabia. "No way they're going to seize the oil fields," he assured General Colin Powell, the JCS chairman.[9] The CENTCOM commander's assigned mission was to ensure the security of Saudi Arabia. He had now done that.

A remarkable convergence of circumstances facilitated this concentration of combat power. Saddam himself helped enormously by doing nothing to impede the arrival of U.S. forces. Additional Iraqi divisions dispatched to Kuwait dug in and sat. By assuming a defensive posture, Saddam forfeited the initiative; for Washington, it was an unearned but welcome gift.[10]

At least as important were changes in the international environment. Less than a year before the Iraqi invasion of Kuwait, the fall of the Berlin Wall had upended global politics. Although the myopic Saddam appeared not to notice, the passing of the Cold War endowed Washington with a freedom of action it had not enjoyed since the mid-1940s. Nowhere was that freedom of action more pronounced than in the military realm. The United States now possessed excess military capacity and vastly greater flexibility when it came to its employment.

George H. W. Bush, the last American president to have acquired meaningful national security experience prior to taking office, was quick to appreciate the implications of this opportunity. Just months before, in a fair imitation of Theodore Roosevelt, he had ordered U.S. forces to oust from power Panama's Manuel Noriega, a longtime CIA asset who had outlived his usefulness. The operation was both an echo from another time and a precursor of things to come. Now the Bush administration set about mobilizing a broad anti-Saddam coalition that left Iraq virtually friendless. Working through a UN Security Council that demonstrated seldom-seen responsiveness and cohesion, the United States isolated Iraq diplomatically and imposed punishing sanctions.[11]

To give the military mission an international face, the administration actively recruited troop contingents from anyone willing to contribute.[12] Countries agreeing to send (mostly token) forces ranged from traditional allies like Great Britain and France to Arab nations such as Egypt and even Syria.[13] To defray the costs of the U.S. military deployment, senior U.S. officials trolled through foreign capitals soliciting financial contributions. Ultimately, the effort known informally as Operation Tin Cup netted a tidy $53 billion.[14] As a consequence, unlike subsequent campaigns in America's War for the Greater Middle East, this particular one did not undermine the U.S. economy or add to the national debt. For the moment at least, policing the region elicited appropriate compensation.

By early October the forces earmarked for Operation Desert Shield were nearly all in place. With Saddam showing no inclination to withdraw from Kuwait, the next move was clearly Bush's to make. The president had two options. He could bide his time to see if sanctions might eventually persuade Saddam to pull out. Or he could evict Iraq from Kuwait forcibly. For the members of Bush's inner circle—General Powell excepted—waiting had next to no appeal.[15]

Already, CENTCOM staff officers under Schwarzkopf's direction were hard at work assessing ways to take the offensive. On October 10, they shared their thinking with Secretary Cheney and Paul Wolfowitz, now the Pentagon's third-ranking civilian as undersecretary for policy. Neither Cheney nor Wolfowitz liked what they heard—a hey-diddle-diddle, straight-up-the-middle attack "directly north into the heart of Iraq's most lethal forces." The concept just "didn't make any sense," Cheney thought.[16] A snarky Pentagon civilian called it the "charge of the Light Brigade into the Wadi of Death."[17] The plan fared no better when briefed to President Bush the following day. So the defense secretary tasked Wolfowitz to come up with something more promising. The policy planner thus became a military planner, an expansion of portfolio that Wolfowitz welcomed.

Not for the last time in America's War for the Greater Middle East, civilian leaders found it necessary to prod the military into thinking more creatively. Drawing on a bit of potted history—a British offensive emanating from Transjordan that captured Baghdad in 1941—and incorporating the advice of a retired general to give the scheme a veneer of professional credibility, Wolfowitz's team devised what became known as the "Western Excursion." The idea was simplicity itself: avoid a frontal assault; insert U.S. forces *behind* the enemy, thereby rendering his position untenable—just like Douglas MacArthur at Inchon in 1950. It was Miles Ignotus all over again.[18]

In 2006, a similar collusion between eggheads and a retired general set the stage for "the Surge," an escalation of the Third Gulf War to which we will attend in due course. In this instance, resenting the intrusion of outsiders into the military sphere, Powell and Schwarzkopf peremptorily rejected the "Western Excursion" as logistically unfeasible but then offered up a somewhat tamer version of the same idea: a fixing attack on dug-in Iraqi defenders, followed by a powerful flanking maneuver—all of this preceded by an extensive bombing campaign.

Here was an approach on which military and civilian leaders could concur. The only hitch: Implementation required a considerably larger force than the one currently at hand. To go on the offensive, Schwarzkopf wanted more of everything: tanks, artillery, bombers, aircraft carriers. He currently had 265,000 troops under his command. He was asking for twice that. Bush and Cheney were not going to argue the point. As Cheney put it later, "We gave them absolutely everything they asked for." There was going to be "no excuse possible for anybody in the military to say that the civilian side of the house had not supported them."[19]

At a press conference on November 8, one day after the midterm elections, President Bush announced that he had ordered additional troops to the Gulf. The aim, he said, was "to ensure that the coalition has an adequate offensive military option should that be necessary to achieve our common goals."[20] The oblique language fooled no one. Unless Saddam Hussein unexpectedly conceded to all U.S. demands, the likelihood of Bush exercising the "option" he was creating approached 100 percent. Schwarzkopf understood that. "Forget the defensive bullshit," he told his commanders.[21] Saddam had started something that the United States was now going to finish.

So over the next two months further reinforcements poured in. From Germany came the U.S. Army's VII Corps, with two mechanized divisions, an armored cavalry regiment, and a host of supporting units. From the United States came the famed 1st Infantry Division—the Big Red One—along with a division of Marines to round out the I Marine Expeditionary Force. Among the new arrivals were many reservists, activated in the biggest call-up since the Korean War. By the time these additional forces all took up their positions in mid-January, Schwarz-kopf's command equaled in total strength the number of U.S. troops serving in Vietnam at the height of that conflict.[22]

In the interim, Bush conscientiously checked the requisite legal and constitutional boxes. On November 29, the so-called international community gave him the go-ahead, UN Security Council Resolution 668 authorizing the use of "all necessary means" to enforce its previous order for Iraq to withdraw from Kuwait. The Security Council gave Saddam until January 15 to comply.

With that deadline approaching, the United States Congress belatedly took up the matter. After a contentious debate, the Congress on January 12 passed a de facto declaration of war, with the Senate voting 52–47 in favor and the House of Representatives 250–183. Nominally, the outcome fell along partisan lines, the vast majority of Republicans supporting the resolution and most Democrats opposed. More accurately, however, the divide was between members still haunted by Vietnam and those determined to jettison Vietnam-induced constraints. The latter camp included a fair number of Democrats such as Senators Al Gore of Tennessee and Joseph Lieberman of Connecticut.[23] Representative Stephen Solarz, an influential Democrat from New York and Vietnam War opponent, co-sponsored the resolution and was among those insisting that Munich, not Vietnam, offered the proper historical analogy. "The great lesson of our times is that evil still exists," he told his colleagues, sounding like Lyndon Johnson or Dean Rusk in 1966, "and when evil is on the march it must be confronted."[24]

There was also a third camp. Senior members of the officer corps, notably including Powell and Schwarzkopf, numbered among those both haunted by Vietnam and determined to undo that war's verdict. Indeed, understanding the campaign to liberate Kuwait, its planning and conduct, requires seeing it in considerable part as a proxy war waged against the past.

Like some ghostly presence, Vietnam hovered over the entire proceedings, both in Washington and in the theater of operations. Although memoirs subsequently penned by the principals in this drama disagree about many things—notably the granting of laurels and the allocation of blame—on one point they are in lockstep. From start to finish, both civilians like Bush and Cheney and soldiers like Powell and Schwarzkopf were intent on ensuring that the war against Iraq was not going to be a rerun of Vietnam. This time, by common agreement, there would no micromanaging by meddling civilians, no gradual escalation, no fighting with one hand tied. This time generals would direct the fight, and the American people would be fully on board. A war against Iraq would be Vietnam done right, with decisive victory the result. No shillyshallying allowed.

For soldiers like Powell and Schwarzkopf, the term *decisive* had specific and concrete meaning, tied directly to the fate now awaiting Saddam's army. "First we're going to cut it off, and then we're going to kill it," Powell promised in a widely reported statement.[25] But the ultimate expression of "it" was the Iraqi Republican Guard, the elite of the Saddam's military. This corps-sized formation consisted of several mechanized divisions with imposing names—Hammurabi, Medina, Nebuchadnezzar, Tawakalna—arrayed in depth behind the Iraqi conscripts strung out along the Saudi border. Victory required their complete liquidation. "We need to destroy—not attack, not damage, not surround—I want you to *destroy* the Republican Guard," Schwarzkopf thundered at his commanders. "When you're done with them, I don't want them to be an effective fighting force. I don't want them to exist as a military organization."[26] Defeating an ostensibly battle-hardened Republican Guard offered the prospect of wiping away the stigma of having failed to defeat an army of Asian peasants.

Yet this preoccupation with settling past accounts occluded a clear understanding of the situation at hand. What the yearned-for battlefield vindication could realistically be expected to yield received only passing attention. So too did the possible implications of deepening direct U.S. military involvement in the Islamic world. Intent on vanquishing the specter of Vietnam, those charged with managing the forthcoming war lost sight of the actual context in which the encounter with Iraq was occurring. The Persian Gulf was not Southeast Asia. The long Cold War had ended. This was something different.

By twentieth-century standards, the Second Gulf War ranks as a moderately large conflict waged for quite limited objectives. By ejecting the Iraqi army that had occupied Kuwait, the forces under Schwarzkopf's command were to restore the sovereignty of that country. (Note that making good on this political requirement did not necessarily require the complete destruction of the Republican Guard; the linkage between Washington's advertised political aim and Schwarzkopf's stated operational objective was tenuous.) Beyond that specified goal of liberating Kuwait lay the vague hope that a demonstration of superior American power might somehow lay the foundation for what President Bush was calling a "new world order."[27]

The operative word was *order*. The pragmatic Bush (in contrast to the next U.S. president to bear that name) entertained no illusions about a war against Iraq advancing the cause of freedom, democracy, and human rights. What the elder Bush sought—and what his administration would happily settle for, especially in the Islamic world—was stability.

In fact, however, there existed little reason to expect that ousting Saddam from Kuwait was going to produce much in the way of secondary benefits. Arab armies had more or less routinely gone down to defeat at Israeli hands. Even so, the underlying causes of disorder and dysfunction, not only in an Arab-Israeli context but elsewhere in the Greater Middle East, had persisted. To fancy that another Arab defeat, this time administered by Americans, would produce a more conclusive outcome required a real leap of faith.

The burden of converting faith into reality fell on Schwarzkopf. With the UN ultimatum about to expire and Saddam still refusing to comply, all eyes turned to the field commander. The impending battle was his to fight. So the lessons of Vietnam dictated. It was, therefore, his to win or to lose.

Schwarzkopf was the first of several generals during America's War for the Greater Middle East to achieve apparent immortality—only to discover that the grant was temporary. When his celebrity was at its peak, a fellow officer who had attended West Point with Schwarzkopf offered this effusive appraisal of his classmate: "Norm is this generation's Doug MacArthur. He's got the tactical brilliance of Patton, the strategic insight of Eisenhower, and the modesty of Bradley."[28] Perhaps.

Yet to an unhealthy extent, Schwarzkopf also shared MacArthur's penchant for theatrics. As with Patton, maintaining his emotional balance required a constant struggle. Like Eisenhower, Schwarzkopf had a volcanic temper, which (unlike Ike) he made little effort to keep in check. And like the thin-skinned Bradley, he was quick to take offense at any perceived slight. Generalship in wartime requires foresight, equanimity, and a supple intelligence. Whatever his other talents, Schwarzkopf was not especially graced with these qualities. The campaign to liberate Kuwait would display his gifts and his flaws in equal measure.

That campaign, dubbed Operation Desert Storm, began at 2:40 A.M. on January 17 with a helicopter attack that destroyed two crucially important Iraqi radar installations. Minutes later F-117 stealth bombers were rolling in on downtown Baghdad while terrain-hugging cruise missiles began pounding high-priority targets such as air defenses and government buildings across the Iraqi capital. These formed the opening salvos of a coalition air offensive that continued with minimal interruption for the next forty days. The limited information parceled out to the public portrayed the air offensive as unprecedented in intensity, accuracy, and effectiveness. In many respects, it was.

On the first night alone, nearly seven hundred combat aircraft, the vast majority of them American, penetrated Iraqi airspace. Remarkably, only one plane, an F/A-18 from the USS *Saratoga* flown by Lieutenant Commander Scott Speicher, was lost.[29] By morning, coalition forces had achieved air superiority. The first wave of attacks crippled Iraqi air defenses and strategic communications. In the days that followed, the target list expanded to include electrical generation plants, petroleum refining and storage facilities, transportation assets, airfields, and suspected weapons of mass destruction sites. Saddam's air force, dominant against Iran but vastly inferior to the coalition air armada, essentially chose not to engage. During the first week of combat, it mustered only thirty sorties per day. By January 27, with Iraqi air assets either destroyed or fleeing to landing fields in Iran, the coalition enjoyed unquestioned air supremacy. The weight of its effort now turned to isolating Saddam's forces in Kuwait, laying into major troop concentrations and then, through what coalition pilots called "tank plinking," incrementally reducing what remained of the Iraqi army's capacity and will to fight.[30]

Saddam responded with reassuring incoherence. He flung Scuds toward Saudi Arabia and Israel, neither country reacting as he anticipated—the Saudis stayed in and the Israelis out.[31] Opening the valves of a Kuwaiti oil terminal, Saddam released thousands of barrels of crude into the Gulf, apparently expecting pollution to give pause to the world's leading polluters. He rashly launched a brigade-sized probe into Saudi Arabia proper. Devoid of air support, the small-scale attack ended in an utter rout. This ill-advised foray served chiefly to reveal the shortcomings of Saddam's army as, in the words of one American general, "the gang that can't shoot straight."[32] The noose was tightening.

For army officers like Powell and Schwarzkopf, that air power alone might suffice to win the war qualified as an inadmissible heresy—like questioning the universality of American values or the perfection of the U.S. Constitution. Where Powell and Schwarzkopf parted company was on the timing of the ground offensive required to administer the coup de grâce. The politically savvy Powell was acutely sensitive to the pressures on President Bush, chiefly coming from impatient allies but also from the press, to move sooner rather than later. The JCS chairman prodded Schwarzkopf to get on with it.

Schwarzkopf pushed back. He had heard whispers that back in Washington people were comparing him to the dilatory Civil War general George McClellan, to any American general officer an intolerable insult.[33] Weighed down by the burdens of command, the CENTCOM chief seemed at times precariously close to coming unglued. "Colin, I think I'm losing it," he complained to Powell at one point. "I feel my head's in a vice."[34] From where he sat, Schwarzkopf could not see what all the hurry was about. With each additional day of bombing, Iraq's army grew perceptibly weaker, the task awaiting American soldiers and Marines less dangerous, and the likelihood of Schwarzkopf himself failing less likely.

On February 22, Saddam's troops began torching hundreds of Kuwaiti oil wells, as if to signal an impending scorched-earth retreat. Almost six weeks of bombing—nearly one hundred thousand sorties plus over three hundred cruise missiles—had left his army (and his country as a whole) reeling. According to U.S. intelligence estimates, frontline Iraq army divisions had suffered 50 percent losses due to casualties and desertions. The Republican Guard had fared somewhat better, but it too had sustained losses of approximately 25 percent.[35] Schwarzkopf finally conceded that the enemy needed no further softening up.

In fact, although these estimates proved reasonably accurate, they told only half the story. From the very outset, CENTCOM had substantially overstated the threat. The Iraqis never had what the Americans thought they had; after weeks of mauling from the air, they had even less. As a consequence, by the last week of February, Schwarzkopf was facing an enemy that was both badly battered and numerically inferior to his own forces, perhaps by as much as a 3:1 margin.[36]

None of this is to suggest that the soldiers and Marines moving into their final attack positions on the night of February 23–24 could rest easy. War is always fraught with hazard. Only by actually encountering their adversary would coalition troops be able to take his measure. And however impressive the achievements of the air campaign, enormous uncertainties remained. Prominent among them was the likelihood that, having ordered the use of chemical weapons in the past, Saddam might do so again. Although U.S. troops routinely trained to fight in such conditions, none had actually done so since World War I. The prospect of doing so now—more or less the equivalent of donning deep-sea diving gear as battledress—evoked little enthusiasm.

Still, when the ground offensive began at 4:00 A.M. on G-Day, February 24, things went astonishingly well. Expected to encounter tough going as they advanced toward Kuwait City, the Marines met light resistance. In the VII Corps sector, forces assigned to breach forward Iraqi defenses did so with remarkable ease. Further west, XVIII Corps, covering VII Corps' open flank, "took off like a rocket."[37] If anything impeded forward movement, it was difficult terrain rather than enemy resistance. Everywhere casualties were well below expectations. To Schwarzkopf's enormous relief, Iraqi forces refrained from using chemical weapons. Meanwhile, the conscripts occupying forward Iraqi defensive positions "declined the role of cannon fodder and surrendered in large numbers."[38] By day's end, Saddam was directing his forces to withdraw from Kuwait. How many Iraqi units actually received this order is difficult to say. Few were in a position to comply.

Early success was throwing CENTCOM's elaborately orchestrated scheme of maneuver out of sync. If the strings are two beats ahead, that leaves the reeds two beats behind. One immediate effect was to exacerbate simmering tensions between Schwarzkopf and the commander of VII Corps, Lieutenant General Frederick M. Franks, Jr. Sharing the same Vietnam-induced hang-ups, Franks and Schwarzkopf differed in both temperament and demeanor. Nicknames told the story. Schwarzkopf's was "the Bear." Among his peers, Franks was known as "Freddy." He was quiet, thoughtful, thorough, and methodical.

The Bear was counting on Freddy to deliver the knockout punch that would dispatch the Republican Guard for good. He had, therefore, provided Franks with a truly imposing force—five heavy divisions and an armored cavalry regiment, with four artillery brigades and seven attack helicopter battalions in support.[39] In all, VII Corps consisted of 50,000 vehicles and 146,000 soldiers.

The plan that Franks devised to employ these assets emphasized deliberation and control. A carefully unfolding sequence of actions would ultimately bring to bear massed combat power against the flanks of the Republican Guard. Conceptually, according to the U.S. Army's official campaign history, the result was "less like the deep rapier thrusts of

Guderian or Rommel" and more like the great wheeling Schlieffen Plan that formed the cornerstone of Germany military strategy in 1914.[40] A monument to detailed staff work, that plan had proved upon implementation to be something of a straitjacket. Something similar occurred here.

As Franks saw it, developments over the course of G-Day affirmed the basic soundness of his approach. Visits to his subordinate commanders in the field corroborated that view. Monitoring events from his command post underneath the Saudi ministry of defense in Riyadh, Schwarzkopf had a different take. So too did Powell, even farther from the action, back in Washington. They wanted Franks to pick up the tempo. To the east, the Marines were well ahead of schedule. To the west, mechanized elements within XVIII Corps were moving farther and faster. Why couldn't Franks do likewise?

This otherwise trivial intramural dispute was to have large implications for America's unfolding War for the Greater Middle East. Franks never did pick up the tempo, at least not enough to suit Schwarzkopf. The disconnect between the two ultimately affected the Desert Storm endgame, yielding an outcome that appeared decisive but was shot through with ambiguity. The victory-that-might-have-been in 1991 promoted fantasies of victories certain to be won by exhibiting the ostensible boldness not seen during Desert Storm.

In the event, when Schwarzkopf checked the situation map on the morning of February 25 and found that VII Corps had not moved overnight, he erupted in fury. Franks needed to get going or else. Yet as pressure on VII Corps to close with the Republican Guard measurably increased, so too did the disparity of perspectives between the two commanders. As Schwarzkopf saw it, the battle was entering the exploitation phase. All that remained was to finish off a beaten enemy. That was not the way it looked in the VII Corps command post. There, it seemed, the real fight still awaited.

Perhaps afflicted with a case of "chateau generalship," Schwarzkopf now showed an increased appetite for risk.[41] Victory beckoned. Seizing the moment began to eclipse other concerns such as casualty avoidance. Meanwhile, Franks, troubled by the number of casualties resulting from friendly fire, was becoming even more risk-averse. It was now his turn to wonder what all the hurry was about.

On the morning of February 26, VII Corps did finally encounter the Republican Guard, inflicting considerable damage. Throughout that day and the next, despite adverse weather, logistics challenges, and growing fatigue, VII Corps units took turns tearing into the badly overmatched enemy. In one engagement, for example, the 2nd Brigade, 1st Armored Division demolished an entire brigade of the Medina Division, destroying sixty-one tanks and thirty-nine other armored vehicles at the cost of a single American killed. The entire fight lasted barely an hour.[42]

In another action, at a spot in the desert that the Americans called 73 Easting, a company-sized American armored unit encountered and utterly obliterated an Iraqi formation roughly four times its size, all without sustaining a scratch. In something like twenty-three minutes, E Troop of the 2nd Armored Cavalry Regiment, commanded by Captain H. R. McMaster, had destroyed twenty-eight enemy tanks along with sixteen personnel carriers and thirty trucks. Army generals saw in this demonstration of total dominance the promise of more such victories to come. The action at 73 Easting, in their estimation, defined the future of war—a bit like researchers announcing a cure for cancer based on a one-time, small-scale trial of an experimental drug.[43]

Desert Storm was a replay of Operation Praying Mantis, albeit on a far grander canvas. By nightfall on February 27, American commanders estimated that given one more day the demolition of the Iraqi army would be complete. Before that day could arrive, however, Desert Storm ended.

In Washington, where destroying the Republican Guard had never figured as a particular imperative, priorities were shifting. Concern for appearances was displacing serious strategic analysis. To some observers, it looked like the Americans were piling on a hapless and defeated foe. The optics were changing in ways that threatened to tarnish perceptions. When to call time was emerging as the question of the moment.

Powell was quick to sense—and embrace—the new mood. "The doves are starting to complain about all the damage you're doing," the closeted four-star dove told Schwarzkopf on a call to Riyadh. "The reports make it look like wanton killing."[44] What would Schwarzkopf think about calling a halt on the 28th? After briefly hesitating, the CENTCOM commander gave way. The idea of winning a Five-Day War, outdoing the vaunted Israelis by one day, caught his fancy. (The several weeks of bombing that had preceded the ground attack did not figure in Schwarzkopf's arithmetic.)

Soon thereafter, Powell updated President Bush and his senior aides in the Oval Office. "Mr. President, it's going much better than expected. The Iraqi army is broken. All they're trying to do is get out," he reported. "By sometime tomorrow the job will be done." Norm concurred in this assessment, Powell emphasized.[45]

"If that's the case," the commander in chief asked, "why not end it today?" Once again, Bush was far in front of his subordinates. Ducking into the president's study, Powell quickly called Riyadh. What if the president terminated hostilities later that very day? "I don't have any problem," Schwarzkopf replied. "Our objective was to drive 'em out and we've done that." In best lessons-learned-from-Vietnam manner, the field commander's views settled the issue. Desert Storm would end at midnight Washington time, the president decided, a nice, tidy one hundred hours after the ground offensive had begun.[46]

With the clock ticking down, Schwarzkopf, channeling MacArthur, seized the moment to lay down his own narrative of the events that had unfolded. In a globally televised presentation subsequently known as the "mother of all briefings"—Saddam had vowed to defeat the Americans in the "mother of all battles"—the CENTCOM commander declared victory. It was a masterful performance, alternately pugnacious, sarcastic, humane, and self-deprecating. His overarching theme emphasized the historic, indeed unprecedented, nature of the U.S.-led coalition's military achievement. In a "classic tank battle," it had all but obliterated the Iraqi army. Any remnants that survived were trapped. "The gates are closed." It was time to stop. "We've accomplished our mission."[47] The problem was that he had not. And the gates were not closed.

Later that same night, Bush himself appeared on television. Absent Schwarzkopf's bombast, he affirmed Schwarzkopf's verdict. "Kuwait is liberated," the president announced. "Iraq's army is defeated. Our military objectives are met." It was time to move on. "This war is now behind us." The first of Bush's claims was indubitably correct, the second partially so. Unfortunately, the last two assertions missed by a wide margin, with considerable implications for the future.[48]

In fact, substantial elements of the Republican Guard remained intact. Nor were they hemmed in. The unilaterally declared ceasefire offered the prospect of escaping back to Baghdad. They wasted little time in doing just that.

Compounding the error, Schwarzkopf bungled the ceasefire's implementation. In a position to impose, he chose instead to concede, with regrettable consequences. The fault was not his alone. Strangely enough, the suspension of operations caught American political and military leaders alike by surprise. No one in a position of authority had given much thought to what should happen next.[49] (This oversight would again crop up in 2003 at a critical juncture of Persian Gulf War 3.0.) Washington had provided CENTCOM no instructions regarding the terms of any agreement to terminate hostilities. So Schwarzkopf drafted his own, which he carried to a meeting with the obscure Iraqi generals whom Saddam Hussein, still alive and well in Baghdad, had appointed to represent him.[50] Schwarzkopf's own views were quite straightforward: "Our side had *won,* so we were in a position to dictate terms."[51]

Yet when that meeting convened on March 3 at Safwan, an Iraqi airfield not far from the Kuwaiti border, satisfying the presumed demands of History competed with more substantive considerations. The atmosphere was rife with grandstanding. Earmarking furnishings for the

Smithsonian Institution "in case they ever wanted to re-create the Safwan negotiation scene" had emerged as a priority. When the proceedings began, Schwarzkopf quickly assured his counterparts, "We have no intention of leaving our forces permanently in Iraqi territory once the ceasefire is signed." He and the soldiers under his command were eager to vamoose. So Saddam Hussein had nothing to worry about on that score. To demonstrate that he harbored no grudges against his adversaries, Schwarzkopf magnanimously granted an Iraqi request to resume their use of military helicopters. "Given that the Iraqis had agreed to all of our requests," he later explained, "I didn't feel it was unreasonable to grant one of theirs." So much for the prerogative of dictating terms. The event adjourned with comradely salutes and handshakes all around.[52]

That was that. The ceremonies may not have quite measured up to those over which MacArthur had presided on the deck of the USS *Missouri* in 1945, but they offered a reasonable facsimile. (Schwarzkopf had actually pondered using the *Missouri*, afloat in the Persian Gulf, only to conclude that assembling all of the various dignitaries there posed too many complications.)[53] In any event, Gulf War 2.0 had officially ended. The Iraqis freed the few coalition troops that they had captured—for Schwarzkopf a key goal. The many tens of thousands of Iraqi POWs in coalition custody were likewise released.

At home, the narrative of Desert Storm as Vietnam-done-right—"a drama of dazzling display, brutal crispness, and amazingly decisive outcome"—gathered momentum and became all but irresistible. As *Time* put it, Desert Storm spelled "the end of the old American depression called the Vietnam syndrome, the compulsion to look for downsides and dooms." Victory in the Gulf heralded "the birth of a new American century—the onset of a unipolar world, with America at the center of it." Such hyperbole commanded widespread assent.[54]

Upon returning to the United States, Schwarzkopf led his troops past cheering throngs during gala confetti-strewn parades in the nation's capitol and through Lower Manhattan's "Canyon of Heroes."[55] Out of victory came a sense of closure and perhaps of national reconciliation. After marching down Constitution Avenue with a contingent from VII Corps, Franks went directly to the Vietnam Memorial. "This one was for you," he thought, as he ran his fingers over the names of fallen comrades.[56] Meanwhile, down in Little Rock, the young governor of Arkansas made a point of including Vietnam vets in the parade honoring local returning Desert Storm heroes. "I'll never forget how moved I was," Bill Clinton recalled, "as I watched them march down the street to our cheers, and saw the Vietnam veterans finally being given the honor they deserved all along."[57] It's hard to imagine two people more dissimilar than Franks and Clinton, the one having lost a leg in Vietnam, the other having made a considerable effort to avoid service there, but on this occasion their views aligned.

Schwarzkopf himself, now an A-list celebrity, was both the most authoritative proponent and the principal beneficiary of this euphoria. Members of the press swooned. Schwarzkopf had "the IQ of a genius" and a "taste for Pavarotti." As "the heartthrob of America," he represented "a new model for male leadership"—"introspective but decisive, caring but competent, one of the guys and a leader." "Schwarzkopf of Arabia" had engineered "a triumph of almost Biblical proportions—his enemy slain in countless numbers, his own soldiers hardly touched by the battlefield's scouring wind." Rather than "a dour martinet like William Westmoreland"—a reference to the Vietnam commander tagged (fairly or not) with getting that war disastrously wrong—Schwarzkopf was "a warrior with a soul." His battlefield achievements were without parallel. "Generations hence military historians will ponder the lessons of the liberation of Kuwait," directly attributable to its commander. Simply put, "no one has done it better than Schwarzkopf."[58]

Personal honors continued to accumulate. From President Bush, Schwarzkopf received the Medal of Freedom, from Congress a gold medal, and from the Queen of England a knighthood. Awed members of Congress proposed his elevation to five-star rank, putting him (and Powell) alongside World War II greats such as Marshall and Eisenhower.[59] He also inked a $5 million contract to write his memoirs, which became a huge bestseller.

Yet virtually from the moment that President Bush had announced a suspension of offensive operations, events on the ground had begun to subvert the victory narrative. Loose ends abounded, as Bush himself vaguely apprehended. An entry in his diary on the morning of February 28 already reflected a growing sense of unease. On the one hand, Bush assured himself, "there's been nothing like this in history." On the other hand, "it hasn't been a clean end."[60]

Evidence that the end was less than clean had begun to accumulate even prior to Schwarzkopf's confab at Safwan. The day before (and therefore three days after Bush had declared the war ended), the 24th Infantry Division (Mechanized) had engaged elements of the Hammurabi Division as they withdrew toward Baghdad. The division commander, Major General Barry McCaffrey, claimed that his troops had come under fire. If so, that fire was notably ineffective. In what became known as the Battle of the Junkyard, American tanks, field artillery, and attack helicopters from the 24th Mech destroyed a roadbound column of some several hundred vehicles. To escape the deadly assault, Iraqi soldiers simply abandoned their equipment and fled. When the action ended after some four hours, U.S. casualties were none killed and one wounded. Whatever the accuracy of McCaffrey's version of events, the incident suggested that Schwarzkopf's "mother of all briefings" had not told the full story. Either the Republican Guard still retained considerable combat capability or U.S. forces had engaged in unnecessary slaughter well after the commander in chief had ordered a halt to the proceedings.[61] That both were true was also a possibility.

Worse was the crisis exploding within Iraq itself—a popular uprising against the continuation of Saddam Hussein's rule. In the midst of the Second Gulf War, President Bush had urged the Iraqi people to rid themselves of Saddam, whom he described as "Hitler revisited."[62] U.S. government propaganda outlets had emphasized the same message.[63] At a press conference on March 1, the president reiterated his solution to the Saddam problem: "The Iraqi people should put him aside." That, he continued, "would facilitate the acceptance of Iraq back into the family of peace-loving nations."[64]

Whether or not they were responding to Bush's suggestion, large numbers of Iraqis, notably Shiites and Kurds who had not fared well under Saddam's Sunni-dominated Ba'ath Party, now launched an effort to oust the dictator. Saddam responded with pitiless repression, which had the intended effect. Thousands were killed. Many hundreds of thousands more fled. In the United States and elsewhere in the West, images of forlorn Kurdish refugees, huddled in the desolate Turkish outback without food, water, or shelter, led nightly news programs. (The largely unseen suffering of Iraqi Shiites garnered less attention.) Meanwhile, the forces under Schwarzkopf's command, still occupying southern Iraq as they prepared to redeploy, did nothing. The result was an epic humanitarian disaster and a huge embarrassment for the United States.

Assuming responsibility for the Kurds had never figured as part of the Bush administration's game plan. Yet once again, the optics were terrible. Surely, Bush's "new world order" was not going to allow such crimes. At his March 1 press conference, Bush had posited that by enhancing American stature and influence, Desert Storm was going to make the world a better and more peaceful place. "I think because of what has happened," he said, "we won't have to use U.S. forces around the world. I think when we say that something is objectively correct, like don't take over a neighbor or you're going to bear some responsibility, people are going to listen."[65] As suggested by the unhappy plight of Iraq's Shiites and Kurds, that message had apparently not sunk in with Saddam Hussein. Through violence, the United States had sought to end violence and impose order. Instead, within Iraq, U.S. intervention had produced conditions conducive to further violence and further disorder—another persistent theme in America's War for the Greater Middle East.

So in remarkably short order, the victory narrative began to unravel. That Saddam had somehow managed to survive now defined the issue. Critics reproached Bush for not having pushed on to Baghdad, with even Schwarzkopf making the misleading claim that his own recommendation had been to "continue to march."[66] New York Times columnist William Safire likened "President Bush's decision to betray the Kurdish people" to debacles such as the Kennedy's Bay of Pigs and Carter's Desert One. (Eisenhower's stone-faced response to the 1956 Hungarian Revolution offered a more apt comparison.) Through inaction, Bush "threw away our newfound pride . . . as a superpower that stands for the right," Safire fulminated. "It seems we defend the rich and sell out the poor."[67] In *The Washington Post*, foreign affairs columnist Jim Hoagland denounced Bush's reluctance to rescue the Kurds as "monumental folly," directly attributable to "the old mind-set about Saddam being a useful tool for U.S. goals." Passivity, he warned, would "tarnish even the most splendid victory."[68] Charles Krauthammer agreed: "We've given Saddam enough chances. The time to finish him is now."[69]

For their part, the president and his defenders offered multiple reasons for not having gone on to Baghdad, chiefly the probable mess waiting there and the refusal of Arab allies to sanction a precedent-setting war aimed at regime change. Redefining the objective as something other than liberating Kuwait would have shattered the coalition. Besides, as Cheney explained, "the assumption from the experts was that Saddam would never survive the defeat."[70] The experts, not the policymakers, had miscalculated.

Yet the most important reason for not going to Baghdad was the one least cited in public. In fact, Hoagland had it more than half-right: The Bush administration was still counting on Iraq to contain Iran. *Washington Post* columnist Mary McGrory stated the matter bluntly. "Bush doesn't want the Shiite fundamentalist rebels to topple Saddam; that would make Iran the top dog in the Middle East."[71] As Brent Scowcroft, Bush's national security adviser, later acknowledged, in making war against Saddam, the United States had sought "to damage his offensive capability without weakening Iraq to the point that a vacuum was created, and destroying the balance between Iraq and Iran"—a neat trick that assumed the ability to mete out punishment with micrometer-like precision.[72]

Yet from the First Gulf War to the Second, this strategic principle had remained sacrosanct: The United States had a compelling interest in positioning Iraq as a counterweight to a dangerous Islamic Republic. By comparison, Saddam's own fate ranked as an afterthought.[73] As for the Kurds, opposing their aspirations for an independent state was the one point on which Iran, Iraq, Syria, Turkey, *and* the United States could all agree. Except among Kurds, carving up existing states to make room for a sovereign Kurdistan generated little support.

Still, in the face of intensifying pressure to "do something" on behalf of Saddam's latest victims, Bush gave way. On April 5, he ordered the U.S. military to begin delivering aid to the Kurds. (Iraqi Shiites were out of luck.) "I want to emphasize that this effort is prompted only by humanitarian concerns," the president insisted—a partial untruth since Turkey's unease with the detested Kurds entering its territory also prompted the course change.[74] Thus began Operation Provide Comfort, a relief mission that in its way equaled Desert Storm in importance. Although nominally the Second Gulf War had ended, something else had already begun. Here was the first indication that the United States military was not going to "go home." Soon enough, more followed.

What then are we to make of Operation Desert Storm? Certainly, the hopes expressed by the war's American architects have not found fulfillment. Had the Second Gulf War "dramatically changed the situation in the Middle East"?[75] Did it create "a far greater opportunity for peace in the Middle East than any of us have ever seen in our lifetimes"?[76] The answers to those questions must be no. With the passing of a quarter-century, judgments about the war will vary depending on the vantage point of the observer.

Viewed as "a war for oil," which indeed it was, Desert Storm produced a satisfactory yet imperfect outcome. The Emir of Kuwait had much for which to be thankful: He had regained his country. For their part, Saudi royals no longer faced the prospect of imminent invasion. The Americans had removed any doubts about their willingness to provide protection. Even so, as long as Saddam Hussein clung to power, he remained a menace and regional stability remained precarious.

Viewed as a postscript to Vietnam, the Second Gulf War qualifies as a clear-cut success that gave rise to problematic second-order effects. For officers such as Powell, Schwarzkopf, and Franks, Desert Storm signified redemption, not least of all because, as Powell put it, "the American people fell in love again with their armed forces."[77] Politically, this brief and seemingly epochal campaign also largely dismantled any restraints on the use of force. At the time, President Bush happily asserted that "By God, we've kicked the Vietnam syndrome once and for all."[78] He was justified in making that claim. But did the new "Desert Storm syndrome" that emerged in its place—a belief that the United States now enjoyed unparalleled military supremacy—mark an improvement? Time would tell. Meanwhile, in the years immediately ahead, the American soldier, showered with popular affection, was going to get one helluva workout.

Viewed in the context of America's expanding military involvement in the Greater Middle East—the primary interest here—Operation Desert Storm accomplished next to nothing. The Bush administration's declaration of victory in 1991 did, in fact, turn out to be premature. That results fell short of expectations stemmed less from flawed generalship, however, than from a fundamental misreading of the overall situation.

Although during the coming decade Washington developed an Ahab-like mania regarding Saddam, the Iraqi dictator was merely a symptom of what the United States was contending with. The real problem had a multitude of aspects: the vacuum left by the eclipse of British imperial power; intractable economic backwardness and political illegitimacy; divisions within Islam compounded by the rise of Arab nationalism; the founding of Israel; and the advent of the Iranian Revolution.

It's hard to imagine how any victory over Iraq, no matter how complete, could have remedied this menu of challenges. After another decade of trying, the United States gave up the attempt. After 9/11, rather than vainly trying to prop up the Greater Middle East, Washington set out to transform it. A fundamental misreading of Desert Storm helped make that attempt appear plausible. The result was a disaster.

PART II

ENTR'ACTE

8

GOOD INTENTIONS

AS WINTER SLOWLY GAVE WAY TO SPRING IN 1991, THE KURDISH crisis was casting a shadow over Desert Storm. To implement Operation Provide Comfort, the Pentagon hastily assembled a scratch force, drawn from various commands, with availability and relative proximity the chief determinants of who would go. At first, the effort had amounted to little more than "throwing popcorn at pigeons."[1] But the popcorn was soon appearing by the pallet-load and began to make a difference. Even so, forlorn refugees in numbers too great to count were still clinging to the sides of barren mountains in southeastern Turkey, exposed to the elements or at best huddling under plastic sheeting. Urgent shortages of food, water, and medical supplies persisted.

Not even the coldest heart could witness misery on such a vast scale without being moved to pity. Yet empathizing was the easy part, qualms of conscience at least partly mollified by airdropping relief supplies. This U.S. Air Force transports were doing with impressive efficiency, while fighter planes provided air cover and several thousand ground troops established a security zone extending from Turkey into northern Iraq itself.[2]

Without doubt, efforts by U.S. and allied forces saved many lives. Yet more difficult was the problem of figuring out what this utterly dissonant postscript to Desert Storm—the equivalent of a wardrobe malfunction disrupting an otherwise impeccably rehearsed show—signified. What warnings did it convey? What did it foreshadow?

For the Bush administration and the U.S. military, Operation Provide

Comfort ranked as little more than a footnote. The epoch-making liberation of Kuwait qualified as the main story. By comparison, the mission to rescue the Kurds was at most an unwelcome but not terribly significant addendum. Desert Storm heralded the future. Provide Comfort looked like a one-off event. So at least U.S. civilian and military leaders expected.

In fact, as America's War for the Greater Middle East continued to unfold, the reverse proved true. Desert Storm—a brief, heroic war immediately followed by long celebratory parades—turned out to be the one-off event. By comparison, Provide Comfort served as a harbinger of morally ambiguous surprises still to come. The seemingly lesser of the two events ended up being the more important.

In retrospect, the policy implications of the Kurdish crisis seem plain as day. Here, for starters, was incontrovertible evidence that America's Saddam problem wasn't going away. The recalcitrant bad boy simply refused to behave. Although for political reasons—a presidential election was approaching—George H. W. Bush kept pretending that the Second Gulf War had produced decisive results, it obviously had not. (Something similar was to occur in 2011 when the Barack Obama administration prematurely declared the Third Gulf War over, only to have it roar back to life.)

By extension, intervention on behalf of the Kurds demolished expectations that the outcome of Desert Storm might allow the United States to police the Persian Gulf from offshore, while Iran and Iraq kept one another in check and thereby ensured a modicum of regional stability. As long as Saddam remained in power, counting on Iraq to contain Iran was going to be a nonstarter. Although stability remained Washington's goal, the burden of ensuring it looked like one the United States itself was going to have to shoulder. That implied unforeseen costs and risks.

Further, while suggesting that the U.S. military was going to have more work to do, the Kurdish crisis simultaneously raised questions about the actual benefits stemming from the military preeminence demonstrated in Desert Storm. Here were hints that those benefits might not fully live up to Washington's expectations. After all, in less than a month, events had invalidated President Bush's prediction that "when we say that something is objectively correct . . . people are going to listen." To be sure, U.S. forces had responded with commendable alacrity in rescuing the Iraqi Kurds. But the very nature of this contingency intimated that the role awaiting the U.S. military was going to involve something more than occasionally beating up some ineptly led third-rate army.

The ongoing evolution of Provide Comfort itself made that very point. To avoid having Iraqi Kurds become permanent refugees—and a permanent problem like the Palestinians displaced back in 1948—the United States needed to persuade them to go back where they came from. From humanitarian assistance, the emphasis now shifted to re-settlement. Yet keeping the Iraqi Kurds where they belonged meant guaranteeing their safety when they got there.

So on July 24, 1991, Operation Provide Comfort gave way to Operation Provide Comfort II. Rather than delivering life-sustaining essentials, the mission had morphed into one focused on providing protection. To accomplish this task, thereby providing the Kurdish returnees with a semblance of normalcy, the Pentagon devised an innovative approach. Averse to using ground troops to defend Iraqi Kurdistan, the United States chose to keep Saddam Hussein at bay and the Kurds in place by relying exclusively on airpower. Operating from Turkish bases, U.S. Air Force combat patrols, with initial assistance from France, Turkey, and the United Kingdom, began enforcing a "no-fly zone" that included all of Iraq north of latitude 36 degrees, an area encompassing Iraqi Kurdistan along with a generous buffer. The immediate aim was to permit the Kurds to enjoy nearly complete autonomy from Baghdad, in effect becoming an independent nation in all but name. More broadly, the aim was to keep a boot on Saddam's neck.

No obvious criteria existed for determining when to declare the mission accomplished. As long as Saddam remained in power, anxiety among the Kurds was going to run high. So once begun, Provide Comfort II kept going, continuing until December 31, 1996. By that time, the air force had flown some forty-two thousand sorties over northern

Iraq, with the allies contributing another twenty thousand.[3] Even then, air operations did not end—they just got a new name. Redesignated Northern Watch, they continued for another several years, while piling up a further thirty-six thousand sorties.

Meanwhile, on August 27, 1992, the United States initiated a southern counterpart, appropriately named Southern Watch. Flying out of bases in Saudi Arabia or from nearby U.S. Navy aircraft carriers, combat aircraft crisscrossed Iraq south of the 32nd parallel, prohibiting Iraqi military activity, not only in the air but also on the ground.[4] Nominally, the purpose of this operation was to shield Iraqi Shiites from Saddam's wrath, although it came too late to help much in that regard. In reality, the point was to put the squeeze on Saddam, part of a larger diplomatic and economic strategy intended to weaken and, with a bit of luck, even depose him. By the time it ended with the start of the Third Gulf War in 2003, pilots enforcing the southern no-fly/no-drive zone had flown over 150,000 sorties.[5]

"What we have effectively done since 1992 is conduct an air occupation of a country." So claimed General Ronald R. Fogelman, U.S. Air Force chief of staff.[6] If so, the occupation was neither benign nor peaceful. In fact, enforcing the no-fly zones resembled the continuous jousting that occurs between Israel and adversaries such as Hamas or Hezbollah. The Israeli term for this is *batash*, roughly translated as "current security." This anodyne phrase refers to everyday warlike actions in circumstances where national survival is not immediately at stake. *Batash* means keeping the other side off-balance or exacting retribution for lesser offenses, with no expectation of achieving decisive results. Over the skies of Iraq, the United States had chosen to get into the *batash* business.[7]

Saddam responded to this appropriation of Iraqi airspace with large quantities of vitriol but only token resistance. In December 1992, a single Iraqi MiG ventured into the southern no-fly zone, only to be promptly downed by a U.S. Air Force F-16. Early the following month other incursions occurred. More troubling, U.S. intelligence detected signs of surface-to-air missiles (SAMs) infiltrating south of the 32nd parallel. On January 13, 1993, the outgoing George H. W. Bush administration responded by attacking Iraqi air defenses throughout the southern no-fly zone. U.S. forces were unopposed and suffered no losses. Saddam claimed that the raid, which involved over one hundred aircraft, had killed nineteen civilians. He vowed to "turn the skies of Iraq into a lava against the oppressors."[8]

On January 17, another MiG tried its luck, this time in the northern no-fly zone. It suffered the same fate as the first, knocked down by another F-16. That same night, in an unrelated incident, several dozen cruise missiles, launched from U.S. Navy warships, slammed into a suspected nuclear facility south of Baghdad, punishment for Saddam's refusal to permit UN weapons inspectors to enter his country. A day later, in a sort of backhanded farewell from an administration due to step down forty-eight hours later, U.S. forces gave Iraqi air defenses one final shellacking. Seventy-five aircraft participated. All returned to base safely. As Bill Clinton took the oath of office as the forty-second U.S. president, hostilities subsided.[9]

They had by no means ended, however. Throughout the 1990s, fighting ebbed and flowed, always one-sided, never yielding a conclusive outcome. Threatened and sometimes actually engaged by Iraqi defenders, U.S. aircraft retaliated in what became a variant of the tank plinking that figured in Desert Storm. Now the plinking focused on taking apart Saddam's air defenses. In a single twelve-month period, Northern Watch aircraft attacked some 225 targets. In the southern zone, from 1999 to 2000 alone, over two thousand American bombs and missiles rained down on Iraqi SAM batteries, radars, and communication nodes. All of this activity attracted minimal public or press attention, largely because during this entire time Iraq failed to hit even a single U.S. aircraft. The gang that couldn't shoot straight had not improved its marksmanship.[10]

This is not to say that U.S. forces suffered no casualties. They did, albeit not at Iraqi hands. In April 1994, Northern Watch F-15s inadvertently shot down two U.S. Army Black Hawks, mistaking them for Russian-built Iraqi helicopters. The twenty-six killed included fifteen

Americans.[11] Then, in June 1996, terrorists attacked Khobar Towers, an apartment complex in Dhahran, Saudi Arabia, used to house U.S. personnel supporting Operation Southern Watch. The bombing killed nineteen and wounded several hundred others. With a swiftness that recalled the *Stark* episode, U.S. and Saudi officials fingered Iran as the perpetrator, a mutually convenient verdict since neither party had any interest in admitting the possible involvement of Saudi citizens. Subsequent evidence suggested that Al Qaeda may have been responsible, retaliation prompted by the continuing presence of infidels in the Land of the Two Holy Places.[12]

Yet all of this, along with periodic eruptions of larger scale violence—a 1993 U.S. cruise missile attack that demolished Iraq's intelligence headquarters in Baghdad and a four-day bombardment of suspected Iraqi weapons of mass destruction facilities in 1998—vanished from memory once the Third Gulf War began in March 2003.[13] This is regrettable. For at least two reasons, restoring the "air occupation" of Iraq to a place of prominence in America's ongoing War for the Greater Middle East is in order.

First, doing so corrects the tendency to dismiss the 1990s as a mere "interwar decade," lying flaccidly between two episodes of enduring importance. On the near side lay the Cold War and on the far side the so-called Global War on Terrorism, the United States having ostensibly dozed off when the former ended in 1989, only to be rudely awakened in 2001 when the latter appeared out of nowhere.

At the very least, the kicks and punches doled out to Saddam Hussein's Iraq complicate that tidy storyline. In fact, the United States did not spend the 1990s sitting on its hands. The venture on which it had embarked back in 1980 continued apace and was intensifying. Being "at war" in the Greater Middle East had now become an everyday proposition, even if the American public generally preferred not to take notice. Only in one sense did the 1990s represent an interwar period: In the ashes left by the Second Gulf War smoldered the embers of a third. U.S. military actions during the 1990s were adding fuel to the fire.

Yet U.S. military operations in Iraq during the 1990s merit attention for a second reason as well. Here was an indication of what the passing of the Vietnam Syndrome portended—a heedless absence of self-restraint, with shallow moralistic impulses overriding thoughtful strategic analysis.

As a consequence, in debates over possible U.S. armed intervention, wariness now gave way to "why not?" One result was to endow the commander in chief with greater latitude, which George H. W. Bush (and Bill Clinton) did not hesitate to exploit in harrying Saddam. When it came to *batash*, presidents could do pretty much whatever they wanted. As long as someone issued a press release or went on TV to explain where the bombs had fallen—and as long as no Americans were killed—few questions were asked.

Yet the passing of the Vietnam Syndrome also had a further impact that impinged on America's War for the Greater Middle East. Faced with some grave injustice or large-scale violation of human rights, presidents now found it increasingly hard to justify inaction. The possession of matchless military capabilities not only endowed the United States with the ability to right wrongs and succor the afflicted, it also imposed an obligation to do just that.

Now more than ever, the old concept of America First, with its preference for keeping the troops at home, seemed unduly selfish, even niggardly. A new sentiment emerged: America Everywhere, open to sending the troops wherever people were in dire straits. When suddenly confronted by the misfortunes besetting the luckless Iraqi Kurds, Bush himself had yielded to this view, setting the 1990s on course to become the "Do something!" decade.

Waiting in the wings were more such episodes, not only in the core of the Greater Middle East but also on the periphery. Yugoslavia, then in the throes of disintegration, offers one example, Afghanistan, soon to fall under the grip of the Taliban, another. To each of these we will attend in due course. But for Bush and then for Clinton, demands for employing the U.S. military as an instrument for doing good focused first on Somalia.

U.S. intervention there, which lasted from August 1992 to March

1994, began with the best of intentions and culminated in a bloody defeat and withdrawal. In the wake of that withdrawal, Somalia became a permanent battleground, one of the lesser theaters in America's War for the Greater Middle East—lesser, that is, except for those living there.

Explaining the incorporation of such an impoverished African country into that larger conflict requires a brief explanation of context. Somalia is a big country, almost as large as Texas, with a coastline more than twice as long as California's. It is also resource-poor. Even its population, consisting almost entirely of Sunni Muslims, is relatively sparse. During the Cold War, Somalia's location on the Horn of Africa had drawn the attention of the world's two superpowers, prompting a minor Soviet-American competition for Somali affections. For Siad Barre, who ran the country from 1969 to 1991, promoting economic development or advancing the well-being of ordinary Somalis rarely figured as priorities. The dictator wanted weapons, which the United States and the Soviet Union took turns providing. When the Cold War reached its conclusion, that competition abruptly ended. Right about the time the outside world was losing interest in Somalia, an uprising by well-armed clan-based militias overthrew Barre and then turned on one another. The country plummeted into chaos, its fragile food and medical systems collapsing. Hundreds of thousands of refugees fled to neighboring countries. Many others faced the prospect of imminent starvation.[14]

In response to a UN Security Council request for assistance, President Bush directed the Pentagon to help, albeit on a modest scale. On August 15, 1992, ten U.S. Air Force C-130s began ferrying supplies from Mombasa, Kenya, to the Somali capital of Mogadishu and other airfields throughout the country. This was Operation Provide Relief, distant cousin of Provide Comfort. Over the next several months, nearly 2,500 sorties transported twenty-eight thousand tons of food and other aid.[15]

Unfortunately, putting food on the ground did not automatically get it into the mouths of people in need. In the midst of ongoing civil war, protecting and distributing relief supplies posed challenges that greatly exceeded the capacity of the few lightly armed peacekeepers that the UN had sent to Somalia. As conditions continued to deteriorate, it became apparent that Provide Relief was coming nowhere close to what the situation required. Media pressure to do more escalated. "Don't Forsake Somalia," *The New York Times* pleaded.[16] "End Somalia's Anguish," *The Christian Science Monitor* urged.[17] Heartrending video clips of malnourished children became daily fare on American television. People were dying in very large numbers. The U.S. Army's official history of this episode describes what happened next: "Unable to explain to the world why the United States, the 'sole remaining superpower' and leader of the 'new world order,' was not able to stop the starvation, President Bush ordered U.S. forces to deploy to Somalia."[18]

On December 5, Provide Relief became Restore Hope, the name change suggestive of larger ambitions. Bush, having now lost his bid for reelection, was going to leave office on a grace note, committing U.S. forces to an act of pure altruism. The mission in Somalia, he explained in an address to the American people, was to "create a secure environment . . . so that food can move from ships overland to the people in the countryside," thereby arresting the ongoing famine.[19] Implicit in that mission was a requirement to bring order out of chaos. Yet the president was adamant that the United States was not going to involve itself in internal Somali politics. Nor were U.S. troops going to stay long, the White House promising—implausibly—to complete their withdrawal by the time Bush left office on January 20, 1993.[20]

Declaring an action apolitical does not make it so, however. Regardless of circumstance, armed intervention in the affairs of another country is an inherently political act, certain to yield political consequences, even if unintended and unforeseen. In this case, framing Restore Hope as an effort to save starving Africans in a failed state obscured two salient facts. First, despite the collapse of central authority, the fifteen or so clans forming the basis of Somali society retained their integrity. In other words, the appearance of rampant anarchy was deceptive. The loyalty commanded by warlords endowed them with power. Second, even if in Western eyes Somalia barely qualified as a nation-state, Somalis themselves were very much part of the larger Islamic world. The arrival of foreign troops, few of them Muslims, was certain to attract notice—and raise alarms—among their fellow believers.

Not everyone shared Bush's expectations of the objects of American solicitude welcoming the arrival of U.S. troops. Smith Hempstone, a cheeky journalist then serving as U.S. ambassador to Kenya, created a stir with a cable (quickly leaked) warning that if the United States decided to "embrace the Somali tarbaby," untoward developments were sure to follow. "If you liked Beirut, you'll love Mogadishu," he cautioned. Somalis "are natural-born guerrillas. They will mine the roads. They will lay ambushes. They will launch hit-and-run attacks. They will not be able to stop the convoys from getting through. But they will inflict—and take—casualties."[21] Above all, time posed a problem. "The warlords will fade away and wait us out," Hempstone predicted. When foreign forces departed, the warlords would simply take up where they had left off.[22]

A reasonably accurate prediction of what actually ensued, this was not what Bush wanted to hear. Hempstone's analysis clashed both with the outgoing president's wish to demonstrate American (and his own) beneficence and with reigning precepts of U.S. military supremacy. That U.S. forces might find local militias difficult to handle was unfathomable. The intervention was going to proceed.

On the night of December 9, a reinforced battalion of U.S. Marines came ashore at Mogadishu, their arrival preceded by teams of commandos. A welcoming party of sorts awaited—"a swarm of journalists" armed with television cameras, spotlights, and flash attachments and eager to record the event for posterity.[23] It made for an inauspicious beginning. This was not a military endeavor encumbered with an excess of seriousness. Fortunately, the Marines met no resistance.

In the days that followed, a steady stream of U.S. troops arrived. From Camp Pendleton, California, came the First Marine Division, from Fort Drum, New York, the army's 10th Mountain Division. Nearly two dozen countries contributed smaller detachments. By the time the deployment was complete, UNITAF, as coalition forces were called, consisted of thirty-eight thousand soldiers, twenty-five thousand of them Americans, all responding to the orders of United States Central Command.[24]

The campaign began on a promising note. The plan devised by General Joseph Hoar, the Marine who had succeeded Schwarzkopf at CENTCOM, called first for establishing control of Mogadishu. After reopening port facilities and the international airport there, Hoar's troops were to fan out, securing the countryside and thereby enabling relief organizations to do their work. With Somali warlords momentarily stepping aside, UNITAF operated in an agreeably permissive environment. One senior U.S. officer in January 1993 reported that "there had been none—no—zero—organized resistance."[25] Soon enough, conditions on the ground improved markedly. To keep busy, coalition forces turned to repairing roads, digging wells, rehabilitating schools, and vaccinating Somali children.[26]

By the time Bill Clinton was making himself comfortable in the Oval Office, the situation in Somalia seemed well in hand. Had the episode ended at this juncture, its relevance to this account would have been minimal. Yet with success seemingly in the offing, problems began cropping up.

Throughout America's War for the Greater Middle East, this phenomenon recurred, typically attributable to a gap between military muscle and political acuity. While the commitment of raw military power might get things off to a good start, a faulty grasp of underlying political dynamics leaves the United States susceptible to ambush, both literal and figurative. Certainly that proved to be the case here.

The challenge that Clinton inherited from his predecessor was to make good on Bush's original promise, leaving Somalia while also preserving all that Restore Hope had accomplished. The approach that soon emerged reflected the naiveté found in almost any newly installed administration, but afflicting the Clinton team more than most. In a nutshell, the Clinton plan called for expanding the mission while passing off to others most of the costs. Humanitarian assistance was to give way to nation-building, described by Madeleine Albright, Clinton's ambassador to the United Nations, as "an unprecedented enterprise aimed at nothing less than the restoration of an entire country as a proud, functioning and viable member of the community of nations."[27]

Simultaneously, to reduce its own exposure, Washington pressed the United Nations into service as America's de facto agent in this ambitious undertaking. In practical terms, this meant the following:

- replacing UNITAF with a motley UN peacekeeping force, but one retaining a small U.S. combat brigade as a quick reaction force (QRF) in case of trouble;
- installing a Turkish officer, Lieutenant General Çevik Bir, to command this new entity known as UNOSOM,[28] but with an American deputy controlling the QRF, while answering to General Hoar back in Tampa; and
- appointing as UN special envoy and chief nation-builder a retired U.S. Navy admiral by the name of Jonathan Howe, who had just recently stepped down from the post of White House deputy national security adviser and who maintained a direct line to Washington.

The defining features of this arrangement were fragmented responsibility and ambiguity of purpose.

A March 1993 document called the Addis Ababa Accords, signed by representatives of various misleadingly named factions such as the Somali Democratic Alliance, the Somali Democratic Movement, the Somali National Democratic Union, the Somali Salvation Democratic Front, and the like, supposedly represented buy-in on the part of the warlords. It did not. Their vision of Somalia's future differed from the UN's. One warlord was particularly displeased. His name was Mohamed Farrah Aidid, self-styled commander of the Somali National Alliance (SNA), a clan-based militia that was neither national nor an alliance. In Mogadishu itself, with its refugee-swollen population of 1.5 million, Aidid had an especially strong presence. This gave him the capacity to make real trouble, which he now proceeded to do.

On May 4, UNITAF handed off the Somalia security mission, now known as Operation Continue Hope, to UNOSOM, which had not yet reached its full strength. Howe and Bir, along with Major General Thomas Montgomery, Bir's American deputy and the commander of the U.S. forces that remained in Somalia, were now nominally in charge.

On June 5, in downtown Mogadishu, Aidid's SNA attacked a contingent of Pakistani peacekeepers, killing twenty-four and wounding many others. As the Pakistanis withdrew, they left behind their dead, which were then subjected to grotesque mutilation. To General Montgomery, the implications of this one-sided firefight were clear: "We were at war."[29]

That accorded with the view of the UN Security Council. With strong American backing, it promptly called for reinforcements and ordered the use of "all necessary means" to punish the perpetrators.[30] Back in Mogadishu, to clarify just who the Security Council was referring to, Admiral Howe put a bounty of twenty-five thousand dollars on Aidid's head and issued a warrant for his arrest. He also started badgering Washington to send reinforcements.

Aidid was unimpressed. Once begun, hostilities rapidly escalated. By early summer, General Hoar later acknowledged, "We lost control of Mogadishu absolutely."[31] The Somali capital now became, in General Montgomery's phrase, "Indian country." Peacekeepers venturing off the UNOSOM compound and into the city proper encountered harassment, demonstrations, unruly mobs, and ambushes. The compound itself, located at the defunct international airport, was subjected to frequent shelling.[32] Meanwhile, American AC-130 gunships began orbiting over Mogadishu, using their 105mm and 40mm cannon to rain fires down on SNA weapons sites, vehicle storage facilities, and radio stations.[33]

The states contributing troops contingents to UNOSOM had signed up to keep the peace, not to wage an urban counterinsurgency campaign. When the SNA beat up a Moroccan battalion on June 17, inflicting heavy casualties—those killed included the battalion commander—UNOSOM effectively exited the fight. Governments now began restricting what they would permit their forces in Somalia to do. With stunning swiftness, Aidid had exposed the limits of both the coalition's military capacity and its political cohesion. The warlord now enjoyed the upper hand.

If anyone was going to fulfill the UN's directive and impose order, it was going to have to be the Americans. So with Hoar's approval and Washington's tacit consent, General Montgomery now began employing the QRF not as UNOSOM's reserve but as an independent strike force. As a direct consequence, the war against Aidid now became America's war rather than the UN's.

Montgomery understood that the QRF, numbering only some thirteen hundred infantrymen, was insufficient to defeat the SNA outright. Yet the American commander was going to have to make do with what he had. Requests for reinforcements to include heavy forces such as tanks had not met with favor back in Tampa. So rather than attempting to defeat the insurgency, Montgomery set out to cripple it by killing or capturing Aidid and his chief lieutenants.[34]

Here we confront another signature of America's military engagement in the Islamic world. Time and again, when confronting situations of daunting political complexity, the United States has personalized the issue. Montgomery assumed that Aidid was, in effect, irreplaceable.[35] To remove him from the scene was to settle matters in Mogadishu, an assumption destined to resurface when the nemesis of the hour was Osama bin Laden, Saddam Hussein, Abu Musab al-Zarqawi, Moamar Gaddafi (on a second go-round), or any of the terrorist "leaders" designated for liquidation by Barack Obama's campaign of targeted assassination. When put to the test, this logic proved defective on two counts. First, few leaders are actually irreplaceable. Get rid of one, and another appears: "The cemeteries are filled with indispensable men," briefly mourned and soon forgotten.[36] Second, the peremptory removal of those few possessing some approximation of indispensability leaves a void, new problems taking the place of those magically solved by getting rid of the villain at the top.

In this case, the decapitation strategy did not receive a full tryout, namely because U.S. military efforts to get Aidid misfired. An action that occurred on July 12 hinted at the problems to come. On that date, elements of the QRF's 1st Battalion, 22nd Infantry raided a building known as Abdi House, thought to contain an SNA command post. U.S. helicopter gunships employed missiles and cannon fire to soften up the target area, before ground troops arrived by helicopter to search the premises. The raiders came up empty-handed but killed a number of bystanders and wounded dozens more.[37] After the Americans left, an angry mob converged on the scene, venting their displeasure on four Western reporters present, whom they beat to death before putting their corpses on grisly display.[38]

Far more than the better-known "Black Hawk Down" firefight of October 3, the Abdi House incident marked the true turning point in the Somalia campaign. Any lingering inclination to exercise restraint now fell away. From this point, Operation Continue Hope could more accurately have been styled Operation Indiscriminate Force. Yet unleashing superior American firepower—one army after-action report subsequently touted the value of using an attack helicopter's "20mm gun in flex mode" as a "great crowd breaker"—played directly into Aidid's hands.[39] By killing women and children, whom Aidid callously but shrewdly thrust into the line of fire, Montgomery's forces provoked further outrage. The level of violence they employed did not suffice to intimidate but was more than ample to inflame.[40]

U.S. troops not only inflicted casualties but also began to sustain them. With UNOSOM effectively sidelined, targeting GIs now became the SNA's priority. One of Aidid's associates succinctly summed up the SNA perspective: "There was no more United Nations, only Americans. If you could kill Americans, it would start problems in America directly."[41] Just so: The killing of four GIs on August 8 when their vehicle hit a mine, for the United States the worst single casualty toll thus far, captured Washington's attention and evoked a response. The Clinton administration decided to double down on U.S. efforts to get Aidid.

The world offered Americans plenty to think about in the summer of 1993, with dramatic events ranging from the ongoing siege of Sarajevo to the signing of the Oslo Accords, promising an end to the Israeli-Palestinian conflict. For the prurient, there was the mysterious suicide of Vince Foster, deputy White House counsel and close friend of the First Lady—the press devoting more attention to Clinton scandals, real or imagined, than to the Clinton administration's approach to governance. In this environment, the worsening situation in Somalia had received only fitful attention.

Even so, two days after the loss of the four U.S. troops, Ambassador Albright felt moved to rebut any looming doubts about what the administration was doing and why. In a *New York Times* op-ed, Albright fingered Aidid as the problem and defined lifting Somalia "from the category of a failed state to that of an emerging democracy" as the self-evident solution. For the United States at this juncture, Somalia represented less a threat than an opportunity. Here was a chance to demonstrate the efficacy of the United Nations. On that score, Albright declared herself pleased with the progress made thus far. "Plans for re-establishing a national government are on track," she insisted. "Traditional Somali leaders and others with civilian leadership skills are starting to assert themselves." The sole responsible option was to "stay the course." Only "advocates of appeasement" would disagree.[42]

This was unalloyed drivel, devoid of the vaguest notion of what launching Somalia on the path toward democracy might actually require. Even so, rather than appeasing, the Clinton administration opted to beef up the forces it had committed to getting rid of Aidid. With the soon-to-retire General Colin Powell concurring, President Clinton on August 22 ordered a small element of specialized army troops to assume primary responsibility for the manhunt. This was Task Force Ranger, commanded by Major General William Garrison, its approximately 440 soldiers drawn from the 75th Ranger Regiment, the super-secret Delta Force, and Task Force 160, the army's special operations aviation unit. The administration was placing a bet that an additional increment of combat power might turn around a failing endeavor. It was a Somalia "surge" before that term had entered the American military lexicon.

The arrival of Task Force Ranger introduced further snarls into already convoluted command relationships. Much as General Bir commanded UNOSOM but not General Montgomery's QRF, Montgomery commanded all U.S. forces in Somalia but not Garrison's task force. Formally at least, both Montgomery and Garrison got their marching orders from General Hoar, located over eight thousand miles away at CENTCOM headquarters in Tampa. Yet Garrison also took his cues from General Wayne Downing, who as commander of U.S. Special Operations Command retained a proprietary relationship with the various bits and pieces forming Garrison's composite organization.[43] Occupying a separate headquarters at Tampa, Downing was Hoar's coequal, with no inclination to defer to CENTCOM. Overall, the arrangement was not conducive to seamless coordination.

The hope was that Montgomery and Garrison might find ways to cooperate. On a very good day in Washington, with nothing much going on, "cooperation" is what the House and the Senate or the CIA and the FBI might be able to manage. In times of stress, such arrangements tend to break down. During wartime in the field, "cooperation" is a recipe for disaster. Such circumstances require unity of command, with absolute clarity about who is in charge. In 1993 Mogadishu, such clarity was nowhere to be found.

Worse still, the Americans underestimated their adversaries. An early chronicler of the intervention charged U.S. commanders with viewing the Somalis as "intellectually primitive, culturally shallow, and militarily craven."[44] Although the judgment may seem unduly harsh, it does not lack for merit. The Americans assigned the mission of taking Aidid out of circulation—Operation Gothic Serpent—assumed that technological superiority conferred advantages. After all, this was—or appeared to be—the great lesson of Operation Desert Storm. Yet here conditions, especially the dense urban environment, differed. In this case, dependence on machines exposed the vulnerabilities of U.S. forces and limited their flexibility. In contrast, Aidid, relatively unencumbered with gadgetry, demonstrated an impressive ability to learn and adapt. Put simply, when it came to agility, the Somalis enjoyed a clear edge.

On August 28, as members of Task Force Ranger settled into their new quarters at Mogadishu International Airport, a routine SNA mortar attack wounded four of the new arrivals. Garrison wasted little time responding. In the early hours of August 30, Gothic Serpent got underway with a neatly executed raid that netted nine detainees, all of whom, embarrassingly, turned out to be United Nations employees rather than SNA operatives. This inauspicious beginning highlighted the dangers of acting in the absence of accurate and timely intelligence.

The first raid served as a template for five more conducted over the next three weeks: Accompanied by Task Force 160 "little boys" providing cover, UH-60 Black Hawks ferried members of Delta Force to the target area; upon arrival, the commandos fast-roped out of their choppers to effect the snatch; rangers arrived in wheeled vehicles to provide backup and to evacuate commandos and captives back to base. According to a declassified history prepared by U.S. Special Operations Command, "These six missions were tactical successes."[45] Yet categorizing them as successful requires a claustrophobically narrow definition of the term. U.S. forces reached the objective area and returned safely: That was success.[46] In other respects, the results proved disappointing. Aidid remained very much at large. In a half-dozen attempts, Task Force Ranger had netted only a single one of his associates.[47] Yet the unit's "aura of invincibility remained intact." Garrison's command, one otherwise sympathetic historian writes, "behaved with a swagger that was irksome at best and reckless at worst."[48]

In the meantime, mortar attacks on UNOSOM continued. Command-detonated mines—U.S. forces had not yet adopted the term *improvised explosive device* (IED)—posed a growing danger. And QRF helicopters were regularly taking—and returning—fire. In their scrupulously balanced account of the Somalia intervention, John Hirsch and Robert Oakley reported that "the use of helicopter gunships against targets in heavily populated areas of south Mogadishu" was becoming commonplace. "A series of incidents between September 5 and 15 resulted in hundreds of Somalis killed and wounded."[49] Although UNOSOM was absorbing far fewer casualties, the lopsided exchange was not indicative of progress. Instead of enforcing order, coalition forces were destroying its last remaining remnants, thereby playing into Aidid's hands.

Then on September 25, an SNA fighter used a rocket-propelled grenade (RPG) to down a UH-60, killing three crewmen. An RPG is an antitank weapon of limited range and accuracy. Its effective employment in an antiaircraft role marked a deeply disturbing development.

Undeterred, Garrison ordered a fateful seventh raid, this time during daylight hours on October 3. But the Americans had telegraphed their punch. This time, Aidid was waiting.[50]

The operation, expected to take thirty minutes from start to finish, began well but ended badly many hours later. During the ensuing period, the SNA shot down two UH-60s belonging to Task Force Ranger and damaged three others. Intense fire complicated efforts to recover killed and wounded crewmen, while pinning down both the rangers who had helicoptered in and those arriving in unarmored trucks.

Chaos reigned. Surrounded, outnumbered, and possibly even outgunned by adversaries they disparaged as "Sammies" or "Skinnies," the elite U.S. troops formed a rudimentary defensive perimeter, returned fire, and hung on. Strafing runs by TF 160 attack helicopters, their crews wearing night vision devices, prevented the Americans from being completely overrun. Even so, there was no disguising the fact that the tables had turned. In the blink of an eye, the hunters had become the hunted.

Summoned to the rescue, General Montgomery cobbled together an extraction force consisting of QRF infantry mounted in Malaysian armored personnel carriers and escorted by a handful of lumbering Pakistani tanks. Getting things organized and moving proved excruciatingly time-consuming. In the meantime, Task Force Ranger, under unrelenting attack, had sustained heavy casualties. By the time the action broke off early the next morning, eighteen American soldiers were dead and another eighty wounded. Somalis had dragged from the wreckage of his aircraft an injured American aviator, Chief Warrant

Officer Michael Durant, whom they now proudly displayed. Estimates of Somali losses ranged widely but certainly numbered in the high hundreds.[51]

The reaction back home followed a predictable script: Shock and anger vied with demands for accountability. A bloodied and dazed-looking Durant made the cover of *Time*, which rather belatedly posed the question, "What in the World Are We Doing?" *Newsweek* aptly described Mogadishu as a "military disaster to rank with Desert One or the bombing of the marine barracks in Beirut."[52] In Washington, it reported, "a frantic search for scapegoats" was underway. Former Ambassador Smith Hempstone took to the pages of *The Wall Street Journal* to weigh in with a hearty I-told-you-so.[53] The "Don't Forsake Somalia" editorial board of *The New York Times* now reversed course: It was "Time to Get Out."[54]

Senator John McCain, a Republican from Arizona, already a prominent voice on military affairs, was furious. U.S. troops were being "killed in a conflict with no clear connection to U.S. national security interests," he complained. "It is time for American forces to come home." McCain cited Ronald Reagan's response to the Beirut bombing as a model. "Reagan's admission of failure prevented the further waste of American lives. The decision to withdraw U.S. forces from Lebanon, frankly, took much more courage than the current administration's decision to escalate our involvement in Somalia."[55]

Yet the impulse to call it quits gained only limited traction. As had been the case after the Beirut bombing, not to mention the *Stark* incident and the shootdown of Iran Air 655, the ensuing inquiry steered clear of issues touching on basic policy. The very pertinent question posed by *Time* went unanswered. Instead, congressional investigators and members of the press became preoccupied with what might have been done to expedite the rescue of Task Force Ranger once the operation of October 3 went awry. The preferred answer: more firepower—Abrams tanks and AC-130 gunships.[56]

Critics pounced on President Clinton, his avoidance of Vietnam service making him an easy target on such matters, for his administration's failure to fill each and every request that commanders in the field had made.[57] That four-stars like Powell and Hoar had opposed those requests did not deter them. Nor did General Garrison's subsequent admission that "if we had put one more ounce of lead on South Mogadishu on the night of 3 and 4 October, I believe it would have sunk."[58]

His instinct for self-preservation kicking into high gear, Clinton did what presidents do to make such troubles go away. He promptly dispatched substantial reinforcements to Mogadishu—to include Abrams tanks and AC-130s—while simultaneously calling off the hunt for Aidid (thereby facilitating Michael Durant's release). To those like Senator McCain who favored a cut-and-run response, he offered a compromise, setting a date-certain of March 31, 1994, for a complete withdrawal. This the Congress accepted. In the interim, rather than courting further trouble, the troops would stay put but keep a low profile, thereby making a show of departing on U.S. terms—much as Reagan had done a decade earlier in Beirut.

Perhaps most important, to placate his critics, Clinton fired his defense secretary, Les Aspin. Compared to all the principals involved, civilian and military alike, Aspin had contributed only tangentially to all that had gone wrong in Mogadishu.[59] But he was eminently expendable. Tagging Aspin as responsible, rather than any of the senior military officers involved, came without any political cost.

With this, the controversy subsided. Almost immediately, the process of transforming the Mogadishu firefight from a small-scale fiasco into an epic worthy of Homer commenced. Thanks to a bestselling book and then a hit movie, the episode that ought to have been known as "the Somalia Campaign, 1992–1994" became simply "Black Hawk Down." Narrowing the aperture enshrined the melee of October 3–4, 1993, as a demonstration of soldierly grit and gallantry while robbing it of context. The Mogadishu firefight became an event that stands alone—like the defense of the Alamo or Custer's Last Stand.

An odd phenomenon ensued: As with the Tet Offensive of 1968 (and as would recur with the Third Gulf War of 2003–2011), mythologists reimagined a self-evident failure as an unrecognized or under-appreciated victory. You just had to see things in the proper light. In General Garrison's estimation, "The Mission was a success." So he wrote soon after the raid in a personal letter to his commander in chief.[60] The journalist Mark Bowden, in his definitive account of the battle, reached a similar conclusion: In "a complex, difficult, and dangerous assignment, and despite terrible setbacks and losses, and against overwhelming odds, the mission was accomplished."[61] By implication, the Mogadishu firefight was something in which Americans could take justifiable pride.

Bowden's claim invites the retort of the North Vietnamese colonel responding to an American officer's insistence at the end of the Vietnam War that, "you know, you never defeated us in battle." Was the American oblivious to the war's outcome? "That may be true," came the reply, "but it is also irrelevant."[62] At the end of the day, the estimable courage demonstrated by the U.S. troops who fought in Mogadishu— two of whom, Master Sergeant Gary Gordon and Sergeant First Class Randy Shughart, were posthumously awarded the Medal of Honor— proved similarly irrelevant to the issue at hand. Aidid had prevailed.

In effect, political and military leaders, not to mention the public at large, found it convenient to expunge from the record all that occurred during the months before that event. Americans had once cited the Battle of New Orleans (an impressive feat of arms) as an excuse to forget the War of 1812 (an ill-advised and badly managed venture). Something similar occurred here, with the travails endured by Task Force Ranger eclipsing Operation Continued Hope and draining it of significance. In the end, Americans overlooked even the most obvious lesson, namely, don't pick a fight with well-armed, highly motivated irregulars in a large city that they own.

Once again, willful forgetting produced nontrivial consequences. In fact, the Somalia campaign that culminated with the Mogadishu firefight had profound relevance for America's ongoing (even if still unacknowledged) War for the Greater Middle East. That was certainly Osama bin Laden's view. For the Al Qaeda leader, who subsequently claimed that his operatives had helped train Aidid's forces, Somalia exposed the "weakness, frailty, and cowardice of the U.S. troops." For Washington, the campaign's outcome warned against further involvement of U.S. forces in cockamamie UN humanitarian schemes. For bin Laden, in contrast, it offered proof that "the American soldier was just a paper tiger." In his view, a U.S. military defeat at the hands of Islam offered cause for celebration. It showed that the United States could be had.[63]

We may opt for a more nuanced view, noting that the American defeat stemmed at least in part from a refusal to provide the wherewithal needed to get the job done. Although additional resources were readily available—the American military establishment in 1993 was generally underemployed—authorities at the White House, in the Pentagon, and at CENTCOM headquarters withheld them, choosing to wage war against Aidid on a shoestring. This serious failure of political will and military judgment was destined to recur in campaigns still to come elsewhere in the Greater Middle East. This was especially true after 9/11, when the United States committed itself to objectives far loftier than taking down the SNA. Time and again, those opting to use force to impose America's will (or, some might say, to uplift and liberate) initiated hostilities without adequately calculating the human, material, fiscal, and political capital required.

Yet more than anything else, the Somalia campaign revealed severe deficiencies in American generalship that went far beyond such obvious lapses as acting without adequate intelligence, allowing tortuous command relationships, and disregarding basic operational security.

For senior commanders, accurately gauging the political environment in which they operate is at least as important as understanding enemy capabilities and intentions. No less than war itself, the exercise of wartime command is an inherently political act. Acute political sensitivity forms an unwritten part of the job description.

Commanders embarking upon a war do so with a finite number of credits—money, lives, time, support on the home front—upon which to draw. Their challenge is to get the job done without depleting those accounts. While Montgomery and Garrison made any number of tactical misjudgments, they erred above all in misidentifying their greatest vulnerability, which was not the threat posed by Aidid but the prospect of a sudden collapse of political support.

By way of comparison, consider Ulysses S. Grant, the exception that proves the rule. When Grant took command of all the Union armies in March 1864, President Lincoln allowed him unlimited drawing rights on the U.S. Treasury, on the fruits of American industry, and most importantly on the military-age manpower of the Union. Lincoln's reelection in November (thanks in large part to the soldier vote) conferred on Grant this further advantage: time. Grant intuitively grasped the opportunity that availed itself. Over the course of a full year, acting with great deliberation, he crushed not only the Rebel armies but also the Confederacy itself in a series of campaigns that exacted staggering costs on both sides. Yet even today, few question whether the result was "worth it." For its part, history celebrates Grant as a great captain.

No other commander in American history—not even those charged with the conduct of World War II—has enjoyed such a free hand. Indeed, the situation facing Montgomery and Garrison was the inverse of Grant's. Whereas Lincoln allowed his general-in-chief to spend freely, the Americans charged with directing the Somalia campaign needed to achieve success within a constrained (if never explicitly specified) budget. Yet in a situation calling for parsimony, Montgomery and Garrison recklessly squandered their limited credits, only to discover that they had spent more than their masters back home—the president, the Congress, and the American people—were willing to cover. Senior U.S. military leaders had never pressed for an answer to the question of how much bringing order to Somalia was actually "worth." The firefight of October 3–4 revealed the answer: not much.

Apparently assuming that generalship was about what you did to the enemy, Montgomery and Garrison (along with their superiors back in Tampa) either ignored or proved unable to decipher the political dimension of the war they were charged with waging. As we shall see, they were by no means the last senior military officers to display this particular failing. Throughout the War for the Greater Middle East, it formed an abiding weakness of American generalship, as, in time, another rule-proving exception made evident. His name was David Petraeus.

9

BALKAN DIGRESSION

MUCH AS MEXICO IS A PART OF LATIN AMERICA LOCATED IN North America, so too the Balkans constitute a fragment of the Islamic world within the confines of Europe. According to one of the prevailing shibboleths of the present age, this commingling of cultures is inherently good. It fosters pluralism, thereby enriching everyday life. Yet cultural interaction also induces friction, whether spontaneously generated or instigated by demagogues and provocateurs.

Until the middle of the last century, the U.S.-Mexican border neatly (if imperfectly) divided Ibero-America, then almost entirely Catholic, from the Anglo-Protestant sphere with which most citizens of the United States, including virtually the entire American elite, identified. In the Balkans, centuries of conflict between Islam and Christendom had long since erased any such line of separation, leaving in its wake a residue of unhappy minorities, unsettled scores, and frustrated ambitions.

For some Americans, even today, the breaching of the barrier that once separated the United States from Latin America remains a source of resentment, and for cynical politicians an opportunity ripe for exploitation. They want the barrier restored. In the Balkans at the end of the Cold War, comparable resentments and even more pronounced cynicism also produced demands for separation. A series of shooting wars resulted, four in all. On two occasions, those conflicts prompted the United States to intervene, first in Bosnia in 1995 and then in Kosovo four years later.

In both cases, the plight of beleaguered Muslims offered the pretext for U.S. military action. In America's ongoing War for the Greater Middle East, the Bosnia and Kosovo campaigns qualified as sideshows. Yet even if soon superseded by larger events, they were hardly trivial. Indeed, of all the various military actions undertaken by the United States in the Islamic world since 1980, these two appear to have come closest to achieving real success. Yet appearances deceive, or at least do not tell the whole story.

That story begins in 1914, when Serbian terrorists assassinated the Austrian Archduke in Sarajevo, triggering a conflagration that, among other things, spelled the end of European global preeminence. In the wake of World War I, the victorious Allies, acting with the same insouciance that they demonstrated in redrawing the map of the Middle East, signed off on a new Balkan political order right out of Rube Goldberg. The result was Yugoslavia, an amalgam of Bosnians, Croats, Montenegrins, Serbs, Slovenes, and others destined to induce political migraines on a scale similar to those produced by other Allied creations such as Iraq and Palestine.[1]

This patchwork arrangement survived for seven decades. With the passing of the Cold War it came apart, as the people-formerly-known-as-Yugoslavs, abandoning multicultural socialism, embraced various forms of religiously and ethnically infused nationalism.

In June 1991, Slovenes and Croats became the first to break away. For Slovenia, which won its independence after a brief "Ten-Day War," the break was relatively painless. For Croatia, things proved more difficult, as a large minority of ethnic Serbs, supported by the Serb-dominated Yugoslav army, resisted. Vicious fighting killed thousands and displaced far larger numbers of Croats and Serbs alike. The suspension of hostilities in January 1992 found Croatia independent but with wide swathes of its territory controlled by a self-declared Republic of Serbian Krajina. Under the auspices of the United Nations, which had already imposed an arms embargo on Yugoslavia, European peacekeepers arrived to maintain a precarious ceasefire.

Then, at the end of February, Bosnians voted to secede from what remained of the Yugoslav federation. Ethnic Serbs within Bosnia-Herzegovina boycotted the referendum and established their own Republika Srpska, aligned with Serbia proper. Soon thereafter, in April 1992, a third Balkan war erupted, as Serbs and Croats set out to dismember now predominantly Muslim Bosnia-Herzegovina. Serb forces laid siege to the Bosnian capital of Sarajevo, in Western eyes a symbol of secular pluralism, now transformed into a scene out of Dante's *Inferno*. "For 400,000 Sarajevans," war correspondent John Burns reported, the siege

> *meant living with sudden death every hour of every day. Children climbing a cherry tree in an orchard are blasted to oblivion by a tank shell. A young mother falls to the sidewalk, mortally wounded by a Serbian sniper, her baby cast from her arms with a leg so severely injured that doctors have to amputate. Mourners grieving over fresh graves in public parks scatter in panic, some falling dead themselves, as Serbian forces fire on them with antiaircraft shells and mortars. Sniper fire is so accurate that surgeons have detected the "personal signature" of individual gunmen in the wounds they inflict—some favoring shots to the head, others to the heart.[2]*

The cordoning off of the Bosnian capital formed just one part of a larger campaign to evict Muslims from territory earmarked for incorporation into a Greater Serbia.[3] UN peacekeepers dispatched to the scene were utterly inadequate to the task.

The United States had made every effort to steer clear of these developments. Other priorities absorbed the attention of the George H. W. Bush administration. With the Cold War winding down, Yugoslavia no longer commanded Washington's attention. The Balkans were Europe's problem. Bush's secretary of state, James Baker, put the matter succinctly: "We don't have a dog in this fight."[4]

Three factors undermined this hands-off approach. The first was the ineptitude of those to whom Washington looked to handle the situation. Demanding an end to violence, European leaders proved incapable of enforcing that demand. To defer to dithering Europeans was, in effect, to become an accessory to murder.

A second factor was the moral framing imposed on the Yugoslav crackup. Among Western elites especially, the fate of Sarajevo and of the Bosnian people more generally assumed a significance reminiscent of the siege of Madrid in 1936–1939. In Bosnia, one of the great moral dramas of the age was being restaged. This contest between "the primitive and the cosmopolitan," as one writer put it, offered Western governments that had failed to rescue the Spanish Republic from the clutches of fascism the chance to get it right this time.[5] Seen in this light, the Bush administration's apparent indifference to the ongoing agony of Sarajevo seemed unconscionable.

Finally, and above all, there was American domestic politics, playing out in a presidential election year. Seeking to unseat an incumbent whose greatest strength lay in foreign policy, Bill Clinton needed some way to portray himself as tough-minded and forward-leaning. President Bush's passivity on Bosnia in 1992 gave his brash young challenger just the opening he was looking for. The Clinton campaign chided Bush for failing to demonstrate "real leadership" in the Balkans. The odious Serb president Slobodan Milošević and his henchmen were made-to-order villains. The solution was obvious: an "economic blockade" to strangle "the renegade regime of Slobodan Milosevic" along with "air strikes against those who are attacking the [Bosnian] relief effort."[6] The candidate himself forthrightly declared, "I would begin with airpower, against the Serbs, to restore the basic conditions of humanity."[7]

When Clinton won the election, however, bellicosity gave way to reticence. The new president's aides postured. Imitating John Kennedy at Berlin, for example, Madeleine Albright flew into the Bosnian capital to announce "Ja sam Sarajevka" and assure her listeners that "America's future and your future are inseparable."[8] Yet such rhetoric notwithstanding, Clinton was no more eager than his predecessor to plunge into any Balkan quagmire. The collapse of the Somalia mission barely eight months into his presidency only reinforced that reluctance.

What ensued was intervention by inadvertence. Clintonites styled their approach "assertive multilateralism." Practically speaking, however, the noun took precedence over the adjective. Assertive multilateralism emphasized consensus over action, process over outcomes. Assertiveness (of a sort) made its appearance only after the exhaustion of all the other alternatives.

Unwilling to proceed unilaterally and unable to persuade U.S. allies to undertake forceful collective action, Clinton found himself in a bind. In early May, European leaders had rejected his "lift and strike" proposal—lifting the arms embargo and using NATO air power to protect the Bosnians. This humiliating diplomatic setback effectively left the administration without a Balkan policy. "In view of your public posture," Secretary of State Warren Christopher gently chided his boss, "what you may not be free to do is to follow the Bush strategy of doing nothing."[9] To paper over their disunity and confusion, the United States and its European allies had at hand a placeholder of sorts. This was Operation Deny Flight, which just the month before had cracked open the door leading to a decades-long U.S. military involvement in the Balkans.

Deny Flight was another exercise in no-fly-zone enforcement, a low-risk way of offering a semblance of protection to Bosnian Muslims threatened by Serb depredations. It was a gesture pretending to be a serious military undertaking.

Acting pursuant to a UN Security Council resolution, twelve NATO nations provided aircraft to Deny Flight. Operating from bases in Italy or aircraft carriers in the Adriatic, U.S. forces contributed far and away the largest share.

As was the case with the Iraqi no-fly zones, Deny Flight offered ample opportunity for boring holes in the sky. In all, between April 1993 and December 1995, NATO aviators flew more than 109,000 sorties. In prohibiting Serbian fixed-wing aircraft from entering Bosnian airspace, the operation did achieve notable success. The weak Serbian air force rarely challenged NATO. When it did, it paid a price. On February 28, 1994, for example, two pairs of U.S. Air Force F-16s encountered six small, subsonic Serbian bombers within the no-fly zone and proceeded to shoot down four without suffering a scratch.[10] In June 1995, the Bosnian Serbs partly evened the score, employing a surface-to-air missile to shoot down an F-16 piloted by air force Captain Scott O'Grady. After successfully ejecting from his aircraft, O'Grady evaded capture for six days until rescued by U.S. Marines in a daring and well-executed recovery operation.

In squadron ready rooms, air victories offered cause for celebration. Back home, O'Grady's exploits made him an instant celebrity, book contracts and cinematic re-creations following in due course.[11] Yet such episodes amounted to the military equivalent of tabloid journalism, diverting perhaps but thin on substance. The action that mattered was occurring not in the air but on the ground. There, unrelenting, primordial violence continued. Although Bosnians (and Croats) were not innocent of crimes, the better-armed Serbs were clearly the worst offenders. As NATO aircraft patrolled overhead, the signatures of the Serbian way of war—random shelling of populated areas, the confinement of military males to squalid concentration camps, and the use of rape as a weapon—all continued undisturbed.[12]

Although authorized to use air strikes to protect peacekeepers—a grant of protection subsequently extended to Bosnians within certain designated "safe areas"—NATO rarely acted on this authority. Between June 1993 and August 1995, Deny Flight aircraft actually released ordnance on a grand total of only ten occasions. The United States and its European allies vaguely hoped that the prospect of more serious military action might induce the Serbs to relent and agree to a negotiated settlement. Yet in terms of impact, Deny Flight amounted to little more than an irritant. Certainly, it did not dissuade the Serbs from intimidating UN peacekeepers or making life hell for Bosnians. The NATO air campaign had become an exercise in military masturbation—a display of ostensibly superior power that served chiefly to reveal Western impotence.[13]

The problem was twofold. On the one hand, procedures for approving air strikes were cumbersome. Under a "dual key" system, both UN and NATO authorities had to assent before a single aircraft could actually attack a single target. Wishing to preserve its nominally non-belligerent status, the UN rarely gave its okay. On the other hand, Serb threats (sometimes implemented) to take peacekeepers hostage damp-ened the enthusiasm for air strikes on the part of those NATO members—not including the United States—that had peacekeeping contingents at risk. So although American officers occupied most of the key posts in the NATO chain of command, they exercised limited actual authority.[14]

As the war dragged on and the body count continued to rise, criti-cism of U.S. policy also intensified. To be sure, not everyone was eager for the United States to become more deeply embedded in the Balkans. Senator John McCain, for one, insisted that this was a problem without a military solution. "Tragic as Bosnia may be," he said in a speech on the Senate floor, "it is a self-inflicted wound which we cannot heal with either airpower or ground troops."[15]

With the passing of time, McCain's became very much the minority view, however. An increasingly energized, if informal, Bosnian Muslim lobby rejected the excuses offered up to explain Clinton's fumbling ef-fort. Already in July 1993, *The Washington Post* was deriding the admin-istration's defense of its Bosnia policy as "petty and embarrassing."[16] That same month, in an amply publicized act of solidarity, Susan Son-tag, doyenne of the American intelligentsia, had gone to Sarajevo. Re-counting her experience in a widely read essay appearing in *The New York Review of Books,* Sontag denounced the United States and the West for "giving the victory to Serb fascism." In the Bosnian capital, she had staged Beckett's *Waiting for Godot,* even though Sarajevans, she ac-knowledged, were actually "waiting for Clinton."[17] By early the follow-ing year, *The New Republic* was castigating the White House for "indifference" and "timidity" in the face of out-and-out genocide. "Poor Bosnia," the editors wrote, "it should have found itself in a trade war. Trade wars we fight. Wars of genocide we watch."[18]

To the influential academic Fouad Ajami, the Bosnians represented the potential for reconciling Islam itself with modernity. Bosnian Serb leaders such as Radovan Karadžić claimed that they were "defending Christianity against militant Islamic fundamentalism."[19] Just the reverse was true, Professor Ajami insisted. Bosnian Muslims were the "true bearers of a universal culture, children of the secular environment of the West."[20]

Here, according to observers such as Ajami, was the reason it was imperative for the United States to come to Bosnia's defense. The typical Bosnian Muslim identified with Islam no more than the average Frenchman identified with Catholicism or the average Brit with the Church of England. In these quarters, religion had become a cultural artifact not worth fighting about. From a strategic perspective, it was incumbent upon the United States to encourage this tendency wherever it existed in the Islamic world. The ultimate objective was not to promote religious tolerance but to make religion itself redundant. Secularization ostensibly facilitated peace.

Concerns related to cultural pluralism, human rights, and protecting Muslims said to share a Western secular outlook kept Bosnia on the front pages. However, they did not suffice to prod the Clinton administration to take the more muscular approach that Bosnia's sympathizers were demanding. What ultimately prompted Clinton to act was a core geopolitical interest: preserving the viability of NATO. For decades, the alliance had formed the cornerstone of Washington's claim to European leadership. Deny Flight represented a first post–Cold War attempt to demonstrate the alliance's continuing relevance. Viewed from this perspective, that operation's evident failure was intolerable. If Bosnian Serbs could defy NATO and get away with it, the alliance was finished, perhaps fatally undermining America's claim to European preeminence.

Throughout this period, well-meaning efforts to negotiate a settlement to the war while preserving Bosnian territorial integrity had proven futile. By the summer of 1995, the Clinton administration accepted that diplomacy had failed. U.S. policy priorities now shifted: Ending the war became imperative, even if that meant accepting de facto ethnic partition. Defeating the Bosnian Serbs militarily (thereby refuting the charge that NATO had become toothless) provided the means to achieve that end.

Although President Clinton's post-Mogadishu aversion to committing U.S. ground troops to combat remained intact, his administration was more than open to collaborating with surrogates. Since 1993, in acts of solidarity more substantial than Sontag's, the governments of Iran and Saudi Arabia (not sharing Sontag's or Ajami's outlook on religion) had competed with one another in funneling weapons worth hundreds of millions of dollars to Bosnian Muslim forces. Although these efforts violated the UN embargo, they reportedly occurred with Washington's knowledge and tacit assent.[21] Several thousand "holy warriors" from Iran, Pakistan, and elsewhere in the Islamic world converged on Bosnia to wage jihad on behalf of their fellow Muslims.[22] Just as they were not innocent, Bosnians were not powerless.

Simultaneously, the United States had been quietly building up Croatian military power. To judge by his retrograde views, the epithet *fascist* fit Croat leader Franjo Tuđman no less than it did Serbs like Milošević and Karadžić.[23] So rather than sullying itself through direct involvement in training and advising Croat forces, the Pentagon sublet the project to a contracting firm run by recently retired U.S. Army generals. Here was another distinguishing feature of America's War for the Greater Middle East, one destined to become more prominent with time: a tendency to farm out traditional military functions to de facto mercenaries.[24] The pursuit of policy objectives was merging with the pursuit of profit.

Still, the upshot was that by the time the Clinton administration finally decided on a policy of coercion, it found local partners ready and willing to forge an anti-Serb axis. With the massacre of some eight thousand Bosnian Muslim men and boys at Srebrenica in mid-July rendering any further "peacemaking" efforts untenable, the United States and its NATO allies now became parties to a war against the Serbs. The shelling of a Sarajevo marketplace on August 28, which killed thirty-

seven Bosnian civilians and wounded dozens more, provided the immediate impetus for implementing the new policy.

On August 30, Operation Determined Force supplanted Deny Flight.
Policing no-fly zones gave way to bombing. Nominally, the purpose of
Determined Force was to prevent further attacks on Bosnian civilians.[25]
The real aim was to "inflict enough pain to compel Serb compliance"
with various NATO demands.[26] Chief among those demands were the
following: lift the siege of Sarajevo, agree to a cessation of hostilities,
and give up aspirations for creating an ethnically pure Greater Serbia.

Operationally, inflicting pain meant degrading Bosnian Serb capabilities rather than pursuing a "cut it off and kill it" approach. So despite its large ambitions, the U.S.-led air campaign, directed by U.S. Air
Force Lieutenant General Michael Short, a fighter pilot and Vietnam
veteran, was limited in scope. Some 220 combat aircraft participated,
operating primarily from the U.S. base in Aviano, Italy, and from the
USS *Theodore Roosevelt,* afloat in the Adriatic. By the time it ended on
September 14, pilots had flown slightly more than thirty-five hundred
sorties—two-thirds of them completed by U.S. forces.[27] NATO had expended 1,026 weapons against forty-eight targets, all chosen with an
eye toward minimizing the risk of collateral damage. Only a single allied aircraft—a French Mirage fighter jet—was lost to enemy action.[28]
All told, the bombing amounted to about one day's effort during Operation Desert Storm.[29]

In terms of careful planning and controlled execution, Determined
Force offered much to admire. As a practical matter, however, it was
largely superfluous. Even before NATO aircraft struck their first target,
developments on the ground had effectively decided the war's outcome. At most, the U.S.-led air campaign drove home the point with
Bosnian Serbs that they were facing imminent defeat.

During the first week of August, a Croat offensive called Operation
Oluja ("Storm") had recaptured the Krajina, the strip of territory running along the Croat-Bosnian border that Serbs had seized back in 1991
and occupied ever since. In liberating this region, an area almost as

large as Connecticut, the Croats had done more than win a decisive victory. They had demonstrated clear-cut superiority over their enemy. A second Croat push called Maestral ("Breeze") exploited the success of the first. The Bosnians also got in the act, launching their own anti-Serb offensive.[30] A dramatic shift in the overall military balance had occurred. According to the CIA's history of the conflict, Bosnian Serb leaders and Milošević himself were quick to recognize the implications. The loss of the Krajina "crystalized their belief that a political-military settlement had to be negotiated as soon as possible."[31]

In the face of this Croat-Bosnian onslaught, Serb civilians fled for their lives. Croat forces occupying the Krajina ousted as many as two hundred thousand Serbs, their plight attracting about as much international sympathy as the Germans expelled from Central and Eastern Europe at the end of World War II. The results met with Washington's quiet approval. "We 'hired' these guys to be our junkyard dogs," one U.S. diplomat wrote of the Croats. Sure, the results were ugly, but now was no time to get "squeamish."[32] Somewhat more delicately, Secretary of State Christopher detected the glimmerings of "a new strategic situation that may turn out to be to our advantage."[33]

For that situation to mature, the war that Washington was seeking to end needed to last a bit longer, as indeed it did. So although NATO had suspended Determined Force two weeks after it began in return for a Bosnian Serb commitment to lift the siege of Sarajevo, fierce fighting persisted for another month. Croat and Bosnian troops "continued to battle for chunks and scraps of disputed territory," further weakening the Bosnian Serb forces.[34] During what proved to be the war's climactic phase, NATO was a bystander. Only after weeks of wrangling did the hostilities finally end on October 12, each of the belligerents now concluding that the costs of continuing outweighed any potential benefits. This ceasefire stuck.

On its heels came a three-week-long peace conference at Dayton, Ohio, convened under U.S. auspices. The resulting agreement did not restore secular multiculturalism to Bosnia-Herzegovina. Indeed, by and large it accepted the reality of ethnic separation there and throughout the former Yugoslavia. Yet the Dayton Accords did cement an end to violence among Serbs, Croats, and Bosnian Muslims, an outcome widely hailed as a triumph of American statecraft. Here, it appeared, was a textbook demonstration of how the deft employment of military might combined with vigorous diplomacy could solve even the most intractable problem.

Seen in this light, the implications extended well beyond the matter immediately at hand. The role that the United States had played in bringing peace to Bosnia affirmed its unique standing in a post–Cold War world. No less importantly, the outcome showed that the American public remained ready to shoulder the responsibilities of global leadership. As Richard Holbrooke, the principal architect of that settlement, wrote, "After Dayton, American foreign policy seemed more assertive, more muscular." Put simply, "America was back."[35]

This at least was the interpretation that the Clinton administration promoted and to which activist American elites readily subscribed. "Our leadership made this peace agreement possible," the president told reporters in announcing the Dayton Accords.[36] Admirers credited Holbrooke with "taming the Balkan bullies." Profiling Holbrooke in *The New York Times*, the journalist Roger Cohen wrote, "Without his outrageousness, without his swagger, America could not have imposed its peace."[37]

Behind Holbrooke's swagger, of course, was American military might. "Deliberate Force infused NATO with a new sense of strength and vibrancy," *The Washington Post*'s Pentagon correspondent observed. It had "also validated force as an effective handmaiden to diplomacy."[38] Here was a template for future action—force employed with great precision in measured doses, allies allotted supporting roles to impart a multilateral gloss, no-nonsense American diplomats thereby empowered to crack heads and get things done.

The view found favor in at least some American military circles. Although the CIA might conclude that it was the junkyard dogs who had finally driven the Serbs "to sit down and negotiate a peace settlement," members of the officer corps thought otherwise.[39] In their view, Operation Determined Force had turned the tide. "Almost at the instant of its application," U.S. Air Force analysts concluded, NATO's abbreviated bombing campaign had accomplished "what three years of factional ground fighting, peacekeeping, and international diplomacy had yet to achieve." In that regard, airpower had "delivered what it promised," bringing peace to Bosnia "quickly, clearly and at minimal cost of blood and treasure."[40]

There was more here than the usual display of American narcissism, and more too than the latest updating of a decades-old claim that airpower offers the most expeditious and humane way to end wars. Rather, with overall U.S. military supremacy a given, traditional notions of what it meant to "win" required some tweaking. The proper role of armed force was not to supplant diplomacy but to make it work. Bosnia supposedly demonstrated that the United States possessed the capacity to do just that. Here was the means to police the "new world order" that George H. W. Bush had glimpsed and Bill Clinton had inherited. Crucially, the Bosnia intervention suggested that Islam as such did not pose an insuperable obstacle to the further application of this template. So, at least, the subsequent implementation of the Dayton Accords seemed to show.

Beginning on December 31, 1995, a robust contingent of some twenty thousand U.S. troops began entering Bosnia to form the core of an even larger NATO peace enforcement mission.[41] The army's 1st Armored Division, commanded by Major General William Nash, provided most of the troops. Fearing a repeat of Mogadishu, the Pentagon had acceded to this assignment with trepidation. The cigar-smoking Nash, an officer who shared more than a little of Richard Holbrooke's swagger, understood that he was to ensure that Bosnia not become a replay of Somalia. His purpose was not to perform good works but simply to maintain a separation between antagonists—to project strength without being excessively intrusive. "We will not be provocative," Nash instructed his troops.[42]

The operation, known as Joint Endeavor, began on an unpropitious note, a direct result of an overly bureaucratic planning process, with too many generals getting in each other's way. Just deploying the troops to the starting line—the Sava River, which forms Bosnia's northern border—involved a frustrating number of snafus. A botched crossing of the Sava, attributable partly to bad weather, partly to gross incompetence, delayed the actual entry of U.S. troops into Bosnia by ten days.[43] Thankfully, the initiative and determination of ordinary soldiers saved the day. One American officer who was present attributed the eventual crossing of the Sava to "a triumph of the human spirit over an insane system, narrowly averting catastrophe."[44] Those wearing stars on their shoulders had not covered themselves with glory.

From that point, although the operation did not lack for anxious moments, problems proved manageable. U.S. commanders were adamant in defining the mission narrowly. Their remit did not include nation-building or even the pursuit of war criminals. Intimidation, not conciliation, defined the spirit of the enterprise. Encased in body armor and wearing Kevlar helmets while armed to the teeth, U.S. troops projected an image of warriors not to be trifled with.[45]

By and large, as a way to enforce order, this approach worked. For anyone nursing expectations of Bosnia becoming a model of multi-ethnic harmony with Christians and Muslims living together in peace, it proved a disappointment. In fact, the overall effect of armed intervention was "to cement wartime ethnic cleansing and maintain ethnic cleansers in power." Four years after the peacekeepers arrived, Bosnia consisted of "three de facto mono-ethnic entities, three separate armies, three separate police forces, and a national government that exists mostly on paper and operates at the mercy of the entities." Even so, the cessation of hostilities negotiated at Dayton had held. That was something.[46]

The U.S. military presence in Bosnia continued for nearly a decade. During that entire period, the total number of troops involved progressively dwindled, with no American lives lost due to hostile action.[47] For a military consumed by the imperatives of "force protection," such an outcome met and even exceeded expectations. For commanders at all levels, mission accomplishment meant "returning home with no casualties." In sharp contrast to the more relaxed attitude of other allied contingents in Bosnia, risk aversion had emerged as a hallmark of the U.S. military's posture. At the unit level, exit strategy meant, in effect, "don't get anyone killed."[48]

More broadly, Joint Endeavor eased concerns that any sustained encounter between American soldiers and non-American Muslims was likely to fuel antagonism. Instead, it appeared that quartering U.S. troops alongside a Muslim population could reassure or pacify. So although painful memories of Somalia lingered—derided by Holbrooke as a "Vietmalia Syndrome"—Bosnia now appeared to define the way forward.[49]

This alluring prospect soon proved chimerical, however. Rather than bringing peace to the Balkans, armed intervention in Bosnia merely set the stage for another intervention on behalf of beleaguered Muslims, this time within Serbia proper.

10

WHAT WINNING MEANS

I HAD WATCHED THE BOSNIA DRAMA PLAY ITSELF OUT FROM A distant and, for me, unfamiliar vantage point. After twenty-three years of service, my own undistinguished military career had reached an unceremonious conclusion. Now out of the army, I was completing an academic apprenticeship of sorts at the School of Advanced International Studies (SAIS) in Washington. My duties as a minor staff functionary provided ample occasion to observe at close hand the various Washington insiders—current and former officials, prominent journalists, and policy-oriented academics—who passed through the SAIS campus just off of Dupont Circle.

For a middle-aged political naïf, the experience proved to both instructive and disheartening. People ostensibly in the know turned out to know not all that much. Even in small off-the-record discussions, the views expressed were predictable and pedestrian. On particular issues, opinions might differ. Yet such differences mattered less than allegiance to an underlying consensus. Rooted in a conviction that Washington itself defined the center of the universe, that consensus took it for granted that the fate of humankind hinged on decisions made there.

In the short run, all appeared uncertain. Crises abounded. To keep the world from cracking up, it was incumbent upon America to lead. In the long run, the outcome—freedom's ultimate triumph—was foreordained. This prospect imparted to American leadership all the justification it required, regardless of past blunders or any obstacles that lay ahead.

A direct legacy of World War II, this consensus had emerged at the dawn of the Cold War. Now, in the 1990s, with the Cold War having ended on a gratifyingly happy note, it appeared incontrovertible. Indeed, the Cold War's outcome affirmed its essential correctness. To question its claims was to commit an unpardonable sin, the punishment for which was excommunication.

As a candidate for the presidency, Bill Clinton had signaled his intention to conform, although his partisan critics were never going to credit him with actually doing so. Ideologues on the right were calling for the United States to exercise "benign global hegemony" as it guided humankind toward "the end of history."[1] The Clinton administration employed a different vocabulary to make the same point, describing the United States as the "indispensable nation" charged with ushering others to join it on "the right side of history."[2]

Conservative columnists like Charles Krauthammer were warning that the United States must not shrink from its responsibility for "laying down the rules of world order and being prepared to enforce them."[3] As if in response, the liberal Anthony Lake, Clinton's first national security adviser, insisted that the administration was intent on doing just that. On a visit to SAIS, Lake outlined a "strategy of enlargement" that was going to expand "the world's free community of market democracies," that is, countries willing to play by American rules.[4] Ethnic and religious differences might survive as cultural curiosities, but in all matters relating to political economy, the imperatives of globalization were destined to win out. The assembled students responded with loud applause.

This neoliberal utopianism found a military counterpart in the Revolution in Military Affairs (RMA). During the 1990s, fostered by a very selective reading of recent events, the RMA became all the rage in national security circles, its influence on successive campaigns in America's War for the Greater Middle East difficult to overstate.

RMA enthusiasts posited that information technology was transforming war's very nature, rendering "existing methods of conducting war obsolete."[5] On future battlefields, the side able to establish and maintain "information dominance" was sure to win.[6]

To the clash of arms that had traditionally involved massive waste and confusion, the RMA would impart precision and control—accelerating the tempo of operations, improving weapons accuracy and lethality, and enabling commanders to "watch battles unfold on computer screens and issue moment-to-moment corrections." Better still, America's overall lead in information technology gave the United States a huge advantage in tapping the RMA's potential. Doing so held out the prospect of victories gained by "disengaged combat," U.S. forces operating "at a healthy distance from the enemy." Remaining beyond the enemy's reach meant fewer American casualties—perhaps none at all—a prospect allowing policymakers greater latitude in deciding when and where to fight.[7]

Reagan's Tanker War had offered a rudimentary glimpse of this future. Bush's Operation Desert Storm had tested it on a larger scale. Bill Clinton's intervention in Bosnia ostensibly affirmed it. Radically enhanced U.S. military effectiveness was making the indispensable nation the unstoppable nation, thereby radically enhancing the overall effectiveness of American statecraft. This defined the promise of the RMA. So at least true believers were prepared to argue.

The U.S. Army's General Wesley Clark was a true believer—or, at least, opportunistically posed as one. During the Cold War, Clark had gained a reputation of being a very ambitious officer with an aptitude for embracing novelty moments before it became accepted convention. He thus appeared to be not only eager but also a quick study.

During the climactic stages of the Bosnia crisis, as a bright-eyed lieutenant general, Clark had served as Richard Holbrooke's chief military adviser, accompanying the American envoy throughout the difficult negotiations that culminated in the Dayton Accords. For Clark, the experience proved to be illuminating. Here, it appeared, was a demonstration of the role military power could play in the post–Cold War world—"a pattern that could be applied again."[8]

Clark grasped what (in his view) most American army officers were too dim to understand. As an overarching rationale for maintaining a large U.S. military establishment, mere deterrence had become obsolete. Deterrence was passive, even timid, when activism was becoming the order of the day. With the Soviet threat gone and the RMA endowing the United States with unprecedented military capabilities, force could now serve as an instrument of "compellence" or "coercive diplomacy."[9]

In mid-1997 President Clinton elevated Clark, now a four-star general, to the post of Supreme Allied Commander Europe (SACEUR), the military head of NATO. In the Balkans, unfinished business remained. Slobodan Milošević still governed what remained of Yugoslavia. In the Serbian province of Kosovo, the next act of that nation's ongoing implosion awaited. The unsettled situation there seemingly offered Clark an opportunity to outdo Holbrooke, while demonstrating his personal mastery of what he liked to call "modern war." So Kosovo became the scene of the next campaign in America's War for the Greater Middle East, one that found the United States and its allies delivering victory to a movement that the State Department classified as a terrorist organization, its membership consisting almost entirely of Muslims with blood in their eyes.

To appreciate Kosovo's political sensitivity, imagine if after the Civil War droves of ex-Confederates had settled in Gettysburg. Imagine further that after achieving majority status, they proceeded to fly the Stars and Bars, teach schoolchildren history from textbooks glorifying the Lost Cause, and agitate for secession. Strongholds of Union sentiment like New York, Chicago, and Boston might take exception.

For Serbs, Kosovo possessed a significance akin to that which many Americans accord to Gettysburg. It was sacred ground, site of an epic, nation-defining battle against the Turks in 1389. Yet the Muslims who had made Kosovo their home since and who now greatly outnumbered the Serbs living there saw it as rightfully *theirs*. Indeed, these Kosovo Albanians, or Kosovars, aspired to follow the precedent of the Slovenes, Croats, Bosnians, and Macedonians in leaving Yugoslavia to go their

own way. Serb alarm at this prospect, further enflamed by the nationalist demagoguery of Slobodan Milošević, made the issue essentially
non-negotiable.

As early as December 1992, George H. W. Bush had warned Milošević
against provoking unrest in Kosovo, threatening "military force against
Serbians in Kosovo and in Serbia proper" if he defied that warning. Yet
as long as the Bosnia crisis was playing itself out, Kosovo enjoyed "a
type of sullen stability," attracting only glancing attention from the outside world.[10]

By nominally (if not actually) preserving a multiethnic Bosnia-
Herzegovina, the Dayton Accords changed all that. To Kosovars, this
suggested that the international community was not going to support
their own aspirations for independence based on ethnic identity. Indeed, U.S. policymakers in particular consistently expressed their opposition to any such outcome. Persuaded that patience would get them
nothing and worried that the influx of Serb refugees from Croatia and
Bosnia being resettled in Kosovo was changing the ethnic balance to
their disadvantage, the Kosovars opted for violence.[11]

The grandly named Kosovo Liberation Army (KLA), created in 1993,
offered the best hope of deliverance. As armies go, the KLA left much
to be desired, however. As late as 1996, it consisted of no more than 150
fighters and commanded little popular following. Yet by early 1998, it
had mustered sufficient capacity to launch a series of harassing attacks
against Serbs in Kosovo. These included assassinations, kidnappings,
and bombings. U.S. officials denounced the KLA as a terrorist organization, giving Slobodan Milošević reason to believe that he had tacit
American permission to crush the group. In the summer of 1998, he set
out to do just that. A heavy-handed campaign of repression dealt the
KLA a severe setback but also created a huge refugee crisis that attracted widespread media attention. For Milošević, the two hundred
thousand Kosovar refugees were a public relations disaster. For the
KLA, they represented a bonanza.[12]

Milošević was playing right into his opponents' hands. The cycle of
KLA incitements and Serb reprisals was ineluctably drawing the United

States and its allies into Kosovo's fight for independence.[13] By October 1998, with the bellicose Madeleine Albright having now replaced the bland Warren Christopher as secretary of state, Washington was issuing ultimatums. Milošević had "not complied fully with the demands of the international community," Albright charged. Either that was now going to stop or Serbia was going to face punitive military action. "We have made it clear to Milosevic and Kosovars," Albright emphasized, "that we do not support independence for Kosovo—that we want Serbia out of Kosovo, not Kosovo out of Serbia."[14] As a practical matter, Albright's stated objectives were inherently at odds with one another. To evict the Serbs was necessarily to hand independence-minded KLA terrorists a victory.

After posting the eviction notice, the United States and its allies paused before enforcing its dictates. Another high-profile mission by Holbrooke extracted concessions from Milošević, which the Serb leader honored just long enough to gain a bit of breathing space. Faced with the prospect of a NATO air attack, Yugoslav forces did withdraw from Kosovo as Washington had demanded. The KLA wasted no time in filling the vacuum. By December, fighting—and the dispossession of civilians in Kosovo—had resumed.

In truth, not everyone in Washington shared Albright's eagerness to force a showdown. Buffeted by multiple crises, the Clinton administration had reached its nadir. For the president himself, the Monica Lewinsky affair was in full swing, with the House Judiciary Committee approving articles of impeachment on December 11. A week later, the latest in a string of confrontations with Saddam Hussein culminated in the four-day bombing campaign known as Operation Desert Fox. Critics called it a wag-the-dog stunt concocted to distract public attention from the troubles assailing the presidency.[15] The charge was not easy to refute.

Secretary Albright anticipated that initiating a war over Kosovo was likely to invite a similar charge. Putting the onus for war on the unsavory Milošević was therefore vital. As State Department spokesman

Jamie Rubin put it, "In order to move towards military action, it has to be clear that the Serbs were responsible."[16] This describes the purpose of a putative peace conference convened under allied auspices at Rambouillet, France, in February 1999. Nominally, the conference represented one last good-faith effort to avert armed intervention by NATO. In fact, its purpose was to remove any remaining barriers to intervention.

Acting under acute American pressure, the Kosovars acquiesced in playing their assigned part. Without even the slightest show of enthusiasm, their delegates agreed to disarm the KLA in return for a promise of self-government *without* independence. A large NATO occupation force allowed access throughout the remnants of Yugoslavia was to guarantee this arrangement.[17] On March 18, Milošević's representatives predictably and obligingly rejected this deal. In doing so, they handed Albright her casus belli.

From his headquarters in Mons, Belgium, General Clark had closely monitored these developments. While presiding over the ongoing occupation of Bosnia, Clark was actively promoting the use of bombing threats to bring Milošević to heel. During trips back to Washington, he collared just about anyone who would listen, whether in the Pentagon, the State Department, or the White House. His efforts at evangelizing did not find favor with Secretary of Defense William Cohen, his immediate boss in the U.S. chain of command, or with JCS chairman General Hugh Shelton, not in Clark's chain of command but someone he could ill afford to alienate. Both began to question not only Clark's propensity for freelancing but also his judgment.[18]

Clark gave them ample reason to do so. On a Pentagon visit in June 1998, he had pressed his views on General Joseph Ralston, a politically savvy officer then serving as vice chair of the Joint Chiefs of Staff. The exchange, recounted in Clark's own memoirs, testifies to his single-minded, not to say tone-deaf self-confidence. Clark had made his standard pitch about getting Milošević to lay off the Kosovars by confronting him with the prospect of a NATO air offensive.

Ralston: "Wes, what are we going to do if the air threat doesn't
  deter him?"

Clark: "Well, it will work. I know him as well as anyone. And it
  will give the diplomats the leverage they need."

Ralston: "OK, but let's just say it doesn't work. What will we
  do?"

Clark: "Well, then we'll bomb. We'll have to follow through."

Yet this qualified at best as a theoretical possibility, Clark insisted. Things were not going to come to actual violence. "I know Milosevic; he doesn't want to get bombed."[19]

Ralston remained skeptical. Clark wrote off his fellow four-star's inability to grasp the obvious as evidence of "the military's innate conservatism."[20] Yet far more striking is Clark's attribution of the problem in Kosovo to the machinations of one particularly nasty individual. Bosnia had taught Clark that "quarrels in the region were not really about age old religious differences but rather the result of many unscrupulous and manipulative leaders seeking their own power and wealth at the expense of ordinary people."[21] By implication, removing or at least intimidating unscrupulous leaders offered the most direct path to giving ordinary people the justice they deserved.

Such a perspective, dismissing political or historical complexities that might impede the use of American power, was by no means peculiar to Clark alone. In hawkish circles, such thinking exerted considerable appeal. In September 1998, for example, a group of foreign policy notables—the sort that convened for luncheons at SAIS—published a full-page letter to President Clinton in The New York Times, urging more forceful action in Kosovo. The title of the letter summarized its message: "Mr. President, Milosevic Is the Problem."[22]

Although nobody dared to propose openly that the United States should simply bump off the Serb leader, here we glimpse yet again the logic destined in time to find expression in a full-fledged policy of targeted assassination. Bad leaders were preventing good outcomes. Solution? Get rid of them. During the years to come, the United States would repeatedly test this proposition, without evident success. Decapitation was to prove a poor substitute for strategy. Whatever problems the United States was facing in the Greater Middle East, they went much deeper than the actions of a few evildoers.

When the Rambouillet conference adjourned without reaching an agreement, Milošević, in effect, was calling NATO's bluff: The mere threat of bombing had not produced the desired results. Indeed, beginning on March 20, Serb reinforcements, both military and paramilitary police forces, started pouring into Kosovo. This marked the beginning of Operation Horseshoe, a Yugoslav offensive aimed at eradicating the KLA and expelling the Muslim interlopers once and for all.

Clark himself was unperturbed. With NATO having authorized itself to use force, the SACEUR had at hand a carefully refined campaign plan ready for implementation. Late on the afternoon of March 23, Shelton called from Washington with the order to execute. From that moment, what the press took to calling "Madeleine's War" became in equal measure "Wes's War."[23]

Operation Allied Force, as it was called, purported to be a humanitarian intervention. But as with its Bosnia predecessor Determined Force, this was a cover story. Its actual purpose was to shore up NATO's credibility by putting a stop to Serb efforts to expel the Muslim inhabitants of Kosovo.[24] In effect, the alliance was going to war to prove that with the passing of the Cold War it still retained the will and capacity to fight. As Clark put it, giving his best imitation of Colin Powell at the outset of Desert Storm, NATO was "going to systematically attack, disrupt, degrade, devastate, and ultimately destroy" Yugoslav forces in and around Kosovo.[25] And with President Clinton having declared that he "did not intend to put our troops in Kosovo to fight a war," Clark was going to accomplish that mission while relying exclusively on air power.[26] Unfortunately, rather than demonstrating that NATO remained alive and well, the ensuing campaign, punctuated by one misstep after another, had the opposite effect.

Shortly after 8:00 P.M. on March 24, Allied Force commenced. Salvos of cruise missiles, along with satellite-guided weapons launched from

B-2 and F-117A stealth bombers, targeted Serb air defenses and strategic communications.[27] Although aircraft from six NATO nations participated in some capacity, the United States flew two-thirds of the combat sorties.

Operationally, the purpose of this "phase one" was to gain complete control of Serb airspace. In that regard, it did not fully measure up. Whether fearful or shrewd, the Yugoslavs kept their radars turned off, which made them difficult to locate. An air defense threat therefore persisted. NATO responded by keeping its aircraft above fifteen thousand feet. Doing so reduced the hazards they faced but also complicated targeting and adversely affected bombing accuracy.

Politically, the aim of phase one was to make a statement expressing NATO's seriousness in causing Yugoslavia to fold without further ado. Certain that they had Milošević pegged, Albright, the war's principal architect, and Clark, its chief engineer, both expected hostilities to end within two or three days. NATO officials in Brussels and most U.S. authorities back in Washington entertained similar views. All miscalculated badly.

In fact, once begun, Allied Force continued for two and a half months, outlasting Desert Storm by several weeks. Crucially, Operation Horseshoe accelerated and expanded. In the face of this onslaught, Kosovars fled en masse, confronting Clark with a crisis that his planners had failed to anticipate. One week into Allied Force, over half a million displaced Kosovars were on the move, with one hundred thousand seeking refuge in Albania and another fifty thousand crossing into Macedonia. The numbers continued to swell.[28]

As phase one gave way to phase two, NATO committed more aircraft to engage a wider array of targets. Phase three waited on tap. Yet the use of such terms belies the confusion that was enveloping Allied Force. By the end of March, according to Clark, "pushing to escalate and intensify was the strategy."[29] In fact, strategy had collapsed, its place taken by a haphazard, at times almost desperate effort to find some way of ending what NATO, egged on by the likes of Albright and Clark, had fecklessly begun.

Almost from the outset—as soon as it became apparent that Milošević intended to put up serious resistance—unity of purpose within NATO gave way to disharmony. A more accurate name for Allied Force would have been Abundant Discord or Abiding Dissonance.

Three cleavages crippled the conduct of the campaign. On each of the three, Clark ended up on the wrong side. Fancying that he exercised authority on a par with that enjoyed by Dwight D. Eisenhower, NATO's first Supreme Commander, Clark was about to learn otherwise. At it turned out, his status was more like that of a university president. Provided with a large house, a fancy office, and some handsome perks, he wielded limited clout even as he was beholden to multiple constituencies, each with its own distinctive agenda.

The first cleavage related to operational priorities. It pitted Clark against his nominal subordinate Lieutenant General Michael Short, charged with orchestrating the air campaign from his headquarters in Vicenza, Italy. That campaign's moral justification rested on the claim that NATO was preventing Milošević from ethnically cleansing Kosovo. That, in turn, implied that taking on the Yugoslav forces actually brutalizing the Kosovars should be a priority.

But those forces, numbering some forty thousand in all, were operating in small units that were difficult to locate and easy to hide. They mixed in with the very population that NATO was supposedly trying to protect. Attacking them was a mission far better suited to ground troops—of which Clark had none available—than to air forces.

Certainly, this described Short's view. In his own encounters with Milošević, Short had concluded, "If you hit that man hard, slapped him up side the head, he'd pay attention."[30] Slapping him "up side the head" translated into going after ministries, infrastructure, airfields, barracks, communications sites, and refineries. As far as Short was concerned, the plight of suffering Kosovars was somebody else's problem.

The air force three-star publicly aired his unhappiness with the priorities established by the army four-star charged with overall responsibility for running the war. "As an airman, I would have done this differently," he complained to *The Washington Post*. "It would not be an incremental air campaign or a slow buildup, but we would go downtown from the first night," bringing home to "the influential citizens of Belgrade" the consequences of defying NATO and the United States.

> If you wake up in the morning and you have no power to your house and no gas to your stove and the bridge you take to work is down and will be lying in the Danube for the next 20 years, I think you begin to ask, "Hey, Slobo, what's this all about? How much more of this do we have to withstand?" And at some point, you make the transition from applauding Serb machismo against the world to thinking what your country is going to look like if this continues.[31]

Scornful of tank plinking, Short refused to do it Clark's way—and ultimately he prevailed.[32]

The second cleavage marked a split between fellow four-stars, pitting the SACEUR against his peers on the Joint Chiefs of Staff. To shield Kosovars caught in the path of Operation Horseshoe, Clark placed an urgent request for AH-64 Apache attack helicopters, potent weapons well suited to plinking Yugoslav mechanized units pushing through Kosovo. Such a commitment entailed risk, however—the AH-64 is fragile as well as powerful. It also hinted at a slippery slope. Given Clark's publicly stated intention to "degrade, devastate, and ultimately destroy" the enemy, committing attack helicopters might open the door to a subsequent commitment of ground troops.

The Joint Chiefs were having none of that. To keep Apaches out of the fight, they debated, delayed, and dragged their feet. "Clearly," Clark later grumbled, "they didn't understand that this was a war, that NATO's future was at stake."[33] More accurately, the JCS had concluded that Clark's priorities differed from their own. They felt a limited obligation to bail out a colleague for whom they felt little affection, especially when doing so meant charging more deeply into a conflict that from the outset they viewed as suspect. By the time the Apaches did finally reach the scene and were ready to launch, the fighting had ended.

Like General Short, the Joint Chiefs had prevailed at the SACEUR's expense.

The third cleavage was between Washington and Brussels, with Clark caught squarely in the middle. Nominally a partnership of co-equals, NATO is actually a tiered organization, with the United States occupying the top tier in solitary splendor. The preeminent symbol of that arrangement is the identity of the SACEUR: An American has always filled the post. Who this officer actually works for, however, is a delicate matter requiring political finesse.

As Allied Force went awry, authorities in Washington expected Clark to put U.S. interests first and to heed their instructions. Clark himself either failed to comprehend or refused to accept that requirement. In televised press conferences convened to explain (implausibly) that all was going according to plan, the SACEUR offered assessments and described intentions that put him at odds with the Pentagon and the White House.[34] Clark gave the impression of viewing himself either as an independent potentate or as an agent of the alliance, rather than as someone who took his marching orders from Washington.

These performances particularly incensed the U.S. secretary of defense, William Cohen, who eventually had had enough. Cohen ordered General Shelton to call Clark with instructions that the JCS chairman read to the SACEUR verbatim: "Get your fucking face off the TV. No more briefings, period."[35] This directive removed any doubts about the hierarchy of authority. But it also exposed the extent to which Clark had forfeited the confidence of those in Washington whose support he badly needed.

Most of this was occurring offstage. In front of the curtain, a war much like any other war was underway, fraught with uncertainty and error and random bloodletting. Yet NATO and U.S. authorities had marketed Allied Force as something other than an actual war. After all, its purpose was to protect the innocent, with violence employed with laserlike precision to minimize casualties and kill only people genuinely deserving to be killed.

So when things that typically happen in war duly occurred, they seemed shocking, as if NATO had suffered a catastrophic failure or was violating some solemn promise. On the night of March 27, for example, a Yugoslav missile downed a U.S. Air Force F-117A. (The pilot, Lieutenant Colonel Dale Zelko, successfully ejected and was recovered.) Given the stealth technology that ostensibly made that aircraft undetectable, the shootdown appeared inexplicable.

On March 31, Serbs captured three GIs on peacekeeping duty in neighboring Macedonia. Clark complained about what he called a "kidnapping."[36] More likely, the soldiers had accidentally wandered across the border and into Serb hands. Even so, published photographs of befuddled young American troops held captive caused widespread dismay. (Once more, the Reverend Jesse Jackson, never publicity-shy, stepped into the breach, traveling to Belgrade to secure the POWs' release.)

Then on April 12, a U.S. Air Force F-15E attacking a railroad bridge struck a passenger train entering the target area at just the wrong time. More than a dozen civilians were killed, with others wounded. Two days later, several F-16s rolled in on what the American pilots thought was a convoy of military vehicles. The convoy actually consisted of tractors pulling farm wagons, packed with fleeing Kosovars. As many as seventy-three noncombatants died as a result.

Worse still was to come on May 7. With the weight of the NATO air effort now shifting to the "strategic" targets that Short preferred, B-2 bombers flying all the way from Whiteman AFB in Missouri put five satellite-guided bombs on a large Belgrade building that turned out to be the embassy of the People's Republic of China. Apologies for what Washington insisted had been an accident did little to mollify the Chinese.

In any real war, incidents such as these—with the possible exception of the embassy bombing—would have qualified as regrettable but insignificant. In Kosovo, they became defining moments, emblematic of an alliance unable to get its act together.

On the American home front, meanwhile, an epidemic of impatience erupted. Politicians and pundits alike expressed consternation over the administration's apparent inability to deliver instantaneous victory. Within a week of the first bombs falling, Senator Richard Lugar, a well-regarded moderate Republican from Indiana, took to the op-ed pages of *The Washington Post* to declare, "We are losing the war in Kosovo."[37] Air power alone wasn't going to suffice. The self-evident solution was to send in ground troops.

A chorus of militant voices rose up to endorse that proposal. Writing in *The Weekly Standard,* for example, Robert Kagan and William Kristol commended Lugar and other Republicans who were calling for escalation. At issue in Kosovo, they wrote, was "the single overriding question of our time: Will the United States and its allies have the will to shape the world in conformance with our interests and our principles . . . ? Or will we allow much of the world to slip into chaos and brutality?" The key was to win a decisive military victory, which meant that the United States needed to "liberate Kosovo" and "drive Milošević from power."[38]

Senator John McCain sounded a similar note. He denounced the Clinton administration for having "waged war on the cheap," with saving Kosovars taking a backseat to avoiding U.S. casualties. McCain professed to find the president's reluctance to invade Kosovo "mystifying." Only a large-scale ground offensive could "rescue the nation's security and honor from the calamity" that Clinton's bungling had produced.[39] In short, the clamor triggered by the absence of immediate military success imparted to Kosovo greatly elevated significance. The stakes at issue there assumed seemingly cosmic proportions.

When and how to mount an invasion, thereby redeeming an increasingly dire situation, became the overriding issue of the day. Observers noted with satisfaction the emergence of an interventionist consensus transcending the usual left-right divisions of American politics. Even peaceniks were coming to appreciate the potential benefits of war.[40] Others assessed the merits of various invasion scenarios.[41] Hovering in the background to provide a simulacrum of historical context was World War II, with Milošević, the latest stand-in for Hitler, engaged in criminal actions akin to those associated with Auschwitz.

In the event, as is so often the case, the kibitzing of critics proved less important than the ongoing rush of events. Given the disparity between the opposing sides, the outcome of the Kosovo War was foreordained—assuming that NATO, which really meant the United States, persevered. Whatever the daily humiliations accruing as a result of a venture gone badly amiss, they paled in comparison to the mortification awaiting the Clinton administration if it admitted outright failure. So, in contrast to Reagan after Beirut or Clinton himself after Mogadishu, the administration refused to quit. Responding to critics, national security adviser Sandy Berger on June 2 identified "four irreducible facts" defining U.S. policy in Kosovo. "One, we will win. Period. Full stop. There is no alternative. Second, winning means what we said it means. Third, the air campaign is having a serious impact. Four, the president has said he has not ruled out any option. So go back to one. We will win."[42]

Berger's fourth point explicitly revoked the administration's previous prohibition on the introduction of ground troops. If phase three of General Clark's air campaign did not produce the desired result, there was indeed going to be a phase four: Invasion.

In fact, by the time Berger staged this demonstration of faux pugnacity, the endgame was already approaching. Phase three of the bombing campaign was now inflicting heavy damage. The forces under General Short's command were doing what he had wanted done all along: closing down oil refineries, dropping bridges across the Danube, knocking out electrical distribution systems, and even blasting the main radio and television broadcast facilities in the center of Belgrade. The Serb people, noisily contemptuous of NATO at the campaign's outset, were showing signs of war-weariness.

Of equal importance, the KLA had bounced back. Under the cover of allied air attacks, they reconstituted their forces and returned to the offensive. As had Operation Determined Force, Allied Force benefited from a proxy ground component.

For Milošević, the last straw came on May 27, when the International Tribunal for the Former Yugoslavia indicted him for war crimes. With Serbia proper under intensifying assault from the air, the KLA on the move, and NATO inching toward invasion, Milošević's interest in terminating hostilities now exceeded even Clinton's. Soon enough, the American, European, and Russian negotiators who had been working unsuccessfully to arrange a ceasefire hammered out terms that Milošević found tolerable.

Once all parties accepted that agreement on June 3, fighting stopped. Military action did not, however. The ceasefire terms required Yugoslav forces to evacuate Kosovo. This they proceeded to do in remarkably good order, exhibiting few signs of defeat. In their place, a force of fifty thousand peacekeepers began arriving in Kosovo on June 12. This was KFOR, an organization primarily built around NATO, with the United States initially contributing seven thousand troops and General Clark in overall command.

Complicating matters was the fact that KFOR also included a Russian contingent. This was part of the price that the West had paid for Moscow's assistance in brokering the ceasefire deal. Yet the Russians were going to play on their own terms. When they jumped the gun by dispatching an armored column from Bosnia to the Kosovo capital of Priština, an angry Clark reacted with characteristic rashness. To prevent the arrival of further Russian reinforcements, he directed KFOR's immediate commander, British Lieutenant General Sir Michael Jackson, to block the runway of Priština's main airport. This Jackson refused to do, provoking a heated exchange with Clark, important for our purposes because it illustrates the impact of the Kosovo war on allied solidarity.

Jackson: Sir, I'm not taking any more orders from Washington.
Clark: Mike, these aren't Washington's orders, they're coming from me.
Jackson: By whose authority?
Clark: By my authority as SACEUR.

Jackson: You don't have that authority.

Clark: I do have that authority. I have the Secretary General
     behind me on this.

Jackson: Sir, I'm not starting World War III for you.

In an effort to resolve the standoff, Jackson placed a call to his British
military boss, General Sir Charles Guthrie, chief of the defense staff
back in London. Jackson explained the situation to Guthrie and then
handed the phone to Clark. "I agree with Mike," Guthrie told the
SACEUR, "and so does Hugh Shelton," effectively cutting off Clark at
the knees.[43] Although Clark didn't know it yet, his military career was
effectively over. He might have salvaged a win against Milošević, but he
was about to lose his job.

Under KFOR's protective eye, the displaced Kosovars began returning home. There, they promptly initiated a vicious ethnic cleansing
campaign aimed at ousting the roughly quarter-million Serbs and Roma
living in the province.[44] The U.S. Army official history offers a concise
account of what newly arrived peacekeepers witnessed:

> Ethnic Albanians, consumed with hatred and resolved to avenge past
> grievances, initiated a wave of destruction that equaled in method if
> not in volume what they had experienced earlier during the Serbian
> ethnic cleansing of the province. Anything Serbian was destroyed or
> vandalized—even abandoned houses and churches. Moreover, much of
> the violence was clearly organized and deliberate. Each day in June,
> American soldiers confronted new expressions of hatred. . . .
>
> Sadly, the violence was not confined to isolated incidents or property
> destruction. Kosovo-Serbs were attacked throughout the province. Even
> before the first week of KFOR occupation ended, at least twenty-seven
> ethnic Serbian men were known to have been abducted by members of
> the KLA. The men were never found. A Serbian school official who had
> protected an Albanian home and family during the Serbian ethnic
> cleansing in 1998 thought he would be safe once the war ended in June
> the following year and Yugoslav forces withdrew. He was not. KLA per-

*sonnel arrived ahead of NATO's KFOR; they killed the man and his
wife and left their bodies hanging in the town square. Other Serbs were
accosted in public buildings, or on the street, and then robbed, beaten, or
"arrested" and detained in jails for several days. Some of them simply
"disappeared." In one community, an estimated five thousand Roma,
who had occasionally cooperated with the Serbs during their reign of
terror, were expelled from their homes, which were then looted and
burned.*[45]

These events challenged the hypothesis attributing Balkan violence
entirely to malevolent politicians like Milošević. Even so, they prompted
little by way of second thoughts in Washington or any other allied capitals. The Kosovo Serbs were written off as incidental, with neither
NATO nor the United States inclined to assume responsibility for their
fate.

By the end of summer 1999, the first half of Secretary Albright's
diktat had found fulfillment: Apart from a small, besieged remnant, the
Serbs were out of Kosovo. As for the second half—that Kosovo was to
remain part of Serbia—this was no longer for authorities in Washington to decide. Allied Force had empowered Kosovar nationalists. Although they waited nearly a decade before declaring their independence,
in 2008 they did just that. A remarkable collaboration between the KLA
and NATO—the one employing terror, the other habitually condemn-
ing its use—had enabled Kosovars to achieve their long-sought political
goal. So although NATO had "won," it was the Kosovars who benefited. Here was a case study in how to make terrorism work, with the
United States and other avowed opponents of such behavior both assisting and subsequently ratifying the results.[46]

Apart from acknowledging that winning ultimately meant what the
Kosovars said it meant, what are we to make of Operation Allied Force?
And how exactly does NATO's intervention in Kosovo, along with its
lesser Bosnian cousin, fit into the narrative of America's War for the
Greater Middle East?

Notably, of all the various campaigns comprising that larger enterprise, Kosovo and Bosnia alone found U.S. forces fighting *on behalf* of Muslims *against* a non-Muslim adversary. In that regard, the two Balkan excursions stand apart. To some this may suggest that the interventions in Kosovo and Bosnia don't belong here—that they actually relate to the story of Europe's post–Cold War reconstitution. In fact, they form part of both stories. To exclude the Balkan campaigns from the narrative of America's War for the Greater Middle East is to overlook weaknesses in U.S. military practice destined to afflict the larger-scale military campaigns just ahead.

Two weaknesses in particular stand out. The first relates to campaign design and the challenges inherent in aligning military plans with political purpose. In Kosovo in particular, the disconnect between the two was nearly absolute. Responsibility for that failure rests primarily, although not entirely, with General Clark. In place of serious engagement with the complexities inherent in using force to move the Serbs out while keeping Kosovo in, Clark substituted amateur psychologizing of Slobodan Milošević. When he got that wrong, nothing remained but to improvise.

The actual conduct of Allied Force served, at least in part, to conceal this fundamental lapse of generalship. Once the shooting began, the United States military did what it traditionally does best, mustering and managing resources on an astonishing scale. Judged from this perspective, Allied Force gives the appearance of being an impressive, even masterful affair, at least statistically.

Over the course of seventy-eight days of combat, while operating out of airfields in several countries, NATO air forces flew over thirty-eight thousand sorties, losing a mere two aircraft to enemy action. Every Yugoslav MiG that rose to offer a challenge was shot down. Despite the expenditure of some twelve thousand tons of munitions—over twenty-eight thousand smart bombs, dumb bombs, and cruise missiles—NATO inflicted relatively few noncombatant casualties. Although errant NATO weapons killed an estimated five hundred civilians and injured another nine hundred, by historical standards these were remarkably small numbers. More astonishing still, the campaign ended without the United States or its allies suffering a single combat fatality.[47]

As measured by numbers of aircraft deployed and weapons delivered, the American contribution to this effort was immense. In all, the U.S. flew two-thirds of all sorties and dropped 83 percent of the munitions. Less visible but arguably even more crucial was the American role in choreographing intelligence collection, targeting, and tasking. Without U.S. participation, NATO could not have sustained and would not have undertaken an operation on the scale of Allied Force. Yet even without NATO, the U.S. military alone could have replicated Allied Force and would probably have done so more efficiently.

So General Clark's characterization of Allied Force as "the most precise and error-free campaign ever conducted" does not lack for merit.[48] Yet even if arguably correct, with the lion's share of the credit going to the United States, his assertion mistakes tactical measures of success for actual victory. This is bit like evaluating Operation Desert Storm based on battlefield exchange ratios while ignoring all the snags that followed once the fighting ended.

In sum, Allied Force offered compelling evidence to suggest that senior U.S. military officers—even supposedly bright ones—were strategically challenged. Although as the designated fall guy Clark found himself soon eased into retirement, recognition of the deficiencies inherent in his conduct of war escaped broader attention. Yet in the campaigns just ahead, those deficiencies reappeared with troubling regularity. In Afghanistan, Iraq, Libya, and elsewhere, U.S. forces continued to post impressive numbers, much as they had in Kosovo and Bosnia. But the generalship required to translate numbers into something approximating permanent and categorical success would prove elusive. By then, of course, Clark was long gone. Yet the flawed approach to wartime command that he represented remained. Operational virtuosity continued to offer a poor substitute for strategic wisdom.

This brings us to the second weakness displayed by Allied Force: the conviction that employing U.S. military power to export universal—that is, Western liberal—values will reduce the incidence of violence globally and holds the best and perhaps only hope for ultimately creating a peaceful world. However imperfectly, this conviction, deeply embedded in the American collective psyche, provides one of the connecting threads making the ongoing War for the Greater Middle East something more than a collection of disparate and geographically scattered skirmishes.

In the Balkans, the United States, along with its allies, subjected this proposition to a very specific test. In Bosnia and Kosovo alike, underlying ideological issues were at stake. In both places, the forces of retrograde sectarianism vied with and were seeking to crush the possibility of secular multiculturalism. Serb nationalists like Milošević represented the former and therefore deserved punishment. Bosnians and Kosovars ostensibly represented the latter and merited protection. By clinging to antipathies, grudges, and resentments traceable back to the heyday of Christendom, the Serbs became, in the eyes of enlightened Westerners, "them." By wearing their Islamic identity lightly, Bosnians and Kosovars became part of "us."

Underpinning this moral drama were unstated assumptions about the proper role of religion in modern life. In the United States and throughout most of the West, the reigning conception of universal values marginalizes faith. In present-day America, individual readers of the Hebrew Bible, the New Testament, or the Qur'an are at liberty to believe that they are encountering the word of God. That such encounters should provide the basis for societal relationships or political arrangements, however, is another thing altogether. In all such matters, real authority derives from sources to which God is not privy.

Yet outside the West, the superiority of cosmopolitan secularism as a basis for organizing societies is not necessarily self-evident. There, imposing on others the West's multifaceted, ever-evolving rights agenda—universal by no means implying fixed or permanent—is as likely to inflame resistance as to foster harmony. In many (although not all) quarters of the Islamic world, values that the West asserts are universal appear empty at best and blasphemous at worst. Even in the Balkans, with Muslims the putative beneficiaries of the West's insistence that universal rights should transcend identity, this proved to be the case.

Here we encounter the Islamic dimension of the war over Kosovo. Although policymakers like Albright and military commanders like Clark regarded the Muslim identity of the Kosovars as incidental, religion was by no means irrelevant to the issue at hand. On the contrary, for observers outside of the West, such considerations loomed large. Much as the government of Israel views attacks on Jews anywhere in the world as matters of Israeli concern, so too many Muslims viewed Serb persecution of Kosovars as an assault on their own. Islamic fundamentalists meeting in London compared the plight of the Kosovars to that of Palestinians forced to flee their homes in 1948. "The massacres perpetrated against Muslims in Afghanistan, Lebanon, Palestine, Albania, and Kosovo" were all part of the same phenomenon. Despite their benign pretensions, organizations such as NATO were directly implicated in orchestrating anti-Muslim violence. Preventing such violence required "the establishment of an Islamic caliphate," which defined "the primary central issue for Muslims all over the world."[49]

Predominantly Muslim nations that had rallied to support Bosnians in their time of trial now competed with one another to assist the Kosovars, with the KLA the ultimate beneficiary. The Saudi government provided millions of dollars of relief supplies to aid the refugees who had fled Kosovo.[50] For its part, Iran had covertly supplied the KLA with funds and arms.[51] Israeli foreign minister Ariel Sharon went so far as to charge Iran with fostering the emergence of an Islamic state in Kosovo.[52] Americans might be insufficiently attuned to Kosovo's relevance to developments elsewhere in the Greater Middle East, but the ever-alert Sharon was not.

No doubt Sharon's worries on that score, stemming from a self-serving Israeli perspective, were overstated. Yet anyone inclined to dismiss such concerns out of hand should consider the fate suffered by the

Serbs who had inhabited Kosovo, some of them for generations, now, in the wake of Allied Force, expelled as ethnic and religious undesirables even as U.S. troops stood by, mutely bearing witness.

As in Bosnia, the proponents of U.S. intervention in Kosovo misconstrued the issue at hand. Military action on behalf of persecuted Muslims in these instances was not going to earn gratitude elsewhere in the Islamic world. The humane and enlightened Professor Ajami might subsequently find it a "mystery" that "no Arab or Muslim leader [had] given the United States thanks or credit for taking military risks on behalf of two Muslim populations in Europe," that America's "good deeds" in Bosnia and Kosovo were somehow "never factored in."[53] But the mystery was a product of Ajami's own wishful thinking, informed by expectations that others would ultimately choose to adhere to the worldview to which he himself subscribed. This failing was by no means confined to Ajami. In American political circles, it runs rampant.

Today, years after NATO came to their rescue, a steady stream of Bosnians and Kosovars leave their homeland and head off toward Syria and Iraq, where they enlist as fighters in the ongoing anti-American, anti-Western jihad.[54] By waging war on behalf of an entirely different set of universal values, these jihadists render a belated verdict on Operations Determined Force and Allied Force. In both cases, appearances of success have proven illusory.

11

PHONY WAR

ALMOST AS AN AFTERTHOUGHT, THE CLINTON ADMINISTRATION initiated a campaign of sorts against Osama bin Laden and Al Qaeda. Like the War for the Greater Middle East as a whole to this point, this campaign was, by any measure, ineffectual. Apart from a vague expectation that projecting sternness might possibly weaken Al Qaeda or give bin Laden pause, it possessed little by way of a sense of direction and less still of a sense of urgency. Not quite certain about what it ought to do, the administration made a show of doing *something*, lest it stand accused of doing nothing. However unwittingly, those charged with formulating U.S. policy gave bin Laden further reason to think that the Americans might not be any tougher than the Soviets had been.

Wealthy son of a Saudi tycoon and something of a popular hero due to his exploits in Afghanistan, bin Laden spent the 1990s struggling to hone Al Qaeda into an instrument of jihad. In that regard, he made no effort to conceal his intentions. A rambling, prolix manifesto penned in 1996 described bin Laden's grievances and outlined his vision. His central complaint was that "the people of Islam had suffered from aggression, iniquity and injustice" at the hands of a "Zionist-Crusader alliance." As a consequence, throughout the Greater Middle East, Muslim "blood became the cheapest and their wealth as loot in the hands of the enemies." In the face of "massacres that send shivers in the body and shake the conscience," the world had done nothing. Armed struggle had therefore become imperative, with an immediate objective of expelling U.S. forces from Saudi Arabia, where they protected an "oppressive and illegitimate" royal family. Apart from belief in Allah, bin Laden wrote, "there is no more important duty than pushing the American enemy out of the holy land."[1]

Two years later, from his sanctuary in Afghanistan, bin Laden added a coda. Ever since Operation Desert Storm, he charged, the United States had been "occupying the lands of Islam in the holiest of places, the Arabian Peninsula, plundering its riches, dictating to its rulers, humiliating its people, terrorizing its neighbors, and turning its bases in the Peninsula into a spearhead through which to fight the neighboring Muslim peoples." To put an end to this intolerable situation, bin Laden now declared it "an individual duty for every Muslim" to kill Americans, soldiers and civilians alike. Evicting foreign armies from "all the lands of Islam" and liberating Muslim holy sites in Mecca and Jerusalem required and justified violence.[2]

These were not secret communiqués but public pronouncements. The challenge for U.S. officials was to decide whether to treat bin Laden's fatwas as the ravings of a madman or as a serious plan of action. After 9/11, the answer appeared self-evident. Yet when these documents first appeared, things were less clear.

Although bin Laden had declared war on the United States, his approach to waging that war took the form of occasional hit-and-run attacks. While hardly trivial, al Qaeda's demonstrated capabilities during the 1990s did not match its leader's grandiose intentions.

Moreover, not every terrorist attack conducted by Al Qaeda targeted Americans, and not every terrorist attack targeting Americans was attributable to Al Qaeda. As the 1990s unfolded, other names on the list of American enemies in the Greater Middle East took precedence. When Bill Clinton became president in 1993, the United States was effectively "at war" with Saddam Hussein and would soon find itself "at war" with Mohamed Farrah Aidid and Slobodan Milošević. It took his administration several years to conclude that the United States was also "at war" with bin Laden.

The Al Qaeda leader himself entertained no doubts in that regard. Moreover, bin Laden detected a pattern in U.S. military actions in Iraq,

Somalia, the Balkans, and elsewhere. The United States, he believed, was intent on dominating the region outright. In truth, as President Clinton deepened U.S. military involvement in the region, he (like his immediate predecessors) never devised anything remotely approximating an actual strategy. Prevailing assumptions about U.S. military supremacy and history's direction seemingly made strategy—which implies establishing priorities, making choices, and matching means to ends—unnecessary.

So as bin Laden's war against the United States unfolded in fits and starts, it took a while for senior officials in Washington to take notice. It took longer still for them to respond. And when that response finally materialized, it amounted to little more than a poorly aimed kick in the shins.

The first known Al Qaeda attempt to kill Americans occurred in December 1992 in Yemen. Bombs detonated outside of two hotels in the Yemeni city of Aden used to billet U.S. troops in transit to Somalia. The attack misfired, causing few casualties, none of them Americans.[3] Occurring in the interval between a U.S. election and the inauguration of a new president, the episode attracted little attention.

The second attack achieved greater success and attracted slightly greater notice. On February 26, 1993, terrorists detonated an explosives-laden van in the parking garage underneath New York's World Trade Center, killing six, injuring a thousand, and causing over $500 million in damages. President Clinton, barely a month in office, used part of his weekly radio address—its main theme was economic policy—to promise federal assistance to state and local authorities investigating the incident. Americans needed to feel "safe in their streets, their offices, and their homes," the president said. "Feeling safe is an essential part of being secure, and that's important to all of us."[4]

The next day Air Force One flew Clinton to Newark for a previously scheduled appearance. Telling reporters that Americans should not "overreact to this at this time," the president chose not to visit the site of the bombing just across the Hudson.[5] Nor did he speculate as to the motives or identity of the perpetrators, who in a statement released to the press identified themselves as members of "the fifth battalion in the Liberation Army."[6] In fact, there was no Liberation Army. The first bombing of the World Trade Center was the handiwork of a small jihadist cell based in the New York metropolitan area.

After a considerable interval, a pair of attacks in Saudi Arabia itself followed. In November 1995, a car bomb blew up outside of a building in Riyadh where Americans trained members of the Saudi Arabian National Guard (SANG), the monarchy's internal security force. Five Americans were killed. The Saudi government arrested, interrogated, and quickly executed four suspects without allowing U.S. investigators to question them.[7]

In June of the following year, another vehicular bomb, this time in Dhahran, ripped apart the Khobar Towers apartment building housing the 4404th Wing (Provisional), the U.S. Air Force unit supporting Operation Southern Watch. Nineteen Americans died, and another 372 were injured by the blast. Less than fully cooperative Saudi authorities steered a team of U.S. investigators led by FBI Director Louis Freeh to the conclusion that Hezbollah, acting on Iran's behalf, had organized the attack. In fact, all of those involved in the attack were Saudis.[8] The Pentagon held the American commander on the scene, Brigadier General Terry Schwalier, responsible for lapses in security and subsequently relocated U.S. forces in Saudi Arabia to more remote and presumably safer locations.[9] Apart from predictable scapegoating and second-guessing by members of Congress, this defined the extent of any response.

Viewing these events from a post–September 2001 vantage point creates a strong urge to see them as unheeded warnings of what lay ahead. And, indeed, in each case, wisps of evidence did hint at bin Laden's possible involvement. So at least some U.S. officials probing the incident at Aden had suspected.[10] From what we now know, an Al Qaeda precursor known as Maktab al-Khidamat, co-founded by bin Laden, probably helped fund the first attack on the World Trade Center. And *after* 9/11, some senior U.S. officials saw bin Laden's hand in the SANG and Khobar Towers incidents. In 2007, for example, William Perry, secretary of defense at the time of the Khobar Towers bombing, recanted his previous views, opining that the attack "was probably masterminded by Osama bin Laden."[11]

At the time, however, bin Laden's involvement in these events was not self-evident. Only with the next major episode, the simultaneous bombing of the U.S. embassies in Kenya and Tanzania on August 7, 1998, did the Al Qaeda leader start garnering serious attention.[12]

The embassy attacks, executed precisely eight years after U.S. forces had first begun arriving in Saudi Arabia, were carefully planned and devastatingly effective. In each case, a truck packed with explosives produced massive structural damage of the intended target. In Nairobi, the attack killed 227, including twelve Americans, and injured several thousand others, the great majority of them Kenyan bystanders. In Dar es Salaam, ten embassy employees, none of them Americans, were killed, and several dozen others were wounded.

Within twenty-four hours, President Clinton took to the airwaves to explain what had occurred. "Americans are targets of terrorism," he said, "because we have unique leadership responsibilities in the world, because we act to advance peace and democracy, and because we stand united against terrorism." The statement was at best incomplete and at worst misleading, designed not to inform but to reassure and thereby to conceal. The smoldering U.S. embassies in Kenya and Tanzania heralded a problem whose complexity—historical, ideological, and religious—the president was not prepared to acknowledge. In place of elucidation, he offered resolve, promising to "continue to take the fight to terrorists."[13] How or against whom the United States was going to fight went unspecified.

In fact, with U.S. intelligence agencies quickly fingering bin Laden as responsible—CIA director George Tenet characterized the evidence as a "slam dunk"—Clinton opted for direct but limited military retaliation.[14] In effect, the scope of America's War for the Greater Middle East was now widening to include Al Qaeda.

Among the distinguishing characteristics of this new adversary, one in particular stood out: It was not a state but a movement. As such, it transcended place. Even so, to initiate their campaign against Al Qaeda, U.S. officials decided on a missile attack targeting a small set of fixed facilities.

Alternatives existed—the employment of piloted aircraft, the commitment of ground troops on a large scale, or a raid by special operations forces—but upon examination they all presented difficulties: longer timelines, the risk of U.S. casualties, the possibility of domestic political opposition. General Shelton, representing the views of the unenthusiastic Joint Chiefs, emphasized those potential difficulties. By comparison, a standoff attack employing ship-launched missiles appeared straightforward and comparatively easy.[15]

On the night of August 20, naval forces under the direction of Marine General Anthony Zinni, now commanding CENTCOM, fired the first salvos in the U.S. military campaign against Al Qaeda. This was Operation Infinite Reach, which despite the grand name was for all practical purposes an El Dorado Canyon do-over.

In the Arabian Sea, several surface ships and a submarine unleashed approximately seventy Tomahawk cruise missiles aimed at an Al Qaeda training camp in Afghanistan. In the Red Sea, two other U.S. Navy surface combatants launched thirteen Tomahawks at a pharmaceutical factory located near the Sudanese capital of Khartoum, where bin Laden himself had lived for a time before decamping to Afghanistan. U.S. intelligence officials like Tenet believed that Al Qaeda leaders, possibly including bin Laden, had convened for a meeting at the camp, located at Khost, southeast of the Afghan capital of Kabul and near the Pakistani border. They also believed that the Al-Shifa pharmaceutical plant, which had opened for business in Khartoum just the year before, was producing chemicals that could be used to manufacture deadly nerve agents likely to end up in Al Qaeda's hands.

On both counts, however, the intelligence proved faulty. The missiles did hit their targets. And needless to say, the U.S. forces involved suffered no losses—no Americans were ever in danger. But by any other standard, Infinite Reach must rate as a disappointment. It was simultaneously flawless and deeply flawed, a well-executed but largely point-less expenditure of high-tech weaponry.

At Khost, the Al Qaeda leadership escaped unscathed. To inflict max-imum casualties, the Tomahawks scattered cluster munitions across the target area, killing a few dozen Al Qaeda foot soldiers along with offi-cers from the Pakistani Inter-Services Intelligence (ISI) present at the scene.[16] But bin Laden was nowhere near the camp, nor were any of his chief lieutenants. Secretary of Defense William Cohen described the Khost facility as "Terrorist University."[17] If it was, then classes had ad-journed and the faculty was nowhere near campus when the missiles made impact. As General Zinni acknowledged, the attack "did not actu-ally do much damage."[18]

Cohen later remarked that the purpose of Infinite Reach was to "send a signal that the United States was coming and was not going to tolerate terrorist activity against America."[19] The signal, if interpreted as such, neither impressed nor intimidated the Al Qaeda leadership.

At Khartoum, meanwhile, Tomahawks demolished the Al-Shifa plant, killing a night watchman and badly injuring a bystander.[20] Yet a subsequent investigation conducted by American scientists cast serious doubts on U.S. claims of the plant being used for nefarious purposes.[21] One thing only appeared certain: The wrecked facility was never going to produce the badly needed antibiotics and antimalarial drugs for which it had been designed.

Back in Washington, senior U.S. officials portrayed the operation as an opening gambit rather than as a decisive stroke. Asked if more at-tacks were to come, Secretary Cohen assured reporters that "we have contingency plans that we are developing, and there may be more in the future." Secretary of State Albright wanted Americans to under-stand that "we are involved here in a long-term struggle," which she described as "the war of the future." But it was a war bereft of mean-ingful context. Albright denounced those "who believe that taking down innocent people is some form of political expression. It is not any form of political expression. . . . It is murder, plain and simple."[22] The characterization staked a moral claim but offered little insight into what waging such a war was likely to require.

From being largely oblivious to bin Laden, the American security apparatus now went to the other extreme, seeing him as the master-mind of a plot with existential implications. Within the Clinton administration, "getting" bin Laden—and thereby presumably leaving Al Qaeda leaderless—became a matter of feverish concern.[23]

This reaction proved deeply problematic. In categorizing the threat posed by Al Qaeda as somehow distinct from other developments already occasioning U.S. intervention in the Islamic world, the United States was committing a fundamental error, exaggerating the danger bin Laden's organization posed even while simultaneously ignoring the circumstances that had produced it. Once again, U.S. policymakers were mistaking symptom (terrorism) for disease (profound political and social dysfunction exacerbated by ill-advised U.S. policies).

It was the equivalent of the British government after the Boston Tea Party fancying that Sam Adams and the Sons of Liberty defined the challenge to the Crown's authority throughout its North American colonies. To imagine that capturing Adams and crushing a gang of rabble-rousing Bostonians would set things right was to indulge in a vast illusion. As in the mid-1770s, so too in the late 1990s: If the "war of the future" was at hand, the world's reigning superpower was utterly clueless about what it was getting into.

On the home front, Infinite Reach evoked little popular support. Critics disgusted with President Clinton's personal misconduct charged him with trying to distract attention from the Lewinsky affair.[24] More hawkish types complained that Infinite Reach didn't go far enough. Reach was one thing, effects were another. They pressed for more robust action. While supporting the attacks on Afghanistan and Sudan, *Washington Post* foreign policy columnist Jim Hoagland detected "troubling signs" that Clinton had once more decided to "stage a pinprick attack [and] announce the problem solved." For Hoagland, once was not enough. "It is hard to believe," he complained, "that one night of attacks has exhausted what Clinton could and should do to stop bin Laden's bloody extremism."[25] Writing in *The Wall Street Journal*, the journalist Max Boot concurred. It was incumbent upon the United States as "the world's policeman" to escalate. Boot called on President Clinton to keep his promise "that recent cruise missile strikes in Sudan and Afghanistan are only the opening salvos in the U.S. campaign against terrorism."[26] For *The New Republic*, killing bin Laden himself had now emerged as a top priority. Its editors wanted the United States to set aside any qualms about assassination. In its "war on terrorism," the United States needed greater "tactical flexibility."[27] Reuel Marc Gerecht, former CIA operative turned foreign policy analyst, went a step further. Americans needed to get over their "civilized desire to minimize the body count," he wrote. Eliminate bin Laden, he promised, and "we will seriously undermine his entire network."[28]

So in America's War for the Greater Middle East, the African embassy attacks served as an important accelerant, reinforcing unhelpful policy inclinations. Rather than prompting a reexamination of first-order assumptions, adding Al Qaeda to Washington's list of antagonists reaffirmed the conviction that military action somehow offered a way to solve the problem.[29] Policy formulation was becoming indistinguishable from targeting.

In fact, Infinite Reach did not become a launching pad for a sustained campaign against Al Qaeda. Even with the CIA now conducting reconnaissance flights over Afghanistan using Predator unmanned aerial vehicles (UAVs), viable targets based on hard intelligence proved hard to come by. Skeptics raised questions about cost-effectiveness. "So we spend millions of dollars' worth of cruise missiles and bombs blowing up a buck fifty's worth of jungle gyms and mud huts again?"[30] The diplomatic pain-to-gain ratio also demanded consideration. U.S. missiles had violated Pakistani airspace en route to their targets in Afghanistan, a reminder that unilateral military action almost inevitably meant annoying some American ally. And as always, the uniformed military's appetite for risk remained low.[31] So although the impulse to have another go at bin Laden produced more than a dozen "specific, detailed, fleshed-out" plans and brought the Clinton administration to the brink of action on multiple occasions, the president never pulled the trigger.[32]

In effect, the United States had impulsively and foolishly responded to bin Laden's declaration of war with a de facto declaration of its own, conferring on Al Qaeda a status it did not deserve. The Clinton administration then compounded the error by refraining from acting on its declaration. Not unlike British and French policy in the fateful winter of 1939–1940, the result, on the American side at least, was a phony war.

The fumbling American response allowed bin Laden to land the next blow. This occurred on October 12, 2000, when the USS *Cole* joined *Stark* and *Samuel B. Roberts* on the list of collateral casualties sustained by the U.S. Navy during America's War for the Greater Middle East.[33]

A guided-missile destroyer that had just transited the Suez Canal and the Red Sea en route to the Persian Gulf, the *Cole* had paused at Aden for a brief "gas-and-go" stop. Shortly after 11:00 A.M., with refueling and other replenishment efforts underway, a small white boat containing two unidentified individuals approached. Crewmen on the *Cole* mistook the craft for a garbage scow, arriving to complete trash removal operations. As the boat neared the destroyer's port side, the two individuals waved and then proceeded to detonate a bomb that ripped open the *Cole*'s hull just above the water line. Engineering spaces flooded with water. Electrical systems failed. Passageways filled with smoke. Seventeen American sailors were killed outright, with another three dozen wounded. Not since World War II had an American warship been lost to enemy action. In an instant, the *Cole* seemed likely to bring that streak to an end.

Valiant efforts by *Cole*'s captain, Commander Kirk Lippold, and his crew of nearly three hundred (including forty-four women), prevented the crippled destroyer from sinking. To save their ship, sailors worked past the point of exhaustion in horrific conditions—temperatures reached 113 degrees Fahrenheit in the shade and 130 below deck. Only after three days of backbreaking labor did they succeed in stabilizing the vessel.[34] Theirs was a heroic achievement that stood in sharp contrast to the muddled policies that sent American warships to places like Aden in the first place.

As usual, those responsible for formulating such policies, both in Washington and at CENTCOM headquarters, got off scot-free. When the arrow of accountability stopped spinning, it once more pointed directly at the commander on the scene. Investigators found that "the ship did not fully protect itself from attack because it lacked deliberate planning and execution of an approved Force Protection Plan." Of the sixty-two required force protection measures, *Cole*'s captain had waived nineteen and failed to accomplish twelve others, several of which "may have prevented the suicide boat attack or mitigated its effects."[35] These findings cost Lippold his career.[36]

In the U.S. military, every operation, large or small, gets a name. For the *Cole* recovery effort, CENTCOM settled on Determined Response. What actually ensued, apart from removing the ship from the scene, more closely approximated Muted Response or even No Response at All.

The *Cole* had visited Aden not only because it needed fuel but also because such port calls formed part of a larger policy of "engagement," stemming from the belief that periodic appearances by U.S. forces in unsettled quarters served to soothe or encourage. According to the Pentagon, engagement meant "helping to shape the international environment . . . to bring about a more peaceful and stable world."[37] In U.S. national security circles, the conviction that engagement promotes peace and stability is not unlike the Christian belief in the Second Coming—it provides the ultimate rationale for the entire enterprise.

According to this logic, that Yemen was anything but peaceful and stable made it ripe for "engagement." Through a program of activities of which the *Cole*'s visit offered but one example, CENTCOM's General Zinni had hoped to keep that country "from becoming another Afghanistan."[38] No one was so naïve to think that any particular action or event was going to have a decisive impact. Yet the expectation that the cumulative effects of engagement would be transformative reflected its own sort of naïveté, to which U.S. officers remained willfully oblivious. So rather than discrediting the concept of engagement, incidents such as the attack on the *Cole* demonstrated the imperative of doubling down. General Tommy Franks, who succeeded Zinni as CENTCOM commander the month before, stated the matter plainly. "Terrorists have declared war on us. We shouldn't back away," he remarked. "I will never recommend disengagement."[39]

For some within the White House, however, the attack on the *Cole* suggested the need for something more than engagement. With U.S. intelligence agencies determining that Al Qaeda had orchestrated the incident, staff members of the National Security Council quickly drafted a multifaceted campaign, "three to five years" in duration, to "roll back" bin Laden's network "to a point where it will no longer pose a serious threat." The plan tagged by name nine other terrorist organizations as parts of that network, even while emphasizing that the actual problem was bigger still. With a presence throughout the West, Al Qaeda itself was operating on a "global basis."

Yet the proposed rollback campaign was anything but global. It focused on Afghanistan, bin Laden's principal base at the time. Key provisions of the plan included providing covert assistance to the local anti-Taliban resistance along with "overt U.S. military action" to destroy Al Qaeda "command/control and infrastructure and Taliban military and command assets." The plan did not speculate on the scope of the military effort required. It did not consider costs or second-order consequences, despite acknowledging that Al Qaeda itself was "as an outgrowth of the international jihad against the Soviet Union in Afghanistan."[40] The previous effort to harness jihadists had produced some unexpected and unintended results. Even so, some within the Clinton White House were keen to give it another go.

In comparison with the thinking behind other U.S. military interventions in the Islamic world undertaken during the previous two decades, this qualified as a bold proposal. Rather than promising quick results, rollback posited the need for sustained action. Rather than a time horizon measured in days or weeks, it assumed that eliminating Al Qaeda would require years of effort.

Even so, we may doubt whether any such campaign would ever have achieved genuinely decisive results. After all, destroying Al Qaeda in Afghanistan would leave intact the conditions giving rise to anti-American jihadism in the first place. But the question of whether or not rollback would have worked is moot: The proposal never made it past the memo stage. In his administration's waning moments, President Clinton had no appetite for opening up a new fighting front. Once the November 2000 election pitting Vice President Al Gore against Texas governor George W. Bush failed to produce a clear winner, mounting a major military campaign against Al Qaeda was out of the question. With the entire country fixated by the recount of the Florida balloting, the attack on the *Cole* went unanswered. When the Supreme Court effectively declared Bush the victor, the phony war begun by Clinton gained a second life.

PART III

MAIN CARD

12

CHANGING THE WAY

THEY LIVE

EVERY NEW ADMINISTRATION ARRIVES IN OFFICE BEARING ITS own foreign policy vision, which rarely survives the encounter with actual events. The vision of the new Bush administration, which came to power on January 20, 2001, was more ambitious and more concrete than most. It derived from specific convictions that President Clinton had willfully disregarded. Chief among those convictions was a belief in military assertiveness as the foundation of American global leadership. For the United States to fulfill its providentially assigned role as history's indispensable nation, possessing and wielding supreme military power formed a sine qua non. Bush's secretary of defense believed that Clinton had given the impression that the United States was "gun-shy" and "risk averse."[1] The Bush team was intent on changing that.

That said, the new president himself, like his predecessor, had acquired little relevant experience prior to assuming his responsibilities as the nation's commander in chief. When it came to national security, he was a novice. So, again like his predecessor, George W. Bush compensated for that inexperience by surrounding himself with seasoned subordinates, known commodities whose very appointment signaled administration intentions.

For our purposes, three appointments in particular stand out. As his running mate, Bush had selected former defense secretary Dick Cheney, now vice president. To preside over the Pentagon, he appointed Donald

Rumsfeld, himself a former defense secretary known to be close to Cheney. As Rumsfeld's deputy, he chose Paul Wolfowitz, a key Cheney lieutenant during the administration of the elder Bush who in Washington circles had by now acquired a reputation for being a broad-gauged thinker.

Although Cheney, Rumsfeld, and Wolfowitz did not see eye to eye on everything, all three subscribed to this proposition: For those with the wit and will to tap its potential, military power is eminently usable. When America's War for the Greater Middle East kicked into high gear—a development that neither Bush nor any of his chief subordinates had anticipated—these three officials seized the opportunity to put that proposition to the test. In doing so they left an indelible mark on U.S. policy. Unfortunately, their achievements proved negligible, their blunders monumental and enduring.

The events of September 11, 2001, occurred on the 234th day of George W. Bush's presidency. Little of what happened on Bush's watch prior to that date merits our attention. Up to that point, the War for the Greater Middle East had continued on autopilot. American warplanes patrolling the northern and southern no-fly zones kept up their occasional bombing of Iraqi targets. The Clinton administration's "dual containment" of both Iraq and Iran remained in effect. While not ignoring bin Laden, Bush's national security team moved with great deliberation as it assessed how to deal with him.[2] Deliberation in this case implied inaction. Al Qaeda ranked as one problem among many. Of somewhat more pressing concern than Fidel Castro's Cuba, it trailed behind the urgent need to field ballistic missile defenses and respond to the strategic challenge posed by the People's Republic of China.

As far as the Greater Middle East was concerned, the Israeli-Palestinian conflict defined the principal point of discontinuity between the outgoing and incoming administrations. President Bush made clear his lack of interest in replicating his predecessor's enthusiasm for trying to settle that dispute. On his watch, brokering peace in the Middle East did not qualify as a priority. As to the larger constellation of problems that had induced one U.S. intervention after another in various quarters of the Islamic world, they received no consideration whatsoever. The new team of old hands had neither the time nor the inclination for any fresh thinking. They arrived knowing everything they needed to know.

They just didn't know enough to avert a horrific attack on the World Trade Center and the Pentagon that killed several thousand innocents and caused an estimated $178 billion in physical damage and lost economic activity.[3]

Success in any surreptitious undertaking, be it bank heist or terrorist attack, requires careful planning, audacious implementation, and a fair dose of plain luck. It also requires a permissive environment, with flimsy defenses and guards asleep at their posts. Although observers may differ over the relative proportions, all of these factors were present on 9/11.

That nineteen young men armed with nothing more than box cutters should so easily hijack four commercial airliners and convert them into devastatingly lethal missiles shook Americans to their core. A people accustomed to taking their own collective safety as a given now experienced a sense of naked vulnerability.

No historical antecedent existed to provide an adequate reference point. Reflexive comparisons to Pearl Harbor did not hold up. In December 1941, Americans had learned about the Japanese attack by tuning in to radio bulletins broadcast after the assault itself had ended. In September 2001, they watched with horror events as they actually unfolded. They witnessed people leaping to their deaths. They saw buildings burn and collapse. For those living in Manhattan or Washington, D.C., the experience overwhelmed the senses. They could taste and smell the destruction.

In the performance of their most fundamental mission—defending the homeland—the Bush administration and the world's largest and ostensibly most sophisticated national security apparatus failed utterly. Yet curiously, in the wake of that failure, not one U.S. official of any rank lost his or her job. No one was reprimanded or demoted. Rallying around the flag and getting on with the business at hand took precedence over fixing accountability.

Was it fair after December 1941 to single out Admiral Husband Kimmel and Lieutenant General Walter Short as personally responsible for the disaster at Pearl Harbor? Probably not. Yet firing these two senior officers and reducing them in rank served at least to acknowledge that an unacceptable failure of leadership had occurred. From the outset of America's War for the Greater Middle East, the cabinet secretaries and four-star military officers charged with formulating and implementing national security policy had remained largely exempt from accountability—the arbitrary firing of defense secretary Aspin after Mogadishu being the exception that proved the rule. Remarkably, that practice survived the events of 9/11. So those who failed to anticipate or prevent the worst ever direct attack on American soil stayed on the job, if anything accruing even greater authority as the officials to whom the public now turned to "keep America safe."

It fell to President Bush himself to explain what had happened, what it meant, and how he would ensure that nothing similar could ever befall Americans again.

In a series of now iconic statements, Bush conceded that the United States found itself engaged in a very large-scale conflict, which he misleadingly and unhelpfully characterized as a "global war on terrorism." In the presidential lexicon, terrorism was interchangeable with evil, so a war to destroy terrorism, as Bush vowed to do, necessarily became a war to destroy evil.

With that in mind, Bush chose to disregard U.S. military actions undertaken pursuant to the Carter Doctrine since 1980. The United States embarked upon the global war on terrorism with a clean slate. So although fifteen of the nineteen hijackers had been Saudis, the president showed no interest in examining the potential implications of that fact. Concern for the security and well-being of Saudi Arabia had prompted the United States to issue the Carter Doctrine in the first place. What did it signify that the perpetrators of this heinous attack came from that very country? The Bush administration treated the question as off-limits.

To place the global war on terrorism in a suitable historical perspective, the president instead described it as a successor to the wars that in collective memory had defined the *prior* century. Whatever the United States may have done militarily in the Islamic world during the previous twenty years counted for less than what it had done in Eurasia from the 1930s to the 1980s. By extension, the central issue was reassuringly familiar.

"We have seen their kind before," Bush said of America's new enemy. "They are the heirs of all the murderous ideologies of the 20th century. By sacrificing human life to serve their radical visions—by abandoning every value except the will to power—they follow in the path of fascism, and Nazism, and totalitarianism. And they will follow that path all the way, to where it ends: in history's unmarked grave of discarded lies." As with World War II and the Cold War, freedom itself was at stake and was destined once more to prevail.[4]

Coming to freedom's defense, however, was going to require wide-ranging offensive action. How specifically such a war was going to unfold was very much up for grabs. A global war on terrorism did not number among the contingencies for which the Pentagon had at hand a ready-made plan. And although the president warned Americans to expect an altogether different conflict—there were "no longer islands to conquer or beachheads to storm"—he did not spell out exactly what those differences implied.[5]

Others in his administration had already taken up the question. The term they devised to describe the enterprise offers a concise expression of their intentions. Not without reason, critics of the "global war on terrorism" have noted the absurdity of waging war against a tactic or, in Bush's preferred formulation, of waging war to eliminate evil. Yet for our purposes the instructive element of that phrase is the administration's insistence on characterizing the war as "global."

To undertake a "global war" was to remove limits on the exercise of American power. Even before 9/11, the Bush administration had chafed against any such constraints and had sought to eradicate them. With the passing of the Cold War, "deterrence is not enough," the president had declared in a speech at the National Defense University not long after entering office. With the world "less certain, less predictable," anticipatory action was becoming the order of the day.[6]

The events of 9/11 created the opportunity to act on this perceived imperative. While any war of even modest scope is fought for multiple purposes, a principal aim of the global war on terrorism was to unshackle American military power. Doing so, Bush and his principal subordinates believed, held the key to preserving the American way of life and all that it entailed. From the outset, in other words, the war's purposes looked beyond any immediate danger posed by Al Qaeda or even by the disordered condition of the Greater Middle East. By now, oil had become an afterthought. Ultimately, the war's architects were seeking to perpetuate the privileged status that most Americans take as their birthright. Doing so meant laying down a new set of rules—expanding the prerogatives exercised by the world's sole superpower and thereby extending the American Century in perpetuity.

Just a week after September 11, Rumsfeld stated the matter with admirable candor. "We have a choice," he told reporters, "either to change the way we live, which is unacceptable, or to change the way that they live, and we . . . chose the latter."[7] No member of the Pentagon press corps pressed Rumsfeld to explain who "they" (not to mention "we") were. But the implication of Rumsfeld's diktat was clear: Any state or group or entity actively supporting, inclined to support, or sympathizing with anti-American terrorism was going to have to mend its ways. Rumsfeld's very first impulse on 9/11 itself was to frame the problem in a broadest possible terms. "Need to move swiftly . . . go massive— sweep it all up, things related and not."[8] Without bothering to count heads, going massive implied an encounter with many millions of people in at least a couple of dozen countries, most if not all of them in the Islamic world.

Over the previous two decades, U.S. military involvement in those precincts had amounted to little more than dabbling. According to the Carter Doctrine, to sustain the American way of life it was incumbent upon the United States to ensure the security of the Persian Gulf and its environs. Each of the younger Bush's predecessors going back to

Carter himself had accepted this proposition, as did Bush himself. Yet to this point, each of these predecessors had shied away from engaging in large-scale, ongoing military action. America's War for the Greater Middle East had lacked seriousness. But that phase had now ended. "If the war does not significantly change the world's political map," Rumsfeld wrote President Bush that same month, "the U.S. will not achieve its aim."[9]

As a military objective, changing the way "they" live possessed a sort of Napoleonic grandeur, either noble or preposterous depending on one's point of view. Making good on such an ambitious aim, thereby redrawing the world's political map, implied a willingness to undertake comparably large exertions.

Oddly, however, the Bush administration balked at providing the wherewithal required. In terms of the stakes involved, the global war on terrorism might bear comparison with World War II or the Cold War. But it was not going to resemble those earlier conflicts in terms of national commitment. Undertaking a global war did not prompt President Bush to mobilize the nation.[10] The state would not exact new taxes or expect shared sacrifice. It would not impose conscription. Everyday existence was to continue as usual, the president charging Americans to "enjoy life the way we want it to be enjoyed."[11] The difficulty of imagining Abraham Lincoln during the siege of Fort Sumter or Franklin Roosevelt following the attack on Pearl Harbor expressing comparable sentiments speaks volumes about the Bush administration's failure to grasp the challenges waiting just ahead. From the outset, in other words, between declared ends and the means available to achieve those ends there yawned a large gap.

In the days and weeks immediately after 9/11, Americans—united in righteous anger—would have done just about anything that Bush as commander in chief asked of them. Apart from passive deference, he asked for next to nothing. While greatly enlarging the scope of America's War for the Greater Middle East, the Bush administration did not expand the role allotted to the American people. Indeed, it minimized that role, thereby establishing a relationship between state and society destined to persist for the duration of Bush's term in office and beyond. The effect was comparable to that of a prenuptial agreement—once signed, difficult if not impossible to renegotiate, especially once the romance begins to wear thin.

Two factors explain the Bush administration's decision to consign the public to the status of spectators. On the one hand, senior U.S. officials, civilian and military alike, assessed public involvement in the war as unnecessary. Properly employed, existing military capabilities would suffice to get the job done. On the other hand, they saw public involvement as inconvenient, more likely to infringe on their own freedom of action than to make any meaningful contribution to victory.

Underpinning these views was a set of expectations about how the contest ahead was going to unfold. Put simply, the capabilities inherent in the Revolution in Military Affairs, if fully exploited and effectively put to use, would determine the war's outcome. Cheney, Rumsfeld, and Wolfowitz all subscribed to the theology of the RMA, now rebranded as "transformation." Bush himself was at least a semi-believer. In that church, technology was God. Quality mattered more than quantity, agility and precision more than brute force. Modern war was a business best left to professionals. On the twenty-first-century battlefield, soldiers cut from the same cloth as those who had fought World War II or Korea or Vietnam were likely to prove a net liability.

The preliminary results achieved in the first post-9/11 military campaign affirmed such expectations. That campaign initiated a new Afghanistan War, with the United States this time playing a direct rather than covert role. The purpose of Operation Enduring Freedom (to avoid offending Muslim sensibilities, the Pentagon jettisoned the initial name Infinite Justice) was twofold: first, to destroy or at least severely weaken Al Qaeda, and second, to make clear the fate awaiting any regime providing support or sanctuary to anti-American terrorists, as the Taliban had done. Although the president's advisers briefly toyed with the notion of going after Saddam Hussein's Iraq—Wolfowitz in particular urging that course—Afghanistan's number-one ranking on the

Bush administration hit list was never seriously in doubt. The demands of vengeance alone would not permit otherwise.

The opening phase of Enduring Freedom was as daring an operation as any undertaken in the annals of U.S. military history. It was also astonishingly successful—even if that success proved incomplete, transitory, and misleading.

Mounting any sort of military campaign in Afghanistan—distant, desperately poor, landlocked, and immense—poses enormous challenges. Even so, the events of 9/11 required action sooner rather than later. Especially in Washington, patience was in short supply. Responsibility for responding to that impatience fell to the CENTCOM commander, General Tommy Franks.

In the U.S. Army, a tradition exists of very senior military officers adopting a persona. Douglas MacArthur cultivated the image of a demigod, George S. Patton a warrior, Omar Bradley a modest, self-effacing "G.I.'s general," Dwight Eisenhower a genial, avuncular, "regular guy." None of these guises was particularly authentic, but each served a purpose.

Tommy Franks came across as a good ol' boy from Texas, perhaps not as smooth as those toadies in the Pentagon but twice as savvy. This meant putting up a crude, boorish front, which Franks excelled at doing. He is, to my knowledge, the only retired general to refer in his memoirs to his fellow four-stars as "motherfuckers."[12] Unfortunately, Franks lacked the gifts to pull off the second half of his act. Imagine Stephen Colbert as a world-class buffoon, but without the incisive wit. That was Franks: a thin-skinned lout, but lacking the smarts to grasp the magnitude of the task that was now his.

Although CENTCOM's AOR included Afghanistan and prior CENTCOM operations had targeted that country, no plan for actually waging war there existed on September 11. Prodded by an impatient Rumsfeld, Franks and his staff quickly corrected that omission, hastily designing a counteroffensive targeting Al Qaeda and the Taliban, although going after the latter first.[13] With some forty-five thousand men under arms, perhaps one-quarter of them non-Afghan "foreign fighters," and a motley collection of leftover Soviet tanks and aircraft, the Taliban did not constitute an especially imposing combat force.[14] Getting to them promised to be the hard part, but getting to Al Qaeda promised to be harder still.

The CENTCOM plan relied on readily available assets—American airpower combining with anti-Taliban proxies who might respond favorably to offers of assistance, even from infidels. Or as General Franks put it, the United States "would leverage technology and the courage of the Afghans themselves to liberate their country."[15] Attributing the Soviet failure to pacify Afghanistan in the 1980s to Russian heavy-handedness, Franks proposed to take a different tack. In fact, however, this was making a virtue out of necessity. Moving large numbers of U.S. ground forces to Afghanistan would require many months of preparation. Any near-term action necessarily meant taking a "light footprint" approach.

On October 7, less than a month after 9/11, that operation began, predictably enough, with air strikes conducted in the dead of night.[16] In all things military, members of the Bush administration had sought to distinguish themselves from their immediate predecessors. Even so, the intensity of the initial assault did not differ appreciably from the start of the Kosovo campaign two years earlier. Featuring a mix of ship-launched cruise missiles, carrier-based strike aircraft, and long-range bombers operating from bases in the United States, the attack delivered blows that were more than symbolic but fell short of being significant.[17] In a humanitarian nod, two U.S. Air Force C-17 transports, flying from Ramstein AFB in Germany, dropped rations and medical supplies near areas subjected to attack. Once begun, the delivery of ordnance and relief supplies continued, albeit without decisive effect. A primitive country like Afghanistan had plenty of people needing to be fed but relatively few targets meriting attack with precision guided munitions. In short order, American warplanes were reduced to "Taliban plinking."[18] An impatient President Bush complained, "We're pounding sand."[19]

In the meantime, contingents of elite U.S. troops were gathering at a former Soviet airbase in Uzbekistan, known to the Americans as K2, to form Task Force Dagger.[20] Commanded by Colonel John Mulholland and drawn principally from the U.S. Army's 5th Special Forces Group, garrisoned at Fort Campbell, Kentucky, TF Dagger consisted of slightly more than three hundred soldiers.[21] Mulholland's mission was as clear-cut as it was daunting: to build a fire under anti-Taliban militants controlling bits of Afghanistan but thus far unable to wrest Kabul and other major Afghan cities from Taliban control. To accomplish this mission, small special operations teams were to link up with Afghan resistance forces and then, employing money, arms, and firepower as blandishments, motivate them to fight.

According to U.S. intelligence estimates, the most promising of such groups was the so-called Northern Alliance located in the Panjshir Valley northeast of the capital. The Northern Alliance qualified as an "alliance" in the same sense that the Republican Party qualifies as a "party." Like the present-day GOP, the Northern Alliance was a loose coalition of unsavory opportunists, interested chiefly in acquiring power. But the several warlords sitting atop the Northern Alliance commanded something on the order of twenty thousand fighters, most of them ethnic Uzbeks and Tajiks. That sufficed to persuade the Bush administration to pursue a marriage of convenience.[22]

On the night of October 19, two helicopters inserted the first of Mulholland's special operators into mountainous terrain with elevations reaching up to sixteen thousand feet. A handful of other teams soon followed and offered their services to anti-Taliban warlords of otherwise dubious reputation.[23] Their offer accepted, the Americans—traveling by horseback on mounts provided by their Afghan hosts—began calling in air strikes on frontline Taliban positions.[24]

With the world's most capable air forces at their beck and call, Northern Alliance commanders launched a major offensive on October 28 toward Mazar-e-Sharif, a Taliban stronghold located on the northern approaches to Kabul. The generous application of American air power fundamentally altered the correlation of forces. Suddenly, thanks to the presence of a handful of Americans wielding laser target designators, the Northern Alliance enjoyed the upper hand. On November 9, Mazar-e-Sharif fell, although intra-Afghan negotiations allowed some Taliban to escape and others to switch sides. As U.S. forces would come to appreciate, the contingent nature of allegiance made it all the more difficult to reach a fixed determination of who was friend and who foe.

These and other realities of the battlefield undermined Bush administration efforts to frame Enduring Freedom as a contest pitting white pakols against black ones. All hats—and hands—were soiled. The vicious nature of the 9/11 attacks had reinforced an American inclination, present from the very outset of its War for the Greater Middle East, to cast the United States in the role of either innocent victim or exponent of righteousness or both.[25] The course of events in Afghanistan made such claims difficult to sustain.

After a battle that ended with Taliban forces surrendering the city of Kunduz, for example, General Abdul Rashid Dostum, a senior Northern Alliance commander, ordered prisoners confined to metal shipping containers. There they remained for days, without food or water. In what became known as the Dasht-i-Leili massacre, large numbers died, estimates ranging from the hundreds to the thousands. Other prisoners were simply shot. But U.S. officials, considering General Dostum to be an exceptionally valuable asset, looked the other way. Then and later, they protected him, suppressing knowledge of the event or minimizing its significance.[26]

Even so, Mazar-e-Sharif seemingly offered concrete evidence that Enduring Freedom was now headed in the right direction. The forward momentum of the offensive continued on toward Kabul, with Taliban defenses outside the Afghan capital essentially giving way without a fight. Once again, Taliban fighters defected in large numbers. Others returned to their villages or fled toward the sanctuary of neighboring Pakistan. In less than a week, the Northern Alliance had seized Kabul itself. Almost immediately, small contingents of U.S. and allied forces arrived to take control of the former Soviet airbase at nearby Bagram.[27]

Attention now turned to Kandahar, the Taliban's spiritual home and last remaining stronghold. Southwest of that city, beginning on No-vember 25, U.S. Marines under the command of Brigadier General James Mattis occupied an abandoned airfield, soon to be known as For-ward Operating Base Rhino. This marked the most substantial commit-ment of conventional U.S. ground forces.[28] Almost imperceptibly at first, the occupation of Bagram and Rhino inaugurated a shift away from the light footprint and toward long-term presence.

Just days before, Franks had assigned army Lieutenant General Paul T. Mikolashek "to direct and synchronize land operations to de-stroy al Qaeda and prevent the reemergence of international terrorist activities" throughout Afghanistan.[29] During his tenure in command, Mikolashek failed to fulfill his mandate, a judgment equally applicable to the eight other three- and four-star generals who succeeded him over the course of the next fifteen years. With Mikolashek situating his head-quarters in far-off Kuwait, Major General Franklin "Buster" Hagen-beck, commanding general of the U.S. Army's 10th Mountain Division, arrived in theater to set up a smaller forward command post. Although Hagenbeck found himself a division commander without a division to command, the apparatus of occupation was beginning to take shape.

By November 28, Northern Alliance forces, now augmented by local Pushtun militants, had laid siege to Kandahar, with both fixed-wing air-craft and Marine attack helicopters pummeling Taliban defenders. Hamid Karzai, the Pushtun exile that Washington was positioning to become Afghanistan's new leader, negotiated a deal allowing the Tali-ban to evacuate. On December 9, escorted by U.S. special operations forces soldiers serving as his security detail, he made a triumphal entry into Kandahar.

Karzai stands in relation to the Afghanistan War as Ngo Dinh Diem stands in relation to the Vietnam War: His credentials as a nationalist untainted by corruption but with a Western orientation made him in Washington's eyes a seemingly ideal partner. In the 1950s, the Eisen-hower administration had sought to use President Diem as its agent in creating a Republic of Vietnam compatible with U.S. national security interests. In the 2000s, the Bush administration sought to use Karzai for similar purposes. Much to their subsequent consternation, U.S. military and civilian officials soon enough discovered, as they had four decades earlier with Diem, that Karzai had a mind of his own.

By now several anti-Taliban factions, too optimistically referred to as the Eastern Alliance, were advancing into the mountainous Tora Bora Valley, a short distance from the Pakistan border. This was the site of a huge cave complex believed to be the last refuge of Al Qaeda and perhaps Osama bin Laden himself. Although provided with extensive air support and reinforced by an elite U.S. hunter-killer team known as Task Force 11, the push into Tora Bora did not get very far.[30] The Eastern Alliance lacked the numbers, cohesion, and energy needed to mount anything more than a desultory offensive. With General Franks disinclined to commit U.S. forces such as the Marines situated at Rhino to block escape routes, bin Laden along with a remnant of Al Qaeda and Taliban fighters slipped into Pakistan unmolested.[31]

On December 18, Operation Enduring Freedom reached a pause that U.S. military officers along with civilian officials back in Washington mistook for victory. Twelve weeks of fighting had badly mauled the enemy without definitively defeating it. Al Qaeda and the Taliban had dispersed, but each retained an ability to reconstitute itself. Osama bin Laden and Taliban leader Mullah Omar were still at large. Much unfinished business remained.

Franks himself believed otherwise. In Kabul on December 22, while attending ceremonies marking Karzai's installation in power, the CENTCOM commander briefly toyed with the image of himself as a "proconsul" wearing "a purple-trimmed toga and a laurel wreath." In his estimation, Operation Enduring Freedom had "destroyed an army the Soviets had failed to dislodge with more than a half million men." Forces under his personal direction had "liberated twenty-five million people and unified the country."[32] This was balderdash, of course. Like Schwarzkopf at the conclusion of Desert Storm, Franks confused partial operational success with permanent mission accomplishment.

Ironically, despite all the emphasis on avoiding Soviet mistakes, Franks had managed to replicate their achievement. He had unleashed

Operation Eagle Claw, 1980: a warning from the gods? (© A. Abbas/Magnum Photos)

Marine peacekeepers depart Beirut, 1982. Not for the last time, events will mock the banner's claim. (US Marine Corps)

Marines survey the rubble, Beirut, 1983. With 241 Americans lost in a single day, Reagan pulls the plug. (SSgt Randy Gaddo/ US Marine Corps)

The Oval Office, 1983: hosting Afghan jihadists.

Rumsfeld in Baghdad, 1983:
The presidential envoy brings
greetings from Washington.
(Iraqi TV)

Operation El Dorado Canyon, 1986.
A one-off raid dings Libya;
Moamar Gaddafi will exact revenge.
(US Department of Defense)

The First Gulf War: In 1987, Saddam Hussein's air force nearly sinks the USS *Stark*, but Washington blames Iran. (US Navy)

Operation Praying Mantis, 1988. In the "largest surface action since the Second World War," U.S. forces pummel Iran's puny fleet. (US Navy)

The Second Gulf War, 1991: Advancing with controlled deliberation, VII Corps closes in on the Iraqi Republican Guard. (US Department of Defense)

Schwarzkopf delivering the "mother of all briefings," 1991: "The gates are closed." Alas, they were not. (Associated Press)

Enforcing the no-fly zones. With few taking notice, the Second Gulf War continues throughout the 1990s. (Staff Sergeant Sean M. Worrell/US Air Force)

Desert Storm homecoming parade, Washington, 1991: well-earned, but sadly premature. (US Department of Defense)

Beleaguered Iraqi Kurds flee Saddam's wrath, 1991. The victory narrative is already unraveling. (© Daniel Lainé/CORBIS)

Mogadishu, 1993: On a wrecked American helicopter,
Somali children celebrate victory. (AP Photo/Dominique Mollard)

Bosnia, 1995: The cavalry arrives to avert further bloodletting.
(US Department of Defense)

Khobar Towers, Dhahran, Saudi Arabia, 1996: Stationing U.S. troops in the Land of the Two Holy Places comes at a price. (US Department of Defense)

Operation Allied Force, 1999: Belgrade burns, and the Kosovo Liberation Army prevails.

9/11: America's War for the Greater Middle East comes home.
(Chief Photographer's Mate Eric J. Tilford/US Navy)

Operation Enduring Freedom, 2001: As Americans charge, the Taliban and Al Qaeda disperse to fight another day. (Scott Nelson/Getty Images)

The Third Gulf War: In 2003, Operation Iraqi Freedom initiates a project of epic ambition. (Gordon A. Rouse/US Marine Corps)

Baghdad, 2003: While American generals chill out, the real fight is just beginning. (Karen Ballard-Pool/Getty Images)

Abu Ghraib: The Freedom Agenda collapses.
(US Military Police Specialist Sabrina Harman)

Liberated Iraq: Snuffing out insurgency or fueling it? (AP Photo)

King David: In Iraq, his achievement was to camouflage failure.
(© Thomas Dworzak / Magnum Photos)

The Afghanistan surge, 2010: Leaflets announce NATO's imminent arrival in Marja and promise "government in a box." (US Army)

Abandoning invade-and-occupy, Washington embraces targeted assassination; not everyone approves. (epa european pressphoto agency b.v. / Alamy Stock Photo)

With AFRICOM joining the fight, U.S. trainers teach their charges new routines.
(Staff Sgt. Steve Cushman/US Marine Corps)

The rise of ISIS enmeshes the United States in a Fourth Gulf War.

upon Afghans the forces of anarchy and seemed oblivious to what the restoration of order was now likely to require. To "stabilize the country," he estimated that a contingent of some ten thousand U.S. troops "seemed about right."[33] Although that assessment soon proved wildly wrong, it illustrates his tenuous grasp of the actual situation. Notwithstanding the CENTCOM commander's self-congratulatory mood, the Afghanistan War had not ended in mid-December 2001. It had only just begun.

At least some senior officials back in Washington seemed to know better. "In some ways," Wolfowitz told an interviewer as Kandahar was about to fall, "the hardest job begins now," emphasizing that "one of the worst mistakes one can make is to leave a half-defeated enemy on the battlefield."[34] A day later, he returned to the same point. Bush and Rumsfeld had issued clear instructions "to keep our eye on the ball, and the ball is still in Afghanistan, and there's a lot of work to do there. It can be very distracting to try to do too many different things at once."[35]

But this was for public consumption. Behind the scenes, eyes and attention were shifting to a different ball. Already on November 27, Rumsfeld had issued oral orders to Franks: Start gearing up CENTCOM to invade Iraq.[36]

As interpreted at the highest levels of the Bush administration, the real significance of Enduring Freedom was that it affirmed America's unquestioned and unprecedented military supremacy. Here, Rumsfeld later wrote, "was a demonstration of the kind of defense transformation that the President envisioned—a mentality of eyes-wide-open situational awareness, can-do determination, and creative adaptability."[37] Rendered into plain English, Rumsfeld was saying that Afghanistan had rendered military orthodoxy obsolete. Big and slow were out. Lean and quick were in.

If anything, previous estimates of U.S. military capabilities now appeared to have been too modest. Wolfowitz characterized the achievements of U.S. forces in Afghanistan as "revolutionary" and "amazing." By way of historical comparison, he cited the World War II Battle of Arnhem, a defeat attributed to planners overestimating Allied capabilities and fatally committing them to "a bridge too far." Now, given "the potential that people on the ground can have for leveraging the capability of long-range air power," Wolfowitz worried, military planners were likely to err in the other direction. Lacking sufficient boldness and imagination, they were prone to producing plans that were not "a bridge too far" but "several bridges too short."[38] For Wolfowitz and other like-minded officials in the national security establishment (and for hawks generally), Enduring Freedom had demolished any need for the United States to constrain its use of force. The risks appeared manageable, the costs modest, the prospective payoff great.

The journalist Charles Krauthammer made the point with typical directness and supreme assurance. "Afghanistan demonstrated that America has both the power and the will to fight, and that when it does, it prevails," he wrote. "The demonstration effect of the Afghan war has already deeply changed the Near East. The area's leaders understand that their future lies with us, not [bin Laden]. Accordingly, they are listening to us."[39] To get people's attention, nothing worked better than throwing your weight around, an expectation animating the next phase of America's War for the Greater Middle East.

This spirit permeated President Bush's State of the Union Address delivered in January 2002. As the president made clear, his administration had already put Afghanistan in its rearview mirror. That prize was already bagged. "In four short months," he crowed, U.S. troops had "captured, arrested, and rid the world of thousands of terrorists, destroyed Afghanistan's terrorist training camps, saved a people from starvation, and freed a country from brutal oppression." Confident that more such successes lay just ahead, Bush flatly declared, "We are winning the war on terror." Yes, more work remained to be done, but not in Afghanistan. Bush vowed to turn next on what he called an "axis of evil" consisting of Iraq, Iran, and North Korea. For those regimes, but above all for Saddam Hussein's Iraq, the day of reckoning was fast approaching.[40] Unfortunately, Bush's verdict on the Afghanistan War proved premature.

Without doubt, the unconventional warriors of TF Dagger had done everything asked of them and more. Also without doubt, the Enduring Freedom air campaign qualified as a marvel of planning and execution, exceeding in precision the feats of Desert Storm and its lesser companions of the previous decade. With more than thirty thousand sorties flown, no aircraft were lost to enemy action. According to Pentagon tabulations, 75 percent of munitions expended hit their intended target, an appreciable improvement over Desert Storm in 1991 and Allied Force in 1999. Given the quantity of ordnance expended—more than twenty-two thousand bombs and missiles—noncombatant casualties were also relatively few in number. Cutting-edge technologies such as laser designators to guide bombs to their targets and UAVs that loitered high above the battlefield to provide intelligence and even launched missiles at ground targets had testified to the U.S. military's technological edge.[41] Best of all, U.S. casualties had been negligible—enough to elicit pious expressions of condolence, not enough to provoke real concern. Of twelve American fatalities, only one—a CIA operative— resulted from enemy action; an errant bomb killed three military personnel; the remaining deaths were due to non-hostile causes.[42] By any of the measures that the Pentagon relied on to assess performance, U.S. forces had shone.

Unfortunately, the measures were incomplete and to some degree beside the point. The initial stages of Enduring Freedom resembled the Tanker War of the 1980s, except on a larger scale. Given the advantages U.S. forces enjoyed in range and lethality, the enemy couldn't even return effective fire.

Those advantages derived from the fact that the Taliban had foolishly chosen to fight as a quasi-conventional force defending fixed positions near major Afghan cities.[43] Yet "defeat" freed the Taliban of any further requirement to fight conventionally. After the fall of Kandahar, they returned to their roots as a guerrilla force, thereby inaugurating a new phase of the Afghanistan War. In that new phase, destined to last years rather than weeks, the "revolutionary" and "amazing" U.S. capabilities on display during the autumn of 2001 proved less than salient.

As a consequence, the victory that President Bush and General

Franks fancied they had won proved ephemeral. A protracted war ensued, waged in a country where the United States was without vital
interests against an adversary that, however repellant, did not directly
threaten U.S. national security. The war against the Taliban became an
exercise in strategic irrelevance—as if in response to Southern secession, Abraham Lincoln had sent the Union Army to Brazil to liberate
the black multitudes held in bondage there. Cleansing Brazil of practices deemed objectionable in American eyes would have posed a
mighty challenge without offering much by way of rewards. So too
with Afghanistan.

Events on the ground almost immediately hinted at the difficulties
to come. In March 2002, U.S. combat forces in Afghanistan—numbering
no more than two thousand at the time—undertook their first significant ground offensive. The shortcomings of this operation, known as
Anaconda, laid bare the limitations of Rumsfeld's lean-and-quick approach to changing the way they live.

The site chosen for this operation was the Shah-i-kot Valley, a rugged
and inhospitable piece of terrain nestled alongside the Pakistan border south of Kabul. Intelligence reports suggested that Taliban or Al
Qaeda kingpins—"high-value targets" or HVTs, in American military
parlance—might have taken refuge there. As measured by body count
or by cities freed from Taliban control, Enduring Freedom had racked
up a series of impressive successes. As measured by HVTs permanently
taken out of circulation, it had proven something of a bust. Anaconda
was going to be a step toward fixing that.[44]

The commanders who authorized and planned Anaconda did not
anticipate serious fighting. Rather than an actual battle, they envisioned
something more like a grouse hunt. A group of several hundred ame-
nable Afghan militants guided by American handlers would enter the
Shah-i-kot to flush the enemy. Blocking forces pre-positioned to cover
the valley's several exits and occupied by U.S. infantrymen would then
do the necessary killing and capturing. From start to finish, the operation would require no more than a couple of days.

Complicating this seemingly straightforward proposition were several factors. First, weather and terrain posed larger than anticipated impediments. Second, intelligence regarding the enemy proved wildly inaccurate. Rather than an estimated 150 to 250 enemy fighters in the valley, actual enemy strength turned out to be two or three times that. Worse, rather than beaten, the enemy was well armed and full of fight. Third, the force assembled for Anaconda was a hodgepodge, made up of bits and pieces from different units, different services, and different countries thrown together without regard for whether the result constituted a workable whole. Fourth, and ultimately decisively, whether through inattention, stupidity, or ornery parochialism, those charged with signing off on Anaconda disregarded the most fundamental precepts of unity of command.

It was left to General Hagenbeck, division commander sans division, to deal with the consequences. In mid-February 2002, Hagenbeck had shifted his demi-headquarters from K2 to Bagram. Lieutenant General Mikolashek, back in Kuwait, charged Hagenbeck with planning and executing Anaconda. For that purpose, General Franks, back in Tampa, gave Hagenbeck control of all forces in Afghanistan *except* unconventional assets grouped together under the heading of Task Force 11. From Prince Sultan air base in Saudi Arabia, air force Lieutenant General T. Michael "Buzz" Moseley would coordinate air support. New to his job, Moseley paid little attention to developments brewing in Afghanistan. That he and Mikolashek reputedly did not care for one another may have exacerbated the problem. Back at Pope Air Force Base in North Carolina, meanwhile, Major General Dell Dailey, commander of U.S. Joint Special Operations Command, directed the actions of "black" units to include TF 11. CIA operatives, still active in the field and reporting up their own independent chain, collaborated with the military at times and on terms of their choosing. Whatever the benefits of this lash-up, tight coordination did not number among them. It was shades of Mogadishu all over again.

The forces provided to Hagenbeck for Anaconda made for an odd mix. In January, the Marines occupying Rhino had departed, their place taken by parts of the 3rd Brigade of the army's 101st Airborne Division,

the "Screaming Eagles." The brigade arrived with two of its three in-
fantry battalions and none of its standard complement of field artillery.
Given an ostensibly negligible threat and a persisting preoccupation
with "footprint," Franks and Rumsfeld deemed it unnecessary to provide the brigade with any significant fire support. Upon appeal, the
CENTCOM commander grudgingly approved the deployment of eight
AH-64 attack helicopters to compensate for the lack of heavy weapons.
Hagenbeck also had a single battalion from his own division. The 1st
Battalion, 87th Infantry had initially deployed to K2 as a security force
but was now reassembling at Bagram. Together, these various units
formed Task Force Rakkasan, commanded by Colonel Frank Wiercinski.[45]

Rakkasan had an indigenous counterpart, which the Americans
styled Task Force Hammer. This imposing name referred to an armed
rabble recruited by an army special forces team, sustained by CIA operatives with plenty of cash to distribute and led by Zia Lodin, son of a
reputedly influential Pushtun tribal chief. A mélange of small clandes-
tine units, some contributed by allies, but including U.S. Navy SEALs,
completed Hagenbeck's order of battle. To describe the overall product
as slapdash would be kind.

Sending infantry into combat without field artillery is like having
unprotected sex with a stranger—you had better be lucky. Luck was
not with General Hagenbeck or the troops under his command when
Operation Anaconda kicked off at night on March 2.

Almost everything that could go wrong did. Traveling by truck over
primitive, nearly impassible roads, TF Hammer made exceedingly slow
progress toward its assigned objective. An orbiting U.S. Air Force AC-
130 gunship mistakenly engaged the advancing convoy, killing one
American and three Afghans and wounding others. Hammer retreated,
regrouped, then resumed its advance, only to encounter enemy mortar
fire. With that, the task force halted and waited for the lavish application of American airpower that had been promised but now was slow
to materialize. Soon thereafter, Zia's Afghans withdrew without even

actually entering the Shah-i-kot. Half of Hagenbeck's plan had fallen apart.

Worse was to come. By his own admission, going into the operation Hagenbeck had assumed that "enemy resistance had all but collapsed" in Afghanistan.[46] As CH-47 Chinook helicopters began delivering elements of TF Rakkasan to landing zones near their assigned blocking positions, the Americans discovered otherwise. The choppers encountered intense fire that damaged one Chinook and put holes in every Apache committed to the fight. An ugly firefight at very close quarters ensued, with the Americans pinned down by small arms and mortar fire. Dozens were wounded. With artillery unavailable and helicopter gunships forced out of the battle, Rakkasan had to rely on fixed-wing air support, which again was slow in coming. Nightfall brought some respite and the welcome return of AC-130 gunships.

On March 3, the situation stabilized as units consolidated, casualties were evacuated, and reinforcements arrived. The night of March 3–4 brought more bad news, however. A CH-47 belonging to TF 160 was shot down while inserting a SEAL team high on a ridgeline called Takur Ghar. A second CH-47 carrying a quick reaction force of army rangers suffered a similar fate. Seven Americans were killed in action. Only after an intense seventeen-hour firefight were these forces finally extracted.

By this time, however, the realization that Anaconda had encountered unexpectedly stiff resistance had roused the various headquarters charged with supporting the U.S. troops fighting for their lives. A massive surge of air support from bombers of all types ensued. By March 6, the infantry fight had effectively ended. Even as elements of TF Rakkasan held their positions, air attacks now superseded action on the ground. Over the next several days, the Shah-i-kot Valley "saw the greatest number of precision munitions dropped into the smallest geographic space in the history of air warfare."[47] On March 10, now augmented by several vintage Soviet armored vehicles, a reconstituted TF Hammer finally entered the Shah-i-kot, where it encountered little of note. By now, enemy forces had either died fighting or successfully made their escape. For its part, TF Rakkasan had already begun to exfil-trate its units and was clear of the valley by March 12. Anaconda ended soon thereafter.

The Pentagon did its best to portray Anaconda as a victory. General Franks pronounced it "an unqualified and absolute success."[48] In reality, it was anything but. The operation did not net any significant HVT. It did not end the Afghanistan War. Abysmally planned and inadequately resourced—shortcomings destined to recur throughout the post-9/11 phase of America's War for the Greater Middle East—the operation had at very considerable cost cleared a piece of nondescript terrain, which U.S. forces promptly abandoned.

With few exceptions, the Americans participating in Operation Ana-conda performed their duties with stoic heroism. Yet in comparison with the extraordinarily light casualties sustained since the Afghanistan War began the previous October, U.S. troops suffered grievous losses. Sadly, these offered but a foretaste of what awaited: In the years to come, well over two thousand Americans were to die in Afghanistan, with another twenty thousand wounded.

To be sure, as they had in every conflict since at least the Korean War, U.S. forces inflicted more casualties than they had sustained. How many more was difficult to say. Just as the Americans had entered the Shah-i-kot not knowing how many enemy soldiers they were to face, they departed not knowing how many they had killed or how many had escaped to fight another day. All they had were estimates, which were in any event beside the point: Casualty ratios do not necessarily correlate with victory.

To anyone willing to assess its implications, Tora Bora and Anaconda warned that the Afghanistan War was far from over. Succumbing to its fixation with Saddam Hussein, the Bush administration chose to pre-tend otherwise. Consigned to the back burner, Afghanistan became yet another phony war, a conflict that the United States had ignited but failed to extinguish and then left to simmer.

13

KICKING DOWN
THE DOOR

WHY DID THE GEORGE W. BUSH ADMINISTRATION CHOOSE TO
invade Iraq in 2003? For our purposes, drilling down on this question is
essential for two reasons. First, doing so situates the Third Gulf War of
2003–2011 within the larger context of America's War for the Greater
Middle East. Second, appreciating what Bush actually meant to achieve
in Iraq reveals in full the magnitude of the failure that the United States
sustained there.

Of course, many answers to that question already exist. The official
one offered by the Bush administration itself and seconded by many of
the war's most ardent supporters cited the putative threat posed by
Iraqi weapons of mass destruction (WMD). Yet in reality, this was a
cover story. As Paul Wolfowitz acknowledged, WMD offered "the one
issue that everyone could agree on," implying the existence of other,
more germane motives.[1]

When the claims of this smoking gun/mushroom cloud school
turned out to lack substance, its adherents insisted that good intentions
should count more than mere veracity.[2] Rumsfeld subsequently dismissed the emphasis on WMD as "a public relations error."[3] Carping
on erroneous or falsified intelligence reports amounted to pointlessly
rehashing issues that the ongoing march of events had rendered moot.
More or less simultaneously, Bush loyalists reverted to a ready-made
fallback position. Liberating oppressed Iraqis now became the adver-

tised war aim. Pressed by a reporter to explain what had happened to the mushroom cloud hypothesis, White House press secretary Scott McClellan neatly summarized the administration's revised position. "We're not going to relitigate the reasons why we went into Iraq," he huffed. That was little history; what beckoned was Big History, in the form of "spreading freedom in the broader Middle East."[4]

Rejecting the official line, critics of Bush's War advanced a number of alternatives. When Iraq's WMDs turned out not to exist and liberating the oppressed proved unexpectedly arduous, these alternatives gained added credibility. Among the explanations floated were these: The United States invaded Iraq to "get the oil," funnel money to the military-industrial complex, provide an excuse for defunding the welfare state, remove a threat to Israel, or allow President Bush the psychic satisfaction of completing a job—deposing Saddam Hussein—his daddy had left unfinished.

Unlike the explanations offered by Bush and his minions, these alternatives had one pronounced advantage: None were self-evidently false. Indeed, each likely contained at least a morsel of truth. Yet neither separately nor in combination do they suffice, for this simple reason: They understate the magnitude of the administration's actual ambitions.

In reality, the Bush administration invaded Iraq in order to validate three precedent-setting and mutually reinforcing propositions. First, the United States was intent on establishing the efficacy of preventive war. Second, it was going to assert the prerogative, permitted to no other country, of removing regimes that Washington deemed odious. And finally, it was seeking to reverse the practice of exempting the Islamic world from neoliberal standards, demonstrating that what Condoleezza Rice called "the paradigm of progress"—democracy, limited government, market economics, and respect for human (and especially women's) rights—was as applicable to the Greater Middle East as to the rest of the world.[5] Here in concrete and specific terms was a strategy to "change the way they live."

As a venue to begin implementing this strategy, Saddam Hussein's Iraq, situated in the very core of the Greater Middle East, appeared uniquely attractive. After all, Saddam had made his country an international pariah—few outside of Saddam's own circle of toadies and dependents were going to mourn his forcible removal from the scene. The Iraqi army was not likely to pose significant opposition, having amply demonstrated its incompetence, even before taking into account the effects of periodic U.S. bombing along with a decade of crippling sanctions. That the Iraqi people were largely secular, upwardly mobile, and united in their yearning for liberation—a fanciful image nursed within the upper reaches of the Bush administration—figured as a bonus. In other words, what made it imperative to invade Iraq was not the danger it posed but the opportunity it presented.

Channeling administration thinking, the journalist Max Boot breezily summarized the argument in an October 2001 essay. "Once Afghanistan has been dealt with, the U.S. should turn its attention to Iraq," he wrote.

> It will probably not be possible to remove Hussein quickly without a U.S. invasion and occupation—though it will hardly require half a million men, since Hussein's army is much diminished since the Gulf War, and the U.S. will probably have plenty of help from Iraqis, once they trust that it intends to finish the job this time. Once Hussein is deposed, an American-led, international regency in Baghdad, to go along with the one in Kabul, should be imposed.
>
> Over the years the U.S. has earned opprobrium in the Arab world for its backing of repressive dictators such as Hosni Mubarak and the Saudi royal family. This could be the chance to right the scales, to establish the first Arab democracy, and to show the Arab people that the U.S. is as committed to freedom for them as it was for the people of Eastern Europe. To turn Iraq into a beacon of hope for the oppressed peoples of the Middle East. Now that would be a historic war aim.[6]

So whether or not Saddam actually had anything to do with 9/11 was beside the point. After all, the ultimate objective of administration strategy, a.k.a. the Freedom Agenda, was not merely to *defend* against the prospect of another 9/11 but to *remove the root causes* of anti-American terrorism in the Greater Middle East. This meant rendering the region itself congruent with American interests and American values. Saddam Hussein's Iraq offered the optimum locale for launching this lofty undertaking.

Try this thought experiment. Imagine that President Bush's famous "Mission Accomplished" speech of May 1, 2003, declaring that "major combat operations in Iraq have ended," had proven accurate; that Vice President Cheney's prediction of U.S. forces being "greeted as liberators" had held, along with Rumsfeld's projections of total war costs coming in at "something under $50 billion"; that Wolfowitz's estimate of Iraq being able to "finance its own costs of reconstruction" had panned out; and that Undersecretary of Defense Douglas Feith's promise of U.S. military action putting "Iraq on a path to become a prosperous and free country" had come to fruition.[7] Imagine, in other words, that Operation Iraqi Freedom had played out as the Bush administration had expected.

How would such an outcome have affected America's standing in the Greater Middle East? In *Leviathan,* Thomas Hobbes wrote, "What quality soever maketh a man beloved, or feared of many; or the reputation of such quality is power; because it is a means to have the assistance and service of many."[8] As applicable to the twenty-first century as to the seventeenth, this aphorism pithily captures the true rationale for Gulf War 3.0. It did not appreciably differ from the motives prompting Saddam Hussein to launch Gulf War 1.0 in 1980 or 2.0 in 1990. Although victory in Iraq might not induce much love for the United States, it would certainly translate into fear and respect. Put simply, by demonstrating the will and the capacity to deal with Iraq, the United States itself would emerge as Leviathan.[9]

General Wesley Clark tells the story of a senior officer on the Joint Staff apprising him just weeks after 9/11 of a Bush administration plan to "take out seven countries in five years," starting with Iraq and Syria and ending with Iran.[10] Absent documentary confirmation, we may question the specifics of Clark's anecdote. We should not, however,

doubt the larger thrust of administration intentions, which the anecdote accurately conveys. To "take out" several countries did not necessarily imply a succession of wars, of course. Indeed, per Hobbes, using
Iraq to illustrate the folly of resisting American power held the promise
of enabling the United States to have its way elsewhere without actually needing to employ that power.

So for all the vituperation U.S. officials heaped on Saddam Hussein,
sending him packing was never more than an interim goal. Acting strategically, Rumsfeld believed, meant doing "something that has three,
four, five moves behind it."[11] Intervention in Afghanistan did not lend
itself to next moves; intervention in Iraq, by contrast, would. As Feith,
the Pentagon's third-ranking civilian, put it, removing Saddam would
"make it easier to confront—politically, militarily, or otherwise—other
state sponsors of terrorism." By way of examples, he specifically cited
Gaddafi's Libya and Bashar al-Assad's Syria. These regimes had "a record of backing down under pressure." As such, they presented problems likely to be "solvable through coercive diplomacy rather than
through military action."[12] Vanquishing Saddam Hussein and destroying his army promised to invest American diplomacy with the power to
coerce.

In short, victory in Iraq would open the door to much else. Indeed,
the logic of the argument extended even to nominal allies such as Pakistan, Egypt, and Saudi Arabia. Each one an incubator of violent Islamism, they too were going to have to start doing things differently.
The overall scope of the Bush administration's domino plan was nothing if not vast. As one Bush administration official remarked, "The road
to the entire Middle East goes through Baghdad."[13]

Given the self-evident centrality of Iraq in this scheme, President
Bush seems never to have made an actual decision to go to war there. It
was simply a given. So the president never convened a meeting to poll
his key advisers on the question. No carefully staffed paper weighing
pros and cons ever made it into the Oval Office. With Afghanistan (assumed to be) finished, going after Iraq emerged by tacit agreement as
the obvious next step. Here was the *real* consensus, in contrast to the

artificially constructed one regarding WMD to which Wolfowitz had alluded. By early 2002 at the latest, *whether* to invade Iraq was not the question, just when and how.[14]

Laying the groundwork for war, a process that spanned the ensuing year, encompassed three major tasks. The first, which fell chiefly to the national security advisor, Condoleezza Rice, was to codify the new norms that war with Iraq was intended to validate. The second task, in which Vice President Cheney showed a keen interest, was to manage domestic opinion, refuting objections to the prospective war raised by naysayers and skeptics. The third task, over which Secretary Rumsfeld claimed ownership, was to produce a war plan guaranteed to deliver victory.[15]

The effort led by Rice yielded a text as critical to understanding America's War for the Greater Middle East as Lincoln's Gettysburg Address is to understanding the American Civil War. That text took the form of a speech delivered by President Bush at the U.S. Military Academy on June 1, 2002. In that speech, Bush made the case for preventive war.

Back in 1946, the Nuremberg Tribunal had categorically condemned preventive war. "To initiate a war of aggression," it declared, "is the supreme international crime differing only from other war crimes in that it contains within itself the accumulated evil of the whole."[16] No presidential administration since that time had dared to question this dictum.

The Bush administration was now seeking to carve out exceptions that would be exclusive to the United States. "The gravest danger to freedom," the president told the graduating West Point cadets, "lies at the perilous crossroads of radicalism and technology." This new danger rendered concepts such as deterrence and containment obsolete. To remain passive was to court disaster. "If we wait for threats to fully materialize," Bush warned, "we will have waited too long." This the United States refused to do: "We must take the battle to the enemy, disrupt his plans, and confront the worst threats before they emerge. In the world we have entered, the only path to safety is the path of action. And this nation will act."

Confronting threats "before they emerge": This defined the essence of what now became known as the Bush Doctrine, which the administration euphemistically referred to as "anticipatory self-defense."[17] Yet that doctrine did not come out of nowhere. It traced its lineage back to Carter's declaration of 1980 that had initiated the War for the Greater Middle East by tying the American way of life to control of the Persian Gulf. Preventive war might be a bastard child of the Carter Doctrine, but there was no denying the genetic similarities.

To invest this freshly asserted prerogative with moral authority, President Bush packaged it within a confident interpretation of history's forward trajectory. "The 20th century," Bush continued, had "ended with a single surviving model of human progress, based on nonnegotiable demands of human dignity." Chief among those demands was "the rule of law, limits on the power of the state, respect for women and private property and free speech and equal justice and religious tolerance." Here the key word was "non-negotiable," the president emphasizing that the "requirements of freedom apply fully" to all people everywhere, to include "the entire Islamic world." So while committed to eliminating threats "before they emerge," the United States was no less committed to enforcing the "non-negotiable demands of human dignity." Bush expressed confidence that preventive war to change the way they live was going to work to the benefit of all.[18]

While Bush soared aloft, his vice president was engaged in somewhat grimier work below. With implacable tenacity, Cheney took it upon himself to bolster the case that Saddam Hussein really did pose a looming menace. Using means both fair and foul, he also sought to discredit or destroy anyone given to contrary views. In this enterprise, intellectual honesty figured at best as optional. As one very senior British official who was well informed about views held in the inner circles of the U.S. government put it, within the administration "the intelligence and the facts were being fixed around the policy."[19] Indeed they were. Along with fixing facts, there was blatant scaremongering. "Time is not on our side," Cheney warned. "The risks of inaction are far greater than the risks of action"—an old chestnut that is the last refuge of the militarist.[20]

Critics of the vice president, who numbered more than a few, professed outrage at his willingness to smear opponents, make bogus claims, and credit dubious information acquired from doubtful sources. In fact, Cheney was merely playing political hardball. However contemptible his conduct, he was hardly the first politician to maneuver his country toward war by relying on demagoguery while playing fast and loose with the facts. In 1917, President Woodrow Wilson had branded senators opposed to the prospect of war with Germany as "a little group of willful men, representing no opinion but their own." Their temerity in refusing to do the president's bidding had "rendered the great Government of the United States helpless and contemptible." In effect, Wilson declared open season on anti-interventionists, who soon found themselves pilloried by the press as "perverse and disloyal obstructionists" and "political tramps" whose names would "go down in history bracketed with Benedict Arnold."[21] Similarly, prior to U.S. entry into World War II, Franklin Roosevelt had slandered anti-interventionists as "Copperheads," a Civil War–era term equivalent to calling someone "pink" or a "fellow traveler" in the 1950s.[22] And the half-truths, untruths, and downright lies that President Lyndon Johnson and members of his administration told in order to justify direct intervention in Vietnam could fill several volumes. But note: In all three cases, an administration hell-bent on war got its way.

So Cheney was merely adhering to a tawdry but hallowed American tradition. Facilitating the initiation of a war abroad meant first engaging in political warfare at home. Cheney viewed his adversaries in Washington precisely as they viewed him: as an enemy to be allowed no quarter.[23]

Meanwhile, shielded from public scrutiny, Rumsfeld took the lead in shaping the actual approach to toppling the first domino. Success required not merely overthrowing Saddam—that outcome was foreordained. For Iraq to serve as strategic catalyst, the United States needed to win a victory of historic proportions—swift, clean, unquestionably decisive, above all serving as a testament to the futility of resisting American power. Rumsfeld disdained the previous administration's incrementalism, where it took weeks and weeks of bombing to defeat a puny country like Serbia. This "gradualism" might be fine for some, he said, but "what it doesn't do is shock and awe, and alter the calculations of the people you're dealing with."[24] For Rumsfeld, the coming war against Saddam was all about altering the calculations of others.

In that regard, CENTCOM's existing war plan—basically a rerun of Desert Storm—was not well suited to producing a sufficiently dazzling outcome. It was fusty and old-fashioned. Even General Franks considered OPLAN 1003 "stale, conventional, predictable," not to mention "too big, too slow, and out-of-date."[25] Rumsfeld readily agreed and was intent on helping Franks devise something better.

The ensuing dialectic revolved around two issues: numbers and sequencing. Rumsfeld the RMA enthusiast did not believe that more "boots on the ground" translated into greater combat power. Fewer could actually be better. He also disliked the U.S. military's preference for gaining control of the air and then pummeling the enemy with bombs *before* introducing ground troops. The step-by-step approach was unnecessarily time-consuming. The defense secretary preferred simultaneity.

To nudge CENTCOM into seeing things his way, Rumsfeld employed a Socratic approach. Possessing truth, he wanted Franks and his staff to join him in discovering that truth as if it were their own. So rather than issuing diktats, Rumsfeld's preferred method was to "poke, prod, and question" and then question some more, until his generals came bearing PowerPoint slides displaying the approved solution.[26] On all matters related to Iraq, he directed his questions to Franks, effectively excluding the Joint Chiefs of Staff from playing any meaningful advisory role. With sufficient tutoring, the CENTCOM commander would come around to seeing the wisdom of Rumsfeld's views.[27]

The asymmetrical collaboration between Rumsfeld and Franks embodied the relationship between the suits and the brass during the post-Vietnam era. As measured by prerogatives and authority, civilian leaders labored to keep senior military officers on a tight leash. Yet for public consumption, they indulged the fiction that in waging war the generals exercised a free hand with the president and secretary of defense acceding to their requirements.

The on-the-shelf version of OPLAN 1003, which predated 9/11, called for an invasion force of a half-million, equivalent in size to the force that had expelled Iraq from Kuwait in 1991. To Rumsfeld, one-fourth of that number sounded better. Franks counter-offered first with 385,000, then 300,000, then 275,000. Rumsfeld was still not satisfied.[28]

They settled on 170,000.[29] They also agreed to a "running start"—once in position, air and available ground forces would attack at the same time. The operative idea was not to pulverize but to shatter, not to defeat in detail but to overwhelm. In contrast to Operation Desert Storm, which had relied on massed combat power, Operation Iraqi Freedom was going to emphasize nimbleness and speed. By the time Saddam and his generals figured out what had hit them, their forces—blinded, bypassed, cut off, isolated—were going to be out of business.

In his memoirs, General Franks goes to great lengths to claim personal authorship of the final Iraq invasion plan, which, he insists, heralded "a true revolution in warfare."[30] In fact, to employ a term attributed to Lenin, Franks was functioning as a "useful idiot." The CENTCOM commander had allowed himself to become captive of the twin obsessions gripping the Bush administration: first, that a military campaign conducted consistent with RMA tenets held the key to validating the Bush Doctrine of preventive war; second, that engineering regime change in Iraq was going to position the United States, acting directly or indirectly, to engineer change elsewhere in the Islamic world.

By indulging these obsessions, Franks misconstrued the challenges awaiting his troops when they entered Iraq. In reality, toppling Saddam did not hold the key to victory. What came next was likely to be the hard part, as at least some senior military officers and more than a few seasoned diplomats warned.[31] After all, persuading Iraqis to accept a new, Washington-mandated political order thereby "changing the way they live," defined the true measure of success. This misapprehension of the war's overarching purpose produced a campaign plan centered on simply getting to Baghdad while giving short shrift to what needed to occur thereafter.

As a serving officer, Franks had an obligation to do the bidding of his superiors. In that regard, he more than fulfilled Bush's and Rumsfeld's expectations. Yet as a military professional, Franks also had an obligation to help those superiors think realistically about war and formulate sound policies. In that regard, Franks failed abysmally. That failure provides the truest measure of his shortcomings as a commander.

Through the winter of 2002–2003, preparations for the Third Gulf War continued. By a comfortable majority in both chambers, Congress had authorized invasion—although political calculation had exercised greater influence on the vote than had careful consideration of the national interest.[32] In effect, the Bush Doctrine thereby received congressional sanction. At the United Nations on February 5, the Bush administration went through the motions of securing Security Council authorization for military action. Finding little support there, the administration surprised no one by deeming such authorization unnecessary.

Popular opposition to the war generated widespread protest that culminated in massive demonstrations around the world on February 15. In New York, London, Paris, Rome, Berlin and literally dozens of other cities, millions took to the streets. Assessing these protests, *The New York Times* concluded that there were actually "two superpowers on the planet: the United States and world public opinion."[33] The Bush administration begged to differ. Unmoved, it simply ignored all the ruckus, the president himself remarking that he was no more inclined to attend to the wishes of demonstrators than he was "to decide policy based upon a focus group."[34] People were entitled to express their opinions, but those opinions didn't matter. The United States government was going to do what it wished to do.

With certain honorable exceptions such as the recently founded

American Conservative and the venerable *Nation* magazine, the editorial position of major newspapers and opinion magazines deferred to the White House and accepted the necessity of war.[35] Some actually welcomed the prospect with enthusiasm. Contemplating the coming war, Max Boot, writing in *The Weekly Standard,* detected "one of those hinge moments in history—events like the storming of the Bastille or the fall of the Berlin Wall—after which everything is different." Historians, Boot predicted, would recall the invasion of Iraq as "the moment when the powerful antibiotic known as democracy was introduced into the diseased environment of the Middle East, and began to transform the region for the better." Victory in Iraq would position the United States "to provide the Middle East with effective imperial oversight." Boot thought it likely that "U.S. victory in Iraq will intimidate" other unenlightened regimes in the neighborhood into biding by Washington's wishes. Should they fail to grasp that opportunity, he wrote, "the United States will have to take more vigorous steps to align our relationships with these countries with our interests and principles."[36]

With the invasion force now assembled and political preparations complete, Bush issued a final ultimatum directing Saddam to leave Iraq. When the Iraqi dictator refused to comply, the president ordered the operation to commence, which it did on March 19.

Franks had envisioned a two-front ground offensive oriented on Baghdad, with the main attack coming from the south, using Kuwait as a base of operations, and a supporting attack in the north out of Turkey. Much to Washington's consternation, Turkish legislators refused to allow the U.S. Army's 4th Division to transit their country to open the northern front. This miscalculation—the Pentagon had spent decades (and billions) courting the Turkish officer corps—offered further evidence that even normally pliant allies were going to think twice before signing on to Bush's crusade.

In the event, Turkey's recalcitrance had little immediate effect on the war's course. The push from the south, employing the U.S. Army's V Corps with two divisions, the 3rd and the 101st, in tandem with the I Marine Expeditionary Force, and the British 1st Armoured Division—

supplemented by the now-standard display of American dominance in the air—more than sufficed to overpower the defenders.[37]

Barely three days into the operation, Franks described Operation Iraqi Freedom for some 1,100 journalists gathered at his forward headquarters in Qatar. Matching the bombast of Schwarzkopf's "mother of all briefings" from a dozen years prior, Franks all but proclaimed victory. "A campaign unlike any other in history" was now well underway, he announced, "a campaign characterized by shock, by surprise, by flexibility, by the employment of precise munitions on a scale never before seen, and by the application of overwhelming force." The balance of his presentation emphasized an absolute mastery of events on the battlefield, gained by employing "forces across the breadth and depth of Iraq, in some cases simultaneously and in some cases sequentially." The plan that was unfolding "provides flexibility so that we can attack the enemy on our terms, and we are doing so," he told reporters. There had been no surprises. The troops were terrific. Saddam was as good as gone. Iraqi weapons of mass destruction were sure to turn up. Success was assured.[38]

Enterprising reporters responded to the general's claims of perfection by highlighting trivial faults, while leaving the campaign's underlying premises unexamined. The ambush of a supply convoy near the Iraqi city of Nasiriyah, with eleven Americans killed and seven captured, became a major story. So too did an offhand comment by a U.S. field commander regarding unanticipated resistance by Iraqi irregulars known as Fedayeen. "The enemy we're fighting is a bit different than the one we war-gamed against," V Corps commander Lieutenant General William S. Wallace remarked. His admission made headlines, garnered a rebuke from Rumsfeld, and provoked Franks to threaten relief. Neither the defense secretary nor the CENTCOM commander was in the mood to tolerate departures from the official script depicting an impeccably choreographed war.[39]

For those doing the actual fighting, the usual fog and friction of battle made their unwelcome appearance. Bad weather and supply shortages hampered the coalition advance. More seriously still, the enemy refused to cooperate. A large-scale attack by AH-64 Apache attack heli-copters targeting the Republican Guard's Medina Division near Karbala went badly awry. Two Apaches were lost, and virtually every other helicopter returned from the mission "riddled with holes."[40]

If Iraqi Freedom had been a Broadway musical, critics would rightly have panned such blown lines and missteps. Yet as a military operation rather than a theatrical production, the drive on Baghdad was actually about as good as it gets. As usual, U.S. troops did all that was asked of them, overcoming uneven but occasionally fierce resistance as they pushed on toward their final objective. As the weather cleared, the at-tack regained momentum. By April 4, U.S. forces had occupied Saddam International Airport outside of the Iraqi capital. A day later, Abrams tanks were rolling through the streets of Baghdad itself. Saddam disap-peared, along with his sons and members of his inner circle. On April 9, the last vestiges of organized resistance collapsed and the transition to "peace operations" commenced.[41] With American soldiers and Marines now entering Baghdad in growing numbers, the press duly recorded a carefully staged performance of jubilant Iraqis toppling Saddam's statue in Al Firdos Square. After advancing over 350 miles in a mere three weeks, while sustaining even fewer casualties than had occurred during Desert Storm, the Bush administration's war of choice—a war intended to jump-start a reordering of the Greater Middle East—appeared to have ended in a definitive victory. Franks certainly thought so, informing Rumsfeld in no uncertain terms that there had "never been a combat operation as successful as Iraqi Freedom."[42]

In fact, rather than ending in just three weeks, the Third Gulf War was destined to continue for another 450. To compare its ultimate dura-tion to the length of the previous paragraph, the fall of Baghdad occurs in the first line between the two letters of "If." And even when U.S. forces finally withdrew, the war itself continued.

As was so often the case during America's War for the Greater Mid-dle East, the outcome of a fight thought to be definitive turned out to be anything but. Like Desert Storm in 1991 or Enduring Freedom in 2001, armed intervention meant to solve a particular problem served chiefly to create new problems of a different order. CENTCOM planners had envisioned the march on Baghdad as marking Operation Iraqi Freedom's "decisive" phase.[43] Yet when U.S. forces thought that they had finished fighting, the decisive phase was just beginning.

Franks himself was oblivious to that prospect. On April 16, he flew into Baghdad for a brief visit. While there, he released a fatuous "Freedom Message to the Iraqi People."[44] Along with his fellow generals, he posed for pictures in one of Saddam Hussein's palaces as if it were the Reich Chancellery in 1945. Soon thereafter, he announced his intention to retire. Post-Saddam Iraq was going to be someone else's headache.

Meanwhile, even before Bush's political team had coordinated the president's "Mission Accomplished" victory lap in early May, things were coming unglued. With Saddam's overthrow, political authority in Iraq collapsed. So too did order, as ordinary Iraqis engaged in an orgy of looting, walking off with "bundles of stolen goods ranging from ceiling fans to mattresses, computers, light bulbs and soccer balls."[45] In Baghdad, Mosul, and Kirkuk, "Looters made off with everything that could be moved."[46] What they could not remove, they ransacked and smashed. The *Los Angeles Times* reported that "plunderers have swept in like a plague of locusts, brazenly breaking into government offices, diplomatic residences, banks, even hospitals, and carting off whatever they can." Within a day of its liberation, the capital of Iraq, a city of nearly five million, had become "a lawless frontier."[47]

Back in Washington, Rumsfeld entertained a different view. The defense secretary mocked journalistic reports coming out of Iraq as exaggerated and misleading. "I picked up a newspaper today and I couldn't believe it," he told attendees at a Pentagon press conference on April 11. "I read eight headlines that talked about chaos, violence, unrest. And it just was Henny Penny—'The sky is falling.' I've never seen anything like it!" The sky was not falling, Rumsfeld insisted. Although things might appear momentarily "untidy," the coalition plan for Iraq was unfolding as intended.[48]

Rumsfeld's reading of the situation was dead wrong. With exhausted U.S. troops lacking the numbers, skills, and necessary direction to provide effective policing, the decisive outcome that was so critical to the Bush administration's goal of transforming the Greater Middle East was slipping away. Validating that strategy required that Saddam's removal elicit either gratitude or at least submission from those freed from his oppressive rule. Unfortunately, neither quality was much in evidence among the Iraqi people. Soon enough, they began turning on their "liberators."

An incident that occurred at the end of April, in the Iraqi city of Fallujah, offered a glimpse of the trials awaiting American troops. Here was an ironic counterpart to the Second Gulf War's legendary action at 73 Easting. In 1991, the small victory won by Captain H. R. McMaster's E Troop had fostered illusions of American military supremacy. Now a comparably small incident laid bare U.S. military shortcomings that soon proved anything but illusory.

The encounter between U.S. troops and Iraqi citizens at a schoolhouse known as Al Qaad saw many shots fired but did not really qualify as a firefight. If it resembled any prior episode in American military history, that episode was the Boston Massacre of 1770. As in Boston, so too in Fallujah, heavily armed soldiers killed civilians protesting against military occupation. Depending on your point of view, the soldiers fired in self-defense or callously gunned down innocents without cause or justification. The difference in viewpoint was irreconcilable and probably irrelevant. What mattered were the consequences stemming from the violence that occurred.

Agreement on certain facts did exist. As part of an American occupation force, soldiers from the newly arrived 82nd Airborne Division had established a presence in Fallujah, a middle-sized Iraqi city with a mostly Sunni population located some forty miles from Baghdad. C Company of the 1st Battalion, 504th Parachute Regiment had commandeered the Al Qaad schoolhouse as their base camp. At least some residents of Fallujah found their presence unwelcome.[49] After nightfall on April 28—Saddam Hussein's birthday—a crowd of some two hundred angry Iraqis, disregarding the curfew imposed by foreign military authorities, gathered at the schoolhouse. There they noisily demanded that the

Americans depart so that classes, suspended for more than a month, could resume.

The demonstrators shouted anti-American slogans, threw rocks, and ignored orders to disperse. They may have fired weapons, either in the air or directly at the U.S. troops, albeit without effect. In either case, the paratroops let loose a fusillade of automatic weapons fire that killed thirteen Iraqis outright and wounded dozens. Although mostly adult males, the dead included at least one woman and one young boy. The Americans suffered no casualties whatsoever.[50]

This was not the first time U.S. troops had killed Iraqi civilians after hostilities had ostensibly ended.[51] Yet the incident at Fallujah differed, becoming the equivalent of a match thrown on dry tinder. Here, observers subsequently concluded, was the event that "breathed life" into the Iraq insurgency.[52] Other violent encounters followed, in Fallujah and elsewhere. In short order, U.S. forces were facing a full-fledged campaign of armed resistance, as complex as it was confusing. "We" were the Redcoats; "they" were the rabble determined to eject the hated occupiers.

To make matters worse, the insurgency erupted precisely at that moment when CENTCOM was executing what in hockey parlance is known as a line change. The major formations that had taken part in the invasion began to depart, their place taken by other units new to the theater of operations. Leaders also rotated. Back at Tampa, General John Abizaid succeeded Franks at CENTCOM commander. When the shuffling of tactical commanders and staffs had finished, responsibility for day-to-day operations in Iraq had devolved upon Lieutenant General Ricardo Sanchez, the most junior and least seasoned three-star general in the U.S. Army. Like the vast majority of his peers, Sanchez had received his commission after the Vietnam War. As a consequence, he had received little schooling and had acquired no firsthand experience dealing with insurgencies. Indeed, he had spent the previous thirty years honing a set of skills only marginally relevant to the task at hand—orchestrating a campaign to pacify a country slightly larger than California with exceedingly porous borders and a fractious population of twenty-five million. It was the equivalent of putting a demolitions expert in charge of restoring a bomb-damaged cathedral.

Complicating that task further was the absence of effective civilian support. To facilitate Iraq's transition to a post-Saddam political order (and to prevent other agencies from horning in on Defense Department turf), Rumsfeld had stood up what he called the Office for Reconstruction and Humanitarian Assistance. Heading this small, hastily devised, and inadequately resourced entity was a retired U.S. Army general named Jay Garner. Back in 1991, at the end of the Second Gulf War, Garner had done an estimable job of organizing aid for displaced Kurds. Now charged with organizing a new government for all of Iraq, he saw his role as akin to that of a midwife: Garner and his team would encourage and coach, but Iraqis themselves would do the hard work of birthing. It was, after all, their country.[53]

Within weeks, the defects of this approach became apparent—chiefly, the prospect of progress made only slowly and incrementally when Washington expected prompt results. Intent on tidying up Iraq sooner rather than later, Rumsfeld shoved Garner aside and appointed in his place L. Paul Bremer. A well-connected former diplomat and Washington operator, Bremer lacked substantive experience in the Arab world but possessed generous stores of self-confidence. He did not fancy playing the role of midwife. As head of what was now called the Coalition Provisional Authority, Bremer intended to govern. In every respect apart from formal title, he saw himself as a viceroy, answering not to Rumsfeld but directly to President Bush himself.

The contrast between Garner and Bremer reflected a division within the administration, which was of two minds about how best to bring the "new" Iraq into existence. In one camp were those favoring an approach akin to the Allied liberation of France in 1944: Vanquish the occupiers, hand over authority to an Iraqi version of General de Gaulle, and have done with it. (Some within the administration saw the urbane Iraqi exile Ahmed Chalabi as Iraq's de Gaulle and Chalabi's Iraqi National Congress as equivalent to the Free French—both absurd propositions.)[54] In the other camp were those who saw the problem as analogous to liberating Nazi Germany after 1945: Only after those implicated in the crimes of the previous regime had been identified and punished could the creation of a new order go forward.

Bremer leaned toward the second approach. Almost immediately after arriving in Baghdad in early May, as if to announce that there was a new boss in town, he issued two directives. The first disbanded Saddam Hussein's Ba'ath Party and prohibited most members from playing any further role in Iraqi public life. The second dissolved the entire Iraqi national security apparatus, which included the army.[55] To some degree, the effect of Bremer's orders was symbolic: They merely affirmed that the old order had passed away. Yet by implication, they also signaled Bremer's intention to replace that old order with something quite different. By grafting onto Iraq Western-style liberalism, democracy, and market economics—principles not hitherto common in that part of the world—he was going to demonstrate their broader applicability to the Greater Middle East. Indeed, the success of the Bush administration's post-9/11 strategy hinged on his ability to do so.

Unfortunately, Bremer proved no better equipped to address the challenges inherent in this undertaking than was General Sanchez as he grappled with a brewing insurgency. For an enterprise that would have tested demigods of empire like Douglas MacArthur or Kitchener of Khartoum, the United States found itself saddled with mere mortals. To make matters worse still, it soon developed that Sanchez and Bremer despised one another.[56] Civil-military tensions undercut unity of effort.

The unhappy union of General Sanchez and Ambassador Bremer lasted barely a year. During that brief interval, the insurgency kicked into high gear. By the time the year ended in the summer of 2004, the administration's strategy of "changing the way they live" had failed irredeemably, even if it took President Bush a bit longer to understand and accept the implications.

The factors contributing to that failure are legion. Yet ranking high among them was the length of time it took senior U.S. commanders to decipher the nature of the conflict and of the opposition. Persuaded that Saddam's overthrow had (or should have) ended the war, explaining why war persisted long after Saddam was gone posed a daunting intellectual challenge.

Who exactly was the enemy? For a full year after the fall of Baghdad, senior U.S. military leaders routinely attributed resistance to thugs and Ba'athist dead-enders. The best way to deal with such a contemptibly shabby threat was to crush it.

In May 2003, Major General Buford Blount, commanding the 3rd Division, told reporters that 90 percent of the opposition in his AOR consisted of "common criminals" responsible for "car thefts, attempted bank robberies, et cetera" with the balance remnants of the ousted regime—individuals who "don't realize that the fight is over" and that they needed to "get on with the new Iraq."[57] A month later, Major General Raymond Odierno, commanding the 4th Division, offered a similar assessment. On a daily basis, his troops were encountering what he called "noncompliant forces" consisting of "former regime members and common criminals." But Odierno disparaged such groups as insignificant: "They are very small, they are very random, they are very ineffective." Mortar and rocket attacks, ambushes, and remotely detonated improvised mines might inflict some casualties, but they did not pose a serious problem. "This is not guerrilla warfare," Odierno insisted. "It is not close to guerrilla warfare because it's not coordinated, it's not organized, and it's not led."[58]

In August—with U.S. combat fatalities since President Bush declared an end to major combat now outnumbering those sustained during the invasion—General Abizaid modified that assessment. "Ba'athist remnants," the recently appointed CENTCOM commander had concluded, were indeed offering organized resistance. They were conducting "a classical guerrilla-type campaign against us." This was a crucial admission. The war had not ended after all. "It's low-intensity conflict," Abizaid concluded, "but it's war."[59]

Winning that war meant finishing the job begun during the invasion. Obliterating what remained of the Ba'ath through unrelenting offensive action would make it clear to all that the old order was gone for good. To flush out insurgent fighters, U.S. forces mounted hundreds of cordon-and-search operations. To kill or capture Ba'athist leaders still on the loose, they launched innumerable raids. By July, Odierno reported, his troops were "conducting search and attack missions, presence patrols and a series of aggressive operations to disarm, defeat and destroy hostile forces, as well as to capture former regime members." The results had been "highly successful, producing a stabilizing effect" throughout his division's AOR.[60]

On July 22, in Mosul, U.S. troops scored a major success: They cornered and then killed Saddam's sons Uday and Qusay. Here, General Sanchez believed, was "a turning point for the resistance and the subversive elements that we're encountering." Although Saddam himself was still at large, "this will prove to the Iraqi people that at least these two members of the regime will not be coming back into power, which is what we stated over and over again."[61]

Yet even as driving a stake through the ousted regime remained the principal military objective, a more complex picture of what coalition forces were up against was beginning to evolve. Just days after taking Saddam's sons off the board, Sanchez himself was explaining on CNN that "we have a multiple-faceted conflict going on here in Iraq. We've got terrorist activity, we've got former regime leadership, we have criminals, and we have some hired assassins that are attacking our soldiers on a daily basis."

Sanchez detected an additional dynamic now coming into play. "This is what I would call a terrorist magnet," he said, "where America, being present here in Iraq, creates a target of opportunity." In effect, rather than producing stability, the U.S. military presence was inciting and attracting anti-American jihadists. That was fine with Sanchez. "This is exactly where we want to fight them," he said. "The key that we must not lose sight of is that we must win this battle here in Iraq. Otherwise America will find itself taking on these terrorists at home."[62]

Yet if the commander's estimate of the situation was changing, his approach to the war remained fixed: Keep the pressure on. His subordinate commanders were doing just that. As the senior Marine commander in Iraq put it, when attacked, "our methods [are] always to respond to force with even greater force."[63] Army and Marine Corps commanders alike persuaded themselves that this approach was working. In Anbar Province, Major General Charles H. Swannack, commanding the 82nd Airborne Division, declared, "We're doing a great job. We're on the glide path to go ahead and get the security situation under control."[64]

General Odierno agreed. In October, he issued an upbeat progress report virtually identical to the one that he had offered in July. "As you all know," he remarked,

> *our soldiers are involved in almost daily contact with terrorists, former regime members and common criminals. To defeat these attacks and continue to improve the security and stability within our area, we are conducting search and attack missions, crisis patrols and a series of aggressive operations to disarm, defeat and destroy hostile forces, as well as to capture mid-level former regime members responsible for organizing anti-coalition activities. These efforts have been highly successful, producing a stabilizing effect throughout the region.*

If in the midst of these highly successful operations violence persisted, Odierno chalked it up to the enemy being on the ropes. The insurgents were "becoming more and more desperate each day," he asserted. The general downplayed reports of foreign fighters entering Iraq in growing numbers, remarking without apparent irony that "what I've found is Iraqis do not like people from other countries fooling in Iraqi business."[65]

For his part, Abizaid was beginning to entertain a more nuanced view. He described an increasingly diverse group of "extremists" who drew their inspiration from a variety of sources not necessarily related to the former regime:

> *They represent religious extremists, they represent national extremists that may or may not have been associated with the Ba'athists, yet nevertheless desire to fight the coalition. . . . There are a small, yet important and well-organized, group of foreign fighters, some of whom have*

been operating in Iraq for a long time, many of whom are infiltrating across various borders. . . . [And] it is also true that there are some anti-coalition Shi'a movements that also aim to destabilize any moderate government that would form in Baghdad.

In other words, Abizaid had now concluded, the war had crosscutting ethnic, sectarian, religious, and nationalist dimensions. The enemy's main aim was not to restore Saddam Hussein but to expel the foreign occupiers. The goal was "not to defeat us militarily," he said, but "to break the will of the United States of America. It's clear, it's simple, it's straightforward. Break our will, make us leave. . . . That's their goal. That's what they're trying to do." By implication, Saddam Hussein, wherever he was, had become irrelevant.[66]

Even so, when U.S. forces finally pulled the bedraggled former Iraqi dictator out of a hole on December 13, Sanchez spied another turning point. "The capture of Saddam Hussein is a defining moment in the new Iraq," he assured reporters in Baghdad. Although the previous month had seen 82 Americans killed and another 336 wounded, Sanchez now glimpsed better days ahead.[67] "I expect that the detention of Saddam Hussein will be regarded as the beginning of reconciliation for the people of Iraq and as a sign of Iraq's rebirth."[68]

His subordinates duly echoed those expectations. "We have turned the corner, and now we can accelerate down the straightaway," remarked General Swannack the following month. "With the capture of Saddam Hussein, we have moved forward because those who had hope for his return no longer have that hope, and those who feared his return no longer have that fear."[69] Odierno shared that view. "The former regime elements we have been combating have been brought to their knees," he said. "Capturing Saddam was a major operational and psychological defeat for the enemy."[70]

In fact, Saddam's capture was beside the point, as events soon demonstrated. The insurgency not only persisted, it intensified, thanks in part to the actions of U.S. forces.

By framing the adversary as a Ba'athist cabal, Sanchez and his fellow commanders had committed a grievous error. But once having done so, they found it difficult to recant, at least in part because doing so would call into question the larger strategic rationale for invading Iraq in the first place—that Iraqis would willingly embrace President Bush's Freedom Agenda, thereby paving the way for a broader transformation of the Greater Middle East.

Imagine if at the end of 1965, just months after U.S. combat troops had arrived in South Vietnam, the American high command in Saigon had come to the realization that nationalism rather than international communism defined the nexus of the ongoing conflict—that the Viet Cong and the North Vietnamese were fighting not to spread a totalitarian ideology around the world but simply to unite an arbitrarily divided country, thereby exercising their right to self-determination. Even to entertain such a heresy would have been to demolish the basis for U.S. intervention.

So too with Iraq. To allow that motives other than restoring Saddam to power were fueling the insurgency would undermine the rationale for continuing the war. This was especially true after the failure to locate Iraqi weapons of mass destruction had discredited that ostensible casus belli. Hence, the doggedness with which senior U.S. military officers clung to the hypothesis that even with Saddam gone the ongoing Iraq War still somehow centered on the deposed dictator.

Just days after Saddam's capture, General Richard Myers visited Baghdad. A reporter asked the JCS chairman to reflect on the possibility that "the people who are killing American soldiers today are not Ba'athists, are not pro-Saddam, are simply nationalists who think you're here as occupiers." Myers was having none of it. "I think that the facts don't support that," he replied. "I think the facts support the people that we've been engaging, the people that we detain—and as you know, we detain hundreds a week—they're not nationalists. These are former regime elements. . . . These are terrorists. These are former regime elements."[71] To admit to other alternatives was to suggest that the entire war might have been a mistake. Hence, the mantra-like recitation of catchphrases that bore scant relation to on-the-ground realities.

That said, Myers was certainly correct in claiming that U.S. forces were incarcerating hundreds of Iraqis every week. Tactically, the detention of military-age males formed the centerpiece of Sanchez's campaign to eradicate the putative Ba'athist threat. Here was Rumsfeld's dictum—"Sweep it all up. Things related and not."—put fully into actual practice. The undisguised aim was to cow the population rather than to win hearts and minds. A report issued by the International Committee of the Red Cross issued in early 2004 succinctly described the methods used. Arrests "tended to follow a pattern," it began.

> *Arresting authorities entered houses usually after dark, breaking down doors, waking up residents roughly, yelling orders, forcing family members into one room under military guard while searching the rest of the house and further breaking doors, cabinets and other property. They arrested suspects, tying their hands in the back with flexi-cuffs, hooding them, and taking them away. Sometimes they arrested all adult males present in a house, including elderly, handicapped or sick people. Treatment often included pushing people around, insulting, taking aim with rifles, punching and kicking and striking with rifles. Individuals were often led away in whatever they happened to be wearing at the time of arrest—sometimes in pyjamas or underwear—and were denied the opportunity to gather a few essential belongings, such as clothing, hygiene items, medicine or eyeglasses. Those who surrendered with a suitcase often had their belongings confiscated. In many cases personal belongings were seized during the arrest, with no receipt being issued.*[72]

Dispatches appearing in mainstream U.S. publications told a similar story. Methods employed by U.S. forces invited comparison with the tactics of intimidation that Israeli troops used in policing the West Bank.[73] These included the destruction of homes belonging to families of anyone suspected of being an insurgent.[74] In a scathing op-ed that appeared in *The New York Times* shortly after Saddam's capture, Marine Lieutenant Colonel Carl E. Mundy III, an Iraq War veteran, wrote that "the 'get tough' approach" employed by Sanchez "resembles tactics used by Israelis in the occupied territories" and was not likely to endear the Americans to Arab Iraqis.[75]

Parallel methods suggested parallel aims. The "get tough" posture of Israel Defense Forces reflected an Israeli determination to maintain a permanent grip on the West Bank. That U.S. forces were taking a similar approach raised the specter of the United States maintaining permanent control of Iraq, Washington's insistence to the contrary notwithstanding. In sum, heavy-handed U.S. pacification techniques were inflaming rather than squelching resistance. "Americans are frequently guilty of excesses that are turning ordinary Iraqis into foes," *Time* magazine bluntly concluded.[76]

The apprehend-detain-interrogate approach was creating a cancer that had already begun to metastasize. To house the growing population of prisoners collared in cordon-and-search operations, U.S. forces had established a network of detention facilities. One such facility was Abu Ghraib, notorious as a prison and torture chamber during the Saddam Hussein era, now holding well over seven thousand Iraqis that U.S. forces had taken into custody. Beginning in October 2003 at the very latest, Abu Ghraib became the scene of "sadistic, blatant, and wanton criminal abuses" perpetrated by American soldiers, with Iraqi detainees their victims. By December, senior U.S. Army leaders knew that they had a problem.[77] An investigation begun the following month by Major General Antonio Taguba documented misconduct that included, in the words of his report:

- Punching, slapping, and kicking detainees; jumping on their naked feet;
- Videotaping and photographing naked male and female detainees;
- Forcibly arranging detainees in various sexually explicit positions for photographing;
- Forcing detainees to remove their clothing and keeping them naked for several days at a time;
- Forcing naked male detainees to wear women's underwear;

- Forcing groups of male detainees to masturbate themselves while being photographed and videotaped;
- Arranging naked male detainees in a pile and then jumping on them;
- Positioning a naked detainee on a [ration] Box, with a sandbag on his head, and attaching wires to his fingers, toes, and penis to simulate electric torture;
- Writing "I am a Rapest" [*sic*] on the leg of a detainee alleged to have forcibly raped a 15-year old fellow detainee, and then photographing him naked;
- Placing a dog chain or strap around a naked detainee's neck and having a female Soldier pose for a picture;
- A male MP guard having sex with a female detainee;
- Using military working dogs (without muzzles) to intimidate and frighten detainees, and in at least one case biting and severely injuring a detainee;
- Taking photographs of dead Iraqi detainees.

Undertaken shortly after Saddam Hussein's capture, Taguba's investigation described the abuse as "systematic." Hoping to dispose of the matter quietly and without undue embarrassment, the U.S. Army classified his report as SECRET.[78]

This effort at problem solving through concealment was doomed from the start. The Taguba report leaked, and in April 2004 the CBS television program *60 Minutes* broke the Abu Ghraib story, broadcasting to the world the photographic evidence on which General Taguba had based his findings.

American authorities in Washington and Baghdad immediately launched into damage control mode. They condemned the lapses in discipline even while insisting that the misbehavior of a few bad apples represented neither the United States military nor U.S. policy in Iraq. They might have saved their breath.

Fair or not, Abu Ghraib affirmed what many Muslims in the Greater Middle East already suspected about American purposes and American culture. Much as a Muslim committing an act of terror thereby affirms for many in the West what they know they know about Islam, the pictorial evidence accompanying the Abu Ghraib scandal affirmed for many Muslims their preexisting impression of the United States as a sinkhole of wantonness, decadence, and sexual perversity.

War is inherently a political act. Abu Ghraib represented a political setback of monumental proportions, so much so that we may date the failure of the Third Gulf War from this point. That is, after Abu Ghraib, U.S. authorities could no longer credibly depict America's War for the Greater Middle East as a benign enterprise informed by sympathy for the people of the Islamic world. Needless to say, the war continued, but the likelihood of Iraq serving as a launch pad from which to pursue a larger strategy of transformation now shrank to zero. Even if the United States somehow managed to eke out a win of sorts in Iraq, that victory would be devoid of any larger purpose. In Baghdad, the road to the Middle East had reached a dead end. Barely out of the starting block, the Bush administration strategy of remaking the Greater Middle East had collapsed.

In June 2004, General Sanchez left Baghdad. Retired in grade, he penned a bitter memoir in which he complained of having been unfairly denied a fourth star.[79] Later that same month, Bremer also departed. With Iraq's sovereignty restored on June 28 through the stroke of George W. Bush's pen, Bremer's successor assumed the title of ambassador. Of course, sovereign Iraq was host to 160,000 foreign troops, who continued to conduct combat operations across the length and breadth of that country.[80] Bremer duly published an account of his tenure as proconsul, blaming others for any problems that had cropped up on his watch.[81] Meanwhile, over the course of many months, seemingly innumerable investigations of the Abu Ghraib scandal played themselves out. In the end, Brigadier General Janis Karpinski, a female reservist, claimed honors as the highest-ranking person to be held accountable. Her punishment was to retire at the lesser rank of colonel. She too penned a self-exculpatory memoir.[82]

At a difficult moment in his presidency, John Kennedy cited "an old saying that victory has a hundred fathers and defeat is an orphan." In the spring of 2003, the Third Gulf War had boasted many proud parents. A year or so later, the ranks had thinned considerably. "I have seen this movie," remarked General Zinni, the former CENTCOM commander, in April 2004. "It was called Vietnam."[83]

In the meantime, the war itself meandered on, with bad news outweighing the good. U.S. forces did come out on top in notable combat actions such as the Battles of Najaf (August 2004) and Second Fallujah (November–December 2004). Yet these encounters had no more bearing on the outcome of the Third Gulf War than the much larger Battles of Second Bull Run (August 1862) or Fredericksburg (December 1862) had on the outcome of the American Civil War. That is, apart from offering bloody markers of an ongoing stalemate, they possessed marginal significance.

Needless to say, casualties continued to mount. By the middle of 2004, the number of American soldiers killed in Iraq had already passed the one thousand mark. Over the course of that year, the monthly toll of those wounded averaged 668. Some months were worse than others. In April, 1,215 U.S. troops were wounded in action. In November that number reached a new peak of 1,431.[84]

Financial costs skyrocketed. By the end of 2004, U.S. war-related expenditures in Iraq were approaching $7 billion per month.[85] In contrast to the Second Gulf War, America's allies did not volunteer to pony up their share. Although President Bush had inherited a budget surplus, the ongoing conflicts in Iraq and Afghanistan combined to generate huge deficits. In 2004, the federal government spent $412 billion more than it took in. Worse was to come. By the time Bush left office in 2009, annual deficits had breached the trillion-dollar mark.[86]

Since 2004 was an election year, winning a second term eclipsed all other presidential priorities. Although success eluded Bush in Iraq, at the polls he fared better. In November, he handily defeated Senator John Kerry of Massachusetts, who tied himself in knots trying to ex-

plain why voting for and then turning against the Iraq War offered reason to anoint him commander in chief. Reelection gave Bush breathing
space. For a time at least, he was free to pretend that Iraq was still going
to come out right, thereby validating the Freedom Agenda as a proper
basis for U.S. policy.

Among the many perverse effects of the American cult of the presidency is the conviction that the outcome of any presidential election
signifies something profound. This notion persists even though the average American votes for candidate A over candidate B not because A
looks to be the next Abraham Lincoln but because B seems the lesser
alternative. Certainly that was the case in the 2004 balloting.

Even so, Bush chose to interpret his reelection as a divine mandate,
as his Second Inaugural Address made clear. In it, Bush committed the
United States to the "goal of ending tyranny in our world." Speaking
with greater eloquence than accuracy, the president declared:

> From the day of our Founding, we have proclaimed that every man
> and woman on this earth has rights, and dignity, and matchless value,
> because they bear the image of the Maker of Heaven and earth. Across
> the generations we have proclaimed the imperative of self-government,
> because no one is fit to be a master, and no one deserves to be a slave.
> Advancing these ideals is the mission that created our Nation. It is the
> honorable achievement of our fathers. Now it is the urgent requirement
> of our nation's security, and the calling of our time.[87]

In reality, as the course of the festering war in Iraq had amply demonstrated, indulging the conceit that America is history's chosen instrument of liberation is more likely to produce grief than glory.

To be sure, Bush's Second Inaugural qualifies as a thoroughly American text, the president reiterating sentiments voiced by more than a
few of his predecessors. Yet the speech also bears the unmistakable imprint of self-indulgent fantasy, of sobriety overtaken by fanaticism.
Bush's expectations of ending tyranny by spreading American ideals

mirrored Osama bin Laden's dream of establishing a new caliphate based on Islamic principles. When put to the test, the president's vision of peace gained by waging preventive war had proven to be just as fanciful as bin Laden's and hardly less pernicious. As adversaries, truly they were made for each other.

14

How This Ends

In June 2004, when General George W. Casey, Jr., arrived in Baghdad to succeed Ricardo Sanchez as overall commander of coalition forces in Iraq, he made an astonishing discovery: There was no plan. Casey's overtaxed predecessor had never formulated a blueprint for conducting the war over which he presided. What was the ultimate objective? What interim steps would move coalition forces toward that objective? No document providing answers to these questions existed. It was as if Anglo-American armies had landed at Normandy on D-Day vaguely understanding that they should head toward Berlin but lacking guidance on how to get off the beaches.

The new commander immediately set out to correct this deficiency. The son of an army general killed in Vietnam, Casey was himself experiencing war for the first time. Deliberate, reflective, devoid of flamboyance, he brought to Baghdad one key attribute that Sanchez had lacked: Coming directly from Washington, he understood that his superiors there were nursing incompatible expectations. Through victory, President Bush was still hoping to resuscitate his Freedom Agenda and thereby preserve some semblance of a purposeful grand strategy. Secretary of Defense Rumsfeld, meanwhile, was keen to move on. He wanted to have done with Iraq as quickly as possible, thereby preventing the American claim to military supremacy from suffering further erosion. To satisfy his bosses fully, Casey needed to win big and get out soon. On-the-ground military realities made that outcome exceedingly unlikely.

The campaign plan that Casey devised and promulgated in August offered Bush and Rumsfeld some of what each wanted, but not all.[1] In essence, he promised something less than outright victory, with even that achieved only after considerable further effort. In his confirmation hearings, Casey had referred to the U.S. goal in terms of building "security" rather than vanquishing the enemy. And "if you want security," he told members of the Senate Armed Services Committee, "you have to have intelligence, and if you want to have intelligence in a counterinsurgency environment, you have to change the perception of the people, first, toward the insurgency and, second, toward the coalition forces."[2] Changing people's perceptions was not a standard U.S. military mission. Implicit in Casey's assessment of the way ahead was a lowering of expectations along with an appeal for patience.

Casey's reference to counterinsurgency was also noteworthy. As a direct consequence of Vietnam, the concept had fallen into disrepute in American military circles. Now Casey was proposing to revive it. Counterinsurgency, or COIN as it came to be known, was to provide the mechanism for changing Iraqi perceptions. Upon his arrival in Baghdad, Casey told President Bush that his number-one priority was to "develop an integrated counterinsurgency plan."[3]

In practical terms, the new commander's version of COIN meant two things: making the U.S. occupation less disagreeable to the occupied while simultaneously creating Iraqi military and political capabilities sufficient to enable that country to manage its own affairs. COIN, in other words, offered the prospect of enabling the United States to make a graceful exit, with December 2005 Casey's target date for completing the mission.[4]

The approach rested on three core assumptions. The first and most important was that a nation-state called "Iraq," inhabited by a people identifying themselves as "Iraqis," actually existed, providing a solid foundation upon which coalition forces could build. The second was that foreign troops, if employing kinder, gentler methods, could make themselves tolerable. The third was that demonstrated progress on the ground would buy enough additional time back in Washington to allow the campaign to play out. Unfortunately, all three assumptions proved to be questionable.

Further complicating matters was the hydra-headed nature of the enemy. In June 2005, Vice President Cheney was assuring Americans that the Iraq insurgency was in its "last throes."[5] More accurately, it was evolving and becoming more complex. Two years after the fall of Baghdad, the armed resistance consisted of Sunni "rejectionists" unhappy with the prospect of the Shia majority exercising political power, Shia militias unhappy with prolonged military occupation, and so-called foreign fighters who were anything but unhappy. Seizing upon the opening created by the invasion of Iraq, they welcomed the opportunity to wage anti-Western jihad there.[6] Crossing into Iraq from neighboring countries, these foreign fighters came from across the Arab world, with some from even more distant quarters of the Greater Middle East. In October 2004, they took to calling themselves Al Qaeda in Iraq, their leader Abu Musab al-Zarqawi pledging fealty to Osama bin Laden. Prior to 2003, in its quest to create a new caliphate, Al Qaeda had not managed to gain a foothold in Saddam Hussein's Iraq. Now, paradoxically, thanks to George Bush's war on terrorism it had.

General Casey commanded coalition forces in Iraq for thirty-two months. During that time, he periodically returned to Washington to provide progress reports. Frequently accompanied by Generals Myers and Abizaid, he journeyed to Capitol Hill to assure the Congress and by extension the American people that events were headed in the right direction. Always careful to note that "challenges" remained, the military leaders directly responsible for overseeing operations in Iraq offered a consistently hopeful appraisal. In their collective judgment, the war there not only remained winnable but had to be won and would be.

In June 2005, for example, Myers assured the Senate Armed Services Committee that "we are on the right course." For his part, Abizaid saw evidence of "good progress" with greater success "undoubtedly ahead." Chiming in, Casey described the mission as "both realistic and achievable." When Senator Edward Kennedy, Democrat of Massachusetts, characterized Iraq as a quagmire, Casey pushed back against such a "misrepresentation of the facts." The insurgents had "no vision, no base, [and] limited popular support," he said. On the other side were the mass of Iraqis committed to democracy and "Iraqi security forces that are fighting and dying for their country every day." That, Casey concluded, "is not a quagmire."[7]

In September, the trio once more trooped back to the Capitol. Myers and Abizaid deferred to the commander in Baghdad to provide an update on Iraq. A "strategy based on proven counterinsurgency principles," Casey testified, was enabling the coalition "to make progress in Iraq every day." He assured senators that "we have a strategy and a plan for success in Iraq and we are broadly on track in achieving our goals." Casey expected improving conditions to allow the United States to begin withdrawing U.S. troops within a year.[8]

By 2006, Myers had retired, his place taken by Marine General Peter Pace. On Iraq, the new JCS chairman affirmed his predecessor's platitudinous assessment. "We have come a long way in Iraq," he told senators in August. Although there still remained "a long way to go," he continued, "we will persist and we will prevail." Speaking after Pace, Abizaid offered a more substantive and far-ranging view, situating Iraq within a much larger struggle that ranged "throughout Central Asia, the Middle East, and the Horn of Africa."

The CENTCOM commander urged senators to see things in a wider perspective. The enemy that U.S. forces were fighting in Iraq was also present "in Afghanistan, Pakistan, Saudi Arabia, Egypt, Jordan, and in Lebanon," he said. "You name the location in the region and they exist there." He continued:

People say the war started on September 11, 2001, but you can make a case for the war having started in October 1983 when Hezbollah destroyed the Marine barracks and killed over 200 American marines that were stationed there. You could say the war played itself out to a certain extent at a lower level in Somalia, where we stayed there for a short period of time and then left. You could say that throwing a few Tomahawk land attack missiles (TLAMs) at this enemy created the circum-

stances by which we had to end up facing this enemy with greater force and greater perseverance and greater patience and courage than we had been able to muster before then.

In the face of this proliferating threat, the immediate challenges facing the United States were threefold, Abizaid believed: first, to "defeat Al Qaeda and its associated movements"; second, to "deter Iranian designs for regional hegemony"; and third, to "find a comprehensive solution to the corrosive Arab-Israeli conflict." Arguing that Iraq "sits at the center of the broader regional problem," Abizaid clung to the proposition that fixing that country was a prerequisite to fixing the rest of the Greater Middle East. Notably, however, he no longer claimed that the armed might of the United States would suffice to restore stability to the country that had become the focal point of U.S. military attention. Ultimately, Iraqis would decide whether Iraq would continue to exist. On that score, Abizaid professed optimism since "there are still many more people in Iraq trying to hold that country together than there are trying to tear it apart."[9]

Yet his rote expressions of can-do spirit notwithstanding, Abizaid in effect conceded that Iraq was merely a subset of a much larger constellation of issues. The Iraq problem was one among many in the Greater Middle East. The CENTCOM commander's testimony offered a made-to-order opportunity to reexamine the actual utility of military power in attempting to repair that region and to consider whether previous U.S. military actions may actually have exacerbated problems there. Here, in short, was an opportunity to reassess strategy. Narrowly preoccupied with Iraq, senators allowed that opportunity to pass unnoticed.

Ultimately, the assurances offered by senior military professionals that things were "broadly on track" proved unavailing. Events in Iraq told a different story. During 2005 and 2006, milestones came and went—elections and referendums yielding a constitution and a new government—without having any noticeable impact on the insurgency.

Timelines slipped. Evidence that Iraq had indeed become a quagmire piled up.

On all sides, the mournful toll of casualties continued to mount. By the end of 2006, cumulative American fatalities in Iraq were approaching the total number of all those killed on 9/11. By that time more than twenty-two thousand U.S. troops had been wounded. Meanwhile, "terrorist" attacks in Iraq, primarily employing IEDs, kept increasing in number and lethality. Although coalition forces reported killing or capturing enemy fighters in impressive numbers, armed resistance showed no signs of slackening.[10] If anything, in the aggregate, it continued to gain strength.[11] Building effective Iraqi security forces, like building effective Iraqi political institutions, too often saw two steps forward followed by three steps back.

In contrast to all previous campaigns in America's War for the Greater Middle East, Operation Iraqi Freedom (along with its neglected Afghan cousin, Operation Enduring Freedom) found U.S. forces caught in the very predicament that military leaders after Vietnam had sworn to avoid: a protracted conflict with little prospect of clear-cut victory at the far end and yet with no apparent way to call it quits without admitting failure. Tactical successes achieved in prior operations such as Praying Mantis, Desert Storm, Determined Force, and Allied Force had sufficed to create a simulacrum of actual victory. As the triumphal march on Baghdad receded into the past, with weeks of fighting turning into months and months into years, the challenge of spinning Iraqi Freedom as a successful enterprise grew proportionally.

So too did the sunk costs. These cumulative costs, whether measured in blood or treasure or credibility, seemingly removed the option of cutting U.S. losses and heading for home. Carter had chosen that course after the abortive Iran hostage rescue mission. So too had Reagan after the Beirut bombing and Clinton after the Mogadishu firefight. This time there was no easy way out. Not without reason, America's armed forces were reputed to be the most formidable the world had ever seen. Yet reputations depend on circumstance. In Iraq, circumstances exposed the limitations of a military once thought to be invincible.

On February 22, 2006, the Third Gulf War did reach a turning point of sorts. On that date, terrorists blew up the al-Askari Mosque in Samarra. The destruction of this site, sacred to Shiites, triggered a spasm of what *The New York Times* called "sectarian fury." Iraq now teetered on the brink of civil war, as "mobs formed across Iraq to chant for revenge."[12] Shiites bent on retribution attacked dozens of Sunni mosques and assassinated Sunni imams. The upshot, as Casey noted with considerable understatement, was "a far more complex environment than we had previously dealt with." As a direct result of the Samarra bombing, he concluded, "the fundamental nature of the conflict had changed from an insurgency against the coalition to a struggle among Iraq's ethnic and sectarian groups for political and economic power in Iraq"— with coalition forces caught in the middle.[13]

If not already a failed state, Iraq was precariously close to becoming one. By October, according to a classified briefing prepared by CENTCOM's intelligence directorate, violence was "at an all-time high [and] spreading geographically." On its color-coded "Index of Civil Conflict," ranging from green (peace) to scarlet (chaos), CENTCOM rated the situation in Iraq as well into the red portion of the spectrum.[14]

American policymakers had not anticipated this situation, to put it mildly. Yet the spike in sectarian fighting within Iraq had implications extending well beyond the boundaries of that country: Iran was now playing a covert but increasingly prominent role in supporting Shia extremists. To put it another way, a war begun with the expectations of putting the United States in the driver's seat now found Washington in the back seat. In a turn of events rich with irony, the initiative now redounded to Iran.

Recall that in the First Gulf War of 1980–1988, with Iran and Iraq vying for regional primacy, the United States had tilted in Baghdad's favor to prevent Tehran from coming out on top. In the Second Gulf War of 1990–1991, the United States had acted to frustrate Saddam Hussein's own hegemonic aspirations. At the outset of the Third Gulf

War, under the guise of advancing President Bush's Freedom Agenda, the United States had made its own bid for regional hegemony. With U.S. forces unable to make good on Bush's promise to pacify Iraq and transform it politically, Iran was now emerging as the principal beneficiary of American overreach. The sequence of U.S. interventionism in the Persian Gulf, initiated with an eye toward curbing Iranian power, was now producing precisely the inverse effect.

Back home Bush's (or Rumsfeld's) War had become increasingly unpopular and the administration's "light at the end of the tunnel" assurances less and less persuasive. The off-year elections of November 2006 served as a referendum of sorts on a conflict now approaching its fourth anniversary. Voters intent on punishing Bush handed Democrats control of both houses of Congress. The president himself got the message. Within a day, he dismissed his secretary of defense, a tacit admission that the war had gone awry. The caustic, confident man once known as "Rumstud," celebrated in his heyday as "a virtual rock star" and "babe magnet," had long since become a political liability.[15] Few shed tears over his departure. Rare bipartisan applause greeted Bush's decision to appoint Robert Gates, a seasoned national security hand, as the next defense secretary.

Yet the election also rendered a judgment on General Casey's stewardship in Baghdad. Called upon to salvage Bush's post-9/11 strategy of transforming the Greater Middle East, he had failed. By not winning, he had lost.

Casey's own days in command were now numbered. In Washington, a plot to oust him, engineered by civilians and retired generals, was gaining steam.[16] It was a replay of the "Western excursion" that had forced a change in the CENTCOM war plan prior to Operation Desert Storm. In that case, General Schwarzkopf survived by modifying his intentions. In this case, a reluctance to change cost Casey his job. In early January 2007, President Bush made it official, announcing that David Petraeus was to replace him forthwith.[17]

In retrospect, Casey's failure appears all but foreordained. Certainly, the cards were stacked against him. He had inherited a mess. While

Casey had counted on Iraqis coming together to shape their own destiny, the fractured nature of Iraqi society militated against that prospect. Al Qaeda's appearance on the scene exacerbated that problem. And although provided with considerable resources, Casey never had sufficient boots on the ground to meet mission requirements.

During his tenure in Baghdad, U.S. troop strength in Iraq varied between 127,000 and 160,000. In historical context, these are not large numbers, especially in light of the importance attached to Operation Iraqi Freedom as the main effort of post-9/11 U.S. military strategy. By comparison, while drawing on a substantially smaller population base (and with women largely excluded from military service), the United States had fielded twice as many troops to fight in Korea and three times as many in Vietnam—neither of which had qualified as the main effort during the Cold War.[18]

Even so, Casey got about as much as the Pentagon was in a position to provide. To lure volunteers, the Congress provided liberal increases in military pay and bonuses. In a policy known as "stop loss," the services prohibited soldiers from leaving active duty at the end of their enlistment contracts. They repurposed sailors and airmen as de facto ground troops. The army reorganized itself to plus up the total number of combat brigades, while subjecting reservists to multiple tours on active duty. Yet rather than offering a remedy, all of these together merely provided a means to manage an ongoing shortage. President Bush's decision not to mobilize the country even as he was embarking upon a "global war" essentially fixed the size of the force available to wage that war.

To narrow the gap between requirements and troops available, the Bush administration greatly expanded the Pentagon's reliance on private security firms to perform functions traditionally done by soldiers. Yet this dubious practice served chiefly to highlight the inadequacies of the American military system. A "nation at war" was incapable of putting even 1 percent of its population in uniform.

Nor did the much-hyped coalition do much to make up any shortfall. Non-U.S. troops under Casey's command peaked at a mere twenty-five thousand. By the end of 2006, that number had plummeted by 40 percent. In terms of quality, moreover, foreign troops tended to be a mixed bag, of limited value when dealing with the critical challenges of imposing order on Baghdad or suppressing Sunni insurgents in Anbar Province. A "coalition of the willing" was not necessarily a "coalition of the capable."

All that said, Casey himself had fallen short, notably so in translating precepts into practice. As much as armies are hierarchical organizations, valuing loyalty and obedience, a gap always exists between what the general-in-chief directs his subordinates to do and what they actually end up doing. During Casey's tenure in command in Baghdad, the gap loomed particularly large.

While Casey himself was settling in for the *longue durée,* the major formations under his command rotated in and out of country. As if per some informal contract, soldiers came to expect that they would deploy together, fight together, and then head home together, after serving a predetermined length of time.[19] This approach stood in sharp contrast to the individual replacement system used in Vietnam. There, the United States military had all but disintegrated under the stress of protracted war. In Iraq, under comparably trying circumstances, U.S. forces demonstrated impressive durability, at least in part thanks to the unit rotation system.

But there was a downside. Units that had fought in Iraq during 2003 and 2004 returned for a second tour in 2005 or 2006 believing that they already had the war figured out. They arrived bearing their own stock of lessons for implementation. As a consequence, they were less than receptive to instructions from on high to try a different approach—especially one that they had been conditioned to view with suspicion.[20]

Imagine some hedge fund manager announcing to his employees that instead of profit, maximizing social value was now the name of the game. Some attentive and enlightened fraction might respond with alacrity to this change in priorities. The remainder either wouldn't hear or wouldn't know where to begin.

So too with Casey's effort to persuade the forces under his command to embrace counterinsurgency. Too many of his subordinates either chose not to hear or didn't know where to begin. As a consequence, brigade and battalion commanders, exercising wide latitude in deciding how to fight, made choices at odds with Casey's intent. Reflecting on the "various operating styles" employed by U.S. units, one careful observer of the war concluded that as late as 2006 tactical commanders were still operating "in a vacuum, with no strategy to guide them because no strategy has been offered." More accurately, Casey had formulated a strategy—one based on counterinsurgency—without adequately spelling out for his subordinates what adhering to its dictates required. "So they fight their own wars, blanketing their sectors with troops and funds right up until the day the Pentagon orders them to let go."[21] Some were implementing a version of COIN; others were freelancing.[22]

The case of Colonel Michael Steele, commanding a brigade of the 101st Airborne Division deployed to Saddam Hussein's hometown of Tikrit in 2005–2006, offers an instructive example. That Steele, a veteran of Mogadishu, was an able and courageous officer is beyond doubt. Yet as one American general put it, he and Casey had a "fundamental difference of opinion about how to prosecute the war in Iraq." A Pattonesque pep talk to his troops summarized Steele's philosophy: "The guy who is going to win on the far end is the one who gets violent the fastest." COIN, with its touchy-feely emphasis, was for wimps. In Steele's outfit—the same Rakkasans who had fought in Operation Anaconda three years earlier—body count became the measure of success, with all military-age males ripe for targeting unless they "stood still with their hands raised," thereby bidding for recognition as noncombatants. Steele made his expectations crystal clear.

In the long history of war crimes, the events that ensued qualify as mere garden-variety atrocities. A handful of Steele's soldiers executed several Iraqi detainees in cold blood. Members of the chain of command orchestrated a clumsy attempt at a cover-up, which inevitably fell apart.[23] Those directly implicated in the killings were tried, convicted, imprisoned, and forgotten. Although reprimanded for having "created a command climate where irresponsible behavior appears to have been allowed to go unchecked," Steele himself was never charged.[24] He served out his tour of duty and took his troops home.

But the episode is a revealing one. From his headquarters in Baghdad, General Casey was issuing directives that said, in effect: "Here's how we will conduct ourselves." In the 3rd Brigade of the 101st, Colonel Steele was deciding otherwise: "Here we do things differently." Responsibility for the climate of command prevailing in the 3rd Brigade began with Steele but did not end there. Clausewitz wrote that the main object in any war is to impose your will on the enemy. But doing so presumes an ability first to impose your will on your own subordinates. Casey's inability to fulfill this preliminary requirement offers one measure of his shortcomings as a war leader.

In any event, on February 10, 2007, the Third Gulf War got its fourth commander, when David Petraeus succeeded Casey in Baghdad. In many respects, Petraeus was an inspired choice for the post. For the war's supporters, no more urgent requirement existed than to reconstitute flagging public support for the ongoing conflict. Sold on false or misleading pretenses, Operation Iraqi Freedom needed to be resold.

President Bush found himself in a predicament similar to that facing Lyndon Johnson back in 1967. With his own credibility shot, LBJ had turned to General William Westmoreland to make the case for staying the course in Vietnam. Forty years later, another president with credibility problems looked to another general to bail him out. The trick was to rebrand Bush's war, widely viewed as futile, as Petraeus's war, with progress visible just around the corner. As luck would have it, not least among his many talents, the new commander was a gifted salesman.

In the years following his graduation from West Point in 1974, Petraeus had punched all the tickets necessary for advancement. If his career path differed from that of other upwardly mobile officers, he set himself apart by managing to punch one particular ticket several times. While some young officers spend a year or so serving as a general's aide-de-camp and a mere handful as aide to a four-star, Petraeus achieved the remarkable distinction of serving as aide-de-camp to three different four-star generals while marrying the daughter of a fourth.[25]

The achievement was emblematic. As army Lieutenant General Daniel Bolger, a peer but not a fan, put it, Petraeus was a charter member of the "AAA Club," consisting of "Aides, Adjutants, and Assholes" who collectively constituted a "careerist self-promotion society that hung out near military throne rooms."[26] Indeed, Petraeus displayed a knack for ingratiating himself with anyone who might someday be of use, not only senior officers but also politicians, academics, and especially journalists.

Whereas in the wake of Vietnam most serving officers viewed reporters with a mix of wariness and hostility, Petraeus saw them as potential assets to cultivate. He expended considerable energy doing just that, beguiling reporters by pretending to take them seriously.

During the first phases of Operation Iraqi Freedom, Major General Petraeus had commanded the 101st Airborne Division. The embedded reporter who spent "all day, every day at his elbow" was Rick Atkinson, a Pulitzer Prize–winning journalist-historian with *The Washington Post*—a bit like an image-savvy World War II general having Ernie Pyle or A. J. Liebling in the back of his jeep as a personal amanuensis. Atkinson came away captivated by Petraeus's "subtle mind" and duly conveyed the general's "cerebral musings" to the *Post*'s influential readership. "Tell me how this ends," Petraeus ruminated to Atkinson in the war's first days. At once sardonic and intimate—and no more spontaneous than Pershing's "Lafayette, we are here" or MacArthur's "I shall return"—the exquisitely calibrated line was designed to seduce. It did just that.[27]

After the fall of Saddam, with the occupation off to a muddled start, Petraeus won plaudits for his energetic efforts to revive the northern city of Mosul. "101st Airborne Scores Success in Reconstruction of Northern Iraq," *The New York Times* reported, describing Petraeus as "steeped in nation building" and "prepared to act while the civilian authority in Baghdad was still getting organized."[28] The achievement proved transitory, however. Petraeus's Mosul was a Potemkin village. Once he departed, the city fell into disarray.[29]

In June 2004, now a lieutenant general, Petraeus returned to Iraq for a second tour, charged by Casey with the task of training Iraqi security forces. *Newsweek* greeted word of his assignment with a fawning cover story that posed the question, "Can This Man Save Iraq?"[30] The implicit answer: yes. Yet when Petraeus departed fifteen months later, the country had not been saved, and the building of an Iraqi army remained a work in progress. *Newsweek* neglected to publish a retraction.

Petraeus's next posting took him to Fort Leavenworth, Kansas, where the U.S. Army thinks about how to fight. Installed as Leavenworth's commanding general, he took personal charge of drafting a new counterinsurgency manual intended to impart greater rigor to what Casey was already purportedly doing in Iraq. The final product, known as FM 3-24, appeared in December 2006 precisely as the Bush administration was grappling with the need for a course change. If nothing else, FM 3-24 was an astonishing public relations triumph, with Petraeus himself the principal beneficiary.[31] The manual announced that salvation was at hand.

We recount these episodes not to question Petraeus's genuinely prodigious talents but to emphasize the one specific quality that set him apart from soldiers like Tommy Franks or Ricardo Sanchez or George Casey. Petraeus was smart, shrewd, and not lacking in physical courage. So were other senior military officers of his day. But unlike others, Petraeus had also acquired a mastery of what Daniel Boorstin decades before had called the "pseudo-event."[32] He had a gift for manipulating appearances so that perception displaces reality. And that, more than anything else, is what the Bush administration required in the winter of 2006–2007: someone who could reimagine the war in Iraq, thereby concealing the irreversible collapse of U.S. strategy in the Greater Middle East.

In his Princeton PhD dissertation, a younger Petraeus had written, "What policymakers believe to have taken place in any particular case is what matters more than what actually occurred."[33] Although not an original thought, it accurately describes the task confronting Petraeus as he took the reins in Baghdad. His first priority was to persuade political elites, the American public, and to some extent the U.S. military

itself to disbelieve in what had actually taken place in Iraq, ignoring the
gap between what had been promised and what had occurred—
substituting instead the image of a war that still might somehow be
redeemed. To succeed was to divert attention from the fact that the war
itself had become devoid of strategic purpose.

Ever so briefly, in the immediate aftermath of 9/11, the Bush administration had devised a strategy of sorts, arguably the first ever since the
United States had inaugurated its War for the Greater Middle East. A
transformed U.S. military, guided by the precepts of the RMA, was
going to transform the core of the Islamic world. Now, a half-dozen
years later, the appointment of General Petraeus represented a tacit
abandonment of that strategy and an abrogation of the RMA. Although
the War for the Greater Middle East continued, U.S. military policy in
the Islamic world from this point forward possessed no more coherence than when Ronald Reagan had supported one side in the Iran-Iraq
War while providing arms to the other. President Bush was counting on
General Petraeus to prevent anyone from noticing.

Petraeus delivered. Temporarily provided with a modest contingent
of thirty thousand additional combat troops, armed with the principles
laid out in FM 3-24, and assisted by General Odierno, now promoted to
three-star rank and responsible for handling day-to-day operations, he
reinvigorated the Third Gulf War through a campaign known as the
"surge." In his confirmation hearings, Petraeus had identified "security
of the population," especially in Baghdad, as his top priority. He promised to establish a "persistent presence" of U.S. troops in even the tough-
est neighborhoods, even while endorsing Casey's muted definition of
victory: Iraqis able to assume responsibility for their own destiny.
"There is no military solution to the problems of Iraq," Petraeus emphasized. Progress would take time, and "there undoubtedly will be
tough days ahead." Yet "hard is not hopeless." Escalation meant hope.[34]

A reasonable facsimile of that forecast ensued. Inserting U.S. forces
into Baghdad's most violent precincts did produce tough days, but by
the fall of 2007 American casualties had begun to taper off. In September, Petraeus was back in Washington. The tide of violence plaguing

Iraq had begun to recede, he reported. Overall civilian casualties had dropped by 45 percent—in Baghdad, by 70 percent. Car bombings and suicide attacks were down. In Anbar Province, Sunnis were turning on Al Qaeda and demonstrating a "newfound willingness to volunteer to serve in the Iraqi army." Petraeus foresaw U.S. troop levels in Iraq returning to pre-surge levels by the following summer. Yet he warned against a "rapid withdrawal" that could release "strong centrifugal forces," thereby squandering hard-won gains.[35]

Here was the new narrative. Petraeus was steering Iraq toward the path to recovery. This time progress was real, not illusory. Even so, challenges remained. The war had to continue.

In an immediate sense, ensuring the war's continuation describes one fundamental purpose of the exercise. By 2007, Americans in growing numbers were sick of Iraq and all that the fighting there entailed. They wanted out and the sooner the better. Yet allowing popular opposition to end the war would jeopardize prerogatives to which members of the national security elite had become accustomed. Since World War II, the president and those enjoying access to the president had determined when, where, and how the United States would fight. With Vietnam the exception that affirmed the rule's importance, the American people had exercised little say. The importance of fending off any further challenge to these arrangements transcended Iraq itself. This the surge did. It bought time and kept the public from intruding into policy.[36]

The various politicians, pundits, academics, and analysts on whom Petraeus had lavished attention saw something more: The surge represented a feat of historically unprecedented proportions, attributable to the general himself. The historian Victor Davis Hanson declared that Petraeus "will enter the annals of military history among figures like Ulysses S. Grant, William Tecumseh Sherman, George Patton, and Matthew Ridgeway [sic]."[37] Better at spelling, the journalist Max Boot readily agreed, anointing Petraeus "the Matthew Ridgway of this war, rescuing a failing war effort just as Ridgway rescued the United States in the Korean War."[38] Michael O'Hanlon and his Brookings Institution colleagues reached further back into America's military past. They assessed Petraeus's surge as "the greatest American military comeback late in a war since Sherman's march to the sea in 1864."[39] Over at the American Enterprise Institute, Frederick Kagan and Kimberly Kagan were not to be outdone. "Great commanders often come in pairs," they wrote: "Eisenhower and Patton, Grant and Sherman, Napoleon and Davout, Marlborough and Eugene, Caesar and Labienus. Generals David Petraeus and Raymond Odierno can now be added to the list."[40] Making the ultimate leap, another writer spied the hand of the divine at work. "God," Jeffrey Bell wrote, "has apparently seen fit to give the U.S. Army a great general in this time of need."[41] In David Petraeus, God had chosen well.

Petraeus-mania left some observers unmoved. Comparing Petraeus and Odierno to Grant and Sherman was a bit like ranking George W. Bush alongside Abraham Lincoln, in their view. Yes, violence in Iraq dramatically subsided in 2007–2008. But, no, Petraeus and the implementation of COIN "best practices" did not provide an adequate causal explanation.

As surge skeptics were quick to point out, the so-called Sunni Awakening—Sunni tribal leaders turning on Al Qaeda and forging marriages of convenience with local U.S. commanders—predated Petraeus's appointment as overall commander in Baghdad. In 2005, H. R. McMaster, hero of 73 Easting during the Second Gulf War and now a colonel commanding the 3rd Armored Cavalry Regiment, had stabilized the city of Tal Afar west of Mosul by taking an approach that emphasized patiently building relationships rather than kicking down doors.[42] In the summer and fall of 2006, Colonel Sean MacFarland, commanding a brigade of the 1st Armored Division successfully (if temporarily) pacified Ramadi, capital of Anbar Province. Like McMaster, MacFarland demonstrated a capacity to cut loose from orthodoxy and innovate on the fly. "I was a bit of a drowning man in Ramadi," he subsequently admitted. "I was reaching for anything that would help me float. And that was the tribes."[43] Yet it was Al Qaeda's excesses rather than the teachings of FM 3-24 that prompted Sunni tribal leaders to suspend their campaign against the Americans, who gratefully responded with subsidies and expressions of warm regard.[44]

In Baghdad itself, a purge had preceded the surge. Many months of fierce fighting between Sunnis and Shia (and among Shiite factions) had effectively ended the commingling of sectarian antagonists in the Iraqi capital. By early 2007, Baghdad appeared intent on replicating mid-twentieth century Boston or Chicago: Mixed neighborhoods had become a thing of the past. Physical separation greatly reduced levels of violence, which Petraeus's troops had not induced but merely affirmed and policed.[45]

Finally, a shadowy kill-or-capture campaign conducted by elite U.S. special operators specifically targeting Al Qaeda was gaining momentum. Lieutenant General Stanley McChrystal, who directed that campaign, reported directly to CENTCOM, not to the American commander in Baghdad. By taking down Al Qaeda in Iraq, McChrystal was regaining some of the territory "lost" to terrorism as a direct result of President Bush's ill-advised 2003 invasion. To credit Petraeus's surge with that success was more or less like crediting the inventors of Facebook with creating the digital age. Others had already done the heavy lifting.[46]

How then are we to situate the Iraq surge within the larger framework of America's War for the Greater Middle East? According to Lieutenant General Bolger, a Petraeus critic, "The surge did not 'win' anything."[47] For his part, Senator John McCain, a Petraeus booster, quickly concluded that "the surge worked" and never budged from that position.[48] Although contradictory, each judgment in its own way has merit.

As an actual event, the surge proved to be little more than a pause. It coincided with and helped further a temporary decline in violence. Unfortunately, Petraeus's achievement in Baghdad in 2007–2008 resembles his achievement in occupying Mosul in 2003–2004: Gains proved fleeting. A genuinely decisive battlefield victory—Midway, for example, or Stalingrad—paves the way for ending a war on favorable terms.

In U.S. military doctrine, the sequel to a successful offensive operation is first *exploitation* and then *pursuit*—in lay terms, going in for the final kill. Neither occurred or was even contemplated in the wake of the Iraq surge.[49] So rather than ending the Third Gulf War, Petraeus's success provided the war's proponents with a rationale for prolonging it. On this score, Bolger surely stands correct. Ultimately, the surge had no bearing whatsoever on the war's outcome.

Yet as a pseudo-event, it qualified as a singular achievement. Styling the surge as an epic victory offered a way to rebut suspicions, growing more prominent the longer Iraq dragged on, that U.S. policymakers were clueless and American military leaders incompetent. To allow such impressions to take hold would be to invite all manner of unwelcome questions about the wisdom of invading Iraq in the first place, of deferring to elites who dreamed up such ideas, and of shoveling ever more money at the Pentagon to persist in a failing enterprise. Most dangerous of all for a nation deeply invested in maintaining global military supremacy were Iraq-induced questions about whether war itself remained a viable instrument of policy.

To all such nitpicking, surge supporters offered this ready reply: Behold the brilliance of King David.[50] Behold, too, his resurrection of COIN as the formula for a new and improved American way of war.[51] Here, Senator McCain's view rather than General Bolger's prevailed. As a preemptive strike against any inclination to reexamine the basic assumptions underlying America's War for the Greater Middle East or to reconsider the militarization of U.S. policy more generally, the surge did succeed and notably so.

The implications became apparent in the 2008 presidential campaign. That contest bore some similarity to the notorious election of 1968 pitting Hubert Humphrey against Richard Nixon. Forty years later, at least in a political sense, Iraq was Vietnam *redux*. Choosing the successor to an incumbent discredited by war required each of the opposing candidates to explain what that war signified and what he intended to do with it.

In the replay, John McCain found himself in the role of Humphrey. Without altogether forsaking the war itself, McCain struggled to avoid having it taint his candidacy. Fortune cast Barack Obama, first-term Democratic senator from Illinois, as Richard Nixon. Like Nixon, Obama ran for the presidency promising to exit the war without damaging the nation's credibility or reputation. Nixon had referred to "peace with honor." Obama chose a similar formulation, pledging "to end this war responsibly."[52] More specifically, Obama promised to shift the weight of the U.S. military effort in the Islamic world. Instead of Iraq, which he had characterized as a "dumb" and "rash" war, Afghanistan would receive top billing. That he depicted as the "war we need to win."[53]

In some respects, the election turned on how the two candidates differed in framing Iraq. For McCain, the surge meant everything. He had supported it while Obama had not. On that basis, McCain argued that he had demonstrated his worthiness to serve as commander in chief whereas Obama had disqualified himself. Of course, even when he had criticized its conduct, McCain had never wavered in supporting the Third Gulf War, which Obama had opposed from day one—indeed, before day one. That, Obama argued, showed that whereas he himself possessed the foresight required of a commander in chief, McCain had revealed his own unsuitability. Crucially, while each candidate impugned the other's judgment, neither questioned the decades-old military enterprise of which Iraq represented one manifestation.

Often in American elections, the outcome of a contest based on ostensibly sharp differences affirms an implicit consensus transcending those differences. Certainly, that occurred here. Obama handily defeated McCain. America's War for the Greater Middle East thereby survived unscathed—which would also have occurred if the polling had produced the opposite result.

The war in Iraq for which Obama assumed responsibility when he became president on January 20, 2009, was already winding down. In his last visit to Baghdad, President Bush had signed off on "a framework for the drawdown of American forces as the fight in Iraq nears a successful end."[54] With success—ostensibly thanks to the surge—so close at hand, the time for U.S. troops to begin packing up for home had arrived. The agreement with the Iraqi government identified December 2011 as the deadline for completing the withdrawal. Preparing to leave office, Bush described Iraq as "a rising democracy, an ally in the war on terror, an inspiring model of freedom for people across the Middle East."[55] Take that at face value, and it looked like "Mission Accomplished" all over again.

In truth, by the one measure that Americans actually cared about—U.S. combat casualties—things were certainly looking up. Yes, fighting continued. But during the first six months of Obama's presidency, the number of Americans killed in Iraq averaged just seventeen per month—a decline of more than 80 percent from two years before. The number of Americans being wounded had also dropped precipitously, with the monthly tally of wounded now smaller than the monthly death toll when the surge was in its early stages.[56] Such signs of progress sufficed to encourage Americans to begin tuning out the war.

Yet once more appearances deceived. In fact, the United States was no closer to "Mission Accomplished" in 2009 than it had been back in 2003, unless, that is, one accepted a severely watered-down definition of what that mission entailed.

Security is a relative term. Although the security within Iraq had improved considerably in the wake of the surge, violence persisted, as did the insurgency itself. During the first six months of President Obama's term, with the surge now officially complete, internecine violence was still claiming an average of 280 Iraqi lives per month. Attacks on coalition forces continued to occur at a rate exceeding 200 per week. From one month to the next, insurgents were killing dozens of Iraqi soldiers and police officers.[57]

Newspaper headlines recording incidents that occurred in a single month hint at the continuing mayhem: "Four Killed in Baghdad Market Blast," June 1, 2009; "Nine Killed in Baghdad Café Bombing," June 4, 2009; "Iraq: Bombing of Minibus in Shiite Area Kills 9," June 8, 2009; "Car Bomb in Iraq Kills About 30 People," June 10, 2009; "Iraq Truck Bomb Kills 64," June 20, 2009; "Iraqis Hunt for Relatives in Rubble of Deadly Truck Bombing," June 21, 2009; "31 Killed in Iraq Attacks as U.S. Pullback Looms," June 22, 2009; "Bomb Strikes Shiite Market in

Baghdad, Killing 69," June 24, 2009; "Motorcycle Bombs Kill 20 in Baghdad," June 26, 2009; "Iraqis Celebrate US Pullback but Bombing Kills
33," June 30, 2009.[58]

In no other country (barring perhaps Afghanistan) would violence
on a scale that Iraqis were continuing to endure qualify as even remotely tolerable. Even so, once in office, President Obama found it
politically expedient to adopt the position of his predecessor. Without
saying so explicitly, his administration accepted the pretense that the
surge had indeed turned the war around. Improved conditions thereby
provided a justification for doing precisely what George W. Bush had
envisioned and what Obama himself had promised to do if elected
president—incrementally reducing the number of GIs present in Iraq.

As often happens when a war drags on for too long, domestic politics
now superseded strategic considerations as a basis for policy. Americans had elected Obama to get the United States out of Iraq. The new
president was fully committed to making good on that expectation. His
challenge was to make withdrawal look like something other than retreat. This describes the mission of U.S. forces in Iraq during the last
two years of the Third Gulf War. As General Zinni or any other veteran
of the Vietnam War in its waning years might have remarked, it was
Vietnamization all over again.

As the Third Gulf War progressed through its several phases, American military leaders displayed a proclivity for gnomic aphorisms of the
sort that in an earlier day might have found favor with Chairman Mao.
General Tommy Franks reduced his theory of modern warfare to just
two words: "Speed kills."[59] When speed alone did not suffice to finish
the job, George Casey devised an alternative: "Al Qaeda out, Sunnis in,
ISF in the lead," a formulation that expressed his determination to eliminate foreign fighters, end sectarian divisions, and prod Iraqi Security
Forces into taking over the fight.[60]

With Petraeus's surge came yet another maxim. "Clear, hold, and
build" was meant to convey renewed resolve, even if the ultimate aim—
finding a way out—remained unchanged. Petraeus departed Iraq in
September 2008, elevated to the post of CENTCOM commander. Nei-

ther Odierno, his immediate successor in Baghdad, nor General Lloyd Austin, who in September 2010 became the sixth U.S. officer to preside over the war, coined a snappy phrase to describe what they were trying to accomplish. Had they done so, something along the lines of "hang on, exit gracefully, fingers crossed" would have fit the bill.

As Operation Iraqi Freedom's last days dwindled down, egress management displaced "kinetic operations" as the focus of attention. Two issues now dominated: the pace of troop withdrawal and the composition of a residual force, if any, to remain behind after the December 2011 end date to which the Bush administration had agreed. Each involved sensitive negotiations between the new commander in chief back in Washington and the general already installed in Baghdad.[61]

As a candidate, Obama had vowed to withdraw all U.S. combat troops from Iraq within sixteen months of taking office. Odierno told his new boss that twenty-three months sounded like a better number. They settled on nineteen. Candidate Obama had implied that all combat troops out meant just that. Supported by Petraeus at CENTCOM, Odierno argued for retaining a backup if the Iraqi army encountered problems it could not handle. Although initially balking at this request, Obama ultimately agreed to a "transitional" force remaining after the U.S. combat role had officially ended. To provide the president with political cover, the Pentagon styled the stay-behind forces as "advise and assist" brigades. In reality, they would be standard U.S. Army combat formations augmented with a small advisory contingent. It was the equivalent of calling an aircraft carrier a hospital ship by adding a few nurses to the crew. Odierno envisioned a total headcount of fifty thousand for this transitional force. Anticipating that this was more than his party's antiwar wing was likely to swallow, Obama countered with an offer of somewhere between thirty-five and fifty thousand, exact numbers to be worked out later.[62]

In Iraq itself, the priority was not tying up loose ends but preventing them from fraying further. Curbing the authoritarian tendencies of the Shiites now wielding power while adjudicating intra-Iraqi disputes to maintain the facade of a functioning government presiding over an actual nation-state absorbed much of Odierno's attention. To his credit, the general studiously avoided claiming that the war was ending in anything even approximating definitive success. When an annoying reporter in September 2009 asked if the Iraq insurgency was now finally in its "last throes"—in this context, a loaded phrase—Odierno responded with irritation. "I will never say last throes," understandably forgetting that six years earlier he had essentially done just that. "And it's not going to end, okay? There'll always be some sort of a low-level insurgency in Iraq for the next five, 10, 15 years. The issue is, what is the level of that insurgency? And can the Iraqis handle it with their own forces and with their government? That's the issue."[63]

The admission could not have been an easy one for an American four-star general to make. Having failed despite herculean efforts to impose its will on the enemy, the U.S.-led coalition had tacitly given up on trying. Indeed, the coalition itself had ceased to exist, the last non-U.S. foreign troop contingents pulling out of Iraq during the summer of 2009. Only the Americans remained.

With the world's most powerful military establishment having initiated a conflict it had proven unable to finish, few palatable options presented themselves. Further prosecution of a war now detached from any larger strategic purpose would amount to sheer lunacy, even assuming that the political will to do so existed, which it did not. Nothing remained but to put the best face on things and leave.

In September 2010, Operation Iraqi Freedom gave way to Operation New Dawn, with General Austin now in overall command. The choice of such an Orwellian appellation was fitting. Although the name change was meant to signal the end of the U.S. combat mission, fighting continued, albeit sporadically. Whether or not anything new was actually dawning, one thing was for certain—U.S. troop strength in Iraq was dropping. In December 2009, 110,000 troops remained in Iraq. One year later the number was 48,000. A year later still and the number was zero, Iraqi authorities having torpedoed U.S. plans to retain a transitional force in country.[64] General Casey had hoped to wrap up the Third Gulf War by December 2005. His estimate was off by precisely six years.

Back in March 1973, at ceremonies marking the inactivation of U.S. Military Assistance Command, Vietnam, General Frederick C. Weyand, MACV's last commander, told the American soldiers in attendance, "You can hold your heads up high for having been a part of this selfless effort." As he prepared to leave Saigon, the general described a glass more than half-full. "Our mission has been accomplished. I depart with a strong feeling of pride in what we have achieved, and in what our achievement represents."[65]

Over thirty-eight years later, departing Baghdad in similar circumstances, General Austin offered an assessment mirroring Weyand's. "What our troops achieved in Iraq over the course of nearly nine years is truly remarkable," he declared. "They removed a brutal dictator and gave the Iraqi people their freedom." In doing so, American soldiers had set the stage for "Iraq's young democracy to emerge as a leader in what has been and what will continue to be a very dynamic region."[66]

Of course, preserving any gains U.S. forces had made in Vietnam by 1973 depended on the ability of the South Vietnamese to fend for themselves. So too with Iraq after 2011. Would Iraqis find it possible to manage on their own? Or, as with the South Vietnamese, would they succumb to a combination of internal and external pressures? Only time would tell. The real "clock" had just begun to tick.

15

GOVERNMENT

IN A BOX

BY ELECTING BARACK OBAMA PRESIDENT, AMERICANS ONCE
more entrusted the highest office in the land to a foreign policy neo-
phyte. With the anomalous exception of George H. W. Bush, this pattern had prevailed throughout America's War for the Greater Middle
East.

All newly elected presidents promise a clean break from past troubles. Obama was no exception. With Russia, there was to be a "reset"
and with China "rigorous and persistent engagement" to preclude the
possibility of a second Cold War. To Iranians, he offered an "extended
hand" in return for a willingness to "unclench their fist." Transcending
these country-specific initiatives in immediate importance was the new
president's vow to "seek a new beginning between the United States
and Muslims around the world." With this new beginning, "common
principles . . . principles of justice and progress; tolerance and the dignity of all human beings" would provide the basis for relations.[1] Good-
bye conflict and suspicion, hello harmony and understanding. In effect,
Obama began his presidency declaring that the War for the Greater
Middle East had become redundant, as if the product of some unfortunate miscommunication. In practice, however, ending that conflict
eluded his grasp, in no small part due to actions on his part that expanded and thereby perpetuated it.

The expansion began in Afghanistan. At the outset of its War for the

Greater Middle East, the United States had sought to destabilize that country. Having succeeded, it tried to ignore the results. Then after 9/11, with regime change now becoming the favored American M.O., the George W. Bush administration toppled the government in Kabul, even as its fixation with Iraq soon thereafter provided an excuse to distance itself once more from the consequences. Loose ends in Afghanistan were not going to prevent the Bush administration from going after Saddam. Yet once begun, Operation Enduring Freedom refused to end. Less by intent than out of miscalculation, Bush found himself stuck with a two-front war.

During World War II, saddled with his own two-front predicament, Franklin Roosevelt had struggled to reconcile the imperatives of waging war against Germany with the imperatives of waging a simultaneous war against Japan. Bush was not into reconciliation. He established clear priorities and stuck with them: Iraq was the main effort and Afghanistan a subsidiary theater. And so it proved to be throughout his term in office. Admiral Michael G. Mullen, who followed Pace as JCS chairman, put the matter succinctly: "In Afghanistan, we do what we can. In Iraq, we do what we must."[2] By "what we can," Mullen meant "not much."

It was a striking admission. During the eight years of the Bush presidency, U.S. military spending, easily the highest in the world, more than doubled from slightly above $300 billion to nearly $700 billion per year. Even so, the Pentagon found it impossible to adequately resource two moderate-sized conflicts. As the Third Gulf War all but consumed the Bush presidency, the Second Afghanistan War dragged on inconclusively, attracting little more than glancing attention.

Upon assuming office, President Obama wasted no time in reversing Bush's priorities. In Afghanistan, he sought to do more with more while moving to get out of Iraq altogether. Escalating in Afghanistan enabled Obama to fulfill an imprudent campaign pledge. Yet doing so had this unintended result: It ensured that the War for the Greater Middle East was going to continue. It also ensured that the strategic void that Bush had bequeathed to Obama would remain intact.

As one facet of a much larger enterprise, Afghanistan was destined to become easily the longest war in American history, a fact difficult to square with that country's modest geopolitical significance. In the wake of 9/11, Bush and his lieutenants had viewed Afghanistan as a strategic dead end. They were not wrong to do so. Eight years later, with President Obama intent on doubling down, the insight remained no less valid, but was now deemed irrelevant.

Indeed, as the fighting in Afghanistan entered its second decade with no end in sight, it was becoming ever more difficult to understand what the United States hoped to achieve by remaining in such a distant country about which most Americans knew little and cared even less. Save Afghanistan from the Taliban? What made Afghans worth the trouble? Why not save Mexico from predatory drug cartels? Why not save Haiti or Venezuela? Both were closer to home, equally in need, and arguably better able to absorb whatever benefactions Washington might be willing to bestow.

After toppling the Taliban, the United States military presence in Afghanistan qualified as hardly more than nominal. During the Bush era, U.S. troop strength had averaged fewer than eighteen thousand, never rising above one-fifth the total number of American military personnel committed to Operation Iraqi Freedom.[3] In comparison to Iraq, casualties also occurred at a modest rate. U.S. losses in Afghanistan averaged fewer than eighty per year.[4]

After the abortive fight at Tora Bora, with Afghanistan nominally liberated, Washington's emphasis had shifted to state-building. The United States and its allies—to justify its existence, NATO was still keen to go "out of area"—set out to create a strong central government in Kabul exercising jurisdiction throughout Afghanistan and headed by the West's chosen leader, the presumably accommodating Hamid Karzai. Such a government would ensure stability, prevent Afghanistan from once more becoming a terrorist safe haven, and create conditions for its long-term modernization.[5]

Although holding the United Nations in generally low regard, the Bush administration looked to the UN and others in the "international community" to take the lead in this very ambitious project. The small contingent of U.S. combat troops retained in Afghanistan were to chase down Al Qaeda remnants along with any of the groups loosely referred to as the Taliban. Where there was fighting to be done, Americans would do it, leaving to others the tasks of occupation and reconstruction. This distribution of labor triggered a tsunami of well-intentioned governmental and nongovernmental organizations eager to respond to the plight of the Afghan people. In short order, twenty-six UN agencies set up shop in Kabul, and over forty countries contributed troops to what became known as the International Security Assistance Force (ISAF).[6]

Unfortunately, results achieved on the ground came nowhere close to meeting the expectations nursed in Western capitals. Despite formal progress made in erecting some semblance of a legitimate government—as in Iraq, interim institutions were created, a constitution was drafted, elections occurred—substantive improvements lagged. Derisively known as the "mayor of Kabul," President Karzai exercised limited authority outside of the Afghan capital. In the countryside, a traditional politics of ethnic and clan identity prevailed. Although donor nations pledged billions in development assistance, some reneged on promises while funds that actually materialized were as likely to go to consultant salaries and corporate profits as to projects actually benefiting Afghans. Corruption was rampant.[7] Only one sector of the domestic economy boomed: opium cultivation and export. Occupied Afghanistan became the source of 90 percent of global opium production.

The disparity between what the occupiers promised and what they delivered created an opening for the Taliban and Al Qaeda to make a comeback. Particularly in the southern and eastern Afghan provinces bordering Pakistan, which had become a sanctuary for militant Islamists, violence intensified. By 2005, suicide bombings and IED attacks, mainstays of the Iraq insurgency, were making their appearance in growing numbers. Security was deteriorating. U.S. allies had imagined that they were signing up for an exercise in armed peacekeeping more or less comparable to Bosnia or Kosovo once aerial bombardment had ceased. The advent of a shooting war came as a disagreeable surprise.[8]

An incident in Kabul itself—an Afghan counterpart to the bloody Fallujah schoolhouse confrontation of April 28, 2003—brought the dimensions of the problem facing the United States and its partners in Afghanistan fully into view.

On the morning of May 29, 2006, a truck driven by American soldiers, part of a U.S. military convoy moving through the crowded streets of the Afghan capital, plowed into roughly a dozen parked vehicles, killing several bystanders and injuring others. As the rest of the convoy tried to leave the scene, angry Afghans surrounded it and began pelting U.S. troops with rocks. Shots were fired, and a full-scale riot erupted. Rampaging through the streets, rioters sacked and burned buildings representing a foreign presence such as aid agencies along with a newly constructed five-star hotel. They angrily denounced the United States and mocked President Karzai as an American lackey. It took six hours for Afghan security forces to restore order. By then sixteen civilians were dead with more than a hundred others hospitalized, many with gunshot wounds.[9]

The U.S. ambassador duly apologized, citing brake failure as the cause of the accident. Many Afghans weren't buying—they charged the Americans with reckless driving, indicative of a general disregard for Afghan life. By no means incidentally, just one week before, an errant U.S. air strike in Kandahar Province had killed at least sixteen and as many as thirty-four Afghan civilians, a group that included women and children, provoking outrage.[10] U.S. authorities had apologized for that unfortunate miscue as well, as they would for many others.[11]

The air strike gone wrong had targeted a resurgent Taliban. No evidence connected the rioters in Kabul to the Taliban or to Al Qaeda. They were merely ordinary Afghans increasingly intolerant of foreigners who enjoyed a privileged status while producing little of apparent value. Afghanistan was becoming a two-front war nested within a larger two-front war. On one front were insurgents intent on overthrowing the government; on the other front was a disaffected populace increasingly inclined to see that government as a tool of the occupiers.

Through 2007 and 2008, conditions in Iraq appeared to be improving. In Afghanistan, they were growing worse. So at least Secretary of Defense Gates concluded during periodic visits to survey the situation. The war there, he later wrote, "was clearly headed in the wrong direction." Statistical indicators, especially as measured by enemy activity, supported that assessment. The problems afflicting Operation Enduring Freedom were legion. According to Gates, they included "insufficient levels of combat troops and trainers, inadequate numbers of civilian experts, confusing command and control, the lack of multinational coordination on the civilian side, and deficient civil-military coordination."[12] On one occasion, flying over the desolate Afghan landscape, the Pentagon chief asked himself, *Why are people fighting over this godforsaken place?*[13] He provided no answer to this pertinent question. Although President Bush agreed to token reinforcements—there were thirty thousand U.S. troops in country when he left office—the Afghan situation appeared increasingly grim.

By the time Obama moved into the White House, army General David McKiernan was commanding U.S. and coalition forces in Afghanistan. He was the sixth American general, beginning with Tommy Franks, to have charge of the Second Afghanistan War. Five more were to follow.

A stolid and phlegmatic officer well versed in the conventions of mechanized warfare, McKiernan confronted a situation in which those conventions did not apply. Candidly describing his war as deadlocked, he did not minimize the obstacles he confronted. Chief among those obstacles were too few troops, too many political restrictions—euphemistically known as "caveats"—that limited the utility of allied contingents, and the existence of de facto jihadist sanctuaries in Pakistan.[14]

McKiernan embraced the view that the war could not be won militarily, by now almost a mantra among senior U.S. military officers. Just

a few years earlier those same officers had insisted with equal conviction that winning wars militarily described what the armed forces of
the United States existed to do. No more. Expectations regarding how
military efforts might contribute to America's War for the Greater Middle East were evolving. McKiernan's own assessment reflected that evolution. Combat operations might continue—"we are not going to run
out of bad people with bad intentions that we could kill or capture"—
but ending the Second Afghanistan War was going to require a political
solution. McKiernan wasn't counting on such a solution to materialize
anytime soon. To reach the "point where we see the light at the end of
this tunnel of this long war" was likely to require years, he said. An officer corps that had expected wars to be brief now took it for granted
that they would be anything but.[15]

What McKiernan wanted from the incoming Obama administration
was quite simple: more troops, to arrive before a Taliban offensive expected for the summer of 2009. Although possessed by an impulse to
do more in Afghanistan, the new administration lacked a clear idea of
how to translate more into a positive outcome of the war. McKiernan's
request and the administration's impulse prompted an early presidential decision, announced on February 17, 2009, to deploy an additional
seventeen thousand troops. These reinforcements were "necessary to
stabilize a deteriorating situation," according to the president.[16] A high-
level policy review to determine what the United States hoped to
achieve beyond stabilization yielded a laundry list of generalities. Un-
veiling the results of that review in late March, Obama vowed "to disrupt, dismantle, and defeat Al Qaida in Pakistan and Afghanistan" but
offered few particulars.[17]

Only on one issue did clarity emerge: McKiernan was not the guy for
the job ahead. On May 6, Secretary Gates flew to Kabul and informed
McKiernan that he was being replaced. Not since Harry Truman fired
Douglas MacArthur in 1951 had a four-star U.S. commander been peremptorily relieved of a wartime command. MacArthur lost his job due
to rank insubordination. McKiernan lost his because he didn't seem the
right fit. He lacked spark. Acting on his defense secretary's strong

recommendation, Obama wasted little time in appointing Stanley McChrystal as McKiernan's replacement.

McChrystal was a remarkable soldier. Like a world-class athlete at the top of his game, he exuded an intensity that allowed little room for anything apart from the mission at hand. He was a laser, not a searchlight. For over four years, from 2004 to 2008, McChrystal had directed anti–Al Qaeda counterterrorism operations, a small covert fragment of a much larger conflict. In Iraq, he declared it his intention to "disembowel" the terrorist network. Killing the leaders of Al Qaeda in Iraq and anyone daring to succeed the deceased, he believed, would ultimately cause "the organization to collapse in on itself."[18] To test that hypothesis, the task force he commanded developed a remarkable aptitude for killing, typically at night, almost always in secret, its members a law unto themselves.

As other senior officers rotated in and out of the war zone, McChrystal had stayed on the job, achieving legendary status even while largely avoiding the limelight.[19] In 2006, a *Newsweek* puff piece had touted him as the "Hidden General."[20] Now, as he prepared to assume responsibility for presiding over the stalemated war effort in Afghanistan, any last vestiges of anonymity disappeared. The Petraeus phenomenon had fostered expectations of the general who singlehandedly saves the day. Reporters now fell all over themselves, describing McChrystal as the next Petraeus. In an admiring profile, journalist Dexter Filkins stated the matter directly: "And so if it was Petraeus who saved Iraq from cataclysm, it now falls to McChrystal to save Afghanistan."[21]

By common consent, he seemed the man for the job. McChrystal was a "warrior-scholar," *The New York Times* reported with satisfaction.[22] He possessed "drive and intellect," *The Washington Post* added, and had won renown for his pronounced "abilities in team-building and problem-solving."[23] He was also something of an ascetic, a "Zen Warrior," according to *Newsweek*.[24] "Fit as a tuning fork," *Time* gushed, McChrystal typically ran ten miles each morning before dawn, subsisted on a diet that would have tested a Trappist monk—he considered eating lunch "a sign of weakness"—and stocked his iPod and Kindle with "serious tomes on Pakistan, Lincoln and Vietnam." McChrystal was going to do things differently, and *Time* approved. "Military policy in Afghanistan is now in the hands of this likable and very, very focused soldier."[25]

The hyperbole had serious implications. McChrystal's civilian superiors were disinclined to place policy formulation in the hands of any general officer, no matter how likable and focused. Yet on the perpetually shifting see-saw of U.S. civil-military relations, the military now enjoyed the upper hand. War was simply too important an enterprise to be left to civilians—so a public disenchanted with Donald Rumsfeld and Paul Wolfowitz (while smitten with David Petraeus) had come to believe. Senior members of the officer corps were quick to exploit the opening that this change in mood presented.

The intensely politicized nature of the civil-military relationship defines one of Washington's prime hidden-in-plain-sight secrets. Yes, ultimately, senior military leaders view themselves as subordinate to civilian authority. So a "Seven Days in May" conspiracy to overthrow the government is well-nigh an impossibility. Shy of orchestrating a coup, however, senior officers (or subordinates acting on their behalf) engage in all sorts of shenanigans to advance the agenda of a particular command, service, or individual. For public consumption, all parties punctiliously observe the requisite proprieties. But these no more define the actual relationship than do the courtesies that a philandering husband extends to his wife on the occasion of their anniversary—as both parties to that relationship fully understand.

Gates sent McChrystal off to his new posting with this charge: Report back within sixty days with a concrete proposal for how to turn around the Second Afghanistan War, using the additional resources Obama had already agreed to provide. The idea was that McChrystal would recommend; the president, taking the counsel of his military and civilian advisers, would decide; and then McChrystal would loyally implement that decision. In war planning, Rumsfeld had employed an intrusive approach to extract the answer he wanted. Gates was inclined to give field commanders greater breathing space. Neither approach lacked for drawbacks.

With characteristic energy, McChrystal went immediately to work. He arrived in Afghanistan in mid-June. Within ten days he had notified Gates that conditions there were far worse than he had anticipated. Within a month, word was reaching the Pentagon that McChrystal's as yet unfinished plan was likely to require troops *beyond* the increment Obama had already approved. By early August, press reports were previewing McChrystal's likely request for reinforcements, as many as forty thousand more, even before he had provided the administration with a rationale for why they might be needed. The general was getting way out in front of his civilian bosses.[26]

On August 30, McChrystal submitted his assessment to Secretary Gates. Containing many assertions but few facts, the sixty-six-page document was long on exhortation and short on reasoned analysis. History received only a passing glance, although McChrystal took a swipe at "the myth advanced in the media that Afghanistan is a 'graveyard of empires,'" which he categorically rejected. Numbers were notable by their absence.

McChrystal began his assessment on a portentous note. "The stakes in Afghanistan are high," he wrote, adding that "the situation in Afghanistan is serious." Although "success is achievable," he emphasized that "it will not be attained simply by trying harder." The key was to win over the population, which "represents a powerful actor that can and must be leveraged." Leveraging Afghan hearts and minds meant that the troops under his command needed "a fundamentally new way of doing business." ISAF required a "new operational culture" that "connects with the powerful will of the Afghan people," implicitly assumed to be of one mind.[27] As a supposed basis for a military campaign, the document was, in a word, squishy.

Most strikingly, in describing the way ahead, McChrystal did not make even a pretense of weighing a range of possible alternatives. His commander's assessment contained no Option A to compare with B and C. There was only A—"a comprehensive counterinsurgency campaign." The acknowledged master of counterterrorism was opting for an entirely different game: COIN. As a course change, this was on a par with Michael Jordan abandoning basketball to give baseball a try.[28]

The Obama administration received this recommendation without enthusiasm. McChrystal's COIN campaign was going to require more troops—within the White House an unwelcome prospect, for both fiscal and political reasons. Worse, McChrystal's presentation deprived Obama of choice. In effect, the general's message to his commander in chief was "Here, rubber-stamp this."

As if to drive home the limits on Obama's freedom of maneuver, General Petraeus, now commanding CENTCOM, chose this particular moment to offer his views on Afghanistan to Michael Gerson, a *Washington Post* columnist of decidedly hawkish persuasion. His standing as a military oracle at its height, Petraeus was especially well regarded in Republican Party circles. Before reinventing himself as a pundit, Gerson had spent years working as a senior aide to President George W. Bush.

Now, Petraeus obligingly shared with Gerson his considered opinion that in Afghanistan "the core principles of counterinsurgency still obtain." True, applying those principles was going to require "a lot more resources." But overall Petraeus seconded the hints coming from McChrystal's headquarters in Kabul. "We have to regain the initiative," he told Gerson. "We have to get ahead of this, to arrest the downward spiral, to revive momentum." COIN offered the means to do just that. By implication, it was incumbent upon Obama to recognize the obvious.[29]

Back in March 1951, to vent his unhappiness with the way President Harry Truman, a Democrat, was interfering with his conduct of the ongoing Korean War, General of the Army Douglas MacArthur sent a letter to Speaker of the House Joseph W. Martin, a Republican. In that letter, quickly released to the public, MacArthur had expressed wonderment that anyone would disagree with his own assessment of the stakes in Korea. Petraeus was arguably the most overtly political senior mili tary officer to grace the American stage since MacArthur. As with MacArthur's letter to Speaker Martin, his September 4 interview with Gerson constituted a veiled challenge to the authority of the commander in chief.

Once again, as had been the case in Iraq, the political clock and the military clock were out of sync. Obama wanted time to deliberate. McChrystal wanted an immediate go-ahead. Petraeus's interview turned out to be only the opening salvo in an effort to pressure the green-as-grass commander in chief without personal military experience into giving the seasoned warfighter whatever he wanted.

A leaked copy of McChrystal's assessment soon made it into the hands of *The Washington Post,* which on September 14 published a long account that included extracts from the actual document.[30] In short order, the full sixty-six pages were available to anyone with access to the internet. McChrystal himself got into the act, appearing on *60 Minutes* and then promoting his plan via a highly publicized presentation in London. After the London speech, a reporter asked McChrystal if he could envision any alternative to a counterinsurgency approach in Afghanistan. "The short answer is: no."[31]

Not everyone agreed. Vice President Joe Biden for one strongly argued against McChrystal's proposal. The U.S. ambassador to Afghanistan, Karl Eikenberry, sided with the vice president. Lending Eikenberry's dissent additional authority was the fact that he was himself a retired army lieutenant general who had presided over the Afghanistan War from 2005 to 2007.

In cables dated November 6 and November 9, Ambassador Eikenberry questioned the relevance of "clear, hold, and build" to actually existing conditions. Acknowledging that U.S. forces would undoubtedly be able to clear parts of Afghanistan, Eikenberry argued that expectations of Afghans moving on to hold and build were wildly unrealistic. A "surge" in Afghanistan would serve chiefly to "increase Afghan dependence," he wrote, thereby postponing rather than advancing the day when foreign troops would be able to depart. More to the point, McChrystal's proposed counterinsurgency campaign was irrelevant to the central issue, which was Pakistan—"the single greatest source of Afghan instability." As long as Pakistani authorities believed that it served their interests for Afghan militants to move freely back and forth across the Pakistani border, the insurgency was going to persist. COIN offered no remedy to that problem. Above all, Eikenberry cautioned against the view that sending more U.S. troops offered the sole plausible policy alternative.[32]

The Eikenberry cables also leaked, thereby handing Obama a ready-made chance to tilt the civil-military balance back in his own favor. The general-turned-diplomat offered the novice commander in chief cover to push back against the demands pressed by Petraeus and McChrystal. Yet pushing back was certain to produce a politically costly confrontation, with the president facing off against the nation's most influential military officer aligned with the highly respected general that Obama himself had only recently placed in charge of the Afghanistan War.

Rather than risking that confrontation, Obama grudgingly acceded to the generals' wishes. Or more accurately, he acceded with caveats attached. In a speech to cadets at West Point on December 1, 2009, the president unveiled his own version of a surge. Thirty thousand additional U.S. troops—ten thousand fewer than McChrystal wanted—would be heading to Afghanistan. Yet theirs was not going to be an open-ended enterprise. "After 18 months," Obama emphasized, "our troops will begin to come home." The aim of the undertaking was "to seize the initiative, while building the Afghan capacity that can allow for a responsible transition of our forces out of Afghanistan."[33]

The speech required decoding. "Building capacity" meant nation-building, which implied counterinsurgency, although Obama steered clear of that baggage-laden term. As for "responsible transition," that had supplanted victory as the ultimate goal. Obama's presentation fell well short of being a full-throated battle cry. Still, McChrystal had gotten most of what he wanted. With technique having now fully supplanted strategy, COIN was going to get a second try.

As a sort of implicit hat tip to his predecessor, Obama was attempting to do in Afghanistan what Bush had ostensibly done in Iraq. The opportunity costs of choosing this path loomed large. By allowing Afghanistan to consume so much of his early attention and above all by handing the war's conduct to McChrystal, Obama effectively foreclosed any prospect of reevaluating the larger predicament confronting the United States as its War for the Greater Middle East prepared to enter its fourth decade. Any presidential predilection favoring fundamental change—an explicit promise of the Obama election—gave way to the demands of continuity. Inertia won out.

To graph changing U.S. troop strengths in Iraq and Afghanistan was to provide a visual representation of this reality. Between May and June of 2010, the lines crisscrossed. Yes, the numbers in Iraq were shrinking. Yes, too, the number of troops in Afghanistan was headed upward, soon to reach a peak just above a hundred thousand—a force three times larger than when Obama had become president.[34] The administration advanced the proposition that this represented progress.

Yet however muted Obama's enthusiasm, McChrystal wasted no time in implementing the president's decision. Having too few forces to implement COIN on a countrywide basis, he chose to concentrate on the two southern provinces of Helmand and Kandahar. More specifically, he identified Marja, a city of approximately eighty thousand, as the right place to validate COIN's relevance to Afghanistan. Located in a region where poppy cultivation flourished, Marja sat well beyond the zone of Afghan government control. As a Taliban stronghold, it appeared ripe for liberation. Here was an Afghan equivalent of Tal Afar before H. R. McMaster had arrived to put things right.

Now, apart from adhering to a common religious tradition, Afghanistan and Iraq are about as much alike as opium and oil. Even so, McChrystal was expecting that just as "clear, hold, and build" had worked its magic in the one country, so too it would surely work in the other. Seldom has the tendency of generals to fight the last war all over again been more vividly on display.

To win support in the Afghan countryside, McChrystal was determined to reduce the number of civilian casualties resulting from ISAF operations, something that President Karzai had been complaining about for years. With that in mind, McChrystal issued rules of engagement that restricted ISAF's use of force other than in self-defense, even though that meant increased risk to U.S. and other coalition forces. Winning Afghan popular support, he insisted, should take precedence over all other considerations. "We must avoid the trap of winning tactical victories—but suffering strategic defeats—by causing civilian casualties or excessive damage and thus alienating the people."[35] Soldiers were to pull triggers, call in artillery, or ask for close air support only when absolutely necessary and when certain that civilians would not be harmed. The policy, which became known as "courageous restraint," was the sort of high-minded concept that looks good on a PowerPoint slide at higher headquarters but might not translate well with a nervous nineteen-year-old lance corporal on foot patrol.

At any rate, the spirit of courageous restraint informed McChrystal's expectations for how events at Marja were to unfold. Code-named Moshtarak (Dari for "together"), the operation began with a prelude of sorts, a leaflet drop instructing Marja's residents to remove themselves from harm's way and, in effect, inviting the Taliban to do likewise. This they did, with considerable numbers fleeing the city. The real action then kicked off overnight on February 13, 2010, with an assault by U.S. Marines, supported by British troops and preceded by U.S. Army special forces teams. After these coalition combat contingents cleared the city of any remaining insurgents, Afghan security forces were to hold it and then, with plenty of outside help, agencies of the Afghan government would swoop in to rebuild. Phase one promised to be doable, phase two challenging, phase three the really hard part. Even so, McChrystal expressed confidence. "We've got a government in a box, ready to roll in," he promised.[36]

Once successfully resurrected, Marja would offer a model for application elsewhere. "Marja is an opening salvo," one senior Pentagon official promised. "It is a first step." Success in Marja would create a "shift in momentum," setting the stage for comparable successes elsewhere in Afghanistan.[37] The expectations of a single liberating act generating irresistible forward progress mirrored those of Iraqi Freedom back in 2003, albeit on a more modest scale.

Actual results achieved quickly punctured such hopes, however. Once more, the application of self-evidently superior American military might failed to yield lasting political success.

With Marines bearing the brunt of the fighting, the initial stages of Moshtarak's clearing phase began reasonably well. During the operation's first week, eight American and three British soldiers were lost to enemy action.[38] Yet by February 25, for the first time in years, the Afghan flag was flying over the city center. "We are in control of all the key populated areas of Marja, we're in control of all the key infrastructure," Brigadier General Larry Nicholson, senior Marine commander, announced. "Our focus now is on markets. Our focus now on getting the roads open and taking care of the people."[39] The transition from clear to hold and even to build seemed well underway.

Again, however, appearances misled. In wartime, it is a mistake to confuse a lull in violence with a cessation of hostilities. Although armed resistance in Marja may have subsided, it had not ended. Instead, the local Taliban regrouped and adapted. In short order, a campaign of intimidation intended to dissuade the local population from cooperating with the outside intruders was taking its toll.[40] The IED threat, once thought eliminated, reappeared. Firefights between Marines and insurgents became commonplace. U.S. forces sustained more casualties in Marja between mid-May and mid-June than they had in the operation's initial stages. In late May, McChrystal himself all but conceded failure. The city intended to serve as a COIN showcase, he conceded, had instead become a "bleeding ulcer."[41]

According to one American journalist who accompanied U.S. Marines during Operation Moshtarak, McChrystal and other COIN true believers had "overpromised and underdelivered."[42] True as far as it goes, the observation does not probe deeply enough the defects inherent in counterinsurgency theory. The troops charged with implementing that theory found that in practice neat distinctions between clear, hold, and build simply did not hold up. Theory didn't translate into reality. Clearing turned out to be partial and reversible. The Afghan forces expected to maintain order once ISAF had secured the city lacked the wherewithal—and perhaps the will—to do so. Worst of all, the promised improvements in everyday life, the essence of McChrystal's "government in a box," failed to materialize.[43] Operation Moshtarak might well have been called Operation Sand Against the Wind. The longer the Marines stayed on, the more apparent it became that theirs was an exercise in futility.[44]

Of the several available explanations for the operation's disappointing outcome, culture—meaning habit, tradition, identity, and religion—deserves pride of place. Here we confront what we might call COIN's Canadian fallacy.

Although Canadians and Americans differ, both sides have learned to bridge those differences, thereby facilitating wide-ranging collaboration. Between "us" and "them" a divide of sorts persists, but over a long period of coexistence, helped by proximity, that divide has shrunk in importance. It's not worth fighting about.

Proponents of counterinsurgency—and of America's War for the Greater Middle East more generally—assume that the Islamic world is filled with Canadians: people who subscribe to or at least lean toward a worldview akin to our own. Alas, Afghans are most emphatically *not* Canadians. The divide separating "us" from "them" is a chasm. Spanning that chasm, even if theoretically feasible, will necessarily require enormous exertions over an exceedingly long period of time. The idea that a couple of battalions of U.S. Marines demonstrating "courageous restraint" could jump-start the process as was absurd as expecting Marines back in 1983 to bring peace to Lebanon.

McChrystal's attempt to pacify just one small Afghan city by applying the latest counterinsurgency principles came nowhere close to succeeding. Months after ISAF's offensive had begun, Marja remained the site of "a full-blown guerrilla insurgency that rages daily across a bomb-riddled landscape of agricultural fields and irrigation trenches."[45] Yet even if not providing a model for application elsewhere in Afghanistan,

Operation Moshtarak did offer an education of sorts for the American general who had conceived it. McChrystal seemed to grasp the underlying explanation for that failure: The problem was ignorance, laced with hubris. Those charged with presiding over the war in Afghanistan, he subsequently remarked, entertained a "superficial understanding of the situation" and "a frighteningly simplistic view of recent history," an indictment in which McChrystal included himself. Present in Afghanistan for nearly a decade, U.S. forces still struggled to understand the place and its people. "We didn't know enough and we still don't know enough," he lamented.[46]

How McChrystal might have applied these insights is impossible to say. The general himself abruptly departed the scene, felled by an embarrassing magazine article appearing in *Rolling Stone*. Having spent the better part of his career in a realm where keeping secrets secret and journalists at arm's length constitute basic survival skills, McChrystal had invited a reporter to become a de facto member of his military household. This unfathomable decision produced predictable results. The reporter affirmed his preexisting antiwar credentials by publishing an exposé that quoted McChrystal's chief aides—"Team America," by their own estimation—mocking senior members of the Obama administration as clueless clowns, with the general himself joining in the fun.[47] In a system of civil-military relations that values the observance of proprieties above all else, the general had committed an unpardonable offense.

Sparing President Obama from having to fire him outright, McChrystal resigned his position and retired. In so doing, of course, he also spared himself from having to confront the reality that his much-hyped campaign to turn around the Afghanistan War had flopped. Dealing with the consequences of that failure now fell to General Petraeus. By agreeing to take the reins in Kabul—in effect, stepping down a notch from his position as CENTCOM commander—Petraeus spared President Obama from having to explain why his previous hand-picked choice to run the war had so quickly flamed out. Both politically and substantively, replacing McChrystal with the maestro of COIN offered the most expeditious way to put the entire episode to rest. Rather than Michael Jordan trying his hand at baseball, here was Barry Bonds, the greatest home run hitter of all time, stepping up to the plate.

Assuming command in July 2010, Petraeus faced many problems, but one in particular demanded immediate attention: ditching the "new operational culture" that McChrystal had sought to infuse in ISAF. This sudden demand for cultural change had not been well received, particularly within the ranks of the United States military. Soldiers socialized to see themselves as heroic warriors did not take kindly to orders from on high to become something between community organizers and cops—especially when doing so endangered themselves and their buddies.

To vent their unhappiness, some troops directed to demonstrate courageous restraint did just the reverse. And some tactical commanders directed to ensure compliance with that policy denounced it as idiotic.

Among those opting for action over restraint was Captain Mathew Golsteyn, an army special forces officer. For gallantry in action at Marja, Golsteyn earned a Silver Star—only to have it subsequently revoked amidst accusations that he had executed an unarmed Afghan suspected of being a bomb-maker. While criminal charges were never filed, Army investigators reported that Golsteyn later said that he had been concerned that freeing the Afghan would put Americans potentially at risk, and that he would not be able to live with himself if more Americans lost their lives.[48] At roughly the same time, a group of U.S. Marines elsewhere in Helmand Province weighed in with their own take on protecting the local population: They videotaped themselves urinating on three Afghan corpses.[49] Similarly, as Moshtarak was unfolding, U.S. troops assigned to the 5th Stryker Brigade in neighboring Kandahar Province perpetrated a series of random killings of Afghan civilians. In one instance they posed for photographs with a victim, a young boy, "as if it were a trophy deer." The apparent motive was thrill-seeking, compounded by a generalized contempt for the local population.[50] These soldiers manifestly did not share McChrystal's view regarding the supreme importance of protecting innocent Afghans. Here, in sum, was a pattern of conduct fundamentally at odds with the commanding general's stated intentions.

Prominent among those overtly challenging the policy itself was Colonel Harry Tunnell, commander of the 5th Stryker Brigade when the atrocities noted above occurred. Tunnell was cut from the same cloth as Colonel Michael Steele, the commander who had rejected General Casey's attempted implementation of COIN in Iraq. Like Steele, Tunnell stubbornly adhered to the conviction that in war there is *always* a military solution: You find it by subjecting your adversary to unremitting pressure. Severely wounded while commanding a battalion in Iraq, Tunnell had penned a brief reflection on his experience there. "Military leaders must stay focused on the destruction of the enemy," he wrote. "It is virtually impossible to convince any committed terrorist who hates America to change his or her point of view—they simply must be attacked relentlessly."[51] That was back in 2005. Nothing that occurred in the intervening years had caused him to modify his views.

Deploying with his brigade to Afghanistan in 2009 as part of the Obama buildup, Tunnell arrived bent on killing insurgents rather than winning friends. In Kandahar Province, he found the fight he was looking for. During his tour of duty, his brigade killed plenty, while losing 37 soldiers with another 238 wounded. Tunnell himself attracted unfavorable attention from his superiors for being more interested in body count than in implementing the latest COIN precepts.[52]

Such criticism, while effectively ending his prospects for further promotion, left him unfazed. Indeed, the defiant Tunnell used his departure from command as an occasion to share his views with Secretary of the Army John McHugh. Those who bowed obsequiously at the altar of COIN were worshipping a false god, Tunnell wrote in a letter addressed to McHugh. Counterinsurgency doctrine was nonsense. It consisted of little more than "musings from amateurs, contractors, plagiarized journal articles." Misguided adherence to bogus COIN theories was contributing to "needless American casualties" while actually "enabling our enemy." As a direct result, the army to which Tunnell had devoted his professional life had become "a chronic failure."

By taking the highly unusual step of taking his complaint directly to the army's senior ranking civilian, Colonel Tunnell signaled his lack of confidence in the general officers occupying positions in the chain of command between himself and the secretary. If doubt remained on that score, his missive removed it by decrying the army's "dysfunctional and toxic leadership environment." Since an inept and spineless general officer corps was not going to remedy the problem, restoring the army to health was going to require vigorous civilian intervention.[53]

Whatever the merits of Tunnell's critique—which, if nothing else, reflected a conception of war to which most ordinary Americans subscribed—it made explicit two great questions dogging America's War for the Greater Middle East as it entered its fourth decade: Are we in this thing to win, or not? And, if not, what's the point of fighting? In combination with troubling incidents of soldier misconduct, Colonel Tunnell's refusal to embrace the theology of COIN hinted at a deep and festering discontent. Left unchecked, that discontent could cause an army to become a mob.

Petraeus moved quickly to address one specific source of that discontent by revoking the rules of engagement issued to implement courageous restraint. The McChrystal ROE had found little favor with U.S. troops, who complained of being "handcuffed by our chain of command."[54] Although the Petraeus revision did not remove those handcuffs, it loosened them considerably. Whereas McChrystal had prioritized protecting civilians, Petraeus now declared it "a moral imperative both to protect Afghan civilians *and* to bring all assets to bear to protect our men and women in uniform."[55] Bringing all assets to bear implied greater latitude in employing heavy firepower.

The new ROE were a portent. During his one year in Kabul, the wizard of COIN played against type. On his watch, there was not going to be a rerun of Marja launched amidst high hopes and big promises. Instead, Petraeus quietly shelved "clear, hold, and build" in favor of something more akin to "find, fix, and kill." The officer most responsible for counterinsurgency's rebirth now effectively abandoned his off-spring.

By the summer of 2010 Afghanistan had come to resemble the latter stages of the Third Gulf War: In the downward revision of war aims, facilitating an orderly exit emerged as priority number one. Even as Operation Moshtarak was still unfolding, a key aide told Petraeus that the best the United States could hope for in Afghanistan was to "get to a point of some transient stability and the appearance of success." Although the appearance was not likely to endure, it "might provide a window for us to withdraw, and to keep things steady for the next three or four years." Bearing down on the Taliban offered the shortest path toward fostering that transient stability.[56]

Toward that end, Petraeus doubled the number of raids conducted by special operations forces. Typically occurring at night—doors bashed in, inhabitants rousted and searched, suspects shot or dragged off for interrogation—these raids remained deeply unpopular with Afghans. But liquidating insurgents, especially those believed to occupy positions in the Taliban hierarchy, now took precedence over concerns about making friends and influencing people. Petraeus also ramped up the number of air strikes, employing both manned aircraft and drones.[57] And for the first time since the war began back in 2001, Abrams main battle tanks appeared on the Afghan battlefield—of no particular value in winning hearts and minds, but exceedingly useful in a serious firefight. According to one unnamed senior official quoted by the *Washington Post*, "We've taken the gloves off."[58]

By certain quantitative measures, the gloves-off approach produced noteworthy results. Between mid-2010 and mid-2011, ISAF claimed that it had removed from circulation some twelve thousand militants. As one charter member of the COIN-is-the-answer club enthused, Petraeus had engineered "an almost industrial-scale counterterrorism killing machine." The man himself expressed satisfaction. "We're seeing progress for the first time in many years," Petraeus proclaimed in the spring of 2011. Although more work remained, "we have halted the momentum of the Taliban in much of the country."[59]

This was wishful thinking. The insurgency showed few signs of slackening. Although precise numbers were hard to come by, most estimates showed that the total number of Taliban fighters was actually increasing.[60] The Petraeus crackdown did have this effect: Civilian casualties jumped considerably, as did the number of Afghans—as many as six hundred thousand—displaced from their homes.[61] Whether coincidentally or as a direct result of the Petraeus approach, a rash of "green-on-blue" incidents—Afghan soldiers attacking ISAF troops—now erupted.[62] Needless to say, the overall tally of U.S. troops killed and wounded also spiked. In the last year of George W. Bush's presidency, U.S. casualties in Afghanistan totaled 798. During the Obama surge, with Petraeus in command, they exceeded five thousand per annum.[63]

Meanwhile, the production of opium, principal source of Taliban funding, flourished. After a brief downtick, the expanse of hectares under poppy cultivation headed upward beginning in 2010, a trend that gained momentum over the next several years.[64] Efforts to create an alternative to the drug economy consumed more money in inflation-adjusted dollars than the United States had spent on the Marshall Plan, with precious little to show for it.[65] Amidst much talk about the need to root out official corruption, Petraeus assigned Brigadier General McMaster, hero of 73 Easting and Tal Afar, to head up a clean government campaign known as Task Force Shafafiyat ("transparency"). The effort went nowhere. In annual rankings of the world's kleptocracies, Afghanistan maintained its place near the bottom of the list, edging out only Somalia and North Korea.[66] Meanwhile, the Afghan forces that ISAF was counting on to assume responsibility for their country's security remained in apparent perpetuity "a work in progress."[67]

Even so, President Obama was undiscouraged. In June 2011, with Petraeus preparing to relinquish command of ISAF to yet another American four-star, the president went on national television to pronounce the Afghanistan surge (to which he had assented with great reluctance) a success (which it was not), with "the light of a secure peace" now visible "in the distance" (an expectation devoid of empirical support). Everything was proceeding according to plan, Obama had persuaded himself. As a result, the scheduled withdrawal of U.S. troops could now begin. By the end of 2014, he promised, the war itself would end.[68] That was the president's story, and his administration was going to stick to it.

Briefing slides that the journalist Ben Anderson came across in 2011 reduced that story to a handful of bullet points prescribing the "Key Tenets of the Afghan Narrative":

- 2011/12 *Notice what is different*
- 2012/13 *Change has begun*
- 2013/14 *Growing confidence*
- 2015 *A new chance, a new beginning*[69]

Not for the first time in America's War for the Greater Middle East, "narrative" was displacing reality. What policymakers in Washington wished to see—a new chance and a new beginning for Afghans— became what they saw, even if the "seeing" required first shutting their eyes. Much as he had with Third Persian Gulf War, Obama had decided upon a date certain when the Second Afghanistan War was going to end, with the great body of Americans, even those who despised the president, willing to pretend that his words made it so. They did not.

In fact, the situation in Afghanistan by the summer of 2011 compared to that phase of the Korean War that occurred after the ceasefire negotiations with the Chinese began at Kaesong in the summer of 1951. Although hostilities in Korea were to continue for another two years, the outcome was foreordained: The peninsula's division into two antagonistic halves was going to persist. When the end finally came, it was shrouded in ambiguity.

Similarly, in Afghanistan, fighting was going to continue, but without any real expectation of affecting the outcome. Rendered ungovernable by the U.S.-led campaign of the 1980s, Afghanistan was destined to remain a shattered country. After more than a decade of exertions aimed at putting the country back together again, the "new" Afghanistan remained a figment of Washington's imagination. Here too, the end, whenever it came, was sure to be shrouded in ambiguity.

On December 28, 2014, President Obama announced that "the longest war in American history" had come "to a responsible conclusion."[70] To this presidential claim, an even semi-attentive public might have replied, "Huh?" In fact, the Afghanistan War had not reached any sort of conclusion, responsible or otherwise. No such conclusion was even dimly visible. Indeed, over ten thousand U.S. troops remained in Afghanistan beyond that date, albeit in what the administration arbitrarily defined as a noncombat role even though Afghanistan remained very much a combat zone.

What set the Afghanistan War apart was not that it was the longest war in U.S. history but that it was more quickly forgotten than any other conflict in which the United States had ever participated. As if by mutual agreement, the American people and their government erased the Afghanistan experience from memory even before the bloodletting had ended.

16

ENTROPY

IN JUNE 2011, WHILE ANNOUNCING THE BEGINNING OF U.S. troop withdrawals from Afghanistan, President Obama said, "We take comfort in knowing that the tide of war is receding."[1] In fact, the tide was not receding. Although Obama's efforts to extricate the United States from Iraq and Afghanistan attracted understandable attention, they tell the lesser part of the story. In other quarters of the Islamic world, the range of U.S. military activities was actually expanding. Even as it sought to convey the impression of striking out boldly in new directions, the Obama administration's chief contribution to the War for the Greater Middle East was to enlarge it.

During the Obama era, the United States initiated military action on many fronts across the Islamic world. Some of those actions marked a return to sites of earlier interventions. Others occurred in locales that the U.S. military had previously considered unimportant and sought to avoid. Having for political reasons jettisoned the phrase "global war on terrorism," the new administration grouped its various and sundry military campaigns under the blandly generic heading of "overseas contingency operations."

What distinguished these campaigns was the absence of any unifying aim or idea. As a consequence, the principal result of Obama's willingness to expend American military might in places as far afield as Libya, Pakistan, Somalia, Yemen, and West Africa was to dissipate energy without notable effect. Prior to 9/11, the abiding defect of U.S. military policy had been ignorance. In the years directly after 9/11, it became hubris. During the Obama presidency, by contrast, the problem was one of diffusion. U.S. forces were increasingly found scattered across the Greater Middle East without actually making a difference anywhere in particular.

This dispersion of effort occurred in rapidly changing political circumstances. Assumptions and preconceptions that had guided U.S. military planning and operations in the Islamic world during the 1980s and 1990s and even in the years immediately following 9/11 no longer pertained. Three changes in particular stand out, one at home, the second abroad, and the third with implications in both realms.

First, the long wars in Iraq and Afghanistan that followed 9/11 pretty much exhausted the willingness of the American people to commit anything more than token numbers of U.S. troops to engage in ground combat. By the beginning of President Obama's second term, a variant of the Vietnam Syndrome, ostensibly "kicked" by Operation Desert Storm, had reasserted itself. This did not translate into the wholesale demilitarization of U.S. policy or even the emergence of an antiwar political party. Indeed, Washington's bipartisan appetite for armed intervention in the Islamic world persisted. By now appetite had become tantamount to addiction.

Yet a public once again averse to casualties and quagmires required changes in method. When Secretary of Defense Robert Gates, shortly before leaving office, told West Point cadets that anyone proposing "to again send a big American land army into Asia or into the Middle East or Africa" needed to "have his head examined," he was acknowledging this shift in public temper.[2] President Obama himself concurred, subsequently remarking that "a strategy that involves invading every country that harbors terrorist networks is naive and unsustainable."[3] Not even the president's sharpest critics contested the point. For the moment at least, the invade-and-occupy-to-liberate phase of America's War for the Greater Middle East had passed.

Further change came in the form of political upheaval sweeping through much of the Greater Middle East, but especially its Arab quarter. In his June 2009 Cairo speech, President Obama had offered a compelling vision of economic opportunity, religious liberty, individual equality, and "governments that reflect the will of the people" ushering in a world order based on tolerance and mutual respect.[4] Echoing George W. Bush and other members of the previous administration, Obama emphasized the universality of that vision. It was as applicable to the Islamic world as to Europe or the United States itself.

Beginning in December of the following year, in a rolling series of uprisings, the will of Arab peoples found concrete expression. Demands for fundamental change assailed regimes that for decades had given every appearance of permanence, first in Tunisia and then in Egypt, Yemen, Bahrain, Libya, and Syria. Although the uprisings resembled one another in energy and spontaneity, the results achieved varied widely. In some instances, the old order collapsed, although not necessarily producing outcomes that found favor in Washington. In others, the old order refused to give way and employed strong-arm tactics to fend off challenges to its authority.

This so-called Arab Awakening posed a huge predicament for the United States. From having ignored democracy in the name of oil at the outset of its War for the Greater Middle East, the United States after 9/11 had declared itself democracy's great champion across the Islamic world. Now, with popular insurrection producing results seemingly at odds with U.S. interests, Washington was having second thoughts. This much alone seemed certain: As a formula for fostering stability, the longstanding U.S. practice of paying lip service to democracy while accommodating autocratic monarchs and presidents-for-life appeared increasingly untenable. The costs associated with hypocrisy were rising.

Then there was change associated with Israel. Through the first three decades of America's War for the Greater Middle East, the U.S.-Israeli relationship had weathered more than a few storms as successive American administrations and Israeli governments labored to temper or, if need be, ignore the tensions between U.S. and Israeli security interests. The key to papering over those differences was to maintain the fiction that authorities in Washington and Jerusalem were equally committed to achieving a two-state solution to the Israeli-Palestinian conflict. The "peace process" held out the theoretical prospect of comprehensive reconciliation between Israel and its Arab neighbors, thereby putting to rest the antagonisms triggered by the founding of the Jewish state in 1948. As long as both parties in the U.S.-Israeli relationship sustained the pretense of being committed to "peace," Washington's unstinting support for Israel, providing it with diplomatic cover along with enormous quantities of arms, remained minimally controversial.

Developments during the Obama era made it increasingly difficult to sustain this arrangement. Within the United States (and more broadly throughout much of the West), public opinion became less inclined to blame the absence of peace on obstreperous Arabs. Relentless Israeli colonization of territories captured in the 1967 war vastly complicated, if not rendering implausible, prospects for creating a viable Palestinian state.[5] As if to drive home the point, a high-profile effort to restart peace talks, launched in 2013 by Secretary of State John Kerry, went nowhere. Meanwhile, periodic punitive actions against Palestinians that inflicted casualties wildly out of proportion with the ostensible provocation—"mowing the lawn," in Israeli parlance—suggested a preference for the calculable effects of collective punishment over the uncertainties of negotiation. In the spring of 2015, running for reelection, Israeli Prime Minister Benjamin Netanyahu all but made it official. Declaring the two-state solution "unachievable," he vowed that none would exist as long as he remained in office.[6] Israeli voters duly awarded him another term.

Within the United States, meanwhile, overt criticism of Israel, previously muted or confined to the political fringes (where it not infrequently carried a whiff of anti-Semitism), was now becoming sharper and more open. This was notably so on college campuses, long the bellwether of change in American political culture. To punish Israel for denying Palestinians their right to self-determination, a grassroots international campaign known as BDS (for boycott, divestment, and sanctions) gained traction, even as it generated controversy.[7]

Acknowledging the existence and influence of a powerful pro-Israel lobby, once taboo, became commonplace.[8] That the West, to include the United States, had a moral obligation to support Israel in atonement for the Holocaust no longer elicited automatic assent. Nor did the argument that Israelis and Americans shared common values that bound the two countries together. Within and between both countries, issues related to identity, religion, democratic practice, and the basic requirements of social justice appeared increasingly at issue. There was no single Israel to align with a single America.

An episode purporting to demonstrate U.S.-Israeli solidarity had the opposite effect, drawing attention to the unseemly underbelly of the relationship. In March 2015, at the invitation of House Speaker John Boehner, Prime Minister Netanyahu presented himself before the United States Congress to address both houses and the American people. Boehner's motives in extending the invitation (without bothering to check with the Obama White House) were nakedly political. As a Republican leader, he was intent on casting his party as Israel's only truly reliable friend. As leader of Israel's rightwing Likud Party, Netanyahu's motives were equally partisan. He was intent on persuading the Israeli electorate that he alone could be counted on to deliver assured American support. Just as Boehner sought to score points at the expense of the Democratic Party, Netanyahu sought to score points at the expense of the Israeli political center and left. Yet while offering the Israeli prime minister an opportunity to flaunt his standing on Capitol Hill, his performance impressed some observers as both smarmy and presumptuous. As for the members of Congress who rewarded Netanyahu's remarks with twenty-nine standing ovations, they came across as supine and puerile.[9]

Netanyahu acted like he owned the place, with the actual owners eagerly conceding the claim. Some Israelis and some Americans found this reassuring, an affirmation of intimate friendship. For others, it was off-putting. The "jumping up and down, up and down, applauding wildly, shouting approval" reminded the acerbic Israeli commentator Uri Avnery of the Reichstag in the 1930s. The spectacle of "members of the most powerful parliament in the world behaving like a bunch of nincompoops" struck him as ridiculous.[10] The comedian and alternative news source Jon Stewart mocked Netanyahu's performance as "the State of the Union Address the Republicans wanted, delivered by the leader they wish they had."[11] The putative guardians of the Israeli-American relationship were making themselves laughingstocks.

All of this—the emergence of an "Iraq Syndrome" with its reluctance to put U.S. troops in harm's way, the turmoil resulting from the Arab Awakening, and signs that attitudes toward Israel were in flux— had implications for the ongoing conduct of America's War for the Greater Middle East.

Moving beyond that war's invade-and-occupy phase had important implications for the American military apparatus, which experienced a substantial reconfiguration during the Obama era. That reconfiguration came chiefly at the expense of the U.S. Army, which in the wake of Iraq and Afghanistan fell out of fashion. Army generals might still entertain visions of brigades and regiments storming enemy lines pursuant to occupying the enemy capital, but no one else was buying. So from a peak of 566,000 at the height of the Third Persian Gulf War, the regular army found itself on a downward glide path toward a projected overall strength of 450,000 by 2018. Although army leaders still insisted that their service existed to fight and win the nation's wars, few Americans wished to test the proposition further.[12]

The principal beneficiaries of the army's fall from grace were special operations forces and anyone able to carve out a piece of the action associated with unmanned aerial vehicles. For policymakers seeking ways to punish without the complications associated with wholesale invasion and occupation, commandos and drones offered a host of benefits. During the fourth decade of America's War for the Greater Middle East, they emerged as the clear weapons of choice.

The presidency of Barack Obama coincided with the "golden age" of America's special operators, according to General Joseph Votel, who in 2014 assumed the reins of U.S. Special Operations Command (SOCOM).[13] In the decades since the embarrassing Iran hostage rescue mission—subsequently enshrined as "our most successful failure" and classified not as a fiasco but as a launch point—the special operations community had grown and prospered.[14] With over seventy-two thousand personnel and further expansion projected, SOCOM by 2015 was on track to surpass the entire British Army in overall size.[15] Over the course of the previous year, SOCOM had operated in an astonishing 150 countries.[16] No military force in history had acquired such a far-flung presence. No institution with a comparably expansive mandate had ever succeeded in maintaining such a low profile, thereby avoiding serious oversight except on its own preferred terms.

Where SOCOM would not or could not go, UAVs offered policymakers an attractive alternative, even if one that U.S. military officers had not immediately recognized. Much as navies initially viewed submarines as a means to conduct reconnaissance rather than as instruments of destruction, the Pentagon initially saw drones as vehicles to gather intelligence or maintain surveillance rather than to kill. Not until February 2001 did the United States successfully weaponize a drone, test-launching a Hellfire missile from a Predator UAV. In November of that year, during the opening stages of the Afghanistan War, a missile from a CIA-operated drone assassinated a senior Al Qaeda operative in Kabul. From this point forward, enthusiasm for exploiting the potential of drones as a means to attack grew progressively. By the time Obama had fully settled into the White House, that enthusiasm knew no bounds, with little apparent interest in the implications of others acquiring drone technology, as they inevitably would.[17] Here was a surviving remnant of the now-discredited Revolution in Military Affairs that had so warped U.S. military practice during the 1990s and immediately after 9/11.

Varying according to purpose, the Obama-era campaigns that superseded Iraq and Afghanistan and brought special operators and drones to the forefront of U.S. military policy fell into three distinct categories. In some, the aim was to *depose*, in others to *suppress*, in others still simply to *retard*. All shared a common determination to minimize risks, keep down costs, and above all avoid anything approximating a quagmire—the very qualities that had made Iraq and Afghanistan each such an ordeal.

Included in the first category were direct intervention in Libya and indirect intervention in Syria. The second category included military actions in Pakistan, Yemen, and Somalia. The third category expanded America's War for the Greater Middle East into Africa, the Pentagon calculating that a modest U.S. military presence in nations with majority or notably large Muslim populations could nip violent jihad in the bud. Regardless of the intended purpose, little of this activity produced the desired effect. Yet overall, the number of active fronts in America's War for the Greater Middle East multiplied—this was President Obama's principal contribution to that war.

The Libyan intervention, launched in March 2011, proved a particular disappointment. The aim of Operation Odyssey Dawn, as the Pentagon called it, was to complete the job left unfinished by Operation El Dorado Canyon a quarter-century before—to rid the planet of Moamar Gaddafi. It did that, but with catastrophic aftereffects.

Ironically, George W. Bush, given to wrapping himself in the mantle of Ronald Reagan, had thrown a lifeline to the Libyan dictator that Reagan had so roundly despised. After the 2003 invasion of Iraq, Gaddafi had volunteered to give up further efforts to develop nuclear, biological, or chemical weapons. The Bush administration accepted the offer—"a significant success," according to Donald Rumsfeld, stemming directly from the fact that Gaddafi "did not want to become the next Saddam Hussein."[18] In return, the State Department removed Libya from its roster of terror-sponsoring nations and restored full diplomatic relations. According to *Time*, parroting the Bush administration's own line, "the onetime international pariah's decision to dismantle his weapons of mass destruction program was primarily the result of the U.S. war on terror and its toppling of Saddam Hussein."[19]

Offering Libya a fresh start, while letting bygones be bygones, served as the first (and last) fruits of Bush's Freedom Agenda. The resulting deal released the Gaddafi regime from various international sanctions and provided Western energy conglomerates access to Libyan oil fields.

To cement this renewal of U.S.-Libyan relations, Secretary of State Condoleezza Rice visited Tripoli in September 2008, calling on Gaddafi at the very residence struck by American bombs two decades prior.[20]

As for Gaddafi's subjects, few tangible freedoms came their way. So during the Arab Awakening, they took matters into their own hands. In February 2011, a popular uprising triggered a full-fledged civil war. Rebel forces seized Benghazi, Libya's second-largest metropolis. With Gaddafi vowing to march on that city and eliminate the "cockroaches" daring to challenge his rule, President Obama reversed his predecessor's policy of conciliation. Secretary of State Hillary Clinton denounced Gaddafi's threat as "completely unacceptable."[21] On March 2, she declared that Gaddafi "must go, now, without further violence and bloodshed."[22] When he refused to comply, the United States set about organizing a coalition to intervene. The advertised aim was to protect civilians and end the turmoil that threatened to destabilize the "entire region."[23] The actual aim was to help Gaddafi's adversaries prevail while validating a new rationale for allowing big countries to interfere in the affairs of small ones, justified by a putative "responsibility to protect." RTP, as it came to be known, was the Bush Doctrine of preventive war in humanitarian drag. Rather than providing protection, its application in Libya sowed the seeds of prolonged disorder.

Odyssey Dawn commenced on March 19. With President Obama having categorically ruled out the commitment of U.S. combat troops, this was to be an air campaign, albeit one facilitated by small numbers of special operations troops on the ground. Odyssey Dawn fell under the purview of United States Africa Command (AFRICOM), newest of the Pentagon's regional commands, ostensibly created not to wage but to prevent wars on that continent. The operation began with the standard volley of Tomahawk missiles launched from ships afloat in the Mediterranean and targeting Libya's weak air defenses and even weaker air force. Attacks by manned aircraft followed, with first France, Great Britain, and several other nations participating on a token basis. Over the next two weeks, according to AFRICOM's air component commander, this summarily assembled coalition "flew well over 2000 sorties, launched more than 200 [cruise missiles], released thousands of pounds of munitions, saved thousands of Libyan civilians from massacre, and eliminated the Libyan Air Force as a threat."[24]

At this point, responsibility for directing the campaign passed from AFRICOM to NATO, headed as always by an American officer, the move intended to endow the operation (which NATO dubbed "Unified Protector") with a multilateral coloration. Under this arrangement, bombing continued through October. By the time operations ended, NATO claimed to have destroyed 5,900 targets to include four hundred artillery pieces and six hundred armored vehicles, all under the guise of protecting civilians. In reality, the United States and its allies were providing a de facto air force for the Libyan resistance while denying air support to Gaddafi's troops. U.S. aircraft, which included Predator drones, completed roughly one-third of the 26,500 NATO sorties flown.[25]

For Gaddafi himself, who fled Tripoli in August, the end came when an armed Predator engaged a convoy in which he was traveling near Sirte, the city of his birth. The deposed dictator was injured in the attack and then captured, beaten, and summarily executed.[26] Secretary Clinton pronounced herself pleased with the outcome. "We came, we saw, he died," she gloated.[27] Her boss the president promptly declared that "the dark shadow of tyranny has been lifted" from Libya and summoned residents of that nation to "build an inclusive and tolerant and democratic Libya that stands as the ultimate rebuke" to the man once known as that country's "Brotherly Leader."[28]

Obama's hopes came to naught, however. It was Iraq all over again: Getting rid of the evil dictator turned out to be the easy part. An intervention justified by the imperative of protecting innocents and averting instability produced the precise opposite of the results intended. Once Gaddafi was gone, the factions that had joined together to overthrow him turned on one another. A country once defined by its leader's zany antics now became synonymous with outright anarchy. The state ceased to function. The plight of desperate Libyans seeking to escape became an international scandal, with thousands losing their lives trying to cross the Mediterranean into Europe. The principal beneficiaries of Gaddafi's removal were human traffickers and radical Islamists as Libya became the site of Al Qaeda's newest franchise. By 2015, the country was a basket case and seemed likely to remain one for the indefinite future.[29]

In Iraq, the presence of U.S. troops on the ground had made the consequences of invasion impossible to ignore. In Libya, the absence of U.S. troops enabled Americans to avert their gaze from what intervention had wrought. While the assassination of the U.S. envoy to Libya in September 2012 stirred a flurry of interest, critics used the death of Ambassador Christopher Stevens not to draw attention to America's role in the crisis enveloping Libya but to score political points at the expense of President Obama and Secretary Clinton. The ill-conceived U.S. intervention in Libya demanded serious reflection, perhaps even contrition. Instead, Washington opted for crude partisanship.

Even so, Libya represented a model of thoughtful planning and competent execution in comparison with Obama's one other foray into regime change. In Syria, the United States responded to a nominally similar situation with impressive rhetoric and desultory action, yielding an outcome at least as calamitous as Libya's.

Among Syrians, the Arab Awakening generated popular demands for the ouster of President Bashar al-Assad and his Ba'athist regime. Assad responded first with minor concessions followed by a crackdown. By April 2011, protest gave way to civil war and escalating violence. Echoing his secretary of state on Gaddafi, Obama declared that Assad "must go."[30] Yet apart from inveighing against any Syrian government use of chemical weapons—violating that "red line" would "change my calculus," the president warned—his administration limited itself to various diplomatic and economic sanctions.[31]

Obama's reluctance to go further became evident in the summer of 2013 when Assad's forces employed chemical weapons against his own people, thereby violating the U.S. red line. To lesser provocations by Gaddafi in the 1980s and Saddam Hussein in the 1990s, Obama's predecessors had responded with punitive action. Obama himself considered that possibility but, sensing an absence of enthusiasm, both at home and among key allies, backed away.[32] Instead, he signed on to a Russian-brokered deal providing for the supervised destruction of Syria's chemical arsenal.

Although the president thereby avoided a war for which he had little appetite, critics took him to task for making a threat and then failing to follow through. Supporters of Israel felt the chill of their security blanket beginning to slip.[33] Even former members of the president's own administration complained. "When the president of the United States draws a red line," said Leon Panetta, who had served Obama as both CIA director and defense secretary, "the credibility of this country is dependent on him backing up his word."[34]

Yet the issue at hand was not credibility, at best an elusive quality, but the difficulty of parsing the substantive U.S. interests at stake in Syria within the larger context of the Greater Middle East. How exactly did Syria matter?

Although U.S. officials had ample justification for calling Assad "a thug and a murderer," his opponents were hardly paragons of virtue.[35] The proportion of Jeffersonian democrats filling the ranks of the Syrian resistance decreased over time, their places taken by radical Islamists more interested in promoting violent jihad than liberal values. Although the administration made a show of trying to funnel assistance to "moderate rebels"—the phrase itself providing instant fodder for satirists—distinguishing moderates from those who were anything but posed a large challenge.[36] So too did getting those moderates into fighting trim. As of late summer in 2015, a CENTCOM training program projected to yield several thousand anti-Assad fighters had graduated only fifty-four, of whom "four or five" actually remained in the field, an achievement entailing the expenditure of $500 million.[37]

In effect, Obama's policy regarding Syria became one of limiting direct U.S. exposure while waiting to see who won and then dealing with the results. The problem was that neither side proved able to gain the upper hand. As a consequence of this impasse, the toll of lives lost and ruined continued to mount, as did the number of those forced to flee their homes. By the autumn of 2015, over two hundred thousand Syrians had been killed, with 4 million refugees having left the country and another 7.6 million internally displaced.[38] As the conflict dragged on and on, Obama stood accused of remaining passive in the face of a vast humanitarian disaster.

Passivity did not describe Moscow's response. American irresolution presented Vladimir Putin with an opening that he unhesitatingly exploited. From the outset of the Syrian crisis, Russia had been providing arms for Assad's forces to misuse. Now in September 2015, Putin ordered a Russian expeditionary task force to take up positions near the Syrian port of Latakia. Post-Soviet Russia possessed only modest power projection capabilities. Even so, Putin's deployment of even small numbers of combat aircraft, tanks, and artillery embarrassed Obama, emphasizing how little control Washington was able to exert over unfolding events. Soon enough Russian bombs were targeting Assad's opponents. Like Israel's Netanyahu, Putin saw the political advantage inherent in openly defying the American president.[39]

More to the point, the confused state of U.S. policy toward Syria—the yawning gap between high-sounding words and half-hearted action—testified to the larger disarray now enveloping Washington's approach to the Greater Middle East. After Libya (not to mention Iraq and Afghanistan), it was impossible to sustain the illusion that eliminating this or that unsavory regime held the key to putting the region back together again. Syria presented Obama with a choice between plunging in and holding back—between a Libya do-over and taking a pass. Reluctant to compound past errors, he resisted—or tried to resist—calls to intervene further in the Syrian civil war.

By no means did this reticence apply across the board. Elsewhere in the Greater Middle East, notably in Pakistan, Somalia, and Yemen, Obama dove right in, going after anti-Western Islamists with a mix of drones and special operations forces. Yet the purpose of these attacks, surreptitiously conducted and announced after the fact (if at all), was merely to curb rather than to eliminate the threat. Here was the American equivalent of the Israeli concept of mowing the lawn.

In terms of scope, the largest of those mowing campaigns occurred in Pakistan. Ostensibly an ally of the United States, Pakistan maintained its own distinct set of interests and priorities, symbolized by its troubling possession of a large nuclear arsenal. Leaders of the Pakistani security establishment—the army and the Inter-Services Intelligence agency (ISI)—were the ultimate arbiters of Pakistani policy, intervening in politics as it suited them to do so. For its part, over the course of decades, Washington had given Pakistani generals good reason to view the United States as capricious and two-faced. This was not a relationship based on trust.[40]

Yet to sustain Operation Enduring Freedom, Washington needed Pakistan, if only because the principal supply routes into landlocked Afghanistan started at the Pakistani port of Karachi and then ran hundreds of miles overland toward Kabul and Kandahar. The United States also looked to Pakistan to deny the Taliban sanctuary in its vast border regions. For at least two reasons, this did not happen, however. First, Pakistani generals saw the Afghan Taliban as potential allies once the Americans inevitably withdrew. Second, preoccupied with other putative threats, above all India, they were unwilling to divert sufficient forces to police their own frontier. The problem was therefore Washington's to address.

Much as President Nixon in his day had extended the ongoing Vietnam War into nominally neutral Laos and Cambodia, President Obama came into office predisposed to extend the ongoing war for Afghanistan into Pakistan. To capture this concept of an enlarged theater of operations, his administration coined the term "AfPak."[41] In 1969, Nixon had unleashed the U.S. Air Force on Laos and Cambodia, a secret bombing campaign later denounced as illegal. By the time Obama unleashed missile-firing UAVs and commandos on Pakistan, few bothered to question the legality of secret attacks in countries with which the United States was not at war. Unless large numbers of U.S. ground troops were involved, the prerogatives enjoyed by the American commander in chief anywhere in the Greater Middle East had by now become pretty much limitless.

Granted, the use of drones to go after militants in Pakistan actually predated the Obama administration. The first such strike had occurred in 2004, during the presidency of George W. Bush. But under Obama the attacks intensified and, perhaps more importantly, became bureaucratically regularized. White House staffers, along with Defense Department and intelligence officials, managed a "disposition matrix" that the president and senior national security aides regularly reviewed, establishing targeting priorities and adding new names of persons to be killed or captured.[42]

Institutionalizing the "kill list" led directly to an increase in the number of UAV strike missions flown. Between 2004 and the day George W. Bush retired from office, the annual tally of U.S. drone strikes in Pakistan reached double digits only once. During Obama's first term, UAV attacks in that country averaged 76 per year, peaking at 128 in 2010. Estimates of resulting casualties varied, but during the Obama presidency drones operating over Pakistan killed at least two thousand and perhaps more than three thousand people.[43] How many of those killed were militants as opposed to innocent bystanders was a matter of dispute, with U.S. officials insisting that the United States went to extraordinary lengths to minimize civilian casualties. Pakistanis unaccustomed to the presence of drones circling overhead along with the possibility of missiles slamming into their village without warning did not share that view.[44]

Much the same story occurred in Yemen and Somalia, the other two principal theaters in Obama's drone war. Of the ninety-nine confirmed U.S. drone strikes in Yemen that occurred between 2002 and mid-2015, all but one occurred on Obama's watch. With Al Qaeda in the Arabian Peninsula (AQAP) the intended target, these strikes killed at least 450 and perhaps as many as 1,000 people.[45] In Somalia, drone strikes began only in 2011, but U.S. special operators, sometimes employing C-130 Spectre gunships, had been active in that country since 2007, as they attempted to curb the activities of Al Shabab, another Al Qaeda–affiliated group.[46]

In each of these three countries (and in Libya following Gaddafi's demise), commando raids supplemented the ongoing drone campaign. The purpose of these missions, typically involving brief insertions of small numbers of elite troops, varied. In some, the aim was to free hostages. Others were snatch-and-grab operations to capture high-value targets and collect intelligence. In others still, like the famous Abbottabad mission of May 2011 that finally ran Osama bin Laden to ground, the object of the exercise was assassination.[47]

Providing a thread of continuity linking these various operations, whether involving drones or forces on the ground, was a stubborn belief in the efficacy of decapitation. With the manifest failure of invade-and-occupy, targeting leaders seemed to offer some prospect of keeping at bay threats to the United States that flourished in the most disordered parts of the Greater Middle East.

Back in 2008–2009, enthusiasm for implementing COIN on a global scale had enjoyed a brief heyday. Now, just a handful of years later, Obama had embarked on a de facto experiment in globalizing counterterrorism techniques of the sort that Stanley McChrystal had made a centerpiece of the Third Gulf War. In American newspapers, the headline "U.S. Kills Militant Leader" now became the Obama-era equivalent of "U.S. Bombs Iraq" during the 1990s. Normalization became a form of concealment. The ho-hum noting of what had become a commonplace occurrence supplanted questions of effectiveness.

But questions of effectiveness haunted U.S. policy during the Obama era. What if U.S. drone strikes and special operations raids, even if tactically successful, were creating more anti-American jihadists than they were eliminating, as even some senior U.S. military officers believed?[48] What if the leaders replacing those that U.S. forces killed turned out to be more vicious than their predecessors—if removing Mr. Bad merely paved the way for Mr. Worse?[49] Or if liquidating those inattentive to the fundamentals of cybersecurity simply paved the way for tech-savvy terrorists—a Darwinian process serving to strengthen the species?[50] These questions defied easy answers. Yet the absence of answers left Obama unable to explain when and how America's War for the Greater Middle East was ever going to end.

Beyond unhappy attempts to depose regimes and inconclusive efforts to suppress terrorist organizations lay one final category of President Obama's military program in the Greater Middle East. This involved experiments in crisis intervention before the source of crisis reached full maturity. In that regard, Africa, hitherto not a Pentagon priority, emerged as a focus of attention, with United States Africa Command, activated in 2008, the agency occupying center stage.

AFRICOM during the Age of Barack Obama compares with CENTCOM during the Age of Ronald Reagan. As an undercapitalized startup, AFRICOM faced real challenges. But with challenges came opportunities and a palpable sense of excitement. As U.S. military officers contemplated Africa, they would have been well served to compare it to the Arab Middle East or to the Indian subcontinent. Here was another locale where the detritus of European colonialism had left a deeply problematic legacy that further Western meddling was unlikely to repair. Instead, oblivious to history, American officers chose to see central and western Africa as virgin territory. In the twenty-first-century scramble for that continent, the United States needed to be a player, which necessarily meant that the U.S. military needed to make its presence felt. Here was an entirely new arena in which to wage America's War for the Greater Middle East.

Yet in contrast to CENTCOM, created with an eye toward fighting the Soviet army in Iran's Zagros Mountains, AFRICOM initially professed no expectation of fighting anyone. The command's original mission statement contained no reference to combat, instead emphasizing "security engagement" undertaken to "promote a stable and secure African environment."[51] At its founding, AFRICOM's declared purpose was simply to nurture competent and professional indigenous forces, inculcating respect for human rights and civilian control, in each of the fifty-three African nations over which its four-star American commander claimed oversight.[52]

Whether genuine or not, this claim of benign purpose ran headlong into a different reality. By 2011, with its anti-Gaddafi bombing campaign, AFRICOM expanded its mandate to include killing and helping people kill. As one U.S. officer put it, Libya marked AFRICOM's transition from a "more congenial combatant command to an actual warfighting combatant command."[53] A duly revised mission statement now declared that AFRICOM "deters and defeats transnational threats in order to advance U.S. national interests"—boilerplate language broad enough to cover just about every contingency from treating disease-afflicted populations to mounting a full-fledged invasion.[54] By 2013, Brigadier General James Linder, officially in charge of AFRICOM's special operations troops but also an energetic proselytizer for the command, was touting Africa as "the battlefield of tomorrow, today."[55]

The specific battlefields to which AFRICOM devoted priority attention lay in countries where radical Islamists had gained a toehold, among them Chad, Mali, Mauritania, Niger, Nigeria, and Cameroon. The enemy in this case consisted of groups such as Ansar Dine, Boko Haram, Al Qaeda in the Islamic Maghreb, and the Lord's Resistance Army. With the exception of the latter, all were offspring of the original Al Qaeda.

Since the onset of the War for the Greater Middle East, the United States had been of two minds about stability, seeking to undermine it in some instances while shoring it up in others. This ambivalence had led Washington to side with Islamists putting a torch to Afghanistan in the 1980s even as it helped Saddam Hussein assail Iranian revolutionaries seeking to put a torch to the Persian Gulf. With regard to Al Qaeda, however, the events of 9/11 had cured Washington of any ambivalence. Here was a disease deemed acutely lethal. Yet the treatment administered by the United States to reduce the presence of the disease in certain organs had accelerated its spread to others. In Africa, the infection appeared rampant.

The Pentagon might have called its response Operation Big Pharma. If the American advertising-pharmaceutical complex believes anything, it's that whatever the complaint, there's some drug that can alleviate it. If the American military-industrial complex believes anything, it's that for any problem there exists a military remedy. It's just a matter of identifying the right prescription and the optimum means of delivery. In

Africa, the United States opted for a low-dose regimen, dispensed partly over and partly under the counter.

In contrast to the other major U.S. regional commands, AFRICOM established only a single officially acknowledged, quasi-permanent base within its AOR. This was Camp Lemonnier in Djibouti. Yet this "small footprint" approach did not prevent AFRICOM from maintaining a constellation of bases-by-other-names, variously known as "forward operating sites," "contingency security locations," and "contingency locations." An approving report in *The Wall Street Journal* deciphered the implications. In Africa, the United States had devised a new way "to maintain its global dominance." Rather than "maintaining large forces in a few" places, the Pentagon "scattered small, nimble teams in many."[56] In this sense, characterizing AFRICOM's presence as a "small footprint" was a misnomer. A more accurate description would have been "few feet but in many places."

Yet even without fixed facilities and a large-scale standing presence, the U.S. military during the Obama era transformed Africa into a beehive of activity, with between five thousand and eight thousand American soldiers or Defense Department contractors present in the theater on any given day. In a novel twist, AFRICOM negotiated "partnerships" between state-level National Guard establishments and individual African nations. Guardsmen from North Carolina were to mentor Botswana's army, with North Dakota charged with Ghana, Michigan with Liberia, Utah with Morocco, Vermont with Senegal, Wyoming with Tunisia, Kentucky with Djibouti, New York with South Africa, and California with Nigeria.[57]

As trainers and models for local forces, teams of U.S. soldiers, both regulars and reservists, were constantly rotating through the continent's central and western reaches, offering instruction in weaponry, fieldcraft, and small-unit tactics while also employing UAVs and other means to provide intelligence support.[58] Meanwhile, largely hidden from sight, special operators collaborated with local partners in attempting to ferret out the enemies of order.[59]

The establishment media took notice and signaled its approval. Back in 1984 the *New York Times* reporter sent to take CENTCOM's measure had come away impressed. Now in 2014 the *Times* correspondent sent to evaluate AFRICOM reached a similar conclusion. Here was an outfit rapidly getting its act together.

The journalist, Eliza Griswold, pegged her story to the formidable and energetic General Linder. Indeed, she all but handed him her laptop. "My job is to look at Africa and see where the threat to the United States is," Linder told her. A South Carolinian, the special operations veteran spoke "with a drawl that does little to soften the blade of his critical intelligence," Griswold swooned. What interested Linder were not local problems but the "connective tissue" that provided context and perspective. Perhaps not surprisingly, the general found precisely what he was looking for—not simply radical Islamism but also drug smuggling, human trafficking, pandemics, desertification, and deep-seated tribal and sectarian rivalries. The list of concerns went on and on. Everything connected to everything else. "We have a real global threat," he insisted to Griswold in driving the point home. "The problems in Africa are going to land on our doorstep if we're not careful."

For Linder, preeminent among those problems was the existence of what he called "ungoverned spaces" beyond the reach of effective state power. AFRICOM's solution was to render these ungoverned spaces governable. Creating local militaries able to provide security was a first step toward doing just that, but only a first step. The overall U.S. military goal in Africa, Griswold concluded, "was to build a society faster than the enemy can take it apart."

Of course, the United States military had recently attempted to do much the same thing elsewhere in the Islamic world, without notable success. Results in Iraq and Afghanistan, where efforts were "poorly planned and poorly placed," had proven disappointing, one of Linder's subordinates, identified only as "Patrick," admitted. But Patrick, a lieutenant colonel and PhD candidate in anthropology to boot, professed optimism. (The field of study was not incidental. In the third decade of America's War for the Greater Middle East, anthropology, along with its cousin sociology, had become a hot discipline. While its infatuation with information technology remained undiminished, the officer corps initiated an intense flirtation with concepts like "mapping human terrain," said to hold the secrets of future victories.)[60] Patrick believed that the United States had learned from its mistakes. Africa was going to be different. "We have to do this right this time." The key was take a deliberate approach. "Give me six weeks, I can make a mess." Patrick said. "Give me a year, I can do something."[61]

Based on the early returns, doing something that actually stuck was going to take much longer than a year. Whatever the benefits of U.S. military tutelage, African armies continued to disappoint. In March 2012, for example, U.S.-schooled Malian officers overthrew their country's democratically elected government.[62] In Nigeria, even with U.S. training, security forces posed a greater danger to their own people than to Boko Haram. In April 2013, as retribution for the killing of one of their own, Nigerian troops sacked the town of Baga, destroying two thousand homes and murdering nearly two hundred residents. The Baga massacre drew a rebuke from Secretary of State Kerry, who charged that "Nigerian security forces are committing gross human rights violations, which, in turn, only escalate the violence and fuel extremism."[63] That summer, a U.S.-sponsored effort to build a Libyan counterterrorism unit got off to an unfortunate start when parties unknown simply walked off with the pistols, assault rifles, and night vision goggles the Americans had provided the trainees.[64] AFRICOM's engagement with Burkina Faso, designed "to promote continued democratization and greater respect for human rights and to encourage sustainable economic development," did nothing to dissuade parts of that country's army from mounting a coup in favor of the deposed dictator in 2015.[65]

Was the U.S. military enterprise in Africa headed in the right direction? The question was a difficult one to answer. While it was easy enough to measure inputs—no one could doubt that AFRICOM was hard at it—results tended to come in the form of promissory notes rather than bankable checks. Clear-cut successes were few in number. Many challenges persisted. In some respects the situation was worsening. As one informed observer remarked in 2013, "The continent is certainly more unstable today than it was in the early 2000s, when the U.S. started to intervene more directly."[66] Taken seriously, the judgment might have sufficed to give policymakers pause. Instead, U.S. military and civilian leaders persuaded themselves that they had no choice except to press on.

This too had become an abiding theme of America's War for the Greater Middle East.

17

IRAQ, AGAIN

IN THE FIRST GULF WAR OF 1980–1988, THE UNITED STATES
had thrown its support behind Saddam Hussein, thereby emboldening
him. In the Second Gulf War, it punished Saddam for overstepping his
bounds and then, through a policy of containment, sought to prevent
him from causing further trouble. In the Third Gulf War, the United
States abandoned containment and forcibly ejected Saddam from
power. It then sought to create a new Iraqi political order capable of
governing and a new Iraqi army capable of defending the Iraqi people.
A Fourth Gulf War, dating from 2013, rendered a definitive verdict on
the Third: When tested, the new Iraqi order proved itself unable to
stand on its own, its manifest deficiencies drawing the United States
into another round of fighting.

Further complicating the situation was the evolving situation in
neighboring Syria. There, the ongoing civil war to which the Obama
administration had reacted with such inconstancy morphed into a
multisided affair involving not only the Assad regime and rebel groups
of various stripes seeking to overthrow Assad but also a new entity bent
on carving out of both Syria and Iraq the beginnings of new pan-Islamic
caliphate. The Fourth Gulf War gave new meaning to the term *convoluted*.

This new entity, variously referred to as Daesh, ISIS, ISIL, or simply
the Islamic State, was not really a state but an anti-state. It aimed to
demolish the state system created by nineteenth- and early-twentieth-
century Europeans who had reconfigured the Greater Middle East to

suit their own imperial purposes. By the twenty-first century, however, the principal architects of this order, above all Great Britain but also France and Italy, retained neither the will nor the wherewithal to prevent its collapse. Europeans looked to the United States, still fancying that it owned the mantle of global leadership, to do just that. Propping up the legacy of empire, despite its manifold defects, seemed to hold out the best chance of stopping the new caliphate in its tracks. Viewed from this perspective, preserving the territorial integrity of Iraq and its neighbors ranked as an urgent priority.

By President Obama's second term in office, however, few Americans could work up much enthusiasm for trying yet again to rescue Iraq. Furthermore, it was not self-evident that ISIS posed an immediate danger to the United States itself. However vile and vicious—qualities proudly displayed by beheadings and other atrocities posted on social media—ISIS possessed limited capacity to project power beyond the Middle East. It lacked an air force and a navy. Its small land forces possessed few heavy weapons. Internationally, apart from other outlawed groups, it had neither allies nor patrons. Even if homegrown terrorists cited ISIS as a source of inspiration, the organization lagged well behind climate change and Chinese hackers as a proximate threat to the United States.

On the other hand, the famous "Pottery Barn Rule" attributed to Secretary of State Colin Powell—"If you break it, you own it"—still lingered to haunt whatever passed for conscience in the inner sanctums of American power. Back in 2003, the George W. Bush administration had indubitably broken Iraq. Subsequent efforts to restore that country had proven a bust, the very existence of ISIS testifying to that fact. Here was the second harvest of poisonous fruit resulting from Operation Iraqi Freedom, the first harvest having produced Al Qaeda in Iraq. While General McChrystal's counterterrorism campaign had depleted AQI, ISIS had emerged as its successor.

Yet what drew the United States into the Fourth Gulf War was less a sense of moral responsibility than sheer monomania. By now, the entire national security apparatus had become so accustomed to seeing the Greater Middle East as a domain of U.S. military action that its ability to think otherwise had withered to the point of nonexistence. Why did Washington choose to reengage militarily in Iraq? Because it couldn't think of anything better to do.

The Islamic State of Iraq and Syria came into existence in April 2013. At that time, the term *ISIS* already applied to a large multinational pharmaceutical company; a 1990s American rock band; the California-based International Self-Improvement Society, offering "religion for the irreligious"; a "mobile wallet platform" supported by AT&T, T-Mobile, and Verizon; the Iowa Student Information System at the University of Iowa; and strangely enough, the Institute for the Secularisation of Islamic Society.

The newest claimant to the title wasted no time in asserting principal ownership, even if it look a while for observers to catch on. In July 2013, when ISIS engineered a spectacular jailbreak that freed hundreds of militants locked up in Iraqi prisons at Abu Ghraib and Taji, *The New York Times* credited the action to "Al Qaeda's Iraq affiliate."[1] Nominally accurate, the characterization missed the point that the affiliate was in the process of superseding the parent organization.[2]

In December, ISIS seized Fallujah, for Americans a city retaining deep resonance as the site of fierce battles that claimed the lives of over a hundred GIs during the previous Gulf War. With this success, ISIS emerged from Al Qaeda's shadows. Early the following month, Abu Bakr al-Baghdadi, the organization's supreme leader, declared the founding of a new caliphate and pronounced himself caliph. ISIS designated the territory over which it presided in Iraq and Syria the Islamic State. AQI was last night's bad dream; Islamic State was tomorrow's nightmare.

Asked to comment on these developments, Secretary of State Kerry emphasized that the United States had no intention of getting dragged back in militarily. "This is a fight that belongs to the Iraqis," he insisted.[3] For his part, Secretary of Defense Chuck Hagel, Obama's third appointee to that post, tried valiantly to put the best face on things. Yes, Iraq was going through a "difficult time." Yet even while admitting that Iraq's new army might not be perfect, Hagel believed that it had "done pretty well." The danger was real, but "Iraq is going to handle it. And we're going to continue to help them and support them."[4] At this point, "help and support" meant "arm and equip." Going back to 2005, the United States had already sold Iraq some $14 billion in weapons and related military materiel. The Pentagon now promised even more, to include M1A1 Abrams tanks, AH-64 Apache attack helicopters, and missiles of various types.[5]

Worse was still to come, however. In June, a force of fewer than a thousand ISIS fighters captured Mosul, Iraq's second largest city, along with Tikrit, hometown of Saddam Hussein. Iraqi defenders—two whole divisions—offered alarmingly little resistance.[6] According to press reports, soldiers in large numbers abandoned their posts, shed their uniforms, and simply fled, setting off a stampede of refugees. Baghdad itself now seemed vulnerable.[7]

In Washington, something akin to panic set in. Senator John McCain described the situation in Iraq as "the greatest threat since the Cold War," notwithstanding that ISIS mustered a grand total of perhaps ten thousand fighters.[8] "Iraq is burning, and the United States of America is watching," military analyst Frederick Kagan fumed. Further inaction, he predicted, "would do far more damage to America than our retreat from Vietnam in 1975."[9] Max Boot spelled out the implications of this dire situation:

> ISIS is well on its way to carving out a fundamentalist caliphate that stretches from Aleppo in northern Syria to Mosul in northern Iraq. The post–World War I borders of the Middle East seem to be unraveling. Syria is being split into two entities, one controlled by Sunni Islamists, the other by Hezbollah. . . . Iraq is being split into three. . . . The only thing that remains to be determined is whether Shiite or Sunni extremists will control the capital—the new battle for Baghdad, which has already begun, is likely to be even bloodier than the previous installment.[10]

All the critics agreed in placing the problem at Obama's feet. When it came to Iraq, he had not cared enough or done enough. None of the critics gave more than passing attention to assessing the consequences of what the United States had already done, not only in Iraq but elsewhere in the region, over the previous several decades. Washington suffered from the inverse of early-onset Alzheimer's. Short-term memory going back a week or ten days was perfectly intact; everything else was gone.

The Obama administration itself shared this disinclination to examine the past, preferring to treat ISIS as sui generis. Without admitting error, it responded to the crisis much as its critics were demanding. So, for example, on June 15, Kagan called for "immediately sending air support; intelligence, surveillance, and reconnaissance assets; air transportation; Special Operations forces; training teams; and more military equipment."[11] Four days later, President Obama announced that he was repositioning U.S. air and naval assets in anticipation of "targeted and precise military action"; had "significantly increased our intelligence, surveillance, and reconnaissance assets"; was dispatching U.S. troops to "train, advise, and support Iraqi security forces"; and was pressing Congress to approve further transfers of military equipment to Iraq.[12] Without saying so, the president also ordered special operations forces into action. The imperatives of partisanship concealed what was, in fact, a broad, if unacknowledged, consensus.

Within days, armed U.S. aircraft, both manned and unmanned, were conducting reconnaissance flights over Iraq.[13] Soon thereafter, U.S. troops arrived to ensure the security of Baghdad International Airport.[14] On August 7, citing the plight of the Yazidi religious sect that ISIS was threatening to exterminate, President Obama announced the beginning of a U.S. air campaign against the Islamic State, even as he assured Americans that "I will not allow the United States to be dragged into fighting another war in Iraq."[15] Air strikes began the next day; by any commonly understood definition of the term, the United States was once more at war in Iraq.

Although the siege of the Yazidis was lifted within days, air operations continued, albeit at a modest tempo. Air force and navy jets, the latter flying from the nuclear aircraft carrier USS *George H. W. Bush,* conducted an average of just five strike missions a day against ISIS ground forces.[16] While the JCS director of operations, army Lieutenant General William Mayville, claimed that these strikes had "temporarily disrupted" the enemy offensive, he conceded that such a meager level of effort was unlikely to make any lasting impact on overall ISIS capabilities. "I in no way want to suggest that we have effectively contained or that we are somehow breaking the momentum of the threat," he emphasized.[17]

So the Obama administration revised and expanded the campaign's objectives. On September 9, the president went back on national television to announce his intention to "degrade and ultimately destroy" the Islamic State "through a comprehensive and sustained counterterrorism strategy."[18] In practical terms, that meant liberating ISIS-occupied cities and regaining control of Iraq's porous borders. Both tasks promised to be challenging. Obama's war-that-was-not-a-war was going to entail major exertions, and it was going to take time. In the American military lexicon, *mission creep* was a term of opprobrium, redolent with connotations similar to Vietnam's "gradual escalation." It suggested action without clearly defined purpose. When it came to ISIS, the mission was undeniably creeping.[19]

That same month, at CENTCOM headquarters in Tampa, Florida, General Lloyd Austin convened a conference of several dozen nations that in one way or another had signaled a willingness to lend a hand against the Islamic State. President Obama had appointed another four-star officer, General John Allen, former CENTCOM commander now retired, as his "Special Presidential Envoy for the Global Coalition to Counter ISIL." Allen's job was to reconcile the various interests and divergent capabilities of coalition members; Austin's was to orchestrate the ongoing military campaign.

In October, that campaign acquired a name, Operation Inherent Resolve. As a call to arms, it was notably muted.

To fulfill President Obama's charge, Austin designed a plan with two distinct dimensions. From the air, where the coalition enjoyed near-impunity, forces under his command would subject ISIS to continuous bombing, not only in Iraq but also in Syria.[20] On the ground, American and other Western advisers would "regenerate and restructure," while also attempting to motivate, Iraqi ground forces. Ultimately, Austin assumed, the war's outcome was going to turn on whether or not Iraqis themselves decided that their country was worth defending.[21]

During the fall of 2014, the air effort ramped up. Between August and December, the monthly tally of weapons actually released increased ninefold.[22] Yet in terms of strike sorties per day, the overall intensity lagged well behind previous bombing campaigns, even lesser episodes such as Bosnia in 1995 and Libya in 2011.[23] One observer derided the bombing as "military tokenism."[24] Even as Austin pronounced himself satisfied with the progress being made, he acknowledged that ISIS was adjusting its tactics so as to limit the effectiveness of coalition air attacks.[25] The fact was that ISIS offered only so many targets worth the price of a PGM. Bombing alone was not going to suffice.

Simultaneously, coalition efforts to train Iraqi security forces picked up momentum, at least as measured by energy expended. In June, President Obama had ordered a first tranche of several hundred trainers to Iraq. The numbers increased incrementally such that by the end of 2014 there were three thousand U.S. military personnel in country. Upon their arrival, the Americans discovered that the Iraqi army so laboriously created during the years of U.S. occupation had all but vanished. Rebuilding meant starting from the ground up.[26]

In terms of operational goals once that rebuilding was underway, regaining control of Mosul ranked as a top CENTCOM priority. General Martin Dempsey, the JCS chairman, had already identified the fight for Mosul as likely to be "the decisive battle in the ground campaign."[27] Austin shared that view. By January, the normally reticent CENTCOM commander was willing to go public with a progress report and a timetable. Things were looking up. Inherent Resolve had already killed an estimated six thousand ISIS fighters, Austin said. ISIS was "beginning to experience a manpower issue." An Iraqi-led counteroffensive to retake Mosul was on track to occur in the spring or summer of 2015.[28]

Testifying before Congress in March of that year, Austin was even more upbeat. As a result of the battering it had sustained from the air, ISIS could no longer "seize and hold new territory," he indicated. The enemy had assumed "a defensive crouch" and was "losing this fight." Ensuring its complete defeat held the key to moving the entire "region in the direction of increased stability and security"—a goal routinely enunciated by CENTCOM commanders over the previous several decades.[29]

Austin's optimism proved misplaced. ISIS demonstrated a remarkable ability not only to replenish its losses but actually to increase its overall strength. By June 2015, with a senior U.S. official now claiming that air operations had killed fully ten thousand ISIS fighters—a number equal to the supposed size of the entire force one year prior—estimates suggested that ISIS now had somewhere between twenty and fifty thousand men under arms.[30] ISIS was also demonstrating an impressive capacity to recruit. While most fighters came from the Middle East and North Africa, others arrived from more remote corners of the Islamic world such as Azerbaijan, Indonesia, the southern Philippines, and, of course, Bosnia and Kosovo. Disturbing numbers came from within the West itself, to include hundreds from European countries such as France, Germany, and the United Kingdom, along with dozens of Australians, Canadians, and even Americans. The figures were imprecise, but the phenomenon itself was troubling.[31] Certainly, there existed no reason to believe that U.S.-led military action was depleting the enemy's ranks. If anything, the opposite was true.

In the late spring of 2015, as if to rebut General Austin's positive assessment, ISIS launched another major offensive. In the previous months, Iraqi forces had regained some lost territory, for example retaking Tikrit. The Peshmerga, the self-defense forces of Iraqi Kurdistan fighting their own distinct war against ISIS, had held their own.[32] Decapitation efforts—including a raid into Syria by U.S. special operations forces that killed a mid-level ISIS functionary—achieved occasional successes.[33] And, of course, the air war continued. With all the regularity of hourly shuttle flights between LaGuardia and Washington National, coalition aircraft traversed Iraqi and Syrian airspace, releasing roughly two thousand bombs and missiles per month.[34] On May 15, Marine Brigadier General Thomas D. Weidley, speaking from Kuwait, went so far as to assure the Pentagon press corps that ISIS was losing "across Iraq and Syria." "They remain on the defensive," he said, adding that "the coalition strategy . . . is on track."[35]

Within the next forty-eight hours, ISIS forces seized Ramadi in Iraq along with the ancient Syrian city of Palmyra. The simultaneous loss of these two cities shattered any illusions that the war was heading in the right direction. For Americans, the fall of Ramadi, by car only a ninety-minute drive from Baghdad, came as a particularly bitter blow. Psychologically, losing this city, site of what had seemed a tide-turning U.S. victory in the previous Gulf War, was the equivalent of the Tet Offensive back in 1968. The light at the end of the Iraqi tunnel was fast receding.

Once again, panic laced with finger-pointing swept Washington. Senator John McCain wasted no time in holding President Obama personally responsible for what he called "a shameful chapter in American history."[36] The loss of Ramadi left "President Obama's strategy against the Islamic State in ruins not only in Iraq but also throughout the Muslim world," Frederick Kagan announced. He too fingered President Obama as directly responsible for a setback that Kagan declared "unnecessary and avoidable." The most recent ISIS offensive had "completely derailed" Obama administration policy and left the region "engulfed in war."[37] Retired army General Jack Keane reached a nearly identical solution. "We are losing this war," he told the Senate Armed Services Committee. The root of the problem was obvious: "There is no strategy to contain the destabilization of the Middle East."[38]

The antidote was equally obvious: escalation. Republican Senator Lindsey Graham of South Carolina felt certain that injecting another ten thousand GIs would surely do the trick.[39] Frederick Kagan went further. He proposed bolstering the existing U.S. commitment to Iraq with another fifteen thousand to twenty thousand U.S. troops—not to engage in large-scale combat operations but to deepen the support being provided the Iraqis. General Keane emphasized the need to expand operations in Syria, which he described as an ISIS safe haven. That meant more (and more effectively conducted) air strikes and many more U.S. special operations raids into Syrian territory.

The administration begged to differ. Secretary of Defense Ashton Carter, a Harvard academic appointed to replace the lackluster Hagel, wasn't going to let Iraqis off the hook. Ramadi had fallen because the units assigned to defend the place had performed abysmally. Although "vastly" outnumbering the attackers, they had "failed to fight," he charged. Ramadi showed that "we have an issue with the will of the Iraqis to fight."[40] General Dempsey, the JCS chairman, offered an even more withering assessment. Iraqi forces had simply turned tail. They weren't "driven out of Ramadi," he said, "they drove out."[41]

Even so, rather than caving to his critics, President Obama stiffed them. At least for public consumption, the mantra of "degrade and destroy" remained intact. The administration affirmed its basic approach to achieving those goals. In truth, few outside of the administration dissented from that basic approach. Even critics inclined to see in ISIS proof that the sky was falling refrained from pressing for the United States to reinvade and reoccupy Iraq.

By this time, the high priests of national security had tried and discarded several approaches to imposing America's will on the Greater Middle East. Time and again, from Lebanon in the 1980s to Afghanistan thirty years later, they had underestimated what it was going to take to do the job right—with Operation Desert Storm the one partial and very temporary exception. However great the danger posed by ISIS, civilian and military leaders alike remained committed to the proposition that eliminating that danger was not going to require anything more than a fragment of the nation's full military strength. As a consequence, the alternatives under active consideration in the summer of 2015 amounted to variations on a single theme. Option 1 was more of the same, option 2 more of the same plus, and option 3 more of the same with a double plus. There was no option proposing an all-out effort to win and none that said, "This isn't working; we need to get out of here."

As was his habit on military matters, the commander in chief chose the middle course. Obama ordered a few hundred additional American trainers to Iraq. Plans to take Mosul were quietly shelved. Regaining control of Ramadi now became the priority—and even that looked to be several months away. The president also promised "the expedited delivery of essential equipment and materiel" not only to Iraq's army but to just about any other Iraqi group willing to fight ISIS. Re-equipping had emerged as a priority due to the Iraqi army's penchant for abandoning its kit on the battlefield. So, for example, the Pentagon announced that it was rushing an order of antitank weapons to Baghdad to help Iraqis defend against the hundreds of captured American-made Humvees that had become the conveyance of choice for ISIS suicide bombers.[42] The United States was rearming an Iraqi army that had become the principal source of arms for the forces that were overrunning Iraq itself.

In the eyes of his critics, Obama's response to the crisis offered the worst of both worlds. It was mission creep combined with gradual escalation.[43] In some quarters, the manifest defects of this approach fed suspicions that Inherent Resolve was mostly for show—a cover story for what was actually a policy of retreat and disengagement.

In particular, an American right wing that loathed Obama as passionately as the left had loathed Obama's predecessor suspected the president of nefariously plotting to get out of Iraq by allowing Iran in. Diplomatic negotiations initiated to prevent Iran from acquiring nuclear weapons, they believed, were actually intended to end that country's exclusion from regional politics. On the surface, the likelihood of an American rapprochement with Iran appeared remote, if only because the government of Israel (not to mention Saudi Arabia), backed by Israel's supporters in the United States, was adamantly opposed. Now, however, the increasingly disordered condition of the Middle East and the failure of past American efforts to quell that disorder, further compounded by the bad blood between Obama and Israeli Prime Minister Netanyahu, suggested that the time might be ripe for a Nixon-goes-to-China moment.

In a sense, the hardliners had good reason to denounce Obama's supposed "appeasement" of Iran. Removing Iran from the official American enemies list—as Obama had already done in the case of Cuba—was likely to have game-changing implications for a raft of existing U.S. commitments and obligations.[44] Obama's real offense was not that he was giving Iran a green light to acquire a nuclear arsenal; it was his refusal to defer to the wishes of Israel and Gulf Arabs, who wanted Iran kept in its box.

Recall that America's War for the Greater Middle East had begun in Iran with the overthrow of the Shah and the subsequent hostage crisis. Since then, apart from the bizarre Iran-Contra episode, Washington had viewed Iran as the "other," to be ignored and isolated. Of course, Iran had returned U.S. hostility with interest. During the next several decades, something between a cold war and a real war had ensued. Intervening on Saddam Hussein's behalf during the First Gulf War, the United States had all but destroyed Iran's navy. Payback came in the Third Gulf War, when Iran provided weapons and technological support to Iraqi Shiite militias who were killing U.S. troops.[45]

Most recently, the United States had collaborated with Israel in orchestrating a series of covert attacks aimed at retarding Iran's suspected efforts to develop nuclear weapons. This was Operation Olympic Games, initiated by President George W. Bush in 2006 and then embraced by his successor. The most notable episode in this campaign occurred in 2010, when the United States employed a computer virus called Stuxnet to penetrate Iran's Natanz nuclear enrichment facility. Although the attack disabled as many as a thousand Iranian centrifuges, Iran wasted little time in repairing the damage. Here was the Hiroshima of cyberwar—an attack launched, like Hiroshima itself, because a capability existed without much thought given to the implications of legitimating its use.[46]

By Obama's second term, however, U.S. policy toward Iran was shifting. Rather than attempting along *with* Israel to disrupt Iran's nuclear program, the United States was seeking *despite* Israel to persuade Iran to curtail that program in return for economic and political concessions. In July 2015, complex and protracted negotiations involving all five permanent members of the UN Security Council plus Germany and Iran produced an agreement—a Joint Comprehensive Plan of Action.

While some celebrated the outcome as a diplomatic triumph, others denounced it as a capitulation. In the latter camp were the several Republicans vying to succeed Obama as president in 2016. Senator Lindsey Graham pronounced the JCPOA a "death sentence for the state of Israel." Rather than curbing Iran's nuclear ambitions, the deal "paves Iran's path to a bomb," former Florida governor Jeb Bush said. Texas Senator Ted Cruz, another presidential hopeful, predicted that as a direct result of the agreement, "millions of Americans will be murdered by radical theocratic zealots." New Jersey governor Chris Christie chastised Obama for having made "humiliating concessions." Former Arkansas governor Mike Huckabee charged the president with marching Israelis "to the door of the oven" and vowed, if elected, "to topple the terrorist Iranian regime and defeat the evil forces of radical Islam."[47] Prime Minister Netanyahu predictably characterized the agreement as "a historic mistake."[48] With trademark hyperbole, Max Boot described the deal as "the date when American dominance in the Middle East was supplanted by the Iranian Imperium."[49] In reality, "American dominance" of the region was a chimera and would remain so.

More to the point, the rush to declare the Iran nuclear deal a disaster was as premature as declaring the overthrow of Saddam Hussein or Moamar Gaddafi a historic victory. The agreement's actual implications would only emerge over time and were likely to differ from the expectations of both proponents and naysayers. In this one respect, diplomacy is akin to war: Long-term outcomes tend to differ from near-term expectations.

Yet even while these negotiations were still underway, Iran itself had effectively enlisted in the war against ISIS. The Islamic Republic might not be an American ally, but it was taking on America's latest enemy in the Greater Middle East. Like the United States, Iran elected to play a limited role. It provided Iraq with materiel, advisers, and air support, all under the aegis of the Quds Force, the functional equivalent of U.S. Special Operations Command.

The resulting alignment of friends and foes was anything but straightforward. The United States and Iran were on the same side, except when they weren't. Within the territorial confines of Iraq, they faced a common enemy while sharing a common near-term objective—preventing ISIS from gaining complete control of that country. That common purpose did not extend to Iraq's future, however. Shiite-majority Iran clearly intended to exercise considerable sway over its Shiite-majority neighbor and wasn't about to ask Washington's permission to do so.

Within the territorial confines of neighboring Syria, the United States and Iran again faced that same immediate adversary. Apart from seeking to defeat ISIS, however, their purposes were radically at odds. The United States clung to the hope of "moderate rebels" ousting the Assad regime, while fearing that radical Islamists might actually succeed in doing so. For its part, Iran was resolutely determined to keep Assad in power in defiance of American insistence to the contrary. For Tehran, having a friendly regime in Damascus was essential.[50]

It was all a bit like Eastern Europe at the end of World War II. FDR had fancied that Poles and Czechs, once liberated from Nazi occupation, might enjoy freedom and independence. Stalin had other ideas. With the fate of Eastern Europe mattering more to the Soviet Union than to the United States, Washington didn't see the issue as worth fighting for. Poland and Czechoslovakia soon slipped behind the Iron Curtain.

As much as Americans might nurse fantasies of Iraq, once liberated from ISIS, enjoying freedom and independence, Iranian authorities clearly had other ideas. And like Stalin in 1945, they enjoyed several advantages, not least of all proximity. Keeping Iran out of Iraq and ejecting it from Syria would come at a very high price. Obama was no more inclined to pay than Roosevelt and Truman had been when tallying up the cost of preventing Eastern Europe's absorption into the Soviet sphere.

In the autumn of 2015, no one could say with certainty how the fight against ISIS was going to turn out. But victory, if achieved, was likely to come at the expense of Iraqis and Syrians—precisely as the Allied victory over Nazi Germany came at the expense of Poles and Czechs. Iran was going to end up the principal beneficiary, with the United States ill positioned to do much more than register protests. This Obama appeared to recognize even if his more bellicose critics did not.

Would defeating ISIS actually solve anything? Probably not, since the conditions that had given rise to ISIS would still persist. Yet focusing on this one specific manifestation of a larger problem provided an excuse to skip lightly past matters of far greater moment. It was like foreign drug cartels and the American epidemic of drug abuse and addiction. You can pretend that attacking the former will reduce the latter, but you're kidding yourself.

In Washington, one subject in particular remained off-limits: the overall progress and prospects of the U.S. military project in the Islamic world. Thirty-five years after Jimmy Carter had issued the Carter Doctrine, that project appeared further removed from completion than when it had begun. By almost any measure, the region was in greater disarray than it had been in 1980. Not only were American purposes unfulfilled, they were becoming increasingly difficult to define with any sort of specificity.

"It's a generational problem," General Dempsey told members of a Senate committee in July 2015.[51] "It," as Dempsey explained on another occasion, was the chaos caused by "loosely connected" groups that "run from Afghanistan across the Arabian Peninsula into Yemen to the Horn of Africa and into North and West Africa." Whether or not civilian officials wanted to hear it or ordinary Americans were prepared to acknowledge it, the fact was that the United States by 2015 found itself mired in something much nastier than simply another Gulf War. The problem was bigger than Iraq and extended far beyond the bounds of the Gulf itself.

Worse still, the issues under dispute went beyond the merely political. It was not just about oil or territory or the perpetuation of some dynasty but about ideology (mostly ours) and religion (mostly theirs). Thwarting this network of groups, "most of which are local, some of which are regional, and some of which are global," was going to entail "a very long contest," Dempsey emphasized.[52] How long? How much longer than it had already run? Wisely, the general did not hazard a guess. No one had a clue.

18

GENERATIONAL WAR

In 1948, George Kennan, State Department director of policy planning, noted that the United States then possessed "about 50% of the world's wealth but only 6.3% of its population." The challenge facing U.S. policymakers, he believed, was "to devise a pattern of relationships which will permit us to maintain this position of disparity without positive detriment to our national security."[1] The overarching aim of American statecraft, in other words, was to sustain the uniquely favorable situation to which the United States had ascended by the end of World War II. It's hard to imagine a statement of purpose more succinct, cogent, and to the point.

Judged by this standard, the stewards of U.S. foreign policy down to the present day have done more than passably well. Today, many decades later, Kennan's position of disparity persists, somewhat diminished but still leaving Americans in a remarkably advantageous position. With less than 5 percent of the population, the United States still controls 25 percent of global net worth.[2] Here is the ultimate emblem of American success, whether as nation or system or ideology. Wealth confers choice. It provides latitude to act or to refrain from acting.

To maintain American preeminence, Kennan and his colleagues devised a strategy that came to be called containment. The term was misleading. Stripped of its immediate Cold War context, a more accurate name was preponderance.[3] That strategy sought not only to check any further expansion of Soviet power but also to overmatch and outlast the Soviet system. Demonstrating the superior allure of American-style freedom—precisely what I experienced driving my Mustang to Chicago back in the summer of 1969—exposed as hollow Soviet promises of utopia. But it did much more. Across much of the planet, whether for better or worse, the American way of life became the principal embodiment of freedom. What we had the world wanted, and we had more of it than anyone else. Here was American primacy made manifest. The arrangement was one that the American people found eminently satisfactory.

With an eye toward sustaining this position of disparity, the United States after World War II consciously chose to become the world's leading military power. In a sharp break from past American practice, it created and maintained on a permanent footing large-scale, heavily armed forces designed for global power projection.

Notably, however, the principal function of these forces was not to wage war but to avert it. By demonstrating a capacity and readiness to fight, the U.S. military was reducing the likelihood of actually having to do so. "Peace Is Our Profession"—so proclaimed the Strategic Air Command, the Cold War–era nuclear strike force that stood ready at a moment's notice to turn large cities into rubble while incinerating millions. Yet SAC's motto was not some clumsy attempt at black humor. It was, or at least was meant to be, a serious statement of purpose.

As long as the Cold War lasted, this paradoxical logic enjoyed widespread acceptance. The advantages of husbanding military power were so apparent as to be self-evident. Here was the rationale routinely employed by representatives of the national security establishment and its affiliates. Calling for more (and better) ships, planes, missiles, and tanks, they did so in the name of keeping the peace. Accumulating weapons of mass destruction of ever greater lethality, they did so for the express purpose of ensuring that such weapons would see no further use.

In retrospect, we may regret the diversion of resources that might have gone to more productive purposes. We may lament the distortion of the American economy and the corruption of American politics stemming from the rise of what President Eisenhower called the military-industrial complex. We may recall with horror the reckless miscalculations that brought the world to the brink of Armageddon during the Cuban Missile Crisis. Even so, the basic approach to national security worked at least tolerably well. World War III didn't happen. Over time, the Cold War's two principal theaters, Western Europe and East Asia, stabilized and achieved a measure of prosperity. When the Cold War itself finally ended, it did so quietly and with American primacy intact, much as Kennan himself had prophesied in its very first days.

Along the way, of course, the United States made many egregious mistakes. The bungled Korean War proved needlessly expensive. The Vietnam misadventure, handiwork of several successive presidential administrations, ended in mortifying defeat. A raft of attempted coups, dirty tricks, and unsavory marriages of convenience made a mockery of Washington's claims to stand for high ideals. The nuclear arms race heedlessly touched off by the United States created hazards that may yet end in unspeakable catastrophe.

Even so, things could have been much worse. Taking the period of the Cold War as a whole, U.S. military policies and American purposes roughly aligned. On balance, this congruence furthered rather than undermining the nation's well-being. For the United States, freedom, abundance, and security went hand in hand.

Yet the Cold War's happy outcome (at least from an American point of view) came with a distinct downside for the U.S. national security apparatus. Among other things, it rendered the paradox underlying postwar U.S. military policy—energetically preparing for global war in order to prevent it—obsolete. In doing so, it brought the armed services and their various clients face to face with a crisis of the first order. With the likelihood of World War III subsiding to somewhere between remote and infinitesimal—with the overarching purpose for which the postwar U.S. military establishment had been created thereby fulfilled—what exactly did that establishment and all of its ancillary agencies, institutes, collaborators, and profit-making auxiliaries exist to do?

The Pentagon wasted no time in providing an answer to that question. Rather than keeping the peace, it declared, the key to perpetuating Kennan's position of disparity was to "shape" the global order. *Shaping* now became the military's primary job. Back in 1992, the Defense Planning Guidance drafted under the aegis of Paul Wolfowitz had spelled out this argument in detail. Pointing proudly to the "new international environment" that had already "been shaped by the victory" over Saddam Hussein the year before, that document provided a blueprint explaining how American power could "shape the future."[4] The sledgehammer was to become a sculptor's chisel.

The Greater Middle East was to serve—indeed, was even then already serving—as the chosen arena for honing military power into a utensil that would maintain America's privileged position and, not so incidentally, provide a continuing rationale for the entire apparatus of national security. That region's predominantly Muslim population thereby became the subjects of experiments ranging from the nominally benign—peacekeeping, peacemaking, and humanitarian intervention—to the nakedly coercive. Beginning in 1980, U.S. forces ventured into the Greater Middle East to reassure, warn, intimidate, suppress, pacify, rescue, liberate, eliminate, transform, and overawe. They bombed, raided, invaded, occupied, and worked through proxies of various stripes. In 1992 Wolfowitz had expressed the earnest hope of American might addressing the "sources of regional instability in ways that promote international law, limit international violence, and encourage the spread of democratic government and open economic systems." The results actually produced over the course of several decades of trying have never come even remotely close to satisfying such expectations.

The events that first drew the United States military into the Greater Middle East and that seemed so extraordinary at the time—the Iranian Revolution and the Soviet occupation of Afghanistan—turned out to be mere harbingers. Subsequent upheavals have swept through the region in waves: revolutions and counterrevolutions, episodes of terror and counterterror, grotesque barbarism and vast suffering. Through it all, a succession of American leaders—Republican and Democratic, conservative and liberal, calculating and naïve—has persisted in the belief that the determined exercise of U.S. military power will somehow put things right. None have seen their hopes fulfilled.

To reflect on this longest of American wars is to confront two questions. First, why has the world's mightiest military achieved so little even while itself absorbing very considerable losses and inflicting even greater damage on the subjects of America's supposed beneficence? Second, why in the face of such unsatisfactory outcomes has the United States refused to chart a different course? In short, why can't we win? And since we haven't won, why can't we get out?

With regard to the first question, one explanation stands out above all others. In stark contrast to the Cold War, American purposes and U.S. military policy in the Islamic world have never aligned. Rather than keeping threats to U.S. interests at bay, a penchant for military activism, initially circumspect but becoming increasingly uninhibited over time, has helped to foster new threats. Time and again, from the 1980s to the present, U.S. military power, unleashed rather than held in abeyance, has met outright failure, produced results other than those intended, or proved to be largely irrelevant. The Greater Middle East remains defiantly resistant to shaping.

Not for want of American effort, of course. Like the armies of World War I desperately searching for ways to break the deadlock on the Western Front, U.S. forces operating in various theaters across the Islamic world have field-tested all manner of novelties, hoping thereby to gain a decisive edge. In World War I that meant tanks and poison gas, rolling barrages and stormtrooper tactics. In America's War for the Greater Middle East, it's been the RMA and COIN, PGMs and UAVs, not to mention such passing fancies as "overwhelming force," "shock and awe," and "air occupation." Yet the introduction of some new battlefield technique does not necessarily signify progress. Too often, it merely offers an excuse to ignore the very absence of progress.

In World War I, the supreme importance assigned to the Western Front made the stalemate there visible to all. The geography of America's War for the Greater Middle East has been more variable. Always there is the Persian Gulf, of course, but at intervals Central Asia, the

Levant, the Maghreb, the Horn of Africa, and even the Balkans have vied for attention. More recently still, West Africa has emerged as an active theater. These periodic changes of venue do not mean that the United States is closing in on its goal, however. Opening up some new front (or reopening an old one) testifies to the reality that U.S. forces in 2016 find themselves caught in a predicament no less perplexing than the one that ensnared the armies of Germany, France, and Great Britain a century ago. Take whatever definition of purpose you want; after more than three decades of trying, for U.S. forces the mission remains unfinished. Indeed, "unfinished" hardly begins to describe the situation; mission accomplishment is nowhere in sight. Put simply, we're stuck.

So why can't we get out? Why in this instance doesn't the ostensibly superior power of the United States confer choice? How can it be that even today, large segments of the policy elite entertain fantasies of salvaging victory if only a smart president will make the requisite smart moves?

To understand the persistence of such illusions requires appreciating several assumptions that promote in Washington a deeply pernicious collective naiveté. Seldom explicitly articulated, these assumptions pervade the U.S. national security establishment.

The first assumption posits that those responsible for formulating U.S. policy in the Greater Middle East—not only elected and appointed officials but also the military officers assigned to senior posts—are able to discern the historical forces at work in the region. Indeed, discernment is theirs as a direct consequence of ascending to high office. Position implies enlightenment, along with adherence to a suitably correct worldview.

The worldview to which individuals rotating through the upper reaches of the national security apparatus subscribe derives from a shared historical narrative. Indeed, their fealty to that narrative, which they routinely affirm by reciting various clichés and platitudes, forms a precondition of their employment.

This narrative recounts the story of the twentieth century as Americans have chosen to remember it. It centers on an epic competition between rival versions of modernity—liberalism vs. fascism vs. communism—and ends in vindication for "our" side. Ultimately, the right side of history had prevailed. Presidents and cabinet secretaries, generals and admirals see no reason why that narrative should not apply to a different locale and extend into the distant future. In other words, they are blind to the possibility that in the Greater Middle East substantially different historical forces just might be at work.

A second assumption takes it for granted that as the sole global superpower the United States possesses not only the wisdom but also the wherewithal to control or direct such forces. In the twentieth century "our" side won because American industry and ingenuity produced not only superior military might but also a superior way of life based on consumption and choice—so at least Americans have been thoroughly conditioned to believe. The United States manufactured a version of freedom that its principal adversaries were hard pressed to match. In Europe and in the parts of Asia that Washington cared about, the competition between glitzy and drab, autonomy and conformity, self-indulgence and self-denial proved to be not much of a contest. That this formula might not work quite so easily in an environment where glitz, autonomy, and self-indulgence may constitute provocations raises the possibility that freedom may not be universal—that it can take alternative forms. Few American policymakers and even fewer senior military officers are able to countenance such a possibility.

A third assumption asserts that U.S. military power offers the most expeditious means of ensuring that universal freedom prevails—that the armed might of the United States, made manifest in the presence of airplanes, warships, and fighting troops, serves as an irreplaceable facilitator or catalyst in moving history toward its foreordained destination. True, not every problem lends itself to a simple and straightforward "military solution." But no problem of any consequence is likely to yield a tolerable solution absent some application of U.S. military power, whether direct or indirect. That the commitment of American armed might could actually backfire and make matters worse is a proposition that few authorities in Washington are willing to entertain.

A final assumption counts on the inevitability of America's purposes ultimately winning acceptance, even in the Islamic world. The subjects of U.S. benefactions will then obligingly submit to Washington's requirements and warmly embrace American norms. If not today, then surely tomorrow, the United States will receive the plaudits and be granted the honors that liberators rightly deserve. Near-term disappointments can be discounted given the certainty that better outcomes lie just ahead.

None of these assumptions has any empirical basis. Each of the four drips with hubris. Taken together, they sustain the absence of self-awareness that has become an American signature. Worse, they constitute a nearly insurmountable barrier to serious critical analysis. Yet the prevalence of these assumptions goes far toward explaining this key failing in the U.S. military effort: the absence of a consistent understanding of what the United States is fighting for and whom it is fighting against.

When Jimmy Carter initiated America's War for the Greater Middle East, this had not been a problem. Then the mission seemed clear: Ensure U.S. access to Persian Gulf oil. The enemy had a name and an address. Indeed, President Carter identified two mutually antagonistic adversaries—Iran in the throes of revolution and an increasingly sclerotic Soviet Union, its own revolution a fading memory. Washington perceived each as posing a looming threat to the Persian Gulf. But if the Gulf's apparent vulnerability offered a proximate rationale for militarizing U.S. policy in the Islamic world, that preliminary assessment soon enough gave way to something more expansive.

This was hardly an unprecedented occurrence. Back in April 1898, the Spanish-American War began as a crusade to liberate Cuba. When in the ensuing months the United States occupied and annexed Hawaii, Guam, the Philippines, and Puerto Rico, that crusade had pretty clearly morphed into something else. So too with America's War for the Greater Middle East. It began as a project centered on protecting Persian Gulf oil. Yet by the time Ronald Reagan sent Marines into Beirut and secret emissaries to Tehran while picking fights with Colonel Gaddafi, U.S. purposes were clearly changing—even if those purposes remained murky to Reagan himself.

Already in the 1980s, in other words, clarity regarding the nature of the mission and the identity of the enemy was evaporating. By fits and starts, America's War for the Greater Middle East was expanding. Increasing its scope undermined its strategic coherence, however, with purposefulness of effort inversely related to the number of countries in which U.S. forces were operating. More meant less. As for "shaping," that remained a mirage, a figment of overheated imaginations back in Washington.

To mask this loss of definition (and perhaps their own confusion), successive presidents framed the overarching problem in generic terms, referring to adversaries as militants, terrorists, warlords, rogue states, or, most recently, "violent extremist organizations."[5] Alternatively, they followed Reagan's example in focusing their ire on specific bad actors. By implication, removing the likes of Gaddafi, Saddam Hussein, Mohamed Farrah Aidid, Slobodan Milošević, Osama bin Laden, Mullah Omar, Abu Musab al-Zarqawi, and Abu Bakr al-Baghdadi held the key to putting things right. Today all but one of these unsavory figures have passed from the scene, their departure bringing the United States not one whit closer to a definitive outcome. And although American air strikes or commandos may one day bag the sole remaining survivor—ISIS leader al-Baghdadi—no reason exists to expect his elimination to have a decisive effect.[6]

Today the problems besetting the Greater Middle East are substantially greater than they were when substantial numbers of U.S. forces first began venturing into the region. We may argue over the underlying sources of those problems and about how to allocate culpability. Multiple factors are involved, among them pervasive underdevelopment, a dearth of enlightened local leadership, the poisonous legacy of European imperialism, complications stemming from the founding of Israel, deep historical divisions within Islam itself, and the challenge of reconciling faith with modernity in a region where religion pervades every aspect of daily life. But there is no arguing that U.S. efforts to alleviate the dysfunction so much in evidence have failed abysmally.

To address this sort of situation, there are two broad ways of employing military power. The first is to wait things out—insulating yourself from the problem's worst effects while promoting a nonviolent solution from within. This requires patience and comes with no guarantee of ultimate success. With all the usual caveats attached, this is the approach the United States took during the Cold War.

The second approach is more direct. It aims to eliminate the problem through sustained, relentless military action. This entails less patience but incurs greater near-term costs. After a certain amount of shillyshallying, it was this head-on approach that the Union adopted during the Civil War.

In the War for the Greater Middle East, the United States chose neither to contain nor to crush, instead charting a course midway in between. In effect, it chose aggravation. With politicians and generals too quick to declare victory and with the American public too quick to throw their hands up when faced with adversity, U.S. forces rarely stayed long enough to finish the job. Instead of intimidating, U.S. military efforts have annoyed, incited, and generally communicated a lack of both competence and determination.

In the ultimate irony, somewhere in the interval between Operation Eagle Claw and Operation Inherent Resolve, the circumstances that had made the Persian Gulf worth fighting for in the first place ceased to pertain. If today the American way of life still depends, for better or for worse, on having access to plentiful reserves of oil and natural gas, then the Western Hemisphere, not the Persian Gulf, deserves top billing in the Pentagon's hierarchy of strategic priorities. Defending Canada and Venezuela should take precedence over defending Saudi Arabia and Iraq. To put it another way, the United States would be better served to secure its own neighborhood rather than vainly attempting to police the Greater Middle East—and it would likely enjoy greater success, to boot.

Even so, shorn of its initial rationale, the War for the Greater Middle

East continues. The line in the sand that Carter drew along Iran's Zagros Mountains now stretches from Central Asia through the Middle East and across the width of Africa. That the ongoing enterprise may someday end—that U.S. troops will finally depart—appears so unlikely as to make the prospect unworthy of discussion. Like the war on drugs or the war on poverty, the War for the Greater Middle East has become a permanent fixture in American life and is accepted as such.

Among the factors contributing to the lack of any serious challenge to the war's perpetuation, four stand out. One is the absence of an antiwar or anti-interventionist political party worthy of the name. The ongoing war has long since acquired a perfidious seal of bipartisan approval, with both Republicans and Democrats alike implicated. As such, the two major parties are equally disinclined to probe too deeply into the origins, conduct, or prospects of a failing and probably irredeemable military endeavor. Within the U.S. Congress, regardless of which party holds the upper hand, partisan considerations and electoral calculations consistently override concern for either U.S. interests or the actual well-being of Americans in uniform—hence the striking absence of any congressional curiosity about what the U.S. military has managed to achieve over the past three-plus decades in the Greater Middle East.

A second reason, directly related to the first, is that politicians aspiring to high office, especially those contemplating a bid for the presidency, find it more expedient to "support the troops" (and therefore the war) than to question the war's efficacy or to propose alternative approaches to satisfying U.S. objectives in the Islamic world. Apart perhaps from free beer and barbeque, nothing beats patriotic bombast when it comes to turning out voters. To the extent that the quadrennial contest to choose a chief executive serves as an opportunity for stock taking, candidates in every election since 1980 have assiduously avoided anything like a serious debate of U.S. military policy among Muslim nations. A particular campaign that goes awry like Somalia or Iraq or Libya may attract passing attention, but never the context in which that campaign was undertaken. We can be certain that the election of 2016 will be no different. The War for the Greater Middle East awaits its Eugene McCarthy or George McGovern.

A third reason, of course, is that some individuals and institutions actually benefit from an armed conflict that drags on and on. Those benefits are immediate and tangible. They come in the form of profits, jobs, and campaign contributions. For the military-industrial complex and its beneficiaries, perpetual war is not necessarily bad news. The alacrity with which the national security apparatus "discovered" the Greater Middle East just as the Cold War was ending does not qualify as coincidental.

Finally, and perhaps most importantly, there is this: Thus far, at least, Americans themselves appear oblivious to what is occurring. Policy-makers have successfully insulated the public from the war's negative effects. Reliance on a professional military places the burden of service and sacrifice onto a very small percentage of citizens and lets everyone else off the hook. The resort to deficit spending to underwrite the war's costs sloughs off onto future generations the onus of paying the bills.

It's not that Americans today actively support the war in the same sense that their grandparents supported World War II. It's that they see no particular reason to attend one way or another to the war's progress or likely outcome. In a fundamental sense, the war is not their concern.

Americans do care, of course, about some things. Promoting the spread of democracy, protecting human rights, curbing global warm-ing, guaranteeing the safety and well-being of Israel: In very substantial numbers, Americans want their country committed to all of these. But they support such worthy causes because they take it as a given that U.S. policy will perpetuate the position of disparity that they consider their due. As in Kennan's day, so also in our own, ensuring that Ameri-cans enjoy their rightful quota (which is to say, more than their fair share) of freedom, abundance, and security comes first. Everything else figures as an afterthought.

But here's the rub. In the twenty-first century, the prerequisites of freedom, abundance, and security are changing. Geopolitically, Asia is eclipsing in importance all other regions apart perhaps from North

America itself. The emerging problem set—coping with the effects of climate change, for example—is global and will require a global response. Whether Americans are able to preserve the privileged position to which they are accustomed will depend on how well and how quickly the United States adapts the existing "pattern of relationships" to fit these fresh circumstances.

Amidst such challenges, the afflictions besetting large portions of the Islamic world will undoubtedly persist. But their relative importance to the United States as determinants of American well-being will diminish, a process even today already well advanced even if U.S. national security priorities have yet to reflect this fact.

In this context, the War for the Greater Middle East becomes a diversion that Americans can ill afford. To fancy at this point that the U.S. military possesses the capacity to "shape" the course of events there is an absurdity. Indulging that absurdity further serves chiefly to impede the ability of the United States to attend to more pressing concerns. Washington finds itself playing yesterday's game and playing it badly, when a more important game with different rules is already well underway elsewhere.

Ultimately, the game that will decide if Americans succeed in preserving their privileged position will play out at home rather than in some far-off place like Iraq or Afghanistan. At the end of the day, whether the United States is able to shape the Greater Middle East will matter less than whether it can reshape itself, restoring effectiveness to self-government, providing for sustainable and equitable prosperity, and extracting from a vastly diverse culture something to hold in common of greater moment than shallow digital enthusiasms and the worship of celebrity.

Perpetuating the War for the Greater Middle East is not enhancing American freedom, abundance, and security. If anything, it is having the opposite effect. One day the American people may awaken to this reality. Then and only then will the war end. When this awakening will occur is impossible to say. For now, sadly, Americans remain deep in slumber.

ACKNOWLEDGMENTS

———

IN WRITING THIS BOOK, I ACCUMULATED MANY DEBTS—SO MANY in fact that I am hard pressed to know where to begin expressing my gratitude to all who helped along the way.

Grace Chang, Harrison Meyer, and Amanda Roth got me started by assisting with preliminary research. As things picked up steam, Derrin Culp became my go-to guy for locating documents and tracking down stray facts. I owe him an immeasurable debt. I am likewise grateful to Professor Mary Ann Tetreault for generously sharing materials that she had collected for a similar project but was unable to complete.

As I turned to the actual writing, Columbia Provost John Coatsworth invited me to spend a semester at the university's School of International and Public Affairs as the first George S. McGovern Fellow. This proved a wonderful opportunity. I thank Provost Coatsworth along with the faculty and staff of SIPA for their kind hospitality.

Once chapters began taking shape, Casey Brower, Chris Gray, Rick Swain, Nick Turse, and Scott Wheeler all read various bits and pieces, offering suggestions and needed encouragement. Kalev Sepp, who knows more about irregular warfare than anyone else of my acquaintance, shared firsthand insights regarding the U.S. occupation of Iraq. My dear friend Lawrence Kaplan read the entire manuscript with a keen eye and offered an invaluable critique.

As the manuscript approached final form, I approached David Lindroth about possibly designing maps to accompany the text. He agreed and in remarkably short order transformed my vague ideas into pleasingly concrete form. It was a treat to work with such a gifted professional. Fred Courtright demystifed the process of locating photos and securing permission for their use.

My thanks to Graham Allison of Harvard's Kennedy School for hosting a luncheon seminar where I could test-drive my conclusions. The feedback from those in attendance was most helpful.

My agent, John Wright, has to be the best in the business. I treasure our relationship. Like John, David Ebershoff, my editor at Random House, is a pro through and through, someone who knows books and loves them. To collaborate with a person of such extraordinary gifts was for me an undeserved blessing. When David moved on to new opportunities, Will Murphy assumed the position of "point man" and saw matters through to completion with efficiency and skill. Others at Random House who played critical roles include Barbara Fillon, Evan Camfield, Toby Ernst, Mika Kasuga, and the estimable Caitlin McKenna. Martin Schneider's copyediting saved me from more than a few gaffes and infelicities. My thanks to one and all.

I have dedicated this book to my wife, Nancy. The day we met, to my amazement now a full half-century ago, remains the luckiest of my life. My dearest hope is that we may grow old together.

NOTES

A Note to Readers

1. Henry James, *Notes on Novelists with Some Other Notes* (New York, 1914), 121.

Prologue

1. For a detailed account of the mission, see Mark Bowden, *Guests of the Ayatollah* (New York, 2006), 223–33, 409–13, 431–68.

2. Jimmy Carter, "Address to the Nation on the Rescue Attempt for American Hostages in Iran" (April 25, 1980). Unless otherwise specified, all presidential speeches and statements, along with other White House documents cited in this book, are readily available at the American Presidency Project, presidency.ucsb.edu.

3. The Pentagon's "Iran Hostage Rescue Mission Report," completed in August 1980 and more commonly known as the Holloway Report, recounted while soft-pedaling some of those errors. A declassified version is available at www2.gwu.edu/~nsarchiv/NSAEBB/NSAEBB63/doc8.pdf, accessed on August 21, 2014. Far more scathing was a report prepared for the Senate Armed Services Committee that cited a "poor commander, poor organization, and failure to anticipate emergencies" as major problems. Nicholas Daniloff, "Hostage Rescue Mission Laid to Poor Command," *The Boston Globe* (June 6, 1980).

4. The "Greater Middle East" exists primarily as a device to facilitate the exercise of Western and especially American power. It is an invention. Yet for the purposes of this book, more traditional terms like "Middle East," "Near East," and "Persian Gulf" do not suffice to describe the scope of U.S. military activities or the ambitions inspiring those activities. So I have chosen to employ the formulation that more accurately accords with Washington's mental map of the world. See Dona J. Stewart, "The Greater Middle East and Reform in the Bush Administration's Ideological Imagination," *Geographical Review* (July 2005), 400–424.

1. War of Choice

1. C. Wright Mills, *White Collar* (New York, 1951), xv, xvii. Other important publications in this vein include David Riesman, *The Lonely Crowd* (New Haven, 1950); William Whyte, *The Organization Man* (New York, 1956); and Vance Packard, *The Hidden Persuaders* (New York, 1957).

2. U.S. Energy Information Administration, "U.S. Field Production of Crude Oil," and "U.S. Imports of Crude Oil and Petroleum Products," eia.gov /dnav/pet/hist/LeafHandler, both accessed August 22, 2014.

3. Nominally, the purpose of putting U.S. forces on alert was to deter any possible Soviet military action. Yet evidence suggests that the Nixon administration was also considering direct military intervention to seize control of Saudi oil. Lizette Alvarez, "Documents Show U.S. Considered Using Force During Oil Embargo," *The New York Times* (January 1, 2004).

4. Richard Nixon, "Address to the Nation About National Energy Policy" (November 25, 1973).

5. Robert W. Tucker, "Oil: The Issue of American Intervention," *Commentary* (January 1975), 21–31.

6. Miles Ignotus, "Seizing Arab Oil," *Harper's* (March 1975), 45–62.

7. Andrew Higgins, "Power and Peril: American Supremacy and Its Limits," *The Asian Wall Street Journal* (February 5, 2004).

8. Beginning in 1949, the U.S. Navy did maintain a token presence, using leased space in a small British base in Bahrain. This so-called Middle East Force consisted of two destroyers and a seaplane tender, which doubled as a flagship. It possessed negligible combat capability.

9. Elliot L. Richardson, *Annual Defense Department Report, FY 1974* (April 10, 1973), 25.

10. James R. Schlesinger, *Annual Defense Department Report, FY 1975* (March 4, 1974), 1, 13–14, 86.

11. Donald H. Rumsfeld, *Annual Defense Department Report, FY 1978* (January 17, 1977), 13, 42, 245.

12. Tucker, "Oil," 21.

13. Although not killed in action, a handful of Americans were murdered while posted in the Greater Middle East. In 1975, for example, assassins killed two U.S. Air Force officers who were serving in Iran. Eric Pace, "Iranian Terrorists Slay Two U.S. Colonels," *The New York Times* (May 22, 1975).

14. Jimmy Carter, "University of Notre Dame—Address at Commencement Exercises" (May 22, 1977).

15. An April 1974 assessment of U.S.-Iranian relations, prepared by an interagency task force, confidently asserted the following: "Iran is the most powerful, politically most stable, and economically most developed state on the Persian Gulf. It shares with us an interest in promoting moderate

elements in the area and in limiting the influence of the Soviet Union and radical forces. Prospects are good for Iran's long-term stability and a continuation of its present international orientation, even if its present leadership leaves the scene." "Paper Prepared by an Interdepartmental Working Group" (April 25, 1974), Document 59, *Foreign Relations of the United States, 1969–1976*, vol. 27, *Iran; Iraq, 1973–1976*.

16. Jimmy Carter, "Toasts of the President and the Shah at a State Dinner" (December 31, 1977).

17. Bernard Gwertzman, "It Was Like Coming Home Again," *The New York Times* (July 29, 1973).

18. The Soviet Union was also selling quantities of arms in the Persian Gulf, notably to Iraq, Iran's traditional rival. U.S. policymakers such as Secretary of State William P. Rogers described Soviet arms exports as "an invitation to trouble," whereas U.S. weapons exports were "a stabilizing influence for peace." Juan de Onis, "Rogers Terms U.S. Arms Sales to Persian Gulf 'Stabilizing,'" *The New York Times* (June 11, 1973).

19. Faisal bin Salman al-Saud, *Iran, Saudi Arabia, and the Gulf: Power Politics in Transition* (London, 2004), 73–77. The Iranian Revolution resulted in the cancellation of some purchases prior to delivery, to include the destroyers.

20. Abbas Milani, "The Shah's Atomic Dreams," *Foreign Policy* (December 29, 2010).

21. Michael Klare, "America's White Collar Mercenaries," *Inquiry* (October 16, 1978), 14–19.

22. Michael C. Jensen, "Retired Generals Employed by Northrop in Various Jobs," *The New York Times* (June 26, 1975).

23. Richard J. Levine, "Oil States' Demand Keeps U.S. Arms Sales at Record Pace as Congress Grows Critical," *The Wall Street Journal* (February 18, 1975); Richard D. Lyons, "U.S. Arms-Sale Rise Stirs Capital Concern," *The New York Times* (October 19, 1975).

24. Leslie H. Gelb, "Study Finds Iran Dependent on U.S. in Using Weapons," *The New York Times* (August 2, 1976).

25. Bernard Gwertzman, "Shah Cautions U.S. Against Arms Cut," *The New York Times* (August 7, 1976).

26. *Department of State Bulletin* (September 4, 1972), 243. Sisco was then assistant secretary for Near East and South Asian affairs. On August 8, 1972, he had testified before the House Subcommittee on the Near East.

27. At the time, the Yemen Arab Republic and the People's Republic of South Yemen were separate countries.

28. OASD (PA & E), "Capabilities for Limited Contingencies in the Persian Gulf" (June 15, 1979). At the time, Wolfowitz was serving as deputy assistant secretary of defense for regional programs.

29. Albert Wohlstetter, "The Uses of Irrelevance," *The New York Times* (February 25, 1979).

30. Albert Wohlstetter, "'Lesser' Excluded Cases," *The New York Times* (February 14, 1979).

31. Fully appreciating the sweep and ambition of Carter's speech requires a careful reading of the entire text. Understanding why it fell short should entail actually viewing the president's delivery. Fortunately, video of the speech is readily available online, for example, at youtube.com/watch?v=kakFDUeoJKM, accessed September 5, 2014.

32. Hendrik Hertzberg, "Foreword to the Paperback Edition," in Kevin Mattson, *What the Heck Are You Up To, Mr. President?* (New York, 2010), xvi.

33. "Generally Good Marks for Carter on Speech," *The New York Times* (July 17, 1979); Keith Richburg, "Carter's Rating Rose Nine Percent After Speech," *The Washington Post* (July 17, 1979).

34. Jimmy Carter, *White House Diary* (New York, 2010), 344.

35. Roger Ricklefs, ". . . And a Misreading of the Nation's 'Soul,'" *The Wall Street Journal* (July 17, 1979).

36. "Reagan and Bush Blame Carter for His Own Woes," *Los Angeles Times* (July 17, 1979).

37. Irving Kristol, "Blame It on the People!" *The Wall Street Journal* (July 17, 1979).

38. George F. Will, "The President Says Too Much That's Bad About America," *Los Angeles Times* (July 19, 1979).

39. In a 1992 episode of *The Simpsons*, the townspeople of Springfield erect a statue in Carter's honor. The pedestal reads "Malaise Forever."

40. Seth G. Jones, *In the Graveyard of Empires* (New York, 2009), 20.

41. Robert M. Gates, *From the Shadows* (New York, 1996), 145. Gates attended the meeting. The official he quotes was Walter Slocombe.

42. Zbigniew Brzezinski, *Power and Principle: Memoirs of the National Security Adviser, 1977–1981* (New York, 1983), 356, 428.

43. "Brzezinski Interview with *La Nouvelle Observateur*" (January 15, 1988), dgibbs.faculty.arizona.edu/brzezinski_interview, accessed September 12, 2014.

44. Brzezinski, *Power and Principle*, 475–76.

45. Mark Bowden, "Among the Hostage Takers," *The Atlantic* (December 2004).

46. On November 20, radical Islamists had seized the Grand Mosque in Mecca. Rumors that the United States was implicated in this incident triggered the embassy attacks. Although the United States was not involved, the occupation of the Grand Mosque, lasting over two weeks and costing several hundred lives, reinforced the impression in Washington that the Greater Middle

East was coming apart, with forceful U.S. action the only plausible antidote.

47. George Ball, "Reflections on a Heavy Year," *Foreign Affairs* (January 1981).

48. Rosalynn Carter, *First Lady from Plains* (New York, 1984), 295.

49. Maxwell Orme Johnson, "Military Force and American Foreign Policy in Southwest Asia, 1979–1982: A Study of the Rapid Deployment Joint Task Force" (unpublished PhD dissertation, University of Virginia, 1982), 25.

50. Johnson, "Military Force and American Foreign Policy," 26.

51. Contemporaneous Soviet documents make this abundantly clear. See "Afghanistan: Lessons from the Last War," a compendium of documents made available by the National Security Archive, www2.gwu.edu /~nsarchiv/NSAEBB/NSAEBB57/soviet.html, accessed September 19, 2014. For an overview, see Artemy Kalinovsky, "Decision-Making and the Soviet War in Afghanistan," *Journal of Cold War Studies* (Fall 2009), 48–51.

52. Zbigniew Brzezinski, Memorandum for the President, Subject: Reflections on Soviet Intervention in Afghanistan (December 26, 1979), www2.gwu .edu/~nsarchiv/NSAEBB/NSAEBB396/docs/1979-12-26%20Brzezinski %20to%20Carter%20on%20Afghanistan.pdf, accessed September 22, 2014. In this memo, Brzezinski expressed expectations of the Soviet intervention succeeding. "The Soviets are likely to act decisively," he wrote, "unlike the U.S. in Vietnam, which pursued a policy of 'inoculating' the enemy."

53. Brzezinski, *Power and Principle,* 356, 427.

54. Transcript, *Meet the Press* (January 20, 1980), search.alexanderstreet.com /media-studies/view/work/2207085, accessed September 30, 2014. President Carter was the television program's sole guest on that date.

55. Theodore L. Eliot, "Afghanistan: Fact and Fiction," *The Wall Street Journal* (January 9, 1980). At that time serving as dean of the Fletcher School of Law and Diplomacy, Eliot insisted that it was "patently ridiculous to believe that the motive for the Soviet invasion" stemmed from any concern about Islamist opposition.

56. Kenneth H. Bacon, "Carter's Shattered Foreign Policy," *The Wall Street Journal* (January 8, 1980).

57. Jimmy Carter, "State of the Union Address" (January 23, 1980).

58. Brzezinski, *Power and Principle,* 444.

59. Brzezinski, *Power and Principle,* 447.

60. I. F. Stone, "Reaping Invasion's Rewards," *The New York Times* (February 29, 1980).

61. Hermann F. Eilts, "Security Considerations in the Persian Gulf," *International Security* (Fall 1980), 88–89.

62. Joseph Kraft, "In the Wake of Afghanistan," *The Washington Post* (March 27, 1980).

63. Robert Moss, "Reaching for Oil: The Soviets' Bold Middle East Strategy," *Saturday Review* (April 12, 1980), 14–15.

64. Richard Pipes, "Soviet Global Strategy," *Commentary* (April 1980), 37. The other half of the pincer was through Scandinavia, where, according to Pipes, the Soviets were putting the squeeze on Finland and Sweden.

65. William Beecher, "Carter's Test," *The Boston Globe* (February 24, 1980).

66. Quoted in Peter C. Stuart, "Soviets on the Move," *The Christian Science Monitor* (February 11, 1980).

67. Quoted in Piero Gleijeses, *Visions of Freedom: Havana, Washington, Pretoria, and the Struggle for Southern Africa, 1976–1991* (Chapel Hill, 1993), 168.

68. George W. Ball, "Checking the Soviets' New Mideast Moves," *Los Angeles Times* (January 27, 1980).

69. Not so incidentally, at this very moment the Wolfowitz Limited Contingency Study was leaked to the press. In reporting on the study's contents, *The New York Times* emphasized the importance of creating a "rapid deployment force" to counter the twenty-three Soviet mechanized divisions said to be available to seize the Persian Gulf. Any U.S. failure to mount an adequate conventional defense would find the United States facing the need to "threaten or make use of tactical nuclear weapons" to defend Persian Gulf oil. Richard Burt, "Study Says a Soviet Move in Iran Might Require U.S. Atomic Arms," *The New York Times* (February 2, 1980).

2. Gearing Up

1. Zbigniew Brzezinski, Presidential Directive/NSC 63, Subject: Persian Gulf Security Framework (January 15, 1981), jimmycarterlibrary.gov/documents/pddirectives/pd63.pdf, accessed September 27, 2014.

2. The administration had been considering the creation of such force since 1977. The Iranian Revolution forced the issue. Ronald H. Cole et al., *The History of the Unified Command Plan, 1946–1999* (Washington, D.C., 2003), 56.

3. P. X. Kelley, "Rapid Deployment: A Vital Trump," *Parameters* (Spring 1981), 50.

4. Kelley, "Rapid Deployment," 51–52.

5. Quoted in Jay LaMonica, "RDF's Bright Star," *The Washington Quarterly* (Spring 1982).

6. Dana Priest, *The Mission* (New York, 2004), 61–98.

7. For the torturous bureaucratic infighting that accompanied the RDJTF's transition to CENTCOM, see Cole et al., *History,* 56–59, 63–67. The CENTCOM AOR did not include Israel, Lebanon, and Syria, which remained under the purview of U.S. European Command. By 2014, the CENTCOM AOR had grown to twenty countries. In the intervening years, it had handed off responsibility for East Africa to the newly created United States Africa Command, but it had also acquired several nations in Central Asia.

8. Since the creation of United States Africa Command (AFRICOM) in 2008, this process is now under way on that continent. See, for example, Kofi Nsia-Pepra, "Militarization of U.S. Foreign Policy in Africa," *Military Review* (January–February 2014), 50–58.

9. Robert C. Kingston, "From RDF to CENTCOM: New Challenges?" *RUSI* (March 1, 1984), 16.

10. Kingston, "From RDF to CENTCOM," 16.

11. "OPLAN 1002 Defense of the Arabian Peninsula," globalsecurity.org /military/ops/oplan-1002.htm, accessed October 1, 2014.

12. "General Sees No Great Soviet Mideast Threat," *Los Angeles Times* (February 16, 1982). In the same article, a spokesman for the secretary of defense disagreed with Kingston's assessment.

13. Frank N. Schubert and Theresa L. Kraus, eds., *Whirlwind War: The United States Army in Operations DESERT SHIELD and DESERT STORM* (Washington, D.C., 1995), 14–20. This is an account prepared by the U.S. Army Center for Military History.

14. Richard Halloran, "Poised for the Persian Gulf," *The New York Times Magazine* (April 1, 1984), 38–40, 61.

15. Curtis Wilkie, "Reagan Pledges to Defend Saudis," *The Boston Globe* (October 2, 1981).

16. A remnant of the British Empire, Diego Garcia remained nominally under British control. Halloran's essay did not mention the expulsion of the indigenous population that had paved the way for the island's conversion into a major U.S. military base. For details, see David Vine, *Island of Shame: The Secret History of the U.S. Military Base in Diego Garcia* (Princeton, 2009).

17. Richard Halloran, "U.S. Intends to Deploy F-4 Fighters in Egypt as Part of Air Buildup," *The New York Times* (June 13, 1980). Halloran was quoting General Lew Allen, chief of staff of the United States Air Force.

18. For an even more optimistic appraisal, see Paul Davis, "Observations on the Rapid Deployment Joint Task Force: Origins, Direction, and Mission" (unpublished paper, June 1982). Davis was an analyst employed by RAND, the government-funded think tank.

19. See, for example, Jeffrey Record, "The RDF: Is the Pentagon Kidding?" *The Washington Quarterly* (Summer 1981); and David Isenberg, "The Rapid Deployment Force: The Few, the Futile, the Expendable," *Policy Analysis* (November 8, 1984).

20. Robert C. Kingston, Senior Officer Oral History Program, U.S. Army Military History Institute (1987), 326, 329.

21. "Soviets Seek Military Lead: Weinberger," *Los Angeles Times* (March 24, 1987).

22. Richard Halloran, "U.S. Altering Strategy for Defense of Arabian Oilfields," *The New York Times* (December 4, 1988).

23. H. Norman Schwarzkopf, *It Doesn't Take a Hero* (New York, 1992), 285.

24. Quoted in Richard Swain, *"Lucky War": Third Army in Desert Storm* (Fort Leavenworth, 1994), 5.

25. Swain, *"Lucky War,"* 7, capitalization in the original.

26. Swain, *"Lucky War,"* 6–7.

27. One explanation, but not the only one. Other contributing factors included the clout wielded by the military-industrial complex; the posturing of office-seekers, particularly Democrats protecting themselves from being portrayed as insufficiently militant; and the collective determination of the national security apparatus to protect its status and prerogatives.

28. Reinhold Niebuhr was the obvious exception, but the impact of his views in policymaking circles did not extend much beyond providing moral justifications for actions policymakers were already inclined to take.

3. Arsenal of Theocracy

1. Quoted in Sean Wilentz, *The Age of Reagan* (New York, 2008), 151.

2. Quoted in George Crile, *Charlie Wilson's War* (New York, 2003), x.

3. Gates, *From the Shadows*, 349.

4. It was also reported that Pakistan was expecting Washington to "turn a blind eye" to its nuclear weapons program. U.S. officials did just that. Michael T. Kaufman, "U.S. Said to Weigh Extensive Arms Sales to Pakistan," *The New York Times* (March 5, 1981).

5. Carl Bernstein, "Arms for Afghanistan," *The New Republic* (July 18, 1981).

6. Strobe Talbott, "Turning the Tables on Moscow," *Time* (April 15, 1985).

7. Marguerite Johnson, "Leaks in the Pipeline," *Time* (December 9, 1985).

8. David B. Ottaway and Patrick E. Tyler, "U.S. Sends New Arms to Rebels," *The Washington Post* (March 30, 1986).

9. Bob Woodward and Charles R. Babcock, "U.S. Covert Aid to Afghans on the Rise," *The Washington Post* (January 13, 1985).

10. Jones, *In the Graveyard of Empires*, 37.

11. Steve Coll in an interview with Amy Goodman and Juan Gonzalez, "Democracy Now!" (June 10, 2004), democracynow.org/2004/6/10/ghost_wars_how_reagan_armed_the, accessed October 23, 2014.

12. Ronald Reagan, "Proclamation 4908—Afghanistan Day" (March 10, 1982).

13. Available at youtube.com/watch?v=uqZ-ToXjCz0, accessed October 23, 2014.

14. Jones, *In the Graveyard of Empires*, 31–34.

15. Crile, *Charlie Wilson's War*, ix.

16. Crile, *Charlie Wilson's War*, 5.

17. Zalmay Khalilzad, "How the Good Guys Won in Afghanistan," *The Washington Post* (February 12, 1989).

18. U.S. Army Command and General Staff College, "Lessons from the War in Afghanistan" (undated [1989]), 4. The entire study is available at the National Security Archive, www2.gwu.edu/~nsarchiv/NSAEBB/NSAEBB57/us11.pdf, accessed November 2, 2014.

19. This was, of course, the thesis of a famous article by Francis Fukuyama. What imbued the "end of history" argument with such allure was not its originality but its timing. Fukuyama caught the mood of the moment in Washington. He put in words what members of the policy elite were already thinking but had not fully articulated. Francis Fukuyama, "The End of History?" *The National Interest* (Summer 1989).

20. Imtiyaz Gul Khan, "Afghanistan: Human Cost of Armed Conflict Since the Soviet Invasion," *Perceptions* (Winter 2012), 212–14.

21. Barnett R. Rubin, "The Political Economy of War and Peace in Afghanistan," *World Development* (2000), 1791–93.

22. Thomas Barfield, *Afghanistan: A Cultural and Political History* (Princeton, 2010), 243.

23. Bruce Riedel, *What We Won: America's Secret War in Afghanistan* (Washington, D.C., 2014).

24. George H. W. Bush, "Statement on the Soviet Withdrawal from Afghanistan" (February 16, 1989).

25. Elaine Sciolino, "To U.S., Afghanistan Seems to Move Farther Away," *The New York Times* (February 12, 1989).

26. Barfield, *Afghanistan*, 251.

27. Leslie H. Gelb, "Rebels, Be Good," *The New York Times* (April 20, 1992). Gelb mocked the State Department spokesperson for imploring of the mujahedin forces closing in on Kabul, "Please do not have violence."

28. Leonard Larsen, "U.S. May Pay High Price for Afghan Aid," Minneapolis *Star-Tribune* (March 16, 1989).

29. Mark Fineman, "Next Step: Have Guns, Will Travel," *Los Angeles Times* (April 7, 1992).

30. Thomas W. Lippman, "Aid to Afghan Rebels Returns to Haunt U.S.," *The Washington Post* (July 26, 1993).

31. Quoted in Lloyd Gardner, *The Long Road to Baghdad* (New York, 2010), 56–57.

4. Silver Screen Six Is Calling

1. David Crist, *The Twilight War* (New York, 2012), 123.

2. Samuel P. Huntington, "The Clash of Civilization?" *Foreign Affairs* (Summer 1993).

3. Benny Morris, *Righteous Victims* (New York, 1999), 516. Other factors may have contributed to Israel's willingness to accept risk. In June 1981, it had

attacked and destroyed Iraq's nuclear reactor at Osirak. In December of that same year it unilaterally annexed the Golan Heights, Syrian territory captured during the 1967 war. In both instances, the United States had complained but then accommodated itself to Israel's actions.

4. Crist, *Twilight War*, 108.

5. Morris, *Righteous Victims*, 516–29.

6. Morris, *Righteous Victims*, 533–37.

7. Quoted in Crist, *Twilight War*, 112.

8. Quoted in Ze'ev Schiff and Ehud Ya'ari, *Israel's Lebanon War* (New York, 1984), 226.

9. Robert J. Hanks, "Send in the Marines?" *Los Angeles Times* (July 8, 1982).

10. At a press briefing, Reagan indicated that if any shooting occurred, he would immediately pull the Marines out. "800 Marines Ordered to Beirut," *Los Angeles Times* (August 20, 1982). The subheadline to this article read, "Will Leave If Attacked, Reagan Says."

11. Benis M. Frank, *U.S. Marines in Lebanon, 1982–1984* (Washington, D.C., 1987), 13, 17. This monograph is the U.S. Marine Corps official history of the intervention.

12. Frank, *U.S. Marines in Lebanon*, 18.

13. Colin Campbell, "U.S. Marines Leave Lebanese Capital," *The New York Times* (September 11, 1982).

14. "U.S. Marines Withdraw from Lebanon," *The Boston Globe* (September 11, 1982).

15. Gemayel's election purchased Phalange party concurrence in the agreed-upon PLO evacuation, expected, in turn, to end the Israeli siege of Beirut. This calculation, along with bribes and threats, secured for Gemayal enough votes from Muslim parliamentarians to gain a majority. Marxist from Lebanon, "Regarding Bashir Gemayel's Elections: The Other Story" (August 30, 2007), marxistfromlebanon.blogspot.com/2007/08/regarding -bashir-gemayels-elections.html, accessed November 6, 2014.

16. Peter Chalk, ed., *Encyclopedia of Terrorism* (Santa Barbara, 2012), 643.

17. George Russell, "Middle East: God—Oh, My God!" *Time* (October 4, 1982).

18. Ronald Reagan, "Statement on the Murder of Palestinian Refugees in Lebanon" (September 18, 1982).

19. Frank, *U.S. Marines in Lebanon*, 22–23. The quote is from the after action report of the 32d Marine Amphibious Unit, dated November 12, 1982. The 32d MAU was the first of several Marine units tasked to perform the "presence" mission in Beirut. The other nations contributing to the multinational peacekeeping force were France and Italy.

20. Ronald Reagan, "National Security Decision Directive Number 64: Next Steps in Lebanon" (October 28, 1982).

21. Ronald Steel, "Keep the Marines out of It," *Los Angeles Times* (July 13, 1982).

22. Michael Getler, "Troops Could Help Rescue Reagan's Plan," *The Washington Post* (September 21, 1982).

23. Leslie Gelb, "U.S. Assumes a Policeman's Lot in Mideast Peace Process," *The New York Times* (October 3, 1982).

24. Frank, *U.S. Marines in Lebanon*, 38–41.

25. Caspar W. Weinberger, *Fighting for Peace* (New York, 1990), 162.

26. Richard Halloran, "A Marine, Pistol Drawn, Stops 3 Israeli Tanks," *The New York Times* (February 3, 1983).

27. Frank, *U.S. Marines in Lebanon*, 80.

28. Frank, *U.S. Marines in Lebanon*, 59–62, 66, 75–82.

29. Timothy J. Geraghty, *Peacekeepers at War* (Washington, D.C., 2009), 60.

30. Geraghty, *Peacekeepers at War*, 61.

31. In military lingo, "six" is traditionally the call sign of a commander.

32. Geraghty, *Peacekeepers at War*, 62–63.

33. Ronald Reagan, *The Reagan Diaries* (New York, 2007), 177.

34. Ronald Reagan, "Addendum to NSDD 103: On Lebanon of September 10, 1983" (September 11, 1983).

35. Frank, *U.S. Marines in Lebanon*, 83, 86, 88.

36. Geraghty, *Peacekeepers at War*, 68–69.

37. George Shultz, *Turmoil and Triumph* (New York, 1993), 226.

38. Thomas Friedman, "Peacekeepers Become Another Warring Faction," *The New York Times* (October 23, 1983).

39. Ronald Reagan, "Remarks to Military Personnel at Cherry Point, North Carolina on the United States Casualties in Lebanon and Grenada" (November 4, 1983).

40. Ronald Reagan, "National Security Decision Directive Number 111: Next Steps Toward Progress in Lebanon and the Middle East" (October 28, 1983).

41. Crist, *Twilight War*, 141–48.

42. Crist, *Twilight War*, 148–49.

43. Ronald Reagan, "National Security Decision Directive Number 123: Next Steps in Lebanon" (February 1, 1984).

44. William E. Smith, "The Marines Leave Lebanon," *Time* (March 5, 1984).

45. Bernard Gwertzman, "New Chapter for Lebanon," *The New York Times* (February 27, 1984).

46. Thomas Friedman, "America's Failure in Lebanon," *The New York Times* (April 8, 1984).

47. "Report of the DoD Commission on the Beirut International Airport Terrorist Act, October 23, 1983" (December 20, 1983). The document is informally known as the Long Commission Report, after its chairman, retired admiral Robert L. J. Long.

48. Augustus Richard Norton, *Hezbollah: A Short History* (Princeton, 2007), 33–34.

5. Mad Dog, Kicked, Bites Back

1. For a concise summary, see Douglas Little, "To the Shores of Tripoli: America, Qaddafi, and Libyan Revolution, 1969–1989," *The International History Review* (2013), 70–99.

2. The issue was, as they say, "complicated." Approximately three thousand Americans were working in Libya, mostly in oil-related jobs. The Nixon administration was reluctant to put those Americans or U.S. access to Libyan oil in jeopardy. With U.S. forces only recently withdrawn from Vietnam, the Pentagon was not keen to get into a fight. "Minutes of a Washington Special Actions Group Meeting" (April 16, 1983), *Foreign Relations of the United States, 1969–1976: Documents on North Africa, 1973–1976* (Washington, D.C., 2014), 20–26; see also "Minutes of a Senior Review Group Meeting" (August 14, 1973), ibid., 67–75. Secretary of State Henry Kissinger chaired both meetings, during the second of which he referred to Gaddafi as "a miserable little sheik running around in the desert."

3. Robert Kimmitt, "Reagan and Gadhafi," *The Washington Times* (August 20, 2006). At the time of the event described, Kimmitt was a member of the National Security Council staff.

4. For a blow-by-blow account, see Joseph T. Stanik, *El Dorado Canyon: Reagan's Undeclared War with Qaddafi* (Annapolis, 2003), 52–56. Stanik describes the Su-22 as "no match for the F-14."

5. "F14 Tomcat Joins Reagan Library," *Los Angeles Daily News* (August 23, 2005).

6. For a compendium, see "Terrorist Attacks on Americans, 1979–1988," pbs.org/wgbh/pages/frontline/shows/target/etc/cron.html, accessed November 24, 2014.

7. Ronald Reagan, "National Security Decision Directive 138: Combating Terrorism" (April 3, 1984).

8. It went without saying that U.S. policy objectives such as enforcing "freedom of navigation" off the coast of Libya *did* possess legitimacy. By extension, so did Washington's reliance on coercive means in pursuit of those objectives, at least as Washington saw it.

9. George Shultz, "Terrorism and the Modern World," *Department of State Bulletin* (December 1984), 16. The article preprints a speech made by Secretary of State Shultz at New York's Park Avenue Synagogue on October 25, 1984.

10. Ronald Reagan, "National Security Decision Directive Number 205 Annex: Acting Against Libyan Support of International Terrorism" (January 8, 1986).

11. Ronald Reagan, *The Reagan Diaries* (New York, 2007), 381. The quotation is from the diary entry dated January 7, 1986.

12. Stanik, *El Dorado Canyon*, 131–40.

13. Quoted in James Gerstenzang, "U.S. Navy Ends Maneuvers in Gulf of Sidra," *Los Angeles Times* (March 28, 1986).

14. Ronald Reagan, "The President's News Conference" (April 9, 1986).

15. French noncooperation may have reflected a certain amount of payback. In Paris, memories of Washington's last-minute withdrawal from a planned joint retaliatory air attack following the October 1983 Beirut bombings remained fresh.

16. Stanik, *El Dorado Canyon*, 162–63.

17. An investigation by *New York Times* correspondent Seymour Hersh concluded that assassinating Gaddafi was, in fact, "the primary goal of the Libyan bombing." Seymour Hersh, "Target Qaddafi," *The New York Times* (February 22, 1987).

18. Twenty-four bombers actually took off, but the plan called for only eighteen to proceed to the target area. The others returned to home base shortly after launch.

19. For a detailed account of the raid, see Stanik, *El Dorado Canyon*, 184–93.

20. Ronald Reagan, "Address to the Nation on the United States Air Strike Against Libya" (April 14, 1986).

21. "U.S. Planes Destroyed 13 Libya Aircraft," *Los Angeles Times* (April 17, 1986).

22. "Joint News Conference by Secretary Shultz and Secretary Weinberger" (April 14, 1984), *Department of State Bulletin* (June 1986).

23. Shultz, *Turmoil and Triumph*, 687.

24. Anthony H. Cordesman, "USCENTCOM Mission and History" (April 1998), 8.

25. David Ottaway, "U.S. Still Certain that Libya Was Behind Nightclub Attack," *The Washington Post* (January 12, 1988).

26. Three months earlier, a similar Libyan plot had killed all 171 people aboard a French airliner over Niger.

6. Rescuing Evil

1. Efraim Karsh, *The Iran-Iraq War, 1980–1988* (Oxford, 2002), 12–29.

2. Jimmy Carter, "Situation in Iraq and Iran: Remarks Concerning the Conflict" (September 24, 1980).

3. Bernard Gwertzman, "Muskie Recommends Two Key 'Principles' to End

Mideast War," *The New York Times* (October 21, 1980). The article quotes Secretary of State Edmund S. Muskie: "We believe the cohesion and stability of Iran is in the interest of the stability of the region as a whole."

4. Karsh, *Iran-Iraq War*, 33–36.

5. The State Department published its first list of state sponsors of terrorism in 1979. Members included Iraq, Libya, South Yemen, and Syria.

6. George P. Shultz to the United States Interests Section in Iraq, "Message from the Secretary for FON MIN Tariq Aziz: Iraqi Support for Terrorism" (May 23, 1983), National Security Archive.

7. United States Embassy in United Kingdom to the Department of State, "Rumsfeld Mission: December 20 Meeting with Iraqi President Saddam Hussein" (December 21, 1983). The cable details Rumsfeld's exchange with the Iraqi leader.

8. Seymour Hersh, "U.S. Secretly Gave Aid to Iraq Early in Its War Against Iran," *The New York Times* (January 26, 1992).

9. The U.S. position was that chemical weapons were bad, but if Iraq used them, Iran was largely to blame. For an example of this logic, see Department of State, Bureau of Near Eastern and South Asian Affairs, "Memorandum from James A. Placke to James M. Ealum [et al.]. [U.S. Condemnation of Iraqi Chemical Weapons Use]" (March 4, 1984), National Security Archive.

10. For a sampling of U.S. involvement, see Douglas Jehl, "Who Armed Iraq? Answers the West Didn't Want to Hear," *The New York Times* (July 18, 1993). See also Douglas Borer, "Inverse Engagement: Lessons from U.S.-Iraq Relations, 1982–1990," *Parameters* (Summer 2003).

11. Precise casualties are not available and estimates vary widely. Yet in toto the Iran-Iraq War probably claimed between four hundred thousand and one million lives. For a range of estimates, see "Secondary Wars and Atrocities of the Twentieth Century" (February 2012), necrometrics.com/20c300k .htm#Iran-Iraq, accessed December 4, 2014.

12. The most comprehensive scholarly account of this episode to date is Malcolm Byrne, *Iran-Contra: Reagan's Scandal and the Unchecked Abuse of Presidential Power* (Lawrence, 2014).

13. The Contras were a guerrilla force, operating primarily out of Honduras, who were attempting with CIA support to overthrow the Sandinista revolutionaries who in 1979 had gained power in Nicaragua. The Contra piece of Iran-Contra worked this way: U.S. officials surreptitiously diverted to these anti-Sandinistas the "profits," amounting to millions of dollars, gained by selling arms to Iran. This too was illegal—a blatant violation of a congressional prohibition on providing such aid to the Contras.

14. Ronald O'Rourke, "The Tanker War," *Proceedings* (May 1988).

15. Harold Lee Wise, *Inside the Danger Zone: The U.S. Military in the Persian Gulf, 1987–1988* (Annapolis, 2007), 7–8.

16. "Historical Crude Oil Prices, 1946–Present" (March 6, 2014), inflationdata .com/Inflation/Inflation_Rate/Historical_Oil_Prices_Table.asp, accessed December 10, 2014.

17. Ronald Reagan, "National Security Decision Directive 139: Measures to Improve U.S. Posture and Readiness to Respond to Developments in the Iran-Iraq War" (April 5, 1984).

18. Caspar W. Weinberger, "A Report to Congress on Security Arrangements in the Persian Gulf" (June 15, 1987), iii.

19. Crist, *Twilight War,* 213; Byrne, *Iran-Contra,* 335.

20. Wise, *Inside the Danger Zone,* 28. The quotation is from a member of the *Stark*'s crew.

21. For a detailed account, see Wise, *Inside the Danger Zone,* 27–41.

22. Wise, *Inside the Danger Zone,* 49.

23. Ronald Reagan, "Question-and-Answer Session with Area Reporters, Chattanooga, Tennessee" (May 19, 1987). The president also stated that "we have been doing everything we can and working with the other nations to try to bring about a peace in that war," with Iraq cooperating and Iran obdurately refusing to do so.

24. George P. Shultz, "Secretary's Letters to the Congress, May 20, 1987," *Department of State Bulletin* (July 1987), 61.

25. "Formal Investigation into the Circumstances Surrounding the Attack on the USS Stark (FFG 31) on 17 May 1987" (June 12, 1987), jag.navy.mil /library/investigations/uss%20stark%20basic.pdf, accessed December 8, 2014.

26. Wise, *Inside the Danger Zone,* 42–45.

27. Patrick Tyler, *A World of Trouble* (New York, 2009), 335.

28. To prevent any recurrence of the *Stark* attack, CENTCOM officers secretly visited Baghdad to negotiate an agreement providing for "a series of electronic winks and nods" permitting Iraqi aircraft to continue their attacks on Iranian vessels while minimizing the likelihood of encountering the U.S. Navy. Crist, *Twilight War,* 231–32.

29. Wise, *Inside the Danger Zone,* 77.

30. Stephens Broening, "U.S. Admonishes Libya Not to Send Mines to Iran," Baltimore *Sun* (September 10, 1987); Elaine Sciolino, "U.S. Sends 2,000 Gas Masks to the Chadians," *The New York Times* (September 25, 1987). According to the second dispatch, U.S. officials had "conclusive evidence that the deliveries took place."

31. Wise, *Inside the Danger Zone,* 75–76, 160.

32. John Kifner, "United States Blows Up Captured Iranian Vessel," *The New York Times* (September 26, 1987).

33. Wise, *Inside the Danger Zone*, 98–103, 113.

34. "Seized Iranian Ship Scuttled by U.S. Forces," *Los Angeles Times* (September 26, 1987).

35. Wise, *Inside the Danger Zone*, 127–30.

36. Wise, *Inside the Danger Zone*, 137–38.

37. Wise, *Inside the Danger Zone*, 142.

38. Wise, *Inside the Danger Zone*, 143–52.

39. In June 1987, Admiral William J. Crowe described the conditions in testimony before the Senate Armed Services Committee. "U.S. Military Forces to Protect 'Re-Flagged' Kuwaiti Oil Tankers" (June 5, 1987), 17.

40. For a full account of the ordeal, see Bradley Peniston, *No Higher Honor* (Annapolis, 2006).

41. Karsh, *Iran-Iraq War*, 57.

42. Crist, *Twilight War*, 339–41.

43. Wise, *Inside the Danger Zone*, 193–214, quotation 210.

44. Crist, *Twilight War*, 337.

45. Harold Lee Wise, "One Day of War," *Naval History* (April 2013).

46. Crist, *Twilight War*, 356.

47. Michael A. Palmer, *Guardians of the Gulf* (New York, 1992), 138.

48. Crist, *Twilight War*, 216.

49. Richard Halloran, "Navy Won't Alter Engagement Rules," *The New York Times* (July 7, 1988).

50. Ronald Reagan, "Letter to the Speaker of the House of Representatives and the President Pro Tempore of the Senate on the Destruction of an Iranian Airliner by the United States Navy over the Persian Gulf" (July 4, 1988).

51. "I will never apologize," *Daily Kos* (July 18, 2014), www.dailykos.com/story/2014/07/18/1314985/--I-Will-Never-Apologize-Iran-Flight-665-Shot-Down-290-Dead, accessed December 11, 2014.

52. "Why the U.S. Navy Is in the Gulf," *The New York Times* (July 6, 1988).

53. "In Captain Rogers's Shoes," *The New York Times* (July 5, 1988).

54. Lou Cannon, "Poll Finds Support for Ship's Action, U.S. Policy in Gulf," *The Washington Post* (July 7, 1988).

55. William J. Crowe Jr., "Formal Investigation into the Circumstances Surrounding Iran Air Flight 655 on July 3, 1988" (August 18, 1988). The document cited is a letter from Admiral Crowe endorsing the findings of the actual investigation.

56. "Statement by Joint Chiefs' Chairman," *The New York Times* (July 4, 1988).

57. David Evans, "One Must Question the Current Value of Military Medals," *Chicago Tribune* (April 6, 1990).

58. John M. Broder, "U.S. Downs Iran Airliner," *Los Angeles Times* (July 4, 1988).

59. Weinberger, *Fighting for Peace*, 426, 428.

60. "The Naval Gap in the Persian Gulf," *The New York Times* (September 12, 1988).

61. "From Nasser to Khomeini," *The New Republic* (August 22, 1988).

62. "Iran: Not in Vain," *National Review* (September 2, 1988).

63. "The Real Winner," *National Review* (September 16, 1988).

7. No Clean Ending

1. Reinhold Niebuhr, *The Irony of American History* (New York, 1952), 2–3.

2. For a concise description of Iraq's severe economic predicament, see Lawrence Freedman and Efraim Karsh, *The Gulf Conflict, 1990–1991* (Princeton, 1993), 37–41.

3. Freedman and Karsh, *Gulf Conflict*, 45–48.

4. George Bush, National Security Directive 26, "U.S. Policy Toward the Persian Gulf" (October 2, 1989).

5. Thomas Friedman, "Bush, Hinting Forces, Declares Iraqi Assault 'Will Not Stand,'" *The New York Times* (August 6, 1990).

6. Schwarzkopf, *It Doesn't Take a Hero*, 305.

7. *The 9/11 Commission Report* (Washington, D.C., 2004), 57.

8. Schubert and Kraus, eds., *Whirlwind War*, 78. This is not to imply that the deployment unfolded without complications. But the problems encountered were of a type that the U.S. military has traditionally possessed a particular aptitude for solving, especially when provided with an open checkbook.

9. Schwarzkopf, *It Doesn't Take a Hero*, 348.

10. In all likelihood, Saddam never had any intention of advancing into Saudi Arabia. Michael R. Gordon and Bernard E. Trainor, *The Generals' War* (Boston, 1995), 65.

11. Only Jordan, Yemen, and the Palestine Liberation Organization professed support for Iraq, although none possessed any meaningful ability to assist.

12. "Anyone" did not include Israel. See note 31 in this chapter.

13. Ultimately, the U.S.-led military coalition included thirty-two countries. Yet of that number the majority contributed fewer than one thousand troops each. Washington saw Egyptian participation as key. It came at a price. In return for President Hosni Mubarak's promise to join the coalition, the United States forgave $10 billion of Egyptian debt.

14. According to Dick Cheney, U.S. expenditures related to the Second Persian

Gulf War equaled $61.1 billion, with foreign governments covering $53.7 billion of that total. Richard B. Cheney, *In My Time: A Personal and Political Memoir* (New York, 2011), 228. Germany, Japan, Saudi Arabia, and Kuwait all kicked in multi-billion-dollar contributions.

15. For one account of Powell's reservations, see Gordon and Trainor, *Generals' War*, 129–31.

16. Cheney, *In My Time*, 198.

17. Henry S. Rowen, "Inchon in the Desert—My Rejected Plan," *The National Interest* (Summer 1995), 35.

18. Henry Rowen, an academic then serving as an assistant secretary of defense, first dreamed up the Western Excursion, also known as Operation Scorpion. Retired lieutenant general Dale Vesser helped flesh out the concept. Rowen recalls Scorpion's genesis in his essay "Inchon in the Desert—My Rejected Plan," 34–39. Rowen's own concerns focused less on how to liberate Kuwait than on how "to keep Scuds from being launched against Israel." Missile attacks against Tel Aviv, he feared, would "kill hundreds of thousands of people in Tel Aviv or Haifa." Israeli retaliation would undermine the anti-Saddam coalition. So Scorpion was primarily a plan to defend Israel.

19. "Oral History: Richard Cheney," *Frontline*, www.pbs.org/wgbh/pages /frontline/gulf/oral/cheney/1.html, accessed December 28, 2014.

20. George H. W. Bush, "The President's News Conference on the Persian Gulf Crisis" (November 8, 1990).

21. Schwarzkopf, *It Doesn't Take a Hero*, 381.

22. By February 1991, U.S. troop strength in the Persian Gulf peaked at over 533,000. Schubert and Kraus, eds., *Whirlwind War*, 157.

23. Granted, a cynic might argue that the governing issue was whether voting for war or against it was more likely to advance the individual member's political ambitions.

24. Sara Fritz and William J. Eaton, "Congress Authorizes Gulf War," *Los Angeles Times* (January 13, 1991).

25. Dan Balz and Rick Atkinson, "Powell Vows to Isolate Iraqi Army and 'Kill It,'" *The Washington Post* (January 24, 1991).

26. Schwarzkopf, *It Doesn't Take a Hero*, 381, emphasis in original.

27. Bush had coined the phrase in a speech to Congress shortly after the Iraqi invasion of Kuwait. George Bush, "Address Before a Joint Session of the Congress on the Persian Gulf Crisis and the Federal Budget Deficit" (September 11, 1990).

28. Brigadier General Ward LeHardy quoted in Otto Friedrich, ed., *Desert Storm: The War in the Persian Gulf* (Boston, 1991), 121.

29. Speicher was classified as missing in action. In a September 2002 speech to the UN General Assembly making the case for war against Iraq, President

George W. Bush included the pilot's unresolved status in his bill of indictment against Saddam Hussein. During the Third Gulf War, U.S. Marines recovered Speicher's remains, thereby confirming that he had been killed in action in January 1991.

30. *Conduct of the Persian Gulf War: Final Report to Congress* (Washington, D.C., 1992), 157, 160, 168, 170, 184. See also Thomas A. Keaney and Eliot A. Cohen, *Revolution in Warfare?* (Annapolis, 1993), 10–13, 18–19. This is the summary volume of "Gulf War Air Power Survey," commissioned by the U.S. Air Force after the Second Gulf War.

31. Keeping Israel on the sidelines militarily had been a U.S. priority from the very onset of the crisis. Washington feared that any Israeli military action against Iraq—by no means implausible, given that Israel had attacked Iraq's Osirak nuclear reactor in 1981—would shatter the anti-Saddam coalition. So the Bush administration pleaded for Israeli self-restraint. Pocketing various promises of security assistance, the government of hardliner Yitzhak Shamir agreed—within limits—to sit tight. The handful of Scuds falling on Tel Aviv and Haifa on January 18—more followed on successive days— tested those limits. In Washington reducing the Scud threat emerged as an urgent priority, one to which Schwarzkopf was largely oblivious—Israel did not even fall within CENTCOM's jurisdiction. Describing himself as "furious," Cheney ordered Schwarzkopf to adjust his priorities. The U.S. also hurriedly dispatched Patriot missile batteries to Israel, providing a semblance of defense. Israel obligingly stayed out of the war. Had the Scuds mounted chemical rather than conventional warheads, a different outcome would have been likely. Cheney, *In My Time*, 215.

32. *Conduct of the Persian Gulf War*, 173–74. The quotation is from Lieutenant General Walt Boomer, senior Marine commander. "Oral History: Walt Boomer," *Frontline*, pbs.org/wgbh/pages/frontline/gulf/oral/boomer/1 .html, accessed December 31, 2014.

33. Schwarzkopf, *It Doesn't Take a Hero*, 361. While commanding the Army of the Potomac during the Civil War, McClellan had proved exceedingly reluctant to engage the enemy. An exasperated President Lincoln remarked, "If General McClellan does not want to use the army, I would like to borrow it for a time."

34. "Oral History: Colin Powell," *Frontline*, pbs.org/wgbh/pages/frontline /gulf/oral/powell/1.html, accessed December 31, 2014.

35. *Conduct of the Persian Gulf War*, 189–91.

36. U.S. estimates of Iraqi forces had ranged up to 545,000 troops. In all likelihood, by February 24, somewhere in the vicinity of 200,000 to 222,000 Iraqi troops remained in the field. Compare Schwarzkopf, *It Doesn't Take a Hero*, 385, with Keaney and Cohen, *Revolution in Warfare?*, 93.

37. "Oral History: H. Norman Schwarzkopf," *Frontline*, pbs.org/wgbh/pages /frontline/gulf/oral/schwarzkopf/1.html, accessed January 5, 2015.

38. Richard M. Swain, *"Lucky War": Third Army in Desert Storm* (Fort Leavenworth, Kan., 1994), 230. The U.S. Army's official history of the Second Gulf War, Swain's book remains the best overall account of that conflict.

39. Swain, *"Lucky War,"* 207. Franks, wanting more, repeatedly petitioned to have the 1st Cavalry Division, initially the theater reserve, also put under his control.

40. Swain, *"Lucky War,"* 229.

41. Swain, *"Lucky War,"* 250. The phrase refers to the practice of some World War I generals to exercise command from comfortable mansions far removed from the fighting front, thereby losing touch with the realities of trench warfare.

42. Swain, *"Lucky War,"* 264.

43. John D. Gresham, "Gulf War 20th: The Battle of 73 Easting and the Road to the Synthetic Battlefield," *Defense Media Network* (February 22, 2011).

44. Schwarzkopf, *It Doesn't Take a Hero,* 468.

45. Colin Powell, *My American Journey* (New York, 1995), 521.

46. Powell, *My American Journey,* 521.

47. Schwarzkopf's end-of-war briefing is available at youtube.com/watch?v=wKi3NwLFkX4, accessed January 2, 2015.

48. George H. W. Bush, "Address on the End of the Gulf War" (February 27, 1991).

49. Swain, *"Lucky War,"* 124.

50. Schwarzkopf's deputy, Lieutenant General Calvin Waller, describes the process of drafting the terms of the ceasefire: "Norman Schwarzkopf said, how do we make this happen, what do we do, and we had a State Department representative in our war room and he said to the State Department representative, what is it we're supposed to do, Mr. State Department rep., and the State Department rep. gave what we called the Iraqi salute, he didn't know, so Schwarzkopf asked for his stenographer to come in and sat him down next to him, he turned in his chair and started dictating to him things that he thought, someone would think of something . . . and give him a little note, he in turn would read that note and, you know, phrase a sentence or a paragraph or whatever needed to be phrased in the proposed document, the navy yeoman went off and typed it up, brought it back in, and he made some slight modifications to it and then we sent it off to the Pentagon and the State Department—that's how it was done." "Oral History: Calvin Waller," *Frontline,* pbs.org/wgbh/pages/frontline/gulf/oral/waller/1.html, accessed January 2, 2015.

51. Schwarzkopf, *It Doesn't Take a Hero,* 480, emphasis in original.

52. Schwarzkopf, *It Doesn't Take a Hero,* 483, 488–89.

53. Schwarzkopf, *It Doesn't Take a Hero,* 473–74.

54. Friedrich, ed., *Desert Storm*, 1, 3.

55. Susan Baer, "Millions Attend Ticker-Tape Parade," Baltimore *Sun* (June 11, 1991).

56. Tom Clancy with General Fred Franks Jr., *Into the Storm* (New York, 1997), 487.

57. Bill Clinton, "A New Covenant for American Security" (December 12, 1991).

58. Richard H. P. Sia, "General H. Norman Schwarzkopf: A Man Wise in the Ways of War," Baltimore *Sun* (March 10, 1991); Ellen Goodman, "The New Model Male," *Chicago Tribune* (March 17, 1991); "Schwarzkopf of Arabia," *Richmond Times-Dispatch* (March 8, 1991); T. Mathews, "A Soldier of Conscience," *Newsweek* (March 11, 1991); R. Watson, "After the Storm," *Newsweek* (March 11, 1991).

59. Jim Kirksey, "Coloradan to Seek 5 Stars for Schwarzkopf and Powell," *The Denver Post* (March 4, 1991).

60. George Bush and Brent Scowcroft, *A World Transformed* (New York, 1998), 486–87.

61. Gordon and Trainor, *Generals' War*, 435–38.

62. Thomas Friedman, "Selling Sacrifice: Gulf Rationale Still Eludes Bush," *The New York Times* (November 16, 1990).

63. Robert Fisk, *The Great War for Civilization* (New York, 2006), 646–47.

64. George Bush, "The President's News Conference on the Persian Gulf Conflict" (March 1, 1991).

65. Bush, "The President's News Conference on the Persian Gulf Conflict" (March 1, 1991).

66. Ann Devroy and Molly Moore, "Winning the War and Struggling with Peace," *The Washington Post* (April 14, 1991).

67. William Safire, "Bush's Bay of Pigs," *The New York Times* (April 4, 1991).

68. Jim Hoagland, "Monumental Folly," *The Washington Post* (March 29, 1991).

69. Charles Krauthammer, "It's Time to Finish Saddam," *The Washington Post* (March 29, 1991).

70. "Oral History: Richard Cheney," *Frontline.*

71. Mary McGrory, "Bush's Peace Problems," *The Washington Post* (March 26, 1991).

72. Bush and Scowcroft, *World Transformed*, 383–84.

73. For further elaboration on this point, see Andrew J. Bacevich, "The United States in Iraq: Terminating an Interminable War," in *Between War and Peace*, ed. Matthew Moten (New York, 2011), 302–22.

74. George Bush, "Statement on Aid to Iraqi Refugees" (April 5, 1991). The

United States owed Turkey. During Desert Storm the Turks had allowed U.S. forces to launch air strikes from Turkish bases.

75. "Oral History: Dick Cheney," *Frontline*.

76. "Oral History: H. Norman Schwarzkopf," *Frontline*.

77. Powell, *My American Journey*, 532.

78. George Bush, "Remarks to the American Legislative Exchange Council" (March 1, 1991).

8. Good Intentions

1. Ann Devroy and Molly Moore, "Winning the War and Struggling with Peace," *The Washington Post* (April 14, 1991).

2. In all, between early April and mid-July of 1991, air force transports supporting Operation Provide Comfort delivered some seven thousand tons of supplies. Daniel L. Haulman, "Crisis in Iraq: Operation Provide Comfort," in *Short of War: Major USAF Contingency Operations*, ed. A. Timothy Warnock (Montgomery, 2000), 181–82. Army and Marine helicopters delivered additional supplies. Ronald T. Brown, *Humanitarian Operations in Northern Iraq, 1991* (Washington, D.C., 1995), 26–30. This monograph is the official U.S. Marine Corps history of Provide Comfort.

3. "Operation Provide Comfort II," globalsecurity.org/military/ops/provide _comfort_2.htm, accessed January 12, 2015.

4. In 1996, this no-fly/no-drive area expanded to the 33rd Parallel just short of Baghdad.

5. William J. Allen, "Crisis in Southern Iraq," *Short of War*, 189–95.

6. Allen, "Crisis in Southern Iraq," 195.

7. For more on the Israeli concept of "current security," see Eliot A. Cohen, Michael J. Eisenstadt, and Andrew J. Bacevich, *Knives, Tanks, and Missiles* (Washington, D.C., 1998), 71–73.

8. Frank Bajak, "U.S. Airplanes Inspect the Damage from Raid," *Deseret News* (January 14, 1993).

9. For a detailed description of these encounters, see Paul K. White, *Crises After the Storm* (Washington, D.C., 1999), 15–28.

10. Andrew J. Bacevich, *American Empire* (Cambridge, 2002), 152.

11. For details, see *Operation Provide Comfort: Review of U.S. Air Force Investigation of Black Hawk Fratricide Incident*, a report prepared by the United States General Accounting Office and published in November 1997, gao.gov /archive/1998/os98004.pdf, accessed January 14, 2015.

12. *The 9/11 Commission Report*, 60; "Al Qaeda Is Now Suspected in 1996 Bombing of Barracks," *The New York Times* (May 14, 2003); "Perry: U.S. Eyed Iran Attack After Bombing" (June 6, 2007), upi.com/Business_News/Security -Industry/2007/06/06/Perry-US-eyed-Iran-attack-after-bombing/UPI

-70451181161509/, accessed January 12, 2015. This United Press International dispatch quotes William Perry, U.S. secretary of defense at the time of the bombing, as saying that "the Khobar Towers bombing was probably masterminded by Osama bin Laden." Al Qaeda was clearly linked to the earlier November 13, 1995, bombing in Riyadh that killed five Americans involved in training the Saudi National Guard.

13. The June 1993 attack, the first military action ordered by the recently inaugurated President Bill Clinton, was in retaliation for a foiled Iraqi plot to assassinate his predecessor during a visit to Kuwait. The December 1998 episode, Operation Desert Fox, was punishment for Saddam's refusal to cooperate with UN arms inspections teams.

14. John L. Hirsch and Robert B. Oakley, *Somalia and Operation Restore Hope* (Washington, D.C., 1995), 3–24.

15. Hirsch and Oakley, *Somalia*, 25.

16. "Don't Forsake Somalia," *The New York Times* (November 4, 1992).

17. "End Somalia's Anguish," *The Christian Science Monitor* (November 30, 1992).

18. Richard Stewart, *The United States Army in Somalia, 1992–1994* (Washington, D.C., 2002), 9.

19. George Bush, "Address to the Nation on the Situation in Somalia" (December 4, 1992).

20. Hirsch and Oakley, *Somalia*, 46.

21. "Think Three Times Before You Embrace the Somali Tarbaby," *U.S. News and World Report* (December 14, 1992). This reprints excerpts of Hempstone's cable.

22. Michael R. Gordon, "Envoy Asserts Intervention in Somalia Is Risky and Not in Interests of U.S.," *The New York Times* (December 6, 1992).

23. Michael R. Gordon, "TV Army on the Beach Took U.S. by Surprise," *The New York Times* (December 10, 1992).

24. Hirsch and Oakley, *Somalia*, 63–64. UNITAF was an acronym for United Task Force.

25. The quote is from Rear Admiral Mike W. Cramer, an intelligence officer with the Joint Chiefs of Staff, testifying before a Senate committee. U.S. Senate, Committee on Armed Forces, *Joint Chiefs of Staff Briefing on Current Military Operations in Somalia, Iraq, and Yugoslavia* (January 29, 1993).

26. Hirsch and Oakley, *Somalia*, 69–70.

27. Quoted in Julia Preston, "U.N. Establishes Force for Somalia; All but 9,000 U.S. Troops to Leave by May," *The Washington Post* (March 26, 1993).

28. Approximately four thousand U.S. troops were to remain in Somalia as part of UNOSOM.

29. "Interview: General Thomas Montgomery (Ret.)," *Frontline*, pbs.org

/wgbh/pages/frontline/shows/ambush/interviews/montgomery.html, accessed January 18, 2015.

30. UN Security Council Resolution 837 (June 6, 1993).

31. "Review of the Circumstances Surrounding the Ranger Raid on October 3–4, 1993, in Mogadishu, Somalia" (September 29, 1995), 19. This document provides the results of a U.S. Senate inquiry into the Somalia intervention. It is commonly referred to as the "Warner-Levin Report" after its principal authors, Senators John Warner (R-VA) and Carl Levin (D-MI).

32. "Interview: Montgomery," *Frontline*.

33. Stewart, *United States Army in Somalia*, 9.

34. "Interview: Montgomery," *Frontline*.

35. "Warner-Levin Report," 23.

36. The sardonic quote, widely attributed to Charles de Gaulle, is likely to have originated much earlier.

37. The precise number of Somalis killed is a matter of dispute, with claims ranging from as few as seven to as many as seventy. Major John Evans, "TF 1-22 Infantry on the Horn of Africa" (2000), 1-22infantry.org/history /somaliapagefour.htm, accessed January 19, 2015.

38. Hirsch and Oakley, *Somalia*, 121.

39. Task Force Raven, "Operation Continue Hope, 27 Aug 93–9 Jan 94, Lessons Learned" (August 20, 1994). This report is on file at the U.S. Army Center for Military History.

40. Overall, U.S. forces killed an estimated 6,000 to 10,000 Somalis during the course of Operation Restore Hope. Eric Schmitt, "Somali War Casualties May Be 10,000," *The New York Times* (December 8, 1993).

41. Quoted in Hirsch and Oakley, *Somalia*, 121.

42. Madeleine K. Albright, "Yes, There Is a Reason to Be in Somalia," *The New York Times* (August 10, 1993).

43. "Garrison and I probably talked once or twice a day most days," Downing later recalled. The talks included guidance. "I kept telling General Garrison not to do anything crazy. . . . Be patient, be careful, eventually you will get a shot at Aideed." "Warner-Levin Report," 39.

44. Jonathan Stevenson, *Losing Mogadishu* (Annapolis, 1995), 115.

45. U.S. Special Operations Command, "Task Force Ranger Operations in Somalia, 3–4 October 1993" (June 1, 1994). This heavily redacted document was originally classified SECRET/NOFORN.

46. Using that criteria, the 1970 Son Tay raid to free American POWs held in North Vietnam also rates as a success. It came up empty-handed, but those involved departed the scene without incident.

47. This was Osman Atto, a wheeler-dealer described as "Aidid's moneyman." Mark Bowden, *Black Hawk Down* (New York, 1999), 27.

48. Robert F. Baumann, *"My Clan Against the World": U.S. and Coalition Forces in Somalia, 1992–1994* (Fort Leavenworth, 2003), 144.

49. Hirsch and Oakley, *Somalia*, 125.

50. As Colonel Lawrence Casper, who commanded QRF aviation assets, subsequently wrote, "through repetition and consistency," those commanding TF Ranger had "telegraphed their mode of operations to those who were interested." Lawrence E. Casper, *Falcon Brigade* (Boulder, 2001), 37.

51. Bowden's *Black Hawk Down* offers a book-length minute-by-minute account. For Garrison's version of events, see his testimony before the Senate Armed Services Committee. "U.S. Military Operations in Somalia" (May 12, 1994), 2–14.

52. Michael Elliott and John Barry, "The Making of a Fiasco," *Newsweek* (October 18, 1993).

53. Smith Hempstone, "In Somalia, My Unheeded Warning Comes True," *The Wall Street Journal* (October 11, 1993).

54. "Somalia: Time to Get Out," *The New York Times* (October 8, 1993).

55. John McCain, "McCain Remarks on Reports from Somalia" (October 4, 1993), mccain.senate.gov/public/index.cfm/speeches?ID=59361aed-af91 -43fd-af0c-f996319d4c67, accessed January 20, 2015.

56. CENTCOM had withdrawn the gunships that had been available earlier that summer.

57. David H. Hackworth, "Making the Same Dumb Mistakes," *Newsweek* (October 18, 1993).

58. James Mayall, ed., *The New Interventionism, 1991–1994* (Cambridge, 1996), 17.

59. To take one example, it had been General Hoar, with General Downing concurring, who had nixed the request to include AC-130s in the Task Force Ranger "force package." Garrison did not view the absence of AC-130s as a problem. In September, Hoar also told Montgomery that he did not support the request for tanks. For his part, Garrison later told congressional investigators, "If I had tanks, I don't know if I would have used them. I never thought of a contingency plan" that included the use of armored vehicles. "Warner-Levin Report," 28–30, 32–33.

60. Bill Clinton, *My Life* (New York, 2004), 553. Garrison defined success as having captured two of Aidid's key aides along with nearly two dozen lesser figures.

61. Bowden, *Black Hawk Down*, 333.

62. Harry Summers, *On Strategy: A Critical Analysis of the Vietnam War* (New York, 1984), 21.

63. Peter L. Bergen, *Holy War* (New York, 2002), 22; *The 9/11 Commission Report*, 60; Tom Zeller Jr., "Back in Somalia, with al Qaeda's Connection More Clear," *The New York Times* (January 9, 2007).

9. Balkan Digression

1. For a concise summary of these events, see Margaret MacMillan, *Paris 1919* (New York, 2001), 109–24.

2. John F. Burns, "The Dying City of Sarajevo," *The New York Times* (July 26, 1992).

3. For a more detailed account, see Steven L. Burg and Paul S. Shoup, *The War in Bosnia-Herzegovina* (Armonk, New York, 1999), 62–127.

4. Laura Silber and Allen Miller, *Yugoslavia: Death of a Nation* (London, 1996), 201.

5. Misha Glenny, "Yugoslavia: The Revenger's Tragedy," *The New York Review of Books* (August 13, 1992).

6. "Partial Text of Clinton Yugoslavia Plan," *Los Angeles Times* (July 28, 1992).

7. Jules Witcover, "Clinton, Gore Begin 2nd Bus Tour by Blasting Bush Foreign Policy," Baltimore *Sun* (August 6, 1992).

8. John Pomfret, "Albright, Shalikashvili Signal U.S. Ties to Bosnia," *Washington Post* (March 31, 1994).

9. Warren Christopher, *In the Stream of History* (Stanford, 1998), 347.

10. Daniel L. Haulman, "Resolution of Bosnian Crisis," in *Short of War*, ed. Warnock, 224.

11. The incident provided the basis for three books, two written by O'Grady himself, and three documentaries, plus a "loosely based on" Hollywood movie.

12. For a concise account, see Burg and Shoup, *War in Bosnia-Herzegovina*, 128–88.

13. Kurt Miller, "Deny Flight and Deliberate Force: An Effective Use of Airpower?" M.A. thesis, U.S. Army Command and Staff College (1997), 48.

14. Haulman, "Resolution of Bosnian Crisis," 224–25.

15. John McCain, "Peacekeeping Efforts in Bosnia and Somalia" (July 1, 1993), mccain.senate.gov/public/index.cfm/speeches?ID=85bcd7dd-a857-4ecf-9a5c-21a264aa6947, accessed January 28, 2015.

16. "The Shame of Bosnia," *The Washington Post* (July 23, 1993).

17. Susan Sontag, "Godot Comes to Sarajevo," *The New York Review of Books* (October 21, 1993).

18. "The Abdication," *The New Republic* (February 28, 1994).

19. Stephen Kinzer, "Belgrade Meeting Backs Peace Plan," *The New York Times* (May 13, 1993).

20. Fouad Ajami, "Standing Up to the Serbs," *U.S. News and World Report* (May 2, 1994).

21. Michael Dobbs, "Saudis Funded Weapons for Bosnia, Official Says," *The Washington Post* (February 2, 1996).

22. Marlise Simons, "Trial Offers Look at Secretive Warriors in Bosnia," *The New York Times* (September 2, 2001).

23. Chris Hedges, "Fascists Reborn as Croatia's Founding Fathers," *The New York Times* (April 12, 1997).

24. Robert F. Baumann et al., *Armed Peacekeepers in Bosnia* (Fort Leavenworth, 2004), 28; David Isenberg, "Soldiers of Fortune, Ltd." (November 1997), aloha.net/~stroble/mercs.html, accessed January 31, 2015. This document is a monograph prepared under the auspices of the Center for Defense Information.

25. The withdrawal of UN peacekeepers eliminated concerns about the Serbs taking them hostage as a way of constraining NATO air attacks.

26. Rick Atkinson, "Air Assault Set Stage for Broader Role," *The Washington Post* (November 15, 1995).

27. Determined Force did not "officially" end until September 20, but during its final week, NATO suspended further air attacks.

28. Earlier that summer, Bosnian Serb forces had succeeded in shooting down a U.S. Air Force F-16. The pilot successfully ejected, evaded capture, and was subsequently recovered.

29. Colonel Robert C. Owen, "The Balkans Air Campaign Study: Part II," *Airpower Journal* (Summer 1997). Supplementing the effort by manned aircraft, the cruiser USS *Normandy* fired thirteen cruise missiles during Deliberate Force.

30. In the "Split Agreement," signed on July 22, 1995, Croat and Bosnian leaders had promised to combine forces against the Bosnian Serbs. A three-way war now became a war of two against one.

31. Central Intelligence Agency, Office of Russian and European Analysis, *Balkan Battlegrounds: A Military History of the Yugoslav Conflict, 1990–1995* (Washington, D.C., 2003), vol. 1, 376. This two-volume work provides a detailed campaign narrative of the entire Balkan War.

32. Robert Frasure quoted in Richard Holbrooke, *To End a War* (New York, 1999), 73.

33. Quoted in Mark Danner, "Operation Storm," *The New York Review of Books* (October 22, 1998).

34. CIA, *Balkan Battlegrounds*, 1:391.

35. Holbrooke, *To End a War*, 361.

36. Bill Clinton, "Remarks Announcing the Bosnia-Herzegovina Peace Agreement" (November 21, 1995).

37. Roger Cohen, "Taming the Bullies of Bosnia," *The New York Times Magazine* (December 17, 1995).

38. Rick Atkinson, "Air Assault Set Stage for Broader Role," *The Washington Post* (November 15, 1995).

39. CIA, *Balkan Battlegrounds,* 1:396.

40. Colonel Robert C. Owen, "Summary," *Final Report of the Balkans Air Campaign Study,* ed. Robert C. Owen (Montgomery, 2000), 513, 515.

41. Although not a NATO member, Russia also participated. Moscow's brief post–Cold War honeymoon with the West was in full swing.

42. Quoted in Harold E. Raugh, Jr., ed., *Operation Joint Endeavor: An Oral History* (Fort Leavenworth, 2010), 63.

43. Overall, the deployment of U.S. Army forces from Germany to Bosnia was an ill-planned and ill-coordinated mess. See Baumann et al., *Armed Peacekeepers,* 70–83.

44. Raugh, ed., *Operation Joint Endeavor,* 10.

45. For further details on Joint Endeavor (subsequently renamed Joint Guard, and then Joint Forge), see R. Cody Phillips, *Bosnia-Herzegovina: The U.S. Army's Role in Peace Enforcement Operations, 1995–2004* (Washington, D.C., [2007]); and Richard Swain, *Neither War nor Not War* (Carlisle Barracks, 2003).

46. International Crisis Group, "Is Dayton Failing? Bosnia Four Years After the Peace Agreement" (October 28, 1999).

47. One American was killed in an incident involving a mine, which General Nash attributed to "ill-discipline on the part of the individual soldier . . . who tampered with the mine." Quoted in Raugh, ed., *Operation Joint Endeavor,* 58.

48. Baumann et al., *Armed Peacekeepers,* 131.

49. Holbrooke, *To End a War,* 217.

10. What Winning Means

1. William Kristol and Robert Kagan, "Toward a Neo-Reaganite Foreign Policy," *Foreign Affairs* (July/August 1996); Francis Fukuyama, "The End of History?" *The National Interest* (Summer 1989).

2. Bill Clinton, "Inaugural Address" (January 20, 1997); Bill Clinton, "Why I'm Going to China," *Newsweek* (June 29, 1998).

3. Charles Krauthammer, "The Unipolar Moment," *Foreign Affairs* (America and the World), 1990.

4. Anthony Lake, "From Containment to Enlargement" (September 21, 1993), mtholyoke.edu/acad/intrel/lakedoc.html, accessed February 6, 2015.

5. Michael J. Mazarr et al., *The Military-Technical Revolution: A Structural Framework* (Washington, D.C., 1993), 16. By the mid-1990s, the term *military-technical revolution* fell out of favor and was superseded by RMA.

6. Andrew Krepinevich, *The Military-Technical Revolution: A Preliminary Assessment* (Washington, D.C., 2002), 12. Although published in 2002, this study

dates from 1992, when it was prepared under the auspices of the Pentagon's Office of Net Assessment.

7. Michael J. Mazarr, "The Revolution in Military Affairs: A Framework for Defense Planning" (June 10, 1994), strategicstudiesinstitute.army.mil/pubs/display.cfm?pubID=242, accessed February 11, 2015.

8. Wesley K. Clark, *Modern War* (New York, 2001), 121.

9. Clark, *Modern War,* 6, 418.

10. Tim Judah, *Kosovo: War and Revenge* (New Haven, 2000), 73, 91.

11. Judah, *Kosovo,* 124–26, 162.

12. Judah, *Kosovo,* 130–31, 136–38, 141, 147, 169–71.

13. Barton Gellman, "The Path to Crisis: How the U.S. and Its Allies Went to War," *The Washington Post* (April 18, 1999).

14. Madeleine K. Albright, "Press Conference on Kosovo" (October 8, 1998). Unless otherwise noted, remarks by State Department officials and State Department documents are available at the department's website, state.gov.

15. The year prior, a movie called *Wag the Dog* directed by Barry Levinson had appeared. In this (quite funny) satire, cynical political operatives invent a fictitious war against Albania to salvage the political fortunes of an American president mired in a sex scandal.

16. James Rubin, "Press Briefing on the Kosovo Peace Talks" (February 21, 1999).

17. The privileges demanded by NATO within Yugoslavia are spelled out in Annex B: Status of Multi-National Implementation Force, Rambouillet Accords, http://peacemaker.un.org/sites/peacemaker.un.org/files/990123_RambouilletAccord.pdf, accessed February 18, 2015.

18. Clark, *Modern War,* 109, 112–13, 127.

19. Clark, *Modern War,* 119.

20. Clark, *Modern War,* 119.

21. Clark, *Modern War,* 68.

22. For text and signatories, including luminaries such as John Bolton, Robert Kagan, Zalmay Khalilzad, William Kristol, and Paul Wolfowitz, see refworld.org/docid/3ae6a6d70.html, accessed August 20, 2015.

23. Walter Isaacson, "Madeleine's War," *Time* (May 9, 1999). For its issue dated July 12, 1999, *The New Republic*'s cover featured a caricature of Albright, referred to as "Secretary of War," wearing the uniform of a three-star general and sporting a chest full of decorations, while striking a pose made famous by the title character in the movie *Patton.*

24. Judah, *Kosovo,* 234–36; Clark, *Modern War,* 171; Madeleine Albright, *Madame Secretary* (New York, 2013), 391.

25. Clark, *Modern War,* 203.

26. Bill Clinton, "Address to the Nation on Airstrikes in the Former Republic of Yugoslavia" (March 24, 1999).

27. The account that follows draws extensively on William M. Arkin, "Operation Allied Force: 'The Most Precise Application of Air Power in History,'" in *War over Kosovo: Politics and Strategy in a Global Age,* ed. Andrew J. Bacevich and Eliot A. Cohen (New York, 2001), 1–37.

28. Clark, *Modern War,* 234. By war's end, the United Nations High Commissioner for Refugees estimated that the total number of displaced Kosovars exceeded 850,000. *UNHCR Global Report 1999* (June 2000), 345.

29. Clark, *Modern War,* 229.

30. Judah, *Kosovo,* 186.

31. William Drozdiak, "Commander of Air War Says Kosovo Victory Near," *The Washington Post* (May 24, 1999).

32. Dana Priest, "United NATO Front Was Divided Within," *The Washington Post* (September 21, 1999).

33. Clark, *Modern War,* 227.

34. At one press conference, for example, Clark stated that it was "always understood that there was no way we were going to be able to stop Serb paramilitary forces who were going in and murdering civilians in villages." By implication, Clark was assigning to parties unknown responsibility for the refugee crisis that he himself had failed to anticipate. Clark, *Modern War,* 207.

35. Clark, *Modern War,* 273.

36. Clark, *Modern War,* 229.

37. Richard G. Lugar, "Send in the Ground Forces," *The Washington Post* (April 1, 1999).

38. Robert Kagan and William Kristol, "Win It," *The Weekly Standard* (April 19, 1999).

39. John McCain, "Will Clinton Trade U.S. Honor for a False Peace?" *The Wall Street Journal* (May 10, 1999).

40. Patricia Cohen, "Ground Wars Make Strange Bedfellows," *The New York Times* (May 30, 1999).

41. Bernard E. Trainor, "How to Mount a Ground War in the Balkans," *The Boston Globe* (May 13, 1999); Warren Bass, "Ground Rules," *The New Republic* (May 17, 1999).

42. Steven Erlanger, "With Milosevic Unyielding on Kosovo, NATO Moved Toward Invasion," *The New York Times* (November 7, 1999).

43. Clark, *Modern War,* 396, 398.

44. Judah, *Kosovo,* 287. In Kosovar eyes, Roma were Serb collaborators.

45. R. Cody Phillips, *Operation Joint Guardian: The U.S. Army in Kosovo* (Washington, D.C., [2007]), 22.

46. In the manner of Zionists such as Menachem Begin and Yitzhak Shamir, various KLA leaders went from being practitioners of terror to becoming mainstream politicians favoring of law and order. For example, the first prime minister of the Kosovo Republic was former KLA leader Hashim Thaçi, who held office for nearly seven years.

47. Two crewmembers of an AH-64 Apache were killed when their helicopter crashed during a training exercise in Albania, one of two Apaches lost in accidents. In the other accident, the crew survived.

48. Clark, *Modern War*, 297.

49. "Fundamentalists Conclude London Meeting, Issue Statement," *Foreign Broadcast Information Service* (May 23, 1999).

50. "Saudi Arabia Expands Aid to Kosovar Refugees," *U.S. Newswire* (April 22, 1999).

51. Raymond Bonner, "NATO Is Wary of Proposals to Help Arm Kosovo Rebels," *The New York Times* (April 4, 1999).

52. "Israel Says Iran Funding Kosovo Separatists," *BBC Monitoring Newsfile* (April 8, 1999).

53. Robert G. Kaiser, "U.S. Message Lost Overseas," *The Washington Post* (October 15, 2001).

54. Timothy Holman, "Foreign Fighters from the Western Balkans in Syria" (June 30, 2014), Combatting Terrorism Center, ctc.usma.edu/posts /foreign-fighters-from-the-western-balkans-in-syria, accessed February 27, 2015; Dzenana Halimoci and Teodorovic Milos, "Mercenaries, Extremists Become Major Balkans Export," *Radio Free Europe Documents and Publications* (August 15, 2014); Gordon N. Bardos, "Jihad in the Balkans," *World Affairs* (September/October 2014).

11. Phony War

1. "Bin Laden Declares Jihad on Americans" (September 2, 1996), *FBIS Report*, fas.org/irp/world/para/ubl-fbis.pdf, accessed March 2, 2015.

2. "Text of Fatwa Urging Jihad Against Americans" (February 23, 1998), *FBIS Report*, fas.org/irp/world/para/ubl-fbis.pdf, accessed March 2, 2015.

3. *The 9/11 Commission Report* (Washington, D.C., 2004), 59–60.

4. William J. Clinton, "The President's Radio Address" (February 27, 1993).

5. Paul West, "Clinton Outlines $7.4 Billion National Service Plan," Baltimore *Sun* (March 2, 1993).

6. Daniel Benjamin and Steven Simon, *The Age of Sacred Terror* (New York, 2002), 13–14.

7. *The 9/11 Commission Report*, 60.

8. David Kirkpatrick, "Saudi Arabia Said to Arrest Suspect in 1996 Khobar Towers Bombing," *The New York Times* (August 26, 2015).

9. "Report to the President and Congress on the Protection of U.S. Forces Deployed Abroad" (August 30, 1996), au.af.mil/au/awc/awcgate/khobar/downing/toc.htm, accessed March 6, 2015. The document is more commonly known as the Downing Report.

10. Bergen, *Holy War*, 176.

11. "Perry: U.S. Eyed Iran Attack After Bombing," United Press International (June 7, 2007).

12. The frequency (or infrequency) with which *The New York Times* has mentioned "Bin Laden" and "Al Qaeda" over time provides one measure of public visibility.

Year	Bin Laden	Al Qaeda
1994	3/1	0/0
1995	0/0	0/0
1996	13/10	0/0
1997	5/5	0/0
1998	213/183	12/23
1999	176/132	2/5
2000	163/142	17/12

Through Proquest, *The New York Times* has two databases for its articles in this period, and they do not produce identical results for any given search term. In each cell, the first number is the number of articles containing the term "Bin Laden" or "Al Qaeda" anywhere in the article, from the *New York Times* "Current File." The second number is the number of articles containing the same item from *The New York Times* "Late Edition/East Coast Edition." I am grateful to Derrin Culp for providing this data.

13. William J. Clinton, "The President's Radio Address" (August 8, 1998).

14. Richard A. Clarke, *Against All Enemies* (New York, 2004), 184.

15. Micah Zenko, "Between Threats and War: U.S. Discrete Military Operations in the Post–Cold War World" (unpublished PhD dissertation, Brandeis University, 2009), 117.

16. Zenko, "Between Threats and War," 127.

17. "Remarks at Press Stake-out on Capitol Hill" (August 21, 1998).

18. Tom Clancy with General Tony Zinni, *Battle Ready* (New York, 2004), 341.

19. Commission on Terrorist Attacks upon the United States, "Staff Statement No. 6—the Military" (March 26, 2004).

20. Zenko, "Between Threats and War," 124.

21. James Risen and David Johnston, "Experts Find No Arms Chemicals at Bombed Sudan Plant," *The New York Times* (February 9, 1999). The investi-

gation was led by Professor Thomas D. Tullius, chairman of the Chemistry Department at Boston University.

22. "Remarks at Press Stake-out on Capitol Hill" (August 21, 1998).

23. Clarke, *Against All Enemies*, 198.

24. Clarke, *Against All Enemies*, 189.

25. Jim Hoagland, "One Raid in a Long War," *The Washington Post* (August 23, 1998).

26. Max Boot, "Victorian Soldiers Have Some Lessons for U.S.," *The Wall Street Journal* (August 25, 1998).

27. "Get Personal," *The New Republic* (September 14 & 21, 1999).

28. Edward G. Shirley, "The Etiquette of Killing bin Laden," *The Wall Street Journal* (August 27, 1998). "Edward G. Shirley" was a pseudonym for Gerecht.

29. There were exceptions, of course, but they carried no weight. An editorial in *The Christian Science Monitor* questioned whether waging war on terrorism was really such a good idea. The *Monitor* suggested that the problem might not be bin Laden but "the alienation and anger rife in parts of Northern Africa, the Middle East, and South Asia." To base U.S. policy on force was to trigger a "cycle of tit-for-tat violence." The *Monitor* anticipated "pressures to suspend civil liberties in order to avert potential terrorist threats on US soil." " 'War' Against Terrorism," *The Christian Science Monitor* (August 24, 1998).

30. Clark, *Against All Enemies*, 201.

31. 9/11 Commission, "Staff Statement No. 6."

32. Hugh Shelton, *Without Hesitation* (New York, 2010), 342–43; Benjamin and Simon, *Age of Sacred Terror*, 280–82, 320.

33. During Operation Desert Storm, two other navy ships, USS *Princeton* and USS *Tripoli*, each struck a mine and sustained serious but not mortal damage.

34. Evan Thomas and Sharon Squassoni, "Desperate Hours," *Newsweek* (March 26, 2001); Hal Pittman, "In the Presence of Heroes," *All Hands* (May 2001).

35. "Command Investigation into the Actions of USS Cole (DDG 67) in Preparing for and Undertaking a Brief Stop for Fuel at Bandar at Tawahi (Aden Harbor), Aden, Yemen on or about 12 October 2000" (November 27, 2000).

36. Lippold disagreed with the investigators' findings. He offers his own version of events in *Front Burner: Al Qaeda's Attack on the USS Cole* (New York, 2012).

37. General John M. Shalikashvili, "Preface," *National Military Strategy of the United States* (Washington, D.C., 1997).

38. Quoted in House Armed Services Committee, "The Investigation into the Attack on the USS Cole" (May 2001), 6. The report is at bits.de/public

/documents/US_Terrorist_Attacks/HASC-colereport0501.pdf, accessed March 10, 2015.

39. "The Investigation into the Attack on the USS Cole," 7.

40. "Strategy for Eliminating the Threat from the Jihadist Networks of al Qida: Status and Prospects" ([January 2001]), www2.gwu.edu/~nsarchiv/NSAEBB /NSAEBB147/clarke%20attachment.pdf, accessed March 11, 2015.

12. Changing the Way They Live

1. "Secretary Rumsfeld Interview with *Time* Magazine" (December 14, 2001). Unless otherwise noted, comments by quotations U.S. defense officials, both military and civilian, can be found at the Department of Defense website, which is defense.gov. In this instance, Rumsfeld was recalling a conversation he had had with George W. Bush in January of that year.

2. Clarke, *Against All Enemies*, 227–38.

3. Shan Carter and Amanda Cox, "One 9/11 Tally: $3.3 Trillion," *The New York Times* (September 8, 2011). The much larger figure reported by the *Times* includes war costs and post-9/11 improvements in domestic security.

4. George W. Bush, "Address Before a Joint Session of Congress on the United States Response to the Terrorist Attacks of September 11" (September 20, 2001).

5. "Remarks to Airline Employees in Chicago, Illinois" (September 27, 2001).

6. "Remarks at the National Defense University" (May 1, 2001).

7. "DoD News Briefing—Secretary Rumsfeld" (September 18, 2001).

8. This is from a note that Rumsfeld dictated to an aide at approximately 2:40 P.M. on September 11, 2001. The note itself is available at "History Commons," historycommons.org/context.jsp?item=a240blameiraq#a240blameiraq, accessed March 14, 2015.

9. Donald Rumsfeld, "Memorandum to the President: Strategic Thoughts" (September 30, 2001).

10. Immediately after 9/11, the Bush administration did call to active duty some thirty-five thousand reservists to bolster homeland defenses and in particular to prevent another aerial attack. This was Operation Noble Eagle, which initially received considerable emphasis and publicity. In March 2002, however, the Pentagon scaled operations down, citing "the high cost of the flights, the drain on Air Force resources and the unlikelihood that the patrols could deter another air attack on the U.S. homeland." In effect, ongoing and anticipated operations abroad took priority. Esther Schrader, "Pentagon Will Reduce Air Patrols over Cities," *Los Angeles Times* (March 19, 2002).

11. "Remarks to Airline Employees."

12. Tommy Franks, *American Soldier* (New York, 2004), 277.

13. Bob Woodward, *Bush at War* (New York, 2002), 25, 43–44.

14. Benjamin S. Lambeth, *Air Power Against Terror* (Santa Monica, 2005), 76–77.

15. Franks, *American Soldier*, 271.

16. CIA paramilitaries had entered the country on September 26 to open negotiations with (and suborn) anti-Taliban Afghans. For a firsthand account, see Gary Schroen, *First In* (New York, 2005).

17. On day one of air operations, U.S. forces, with a minor British augmentation, hit a grand total of only thirty-one targets. Day two involved fewer aircraft than day one and struck only thirteen targets. Lambeth, *Air Power Against Terror*, 85–86, 88.

18. Lambeth, *Air Power Against Terror*, 95–96.

19. Woodward, *Bush at War*, 212.

20. After 9/11, in return for substantial financial compensation, the government of Uzbekistan agreed to allow U.S. forces access to the airfield at Karshi-Khanabad. From 2001 to 2002, U.S. aid to Uzbekistan quadrupled. Donald P. Wright et al., *A Different Kind of War: The U.S. Army in Operation Enduring Freedom* (Fort Leavenworth, 2010), 38. U.S. forces continued to use this facility, known informally as K2, as a logistics support base for operations in Afghanistan until 2005. At that time, irritated by U.S. pressure related to human rights, Uzbekistan revoked the agreement and evicted the Americans.

21. Dana Priest, " 'Team 555' Shaped a New Way of War," *The Washington Post* (April 3, 2002).

22. Woodward, *Bush at War*, 51.

23. Lambeth, *Air Power Against Terror*, 71.

24. For a detailed account of the role of U.S. special forces in the campaign to depose the Taliban, see Wright et al., *Different Kind of War*, 75–82, 96–112.

25. A few notables registered their dissent. Susan Sontag for one, just a week after 9/11, complained about the "self-righteous drivel and outright deceptions being peddled by public figures and TV commentators" who refused to acknowledge that the terrorist attack occurred as a "consequence of specific American alliances and actions." In place of what she derided as "grief management," Sontag advocated "a few shreds of historical awareness" to help understand "what has just happened, and what may continue to happen." Susan Sontag, "Tuesday, and After," *The New Yorker* (September 24, 2001).

26. James Risen, "U.S. Inaction Seen After Taliban P.O.W.'s Died," *The New York Times* (July 10, 2009).

27. Lambeth, *Air Power Against Terror*, 132–33.

28. On the night of October 19–20, approximately two hundred troops from the army's 3d Battalion, 75th Ranger Regiment had parachuted into the same airfield. The Rangers' principal mission was to support a Delta Force

raid aimed at getting the Taliban leader Mullah Omar. That effort came up empty-handed. After a stay of several hours, C-130s safely extracted the Rangers.

29. Richard W. Stewart, *Operation Enduring Freedom: October 2001–March 2002* (Washington, D.C., [2004]), 19. Stewart was TF Dagger's official historian.

30. Task Force 11 was one of several "black" special forces units participating in Enduring Freedom, their existence classified, their presence not officially acknowledged.

31. Wright et al., *Different Kind of War*, 113–20.

32. Franks, *American Soldier*, 314, 325.

33. Franks, *American Soldier*, 324.

34. "Deputy Secretary Wolfowitz Interview with CNN Late Edition" (December 9, 2001).

35. "Deputy Secretary Wolfowitz Interview with Middle East Broadcasting Center" (December 10, 2001).

36. Franks, *American Soldier*, 315.

37. Donald Rumsfeld, *Known and Unknown* (New York, 2011), 405.

38. "Deputy Secretary Wolfowitz Interview with Los Angeles Times" (December 14, 2001).

39. Charles Krauthammer, "Where Power Talks," *The Washington Post* (January 4, 2002).

40. "Address Before a Joint Session of Congress on the State of the Union" (January 29, 2002).

41. Lambeth, *Air Power Against Terror*, 247–53.

42. The figures come from icasualties.org/oef, accessed March 20, 2015.

43. Wright et al., *Different Kind of War*, 120.

44. The following draws on Sean Naylor, *Not a Good Day to Die* (New York, 2005), which is the definitive account of Operation Anaconda. But see also, Lambeth, *Air Power Against Terror*, 163–200; and Wright et al., *Different Kind of War*, 127–73.

45. Dating from its service in post–World War II Japan, the 187th Infantry Regiment had acquired the nickname Rakkasans. The infantry battalions forming Wiercinski's brigade of the 101st came from that regiment.

46. Naylor, *Not a Good Day*, 120.

47. Lambeth, *Air Power Against Terror*, 194.

48. Brian Knowlton, "U.S. Offensive 'Absolute Success' but More Fighting Seen Ahead," *The New York Times* (March 19, 2002).

13. Kicking Down the Door

1. "Deputy Secretary Wolfowitz Interview with Sam Tannenhaus," *Vanity Fair* (May 9, 2003). In his memoir, Douglas Feith affirms this point, writing that Saddam's alleged possession of weapons of mass destruction "was *not* a cornerstone of our rationale for going to war." WMD merely offered a convenient argument, useful in attempting to persuade skeptics at home and abroad. Douglas J. Feith, *War and Decision* (New York, 2008), 228, emphasis in original.

2. The allusion is to the famous quote by Bush national security adviser Condoleezza Rice making the case for preventive war against Iraq and warning that "we don't want the smoking gun to be a mushroom cloud." *CNN Late Edition with Wolf Blitzer* (September 8, 2002), http://transcripts.cnn.com /TRANSCRIPTS/0209/08/le.00.html, accessed March 28, 2015.

3. Rumsfeld, *Known and Unknown*, 435.

4. "Scott McClellan Holds White House Regular News Briefing" (December 6, 2005).

5. "Remarks by National Security Advisor Condoleezza Rice on Terrorism and Foreign Policy" (April 29, 2002).

6. Max Boot, "The Case for American Empire," *The Weekly Standard* (October 15, 2001).

7. George W. Bush, "Address to the Nation on Iraq from the U.S.S. *Abraham Lincoln*" (May 1, 2003); Dick Cheney, interview on *Meet the Press* (March 16, 2003); Donald Rumsfeld, "Secretary Rumsfeld Media Stakeout" (January 19, 2003); Paul Wolfowitz, "Testimony Before House Appropriations Committee" (March 27, 2003); Douglas J. Feith, "Statement to the Senate Committee on Foreign Relations" (February 11, 2003).

8. Thomas Hobbes, *Leviathan* (rpt., London, 1886), 48.

9. During his confirmation hearings in 2001, Rumsfeld had previewed the logic. The ultimate goal of U.S. national security policy, he testified, "ought to be to be so strong and so powerful that you can dissuade people from doing things they otherwise would do. You do not have to even fight the war." *Nominations Before the Senate Armed Services Committee, First Session, 107th Congress* (January 11, 2001), 55.

10. *Democracy Now* (March 2, 2007), youtube.com/watch?v=SXS3vW47mOE, accessed March 30, 2015.

11. Feith, *War and Decision*, 49.

12. Feith, *War and Decision*, 52.

13. Quoted in Hal Brands, *What Good Is Grand Strategy?* (Ithaca, 2014), 163.

14. John Prados and Christopher Ames, "Was There Even a Decision?" (October 1, 2010), National Security Archive, nsarchive.gwu.edu/NSAEBB /NSAEBB328/, accessed March 31, 2015.

15. Some might suggest that there was a fourth task—making the case internationally that invading Iraq was legitimate and justified. This task fell to Secretary of State Colin Powell, but apart from Powell himself, other senior Bush administration officials did not see it as of very great moment.

16. Philip Reichel, ed., *Handbook of Transnational Crime and Justice* (Thousand Oaks, Calif., 2005), 205.

17. Douglas Feith, "Sovereignty and Anticipatory Self-Defense" (August 24, 2002), papers.rumsfeld.com, accessed April 12, 2005.

18. "President Bush Delivers Graduation Speech at West Point" (June 1, 2002). In September 2002, the White House released a new *National Security Strategy of the United States of America* that embellished these themes.

19. "Downing Street Memo," *Sunday Times* (May 1, 2005). The memo itself, minutes of a meeting between British Prime Minister Tony Blair and his key security advisers, was dated July 23, 2002.

20. "Cheney Cites 'Risks of Inaction' with Iraq," *CNN.com/Inside Politics* (August 27, 2002).

21. Robert C. Byrd and Mary Sharon Hall, *The Senate, 1789–1989*, vol. 1 (Washington, D.C., 1988), 417.

22. Thomas Morrow, "Wheeler Flays F.D.R. Smear of Col. Lindbergh," *Chicago Tribune* (April 26, 1941).

23. In *The New York Review of Books*, the journalist Mark Danner has contributed several acutely insightful essays on Cheney's methods and the results he achieved. They include "In the Darkness of Dick Cheney" (March 6, 2014), "He Remade Our World" (April 3, 2014), and "Cheney: The More Ruthless the Better" (May 8, 2014).

24. Quoted in Thomas K. Adams, *The Army After Next* (Westport, 2006), 136.

25. Franks, *American Soldier,* 331.

26. It was literally the case that PowerPoint slides supplanted more orthodox planning methodologies. Here, too, Rumsfeld was expressing his disdain for military convention. Thomas E. Ricks, *Fiasco* (New York, 2006), 75.

27. Michael R. Gordon and Bernard E. Trainor, *Cobra II* (New York, 2006), 5–7, 22–23; Ricks, *Fiasco,* 42–43.

28. Gordon and Trainor, *Cobra II,* 4, 29, 31–32.

29. Franks, *American Soldier,* 428.

30. Franks, *American Soldier,* 416. Franks devotes over a hundred pages (328–437) to detailing plans and preparations for Operation Iraqi Freedom and barely fifty (478–530) to its actual execution.

31. Most famously, General Eric Shinseki, then serving as army chief of staff, stated publicly in February 2003 that occupying Iraq was likely to require a force of several hundred thousand troops. Senior civilian officials in the Bush administration dismissed this projection as "wildly off the mark."

Eric Schmitt, "Pentagon Contradicts General on Iraq Occupation Force's Size," *The New York Times* (February 28, 2003).

32. With the vote occurring in October 2002, just prior to the off-year elections, the count was 77–23 in the Senate and 296–133 in the House of Representatives. Prior to the Second Persian Gulf War, members of Congress nursing presidential ambitions who had voted against the resolution authorizing the use of force had paid a steep political price. Opposing Desert Storm was subsequently deemed a disqualifying error. This time around, ambitious senators such as Joe Biden, Hillary Clinton, and John Kerry had no intention of suffering a similar fate. All three were among the prominent Democrats who joined Republicans in voting for war.

33. Patrick E. Tyler, "A New Power in the Streets," *The New York Times* (February 17, 2003).

34. Anne E. Kornblut, "President Undeterred by Antiwar Protests," *The Boston Globe* (February 19, 2003).

35. For samples of prescient opposition to war, see Eric S. Margolis, "Iraq Invasion: The Road to Folly," *The American Conservative* (October 7, 2002); and "An Open Letter to the Members of Congress," *The Nation* (October 14, 2002).

36. Max Boot, "The End of Appeasement," *The Weekly Standard* (February 10, 2003).

37. During the campaign to overthrow Saddam, coalition air forces flew over twenty thousand combat sorties, three-fourths of them against Iraqi ground forces. The latter figure reflects the degraded state of Iraqi air defenses and command-and-control capabilities when the war began—there wasn't much left to attack. U.S. forces provided over 90 percent of the aircraft involved. Of the twenty-eight thousand pieces of ordnance expended, over 70 percent were precision guided munitions. The number of fixed-wing aircraft lost to enemy action was one—a U.S. Air Force A-10 Warthog. "Operation Iraqi Freedom—By the Numbers" (April 30, 2003), afhso.af.mil /shared/media/document/AFD-130613-025.pdf, accessed April 18, 2015. This document is a statistical compendium assembled by CENTCOM's air component.

38. "This Will Be a Campaign Unlike Any Other in History," *The Wall Street Journal* (March 22, 2003). The article provides a complete transcript of CENTCOM press briefing.

39. Jim Dwyer, "A Gulf Commander Sees a Longer Road," *The New York Times* (March 28, 2003).

40. Gregory Fontenot et al., *On Point: The United States Army in Operation Iraqi Freedom* (Washington, D.C., 2004), 89. This U.S. Army publication provides a preliminary official history of the Third Persian Gulf War's first phase.

41. Fontenot et al., *On Point*, 339.

42. Franks, *American Soldier*, 524.

43. CENTCOM's OPLAN 1003V broke into four phases. Phase I was "Preparations." Phase II was "Shape the Battlespace." Phase III was "Decisive Operations," which meant getting to Baghdad. Phase IV dealt with post-combat actions. "U.S. Central Command Slide Compilation, ca. August 15, 2002; Top Secret / Polo Step, Tab K," National Security Archive, nsarchive.gwu .edu/NSAEBB/NSAEBB418/, accessed April 15, 2015.

44. It began: "I, General Tommy R. Franks, Commander of Coalition Forces, do hereby proclaim that: Coalition Forces in Iraq have come as liberators, not as conquerors." It went on to promise that the forces under his command would help Iraqis "heal their wounds," while building a representative government and protecting Iraqi oil. Franks, *American Soldier,* 528–29.

45. Roger Roy, "In Free Baghdad, Looters Claim Everything They Can Carry," *Orlando Sentinel* (April 10, 2003).

46. Mark McDonald, Jonathan S. Landay, and Drew Brown, "Chaos Reigns on Streets in Baghdad, Mosul, Kirkuk as Looters Take Everything," Knight Ridder Tribune News Service (April 11, 2003).

47. John Daniszewski and Geoffrey Mohan, "Looters Bring Baghdad New Havoc," *Los Angeles Times* (April 11, 2003).

48. "DoD News Briefing—Secretary Rumsfeld and Gen. Myers" (April 11, 2003).

49. According to rumor, GIs were distributing pornography to Iraqi children and using night vision devices to ogle Iraqi women. "Violent Response: The U.S. Army in Al-Falluja," *Human Rights Watch* (June 2003), 5.

50. Elizabeth Neuffer, "U.S., Iraqis at Odds on Protesters' Deaths," *The Boston Globe* (April 30, 2003); Christine Spolar, "13 Iraqis Killed at Protest, Scores Injured," *Chicago Tribune* (April 30, 2003).

51. In an incident at Mosul two weeks earlier, U.S. Marines had killed ten Iraqi demonstrators. David Rohde, "Clash in Mosul Complicates Already Troubled U.S. Arrival," *The New York Times* (April 15, 2003).

52. William Knarr and Robert Castro, "The Battle for Fallujah," Institute for Defense Analysis (September 2009), 12.

53. "General Jay Garner on Iraq," *BBC Newsnight* (March 19, 2004), transcript at gregpalast.com/bbc-newsnight-reportgeneral-jay-garner-on-iraq/, accessed April 17, 1015.

54. Douglas Feith reputedly wanted Garner simply to "declare Chalabi president." Dov S. Zakheim, *A Vulcan's Tale* (Washington, D.C., 2011), 163. Zakheim was a senior Pentagon official during George W. Bush's first term.

55. The text of both orders is available at the CPA website, iraqcoalition.org /regulations/, accessed April 17, 2015.

56. Ricks, *Fiasco,* 324.

57. "Third Infantry Division Commander Live Briefing from Iraq" (May 15, 2003).

58. "Maj. Gen. Odierno Videoteleconference [*sic*] from Baghdad" (June 18, 2003).

59. "DoD News Briefing—Mr. Di Rita and Gen. Abizaid" (July 16, 2003).

60. "Videoteleconference [*sic*] from Iraq with Maj. Gen. Odierno" (July 25, 2003).

61. "Lt. Gen. Sanchez Briefing on the Confirmation of the Deaths of Uday and Qusay Hussein" (July 23, 2003).

62. "Lt. Gen. Sanchez Interview on CNN" (July 27, 2003).

63. "Briefing on the First Marine Expeditionary Force in Iraq" (September 9, 2003). The speaker was Lieutenant General James T. Conway.

64. "Army Maj. Gen. Swannack, Jr. Video Tele-conference from Baghdad" (November 18, 2003).

65. "Commander, 4th Infantry Division, Maj. Gen. Raymond Odierno, via Teleconference from Tikrit, Iraq" (October 27, 2003).

66. "Live Video Teleconference with General Abizaid" (November 13, 2003).

67. Casualty figures come from icasualty.org, accessed April 23, 2015.

68. "Ambassador Bremer Briefing from Baghdad" (December 14, 2003).

69. "82nd Airborne Division Commanding General's Briefing from Iraq" (January 6, 2004).

70. "4th Infantry Division commanding General's Briefing from Iraq" (January 22, 2004).

71. "Media Availability from Baghdad, Iraq" (December 16, 2003).

72. "Report of the International Committee of the Red Cross (ICRC) on the Treatment by Coalition Forces of Prisoners of War and Other Protected Persons by the Geneva Conventions in Iraq During Arrest, Internment, and Interrogation" (February 2004).

73. Dexter Filkins, "Tough New Tactics by U.S. Tighten Grip on Iraq Towns," *The New York Times* (December 7, 2003).

74. Jeff Wilkinson, "U.S. Blasts Iraqi Homes of Suspects," *The Philadelphia Inquirer* (November 18, 2003).

75. Carl E. Mundy III, "Spare the Rod, Save the Nation," *The New York Times* (December 30, 2003).

76. Brian Bennett et al., "Losing Hearts and Minds," *Time* (December 8, 2003). For a detailed critique of U.S. tactics in this phase of the war, see Ricks, *Fiasco*, 214–69.

77. Josh White, "U.S. Generals in Iraq Were Told of Abuse Early, Inquiry Finds," *The Washington Post* (December 1, 2004).

78. "Article 15-6 Investigation of the 800th Military Police Brigade" ([March 2004]).

79. Ricardo S. Sanchez, *Wiser in Battle* (New York, 2008).

80. Donald P. Wright et al., *On Point II* (Washington, D.C., 2008), 169.

81. L. Paul Bremer, *My Year in Iraq* (New York, 2006).

82. Janis Karpinski, *One Woman's Army* (New York, 2005).

83. Quoted in Ricks, *Fiasco*, 362.

84. Available on icasualties.org, accessed April 24, 2015.

85. Amy Belasco, "The Cost of Iraq, Afghanistan, and other Global War on Terror Operations Since 9/11" (December 8, 2014), 14. This is a report issued by the Congressional Research Service.

86. "Budget Deficit History," usgovinfo.about.com/od/federalbudgetprocess/a/Budget-Deficit-History.htm, accessed April 24, 2015.

87. George W. Bush, "Second Inaugural Address" (January 20, 2005).

14. How This Ends

1. The breadth of the mission statement drafted by Casey and U.S. Ambassador John Negroponte suggests the shift away from the certainties that had informed Operation Iraqi Freedom at the outset. It read: "To help the Iraqi people build a new Iraq, at peace with its neighbors, with a constitutional, representative government that respects human rights and possesses security forces sufficient to maintain domestic order, and deny Iraq as a safe haven for terrorists." Quoted in George W. Casey Jr., *Strategic Reflections* (Washington, D.C., 2012), 26.

2. U.S. Senate, Committee on Armed Services, "Nomination of Gen George W. Casey, Jr., USA for Reappointment to the Grade of General and to be Commander, Multi-National Force, Iraq" (June 24, 2005).

3. Casey, *Strategic Reflections*, 20.

4. As late as December 2004, Casey was still publically predicting mission accomplishment by December of the following year. John D. Banusiewicz, "Bombs Create Illusion of Powerful Insurgency, Commander Says," *DoD News* (December 16, 2004).

5. "Iraq Insurgency in 'Last Throes,' Cheney Says," CNN.com (June 20, 2005).

6. Iraqi Kurds, comprising roughly one-fifth of Iraq's total population, were also happy. Without raising much of a fuss, they had unofficially but effectively seceded, establishing an autonomous and mostly peaceful Kurdistan in territory that was nominally northern Iraq. If the United States had invaded Iraq in order to let Iraqi Kurds go their own way, the war rated as a success.

7. United States Senate, Committee on Armed Services, "U.S. Military Strategy and Operations in Iraq" (June 23, 2005).

8. United States Senate, Committee on Armed Services, "U.S. Military Strategy and Operations in Iraq" (September 29, 2005).

9. United States Senate, Committee on Armed Services, "Iraq, Afghanistan, and the Global War on Terrorism" (August 3, 2006).

10. "Iraq Index" (December 21, 2006), brookings.edu/fp/saban/iraq /index20061221.pdf, accessed May 3, 2015.

11. In February 2005, General Casey testified that coalition forces had taken fifteen thousand insurgents out of circulation over the previous year. This was thousands more than the estimated number of insurgents said to exist at that time. Either U.S. intelligence estimates were wrong or U.S. forces were creating more "terrorists" than they were eliminating.

12. Robert F. Worth, "Blast at Shiite Shrine Sets off Sectarian Fury in Iraq," *The New York Times* (February 23, 2006).

13. Casey, *Strategic Reflections,* 93, 104.

14. Michael R. Gordon, "U.S. Central Command Charts Sharp Movement of the Civil Conflict in Iraq Toward Chaos," *The New York Times* (November 1, 2006). The print edition of the news article reprinted in color a leaked PowerPoint briefing slide.

15. Larissa MacFarquhar, "Midge's Mash Note," *The New Yorker* (November 3, 2003). In 2002, Rumsfeld, then seventy years old, had landed on *People* magazine's list of "sexiest men alive."

16. Fred Kaplan, *The Insurgents* (New York, 2013), 223–43.

17. Casey himself was "kicked upstairs" to become army chief of staff.

18. U.S. troop strength during the Korean War peaked at 326,000; for Vietnam, the equivalent figure was 536,000.

19. In the summer of 2006, Casey requested that the 172nd Stryker Brigade be extended for four months beyond its designated redeployment date. Approving the request, Secretary of Defense Rumsfeld felt obliged to visit the brigade's home station at Fort Wainwright, Alaska, to explain his decision to affected families.

20. William C. Hix and Kalev Sepp, "Assessing Counterinsurgency: Iraq War, 2004–5," unpublished paper (2015). Hix and Sepp had advised Casey on counterinsurgency matters.

21. Lawrence F. Kaplan, "Letting Go," *The New Republic* (July 10, 2006).

22. Hix and Sepp, "Assessing Counterinsurgency."

23. Stjepan G. Mestrovic, *The "Good Soldier" on Trial* (New York, 2009), 57–65.

24. Raffi Khatchadourian, "The Kill Company," *The New Yorker* (July 6, 2009).

25. The three were Generals John Galvin, Carl Vuono, and Henry Shelton. Petraeus's father-in-law was General William Knowlton.

26. Daniel Bolger, *Why We Lost* (Boston, 2015), 181.

27. Rick Atkinson, "A Long and Blinding Road to Battle in Iraq," *The Washington Post* (March 7, 2004).

28. Michael Gordon, "101st Airborne Scores Success in Reconstruction of Northern Iraq," *The New York Times* (September 4, 2003).

29. A research paper prepared by three serving military officers attending the Naval Postgraduate School in Monterey, California concluded that "insurgent organization and violence increased throughout the year" while Petraeus's troops were occupying Mosul. Insurgent violence and influence increased even further the following year. By 2005, Mosul was "a city under siege." Jarett D. Broemmel, Shannon E. Nielsen, and Terry L. Clark, "An Analysis of Counterinsurgency in Iraq: Mosul, Ramadi, and Samarra from 2003–2005" (unpublished M.A. thesis, Naval Postgraduate School, 2006), 27, 52, 68. The authors were majors in the U.S. Army.

30. *Newsweek* (July 5, 2004).

31. Within a month of its appearance, internet users had reportedly downloaded FM 3-24 1.5 million times. The University of Chicago Press quickly published a paperback version of the text, to which Petraeus himself appended an endorsement, in effect blurbing his own book: "Surely a manual that's on the bedside table of the president, vice president, secretary of defense, 21 of 25 members of the Senate Armed Services Committee and many others deserves a place at your bedside too."

32. Daniel J. Boorstin, *The Image, or What Happened to the American Dream* (New York, 1962).

33. David Howell Petraeus, "The American Military and the Lessons of Vietnam" (unpublished PhD dissertation, Princeton University, 1987), 13.

34. United States Senate, Committee on Armed Services, "Nomination of LTG David H. Petraeus, USA, to be General and Commander, Multinational Forces, Iraq" (January 23, 2007).

35. United States Senate, Committee on Armed Services, "The Situation in Iraq and Progress Made by the Government of Iraq in Meeting Benchmarks" (September 11, 2007).

36. Petraeus himself understood this. "The Washington clock is moving more rapidly than the Baghdad clock," he remarked to an interviewer in April 2007. "So we're obviously trying to speed up the Baghdad clock a bit and to produce some progress on the ground that can, perhaps . . . put a little more time on the Washington clock." Thomas E. Ricks, "Politics Collide with Iraq Realities," *The Washington Post* (April 8, 2007). In his memoir, Robert Gates, who had succeeded Rumsfeld as defense secretary, used an identical comparison to describe the surge. "My role was to figure out how to buy time," he wrote, to figure out "how to slow down the Washington clock, and how to speed up the Baghdad clock." Robert M. Gates, *Duty* (New York, 2014), 49.

37. Victor Davis Hanson, "Iraq, Round Three," *Policy Review* (November/December 2008).

38. Max Boot, "We Are Winning, We Haven't Won," *The Weekly Standard* (February 4, 2008).

39. Jason Campbell, Michael O'Hanlon, and Amy Unikewicz, "The State of Iraq: An Update," *The New York Times* (December 22, 2007).

40. Frederick W. Kagan and Kimberly Kagan, "The Patton of Counterinsurgency," *The Weekly Standard* (March 10, 2008).

41. Jeffrey Bell, "The Petraeus Promotion," *The Weekly Standard* (May 5, 2008).

42. For a sympathetic journalist's account, see George Packer, "The Lesson of Tal Afar," *The New Yorker* (April 10, 2006).

43. Jim Michaels, "An Army Colonel's Gamble Pays Off in Iraq," *USA Today* (May 1, 2007).

44. For MacFarland's own account, see Niel Smith and Sean MacFarland, "Anbar Awakens: The Tipping Point," *Military Review* (March–April 2008). But see also Gian Gentile, *Wrong Turn* (New York, 2013), 87–88, 96–98; and, Douglas Porch, *Counterinsurgency* (Cambridge, 2013), 309.

45. Gentile, *Wrong Turn,* 89.

46. Gentile, *Wrong Turn,* 101. For a commander's perspective on that campaign, see Stanley McChrystal, *My Share of the Task* (New York, 2013), chs. 7–15.

47. Daniel P. Bolger, "The Truth About the Wars," *The New York Times* (November 10, 2014).

48. John McCain and Joe Lieberman, "The Surge Worked," *The Wall Street Journal* (January 10, 2008).

49. "A pursuit is an offensive operation against a retreating enemy force. It follows a successful attack or exploitation and is ordered when the enemy cannot conduct an organized defense and attempts to disengage. The object of the pursuit is destruction of the opposing force." U.S. Army, FM 100-5 *Operations* (Washington, D.C., 1993), 7–9.

50. The sobriquet awarded to Petraeus was either admiring or sardonic depending on the point of view of the speaker. Mark Bowden, "The Professor of War," *Vanity Fair* (May 2010).

51. COIN enthusiasts were soon promoting visions of what they unhesitatingly called "global counterinsurgency." The proper application of COIN principles, wrote Colonel James Johnson, would enable the United States to create "an environment of political, ideological and economic freedom across the globe." "A Global Counter-Insurgency Plan for the War on Terror," *CTC Sentinel* (June 15, 2008). See also Colonel Daniel S. Roper, "Global Counterinsurgency: Strategic Clarity for the Long War," *Parameters* (Autumn 2008).

52. "Obama's Speech on Iraq" (March 18, 2008), cfr.org/elections/obamas-speech-iraq-march-2008/p15761, accessed May 11, 2015.

53. "Obama's Speech Against the Iraq War" (October 2, 2002); "Remarks in Washington, D.C.: 'The War We Need to Win'" (August 1, 2007).

54. George W. Bush, "Remarks at the United States Military Academy at West Point" (December 9, 2008).

55. "Remarks on Presenting the Presidential Medal of Freedom at the Department of State" (January 15, 2009).

56. Available at icasualties.org.

57. Brookings Iraq Index (December 11, 2009), brookings.edu/~/media /Centers/saban/iraq-index/index20091211.PDF, accessed May 13, 2015.

58. "Four Killed in Baghdad Market Blast," Agence France Presse (June 1, 2009); "Nine Killed in Baghdad Café Bombing," Agence France Presse (June 4, 2009); "Iraq: Bombing of Minibus in Shiite Area Kills 9," Associated Press (June 8, 2009); "Car Bomb in Iraq Kills About 30 People," Associated Press (June 10, 2009); "Iraq Truck Bomb Kills 64," Agence France Presse (June 20, 2009); "Iraqis Hunt for Relatives in Rubble of Deadly Truck Bombing," Agence France Presse (June 21, 2009); "31 Killed in Iraq Attacks as U.S. Pullback Looms," Agence France Presse (June 22, 2009); "Bomb Strikes Shiite Market in Baghdad, Killing 69," Associated Press (June 24, 2009); "Motorcycle Bombs Kill 20 in Baghdad," Associated Press (June 26, 2009); "Iraqis Celebrate US Pullback but Bombing Kills 33," Associated Press (June 30, 2009).

59. Franks, American Soldier, 400.

60. Casey, Strategic Reflections, 68.

61. A third issue receiving attention was that of removing equipment—some 2.8 million tons worth, in 88,000 shipping containers, along with 41,000 vehicles of various types. "DoD News Briefing with Lt. Gen Webster from Kuwait" (April 2, 2010).

62. Michael R. Gordon and Bernard E. Trainor, The Endgame (New York, 2012), 560–70, 573–74.

63. "DoD News Briefing with Gen. Ray Odierno from the Pentagon Briefing Room" (May 8, 2009).

64. The United States was demanding that any U.S. troops remaining in Iraq beyond the December 31, 2011, deadline for withdrawal to which the Bush administration had agreed should be immune from Iraqi law. The government of Iraq rejected this infringement of national sovereignty.

65. Joseph B. Treaster, "U.S. Forces out of Vietnam; Hanoi Frees the Last P.O.W.," The New York Times (March 30, 1973).

66. "Obama Gives Top U.S. Commander in Iraq Understated Welcome Home," Associated Press (December 20, 2011); "U.S. General Brings Baghdad Standard Home," CNN.com (December 20, 2011).

15. Government in a Box

1. "Remarks in Cairo," June 4, 2009.

2. Julian E. Barnes, "U.S. Calls Iraq the Priority," *Los Angeles Times* (December 12, 2007).

3. Amy Belasco, "Troop Levels in the Afghan and Iraq Wars, FY2001–FY2012: Cost and Other Potential Issues" (July 2, 2009). This is a Congressional Research Service report.

4. Available at icasualties.org/oef.

5. Barfield, *Afghanistan*, 293–305.

6. UN agencies included the Mine Action Coordination Centre of Afghanistan, the United Nations Information and Communication Technologies Task Force, the United Nations Framework Convention on Climate Change, and the United Nations Common Supplier Database. For a complete list, see the website of the United Nations Assistance Mission in Afghanistan, http://unama.unmissions.org, accessed May 20, 2015. The United Kingdom, its army having failed on multiple previous occasions to pacify Afghanistan, contributed by far the largest ISAF contingent, followed by Germany, France, Canada, and Italy. See the "ISAF Placemat" for January 2009, at nato.int/isaf/placemats_archive/2009-01-12-ISAF-Placemat.pdf, accessed May 20, 2015.

7. In 2007, for example, Afghanistan ranked 172nd out of 179 on Transparency International's annual corruption index, coming in slightly ahead of Iraq and Somalia. transparency.org/research/cpi/cpi_2007/0/, accessed May 22, 2015.

8. Barfield, *Afghanistan*, 312–20.

9. Carlotta Gall, "Convey Crash Sparks Kabul Riots," *The New York Times* (May 29, 2006); Rachel Morarjee, "Riots Breach Kabul 'Island'," *The Christian Science Monitor* (May 30, 2006); Carlotta Gall, "Ruffians Blamed in Afghan Raids," *The International Herald Tribune* (June 1, 2006).

10. Pamela Constable, "Dozens Are Killed in Afghan Fighting," *The Washington Post* (May 23, 2006).

11. In 2006, coalition airstrikes killed 116 civilians, a number that rose to 321 the following year. Human Rights Watch, "'Troops in Contact': Airstrikes and Civilian Deaths in Afghanistan" (September 2008), 14.

12. The reference to confusing command and control alluded to the fact that NATO, CENTCOM, and U.S. Special Operations Command—each headed by a different American four-star—each "owned" part of the action in Afghanistan. Unity of command took a backseat to the protection of bureaucratic turf.

13. Gates, *Duty*, 199, 209, 211, emphasis in original.

14. "A Counter-Insurgency Takes a Long Time, Longer Than We Thought," *Spiegel Online* (November 8, 2008).

15. Dan Rather, "The Commander," *Dan Rather Reports* (January 6, 2009).

16. "Statement on United States Troop Levels in Afghanistan" (February 17, 2009).

17. "Remarks on United States Military and Diplomatic Strategies for Afghanistan and Pakistan" (March 27, 2009).

18. McChrystal, *My Share of the Task*, 162.

19. A notable misstep occurred in 2004 when McChrystal recommended a deceased army ranger, former NFL football player Pat Tillman, for a posthumous award for gallantry, concealing the fact that Tillman had died from friendly fire.

20. John Barry, "The Hidden General," *Newsweek* (June 25, 2006).

21. Dexter Filkins, "Stanley McChrystal's Long War," *The New York Times Magazine* (October 14, 2009).

22. Elisabeth Bumiller and Mark Mazzetti, "General Steps from the Shadows," *The New York Times* (May 13, 2009).

23. Ann Scott Tyson, "Manhunter to Take on a Wider Mission," *The Washington Post* (May 13, 2009).

24. Evan Thomas, "General McChrystal's Plan for Afghanistan," *Newsweek* (September 25, 2009).

25. Mark Thompson and Aryn Baker, "Starting Anew," *Time* (July 20, 2009).

26. Gates, *Duty*, 352–53.

27. "COMISAF's Initial Assessment" (August 30, 2009), washingtonpost.com /wp-dyn/content/article/2009/09/21/AR2009092100110.html, accessed May 25, 2015.

28. In his first nine seasons playing for the Chicago Bulls in the NBA, Jordan had averaged over 30 points per game. In his one season as an outfielder with the Double-A minor league Birmingham Barons, he hit .202.

29. Michael Gerson, "U.S. Has Reasons to Hope for Afghanistan," *The Washington Post* (September 4, 2009).

30. No one claimed responsibility for the leak. Secretary of Defense Gates fingered a member of McChrystal's staff, acting "out of impatience." Gates, *Duty*, 368.

31. John F. Burns, "McChrystal Rejects Scaling Down Afghan Military Aims," *The New York Times* (October 1, 2009).

32. The Eikenberry cables are readily available online at documents.nytimes .com/eikenberry-s-memos-on-the-strategy-in-afghanistan, accessed May 31, 2015.

33. "Remarks by the President in Address to the Nation on the Way Forward in Afghanistan and Pakistan" (December 1, 2009).

34. Amy Belasco, "The Cost of Iraq, Afghanistan, and Other Global War on Terror Operations Since 9/11" (December 8, 2014). Appendix A provides details.

35. Headquarters, International Security Assistance Force, Kabul Afghanistan, SUBJECT: Tactical Directive (July 6, 2009). This two-page document explains the rationale for the more restrictive rules of engagement that McChrystal was imposing.

36. Dexter Filkins, "Afghan Offensive Is New War Model," *The New York Times* (February 12, 2010).

37. Michelle Flournoy, undersecretary of defense for policy, testifying before the Senate Armed Services Committee, "Briefing on Operation Moshtarak in Helmand Province, Afghanistan" (February 22, 2010).

38. Rod Nordland, "12 in Allied Forces Die in Afghanistan," *The New York Times* (February 19, 2010).

39. Zoe Magee, "Afghan Flag Raised Over Marja After Battling Taliban for 12 Days," ABCNews.go.com (February 25, 2010).

40. Rod Nordland, "Taliban Hit Back With a Campaign of Intimidation," *The New York Times* (March 18, 2010).

41. Rajiv Chandrasekaran, " 'Still a Long Way to Go' for U.S. Operation in Marja, Afghanistan," *The Washington Post* (June 10, 2010).

42. Bing West, *The Wrong War* (New York, 2011), 223.

43. The individual appointed to govern liberated Marja became an ironic symbol of the obstacles to honest and competent administration. He turned out to be a convicted felon who had served a four-year prison term in Germany. "Officials: New Marjah Leader's Criminal Past to Be Probed," *USA Today* (March 6, 2010).

44. To appreciate the frustrations that the Marines experienced, see Ben Anderson's superb 2011 HBO documentary *The Battle of Marjah*, youtube.com/watch?v=b9Pq5JZ2Fd8, accessed May 28, 2015.

45. Todd Pitman, "Marines in Marjah Face Full-Blown Insurgency," *The Boston Globe* (October 8, 2010).

46. "CFR Events: HBO History Makers Series with Stanley McChrystal" (October 6, 2011).

47. Michael Hastings, "The Runaway General," *Rolling Stone* (July 8, 2010).

48. Dan Lamothe, "Inside the Stunning Fall and War-Crimes Investigation of an Army Green Beret War Hero," *The Washington Post* (May 19, 2015).

49. Graham Bowley and Matthew Rosenberg, "Video Inflames a Delicate Moment for U.S. in Afghanistan," *The New York Times* (January 12, 2012).

50. Mark Boal, "The Kill Team," *Rolling Stone* (April 14, 2011).

51. Harry D. Tunnell IV, *Red Devils: Tactical Perspectives from Iraq* (n.p., 2006), 53.

52. Anna Mulrine, "Pentagon Had Red Flags About Command Climate in 'Kill Team' Stryker Brigade," *Christian Science Monitor* (October 28, 2010).

53. Memorandum for the Honorable John McHugh, Subject: Open Door Policy—Report from a Tactical Commander (August 20, 2010), michaelyon-online.com/images/pdf/secarmy_redacted-redux.pdf, accessed June 2, 2015.

54. Rajiv Chandrasekaran, "Petraeus Reviews Directive Meant to Limit Afghan Civilian Deaths," *Washington Post* (July 9, 2010).

55. "General Petraeus Issues Updated Tactical Directive" (August 4, 2010), rs.nato.int/article/isaf-releases/general-petraeus-issues-updated-tactical-directive-emphasizes-disciplined-use-of-force.html, accessed June 1, 2015. This NATO website provides unclassified extracts from Petraeus's classified directive, dated August 1, 2010, emphasis in the original.

56. Bob Woodward, *Obama's Wars* (New York, 2010), 346.

57. As measured by "weapons releases," ISAF air strikes increased by 22 percent from 2009 to 2010, with an additional 6 percent the following year. "Combined Forces Air Component Commander, 2007–2012 Airpower Statistics" (October 31, 2012), wired.com/2012/11/drones-afghan-air-war/, accessed June 5, 2015.

58. Rajiv Chandrasekaran, "U.S. Deploying Heavily Armored Battle Tanks for First Time in Afghan War," *The Washington Post* (November 19, 2010).

59. "Kill/Capture," *Frontline* (May 10, 2011). The quotation is from John Nagl, who had collaborated in drafting FM 3-24.

60. Tim Foxley, "How Many Taliban Are There?" *Afghanhindsight* (November 2012), afghanhindsight.wordpress.com/2012/11/08/how-many-taliban-are-there/, accessed June 7, 2015.

61. Susan D. Chesser, *Afghanistan Casualties: Military Forces and Civilians* (December 6, 2012). This is a Congressional Research Service report.

62. The number of such episodes increased from five in 2010 to sixteen in 2011 and then to forty-four the following year. Bill Roggio and Lisa Lundquist, "Green-on-Blue Attacks in Afghanistan: The Data," *The Long War Journal* (April 8, 2015).

63. "U.S. Military Casualties—Operation Enduring Freedom (OEF) Casualty Summary by Month," dmdc.osd.mil/dcas/pages/report_oef_month.xhtml, accessed June 7, 2015.

64. United Nations Office on Drugs and Crime, *Afghanistan Opium Survey 2014* (November 2014), 60.

65. Joel Brinkley, "Money Pit: The Monstrous Failure of U.S. Aid to Afghanistan," *World Affairs* (January–February 2013).

66. Transparency International, *Corruptions Perceptions Index, 2013,* transparency.org/cpi2013/results, accessed June 6, 2015.

67. A web search that combines "Afghan security forces" with "work in prog-

ress" yields thousands of reports, articles, and news stories using the latter phrase to describe the former between 2007 and 2015.

68. "Address to the Nation on the Drawdown of United States Military Personnel in Afghanistan" (June 22, 2011).

69. Ben Anderson, "TIA: This Is Afghanistan," *Port* (August 14, 2013).

70. "Statement by the President on the End of the Combat Mission in Afghanistan" (December 28, 2014).

16. Entropy

1. "Remarks by the President on the Way Forward in Afghanistan" (June 22, 2011).

2. "Secretary of Defense Speech" (February 25, 2011).

3. "Remarks by the President at the United States Military Academy Commencement Ceremony" (May 28, 2014).

4. "Remarks in Cairo" (June 4, 2009).

5. By 2015, more than 350,000 Israelis were living in the occupied territories, with the rate of settlement increasing in recent years. Jodi Rudoren and Jeremy Ashkenas, "Netanyahu and the Settlements," *The New York Times* (March 12, 2015).

6. Jodi Rudoren, "Netanyahu Says No to Statehood for Palestinians," *The New York Times* (March 16, 2015).

7. According to some projections, BDS was likely to cost the Israeli economy billions. See, for example, John Reed, "Israel: A New Kind of War," *Financial Times* (June 12, 2015). Whatever its economic impact, BDS generated outrage tinged with panic among Israel's supporters. See for example the series of reports in *Commentary* magazine at commentarymagazine.com/topic/bds-movement/, accessed June 15, 2015.

8. The book that first violated and thereby destroyed that taboo was John J. Mearsheimer and Stephen M. Walt, *The Israel Lobby* (New York, 2007).

9. For a complete inventory, see Justin Elliott, "Netanyahu Gets More Standing Ovations Than Obama," *Salon* (May 24, 2015).

10. Uri Avnery, "The Speech," *Gush Shalom* (March 6, 2015).

11. *The Daily Show with Jon Stewart* (March 3, 2015), thedailyshow.cc.com/videos/p87z5f/bibi-s-big-adventure--the-media-comeback-kid, accessed June 14, 2015.

12. John M. McHugh and Raymond T. Odierno, "On the Posture of the United States Army" (March 11, 2015).

13. William R. Levesque, "Gen. Joseph Votel Takes Over U.S. Special Operations Command During Ceremony in Tampa," *Tampa Bay Times* (August 28, 2014).

14. Mark Bowden, "1980 Iran Incident Was Our Most Successful Failure," *The Philadelphia Inquirer* (May 9, 2010).

15. In 2015, the British Army consisted of eighty-two thousand soldiers, with the government of Prime Minister David Cameron promising further cuts.

16. Nick Turse, "A Shadow War in 150 Countries," *TomDispatch* (January 20, 2015).

17. Michael P. Kreuzer, "Remotely Piloted Aircraft: Evolution, Diffusion, and the Future of Air Warfare" (unpublished PhD dissertation, Princeton University, 2014), 66–70.

18. Rumsfeld, *Known and Unknown*, 630.

19. Scott MacLeod, "Behind Gaddafi's Diplomatic Turnaround," *Time* (May 18, 2006).

20. Gaddafi was much taken with the American secretary of state, referring to her as "my darling black African woman." In an interview, he professed to be "very proud of the way she leans back and gives orders to the Arab leaders." Gaddafi continued: "Yes, Leezza, Leezza, Leezza. . . . I love her very much." Helene Cooper, "Isolation Over, Libyan Leader Meets with Rice," *The New York Times* (September 5, 2008).

21. "Libya Protests: Defiant Gaddafi Refuses to Quit," BBC News (February 22, 2011).

22. "Testimony to Senate Foreign Relations Committee" (March 2, 2011).

23. Barack Obama, "Remarks on the Situation in Libya" (March 18, 2011).

24. Major General Margaret Woodward, "Defending America's Vital National Interests in Africa" (September 21, 2011).

25. North Atlantic Treaty Organization, "Operation Unified Protector Final Mission Stats" (November 2, 2011), nato.int/nato_static/assets/pdf/pdf _2011_11/20111108_111107-factsheet_up_factsfigures_en.pdf, accessed June 16, 2015; Florence Gaub, *The North Atlantic Treaty Organization and Libya: Reviewing Operation Unified Protector* (Carlisle Barracks, 2013), 7.

26. Thomas Harding, "Col. Gaddafi Killed: Convoy Bombed by Drone Flown by Pilot in Las Vegas," *The Telegraph* (October 20, 2011).

27. Corbett Daly, "Clinton on Qaddafi: 'We Came, We Saw, He Died,'" *CBS News* (October 20, 2011).

28. "Remarks on the Death of Former Leader Muammar Abu Minyar al-Qadhafi of Libya" (October 20, 2011).

29. Alan J. Kuperman, "Obama's Libya Debacle," *Foreign Affairs* (March/April 2015).

30. "The President's News Conference with King Abdullah II of Jordan in Amman, Jordan" (March 22, 2013).

31. Mark Landler, "Obama Threatens Force Against Syria," *The New York Times* (August 20, 2012).

32. Chuck Todd, "The White House Walk-and-Talk That Changed Obama's Mind on Syria," *NBC News* (August 31, 2013).

33. Jodi Rudoren, "U.S. Backing of Russian Plan Leaves a Wary Israel Focusing on Self-Reliance," *The New York Times* (September 12, 2013).

34. Thom Shanker and Lauren D'Avolio, "Former Defense Secretaries Criticize Obama on Syria," *The New York Times* (September 18, 2013).

35. "Kerry's Remarks on Chemical Weapons in Syria," *The New York Times* (August 30, 2013).

36. Andy Borowitz, "Moderate Syrian Rebel Application Form," *The New Yorker* (June 27, 2014).

37. Helene Cooper, "Few U.S.-Trained Syrians Still Fight ISIS, Senators Told," *The New York Times* (September 16, 2015).

38. Karen Yourish et al., "Death in Syria," *The New York Times* (September 14, 2015); "Syria's Refugee Crisis in Numbers," *Amnesty International* (September 4, 2015).

39. Eric Schmitt and Neil MacFarquhar, "Russia Expands Fleet in Syria with Jets That Can Attack Targets on Ground," *The New York Times* (September 21, 2015).

40. For a critical, yet balanced account of the U.S.-Pakistani relationship with all its ups and downs, see Husain Haqqani, *Magnificent Delusions* (New York, 2013).

41. Richard Holbrooke may have been the first to use the term. In a speech delivered in February 2009 at Munich, just beginning his ill-fated term as Obama's special envoy to Afghanistan and Pakistan, Holbrooke riffed on "the problem AfPak, as in Afghanistan Pakistan." The use of the term was "not just an effort to save eight syllables," he said. "It is an attempt to indicate and imprint in our DNA the fact that there is one theater of war, straddling an ill-defined border, the Durand Line, and that on the western side of that border, NATO and other forces are able to operate. On the eastern side, it's the sovereign territory of Pakistan. But it is on the eastern side of this ill-defined border that the international terrorist movement is located." Michael Quinion, *World Wide Words*, worldwidewords.org/turnsofphrase/tp-afp1.htm, accessed June 18, 2015.

42. Greg Miller, "Plan for Hunting Terrorists Signals U.S. Intends to Keep Adding Names to Kill Lists," *The Washington Post* (October 23, 2012).

43. "CIA Drone Strikes in Pakistan, 2004–Present," *The Bureau of Investigative Journalism* (June 2015).

44. On the unpopularity of U.S. drone operations among Pakistanis, see the polling data at *Pew Research Center Global Attitudes and Trends,* pewglobal.org/question-search/?qid=225&cntIDs=&stdIDs=, accessed June 19, 2015.

45. "U.S. Strikes in Yemen, 2002 to Present," *The Bureau of Investigative Journalism* (June 2015).

46. "U.S. Strikes in Somalia, 2007–Present," *The Bureau of Investigative Journalism* (June 2015). For even more detail on Obama era drone operations, see "The Drone Papers," *The Intercept* (n.d. [October 2015]), theintercept.com /drone-papers/, accessed October 29, 2015.

47. James Kitfield, "5 Takeaways from the U.S. Special Ops Raids in Somalia and Libya," *Defense One* (October 8, 2013).

48. Murtaza Husain, "Retired General: Drones Create More Terrorists Than They Kill," *The Intercept* (July 16, 2015). The officer referred to was army Lieutenant General Michael Flynn, an intelligence specialist.

49. In his important book *Kill Chain* (New York, 2015), Andrew Cockburn makes precisely this point.

50. A point made by Malise Ruthven, "Inside the Islamic State," *The New York Review of Books* (July 9, 2015).

51. For the original AFRICOM mission statement, see Major General Buz Altshuler, "United States Africa Command" (October 16, 2008).

52. The AFRICOM AOR was formed out of countries previously falling under the purview of United States European Command, Central Command, and Pacific Command. Although part of Africa, Egypt remained within the CENTCOM AOR.

53. Nick Turse, *Tomorrow's Battlefield* (Chicago, 2015), 90.

54. "United States Africa Command: Mission," africom.mil/about-the -command, June 20, 2015.

55. Turse, *Tomorrow's Battlefield*, 3.

56. Michael M. Phillips, "New Way the U.S. Projects Power Around the Globe: Commandos," *The Wall Street Journal* (April 24, 2015).

57. United States Africa Command, "2012 Posture Statement" (March 1, 2012).

58. For all of these developments, the best primer to date is Turse, *Tomorrow's Battlefield*.

59. Eric Schmitt, "Elite U.S. Troops Helping Africans Fight Terror," *The New York Times* (May 27, 2014).

60. For further elucidation, see Lieutenant Colonel Jack Marr et al., "Human Terrain Mapping: A Critical First Step to Winning the COIN Fight," *Military Review* (March–April 2008).

61. Eliza Griswold, "The Next Front," *The New York Times Magazine* (June 15, 2014).

62. Adam Nossiter, "Soldiers Overthrow Mali Government in Setback for Democracy in Africa," *The New York Times* (March 22, 2012). The coup leaders were unhappy with the government's effort to quash a rebellion in northern Mali instigated by Toureg tribesmen, who had fled Libya in the way of Gaddafi's overthrow. The Toureg had hired themselves out to Gaddafi as

mercenaries. With his removal, there were no more paychecks, so it was time to head home.

63. Adam Nossiter, "In Nigeria, More Attacks on Militants," *The New York Times* (May 17, 2013).

64. Turse, *Tomorrow's Battlefield*, 100.

65. "Burkina Faso," africom.mil/africa/west-africa/burkina-faso, accessed September 29, 2015.

66. Turse, *Tomorrow's Battlefield*, 37.

17. Iraq, Again

1. Michael R. Gordon and Duraid Adnan, "Brazen Attacks at Prisons Raise Worries of Al Qaeda's Strength in Iraq," *The New York Times* (July 23, 2013).

2. In February 2014, Al Qaeda disowned ISIS, which now gained recognition as a distinct entity. Liz Sly, "Al Qaeda Disavows Ties to Hard-Line Iraqi-Syrian Affiliate Fighting Assad," *The Washington Post* (February 4, 2014).

3. "Remarks at Solo Press Availability" (January 5, 2014).

4. "Remarks by Secretary Hagel at Brooke Army Medical Center in San Antonio, Texas" (January 8, 2014).

5. Richard Sisk, "U.S. to Ramp Up Arms Deliveries to Iraq," Military.com (January 6, 2014).

6. Andrew Tilghman and Jeff Schogol, "How Did 800 ISIS Fighters Rout Two Iraqi Divisions?" *Military Times* (June 12, 2014).

7. Liz Sly and Ahmed Ramadan, "Insurgents Seize Iraqi City of Mosul as Security Forces Flee," *The Washington Post* (June 10, 2014).

8. Martin Matishak and Alexander Bolton, "McCain: Obama's Entire National Security Team Should Resign over Iraq," *The Hill* (June 12, 2014).

9. Frederick Kagan, "Put Out This Fire," New York *Daily News* (June 15, 2014).

10. Max Boot, "Obama's Iraq," *The Weekly Standard* (June 23, 2014).

11. Kagan, "Put Out This Fire."

12. "Remarks on the Situation in Iraq and an Exchange with Reporters" (June 19, 2014).

13. "Press Briefing with Rear Adm. Kirby in the Pentagon Briefing Room" (June 27, 2014).

14. "Statement from Pentagon Press Secretary, Rear Admiral John Kirby on Additional Security Forces to Iraq" (June 30, 2014).

15. "Statement by the President" (August 7, 2014).

16. "U.S. Military ISIS Air Strikes in Iraq: Day-by-Day Breakdown," *The Guardian* (September 3, 2014). This article provides CENTCOM data on sorties and targets.

17. "Department of Defense Press Briefing by Lt. Gen. Mayville in the Pentagon Briefing Room" (August 11, 2014).

18. "Statement by the President on ISIL" (September 10, 2014).

19. President Obama neither requested nor received congressional approval to begin this military operation, citing as sufficient the Authorization for Use of Military Force passed on September 14, 2001, in response to the 9/11 attacks. In February 2015, Obama went through the motions of asking Congress for a specific authorization. Congress did not act on that request, implicitly ceding to the president the authority to interpret the September 2001 law however he wished.

20. The first U.S. airstrike in Syria occurred on September 22, 2014. To give the operation an Arab coloration, aircraft from Bahrain, Jordan, Qatar, Saudi Arabia, and the United Arab Emirates participated in a supporting role.

21. "Department of Defense Press Briefing by General Austin in the Pentagon Press Briefing Room" (October 17, 2014).

22. In August, the number was 211; by December, it was 1,867. "Combined Forces Air Component Commander, 2010–2015 Airpower Statistics" (May 31, 2015), www.defense.gov/home/features/2014/0814_iraq/docs/31%20May%202015.pdf, accessed July 3, 2015.

23. Micah Zenko, "Chart: The Airstrikes in Iraq and Syria vs. Previous Military Campaigns," Defense One (July 6, 2015).

24. Anthony H. Cordesman, "The Air War Against the Islamic State" (October 29, 2014), csis.org/publication/air-war-against-islamic-state-need-adequacy-resources, accessed July 5, 2015.

25. "Department of Defense Press Briefing by General Austin," (October 17, 2014).

26. Loveday Morris, "The U.S. Military Is Back Training Troops in Iraq, but It's a Little Different This Time," The Washington Post (January 8, 2015); Rod Nordland, "U.S. Soldiers, Back in Iraq, Find Security Forces in Disrepair," The New York Times (April 4, 2015).

27. Sebastian Payne, "Gen. Martin Dempsey: U.S. Called in Apache Helicopters to Protect Baghdad Airport," The Washington Post (October 12, 2014).

28. Julian E. Barnes, "U.S., Iraq Prepare Offensive to Retake Mosul from Islamic State," The Wall Street Journal (January 22, 2015).

29. U.S. Senate, Committee on Armed Services, "Hearing to Receive Testimony on U.S. Central Command . . ." (March 26, 2015).

30. Bill Roggio, "U.S. Claims 10,000 Islamic State Fighters Killed Since Start of Air Campaign," Long War Journal (June 3, 2015).

31. Jessica Stern and J. M. Berger, "ISIS and the Foreign Fighter Phenomenon," The Atlantic (March 8, 2015).

32. Among the forces fighting against ISIS, the Peshmerga probably rated as most willing and most capable. Yet arming and assisting the Kurds, widely

suspected of seeking to create a fully sovereign Kurdish state, necessarily alarmed other important allies in the region such as Turkey. The United States found itself obliged to walk a fine line. Rukmini Callimachi, "Inside Syria: Kurds Roll Back ISIS, but Alliances Are Strained," *The New York Times* (August 10, 2015).

33. Helene Cooper and Eric Schmitt, "ISIS Official Killed in U.S. Raid in Syria, Pentagon Says," *The New York Times* (May 16, 2015).

34. "Combined Forces Air Component Commander, 2010–2015 Airpower Statistics" (May 31, 2015).

35. "Department of Defense Press Briefing with General Weidley via Teleconference from Southwest Asia" (May 15, 2015).

36. "McCain: 'Black Flag of ISIS' Flies Where Soldiers Died" (May 25, 2015), 12news.com/story/news/politics/2015/05/25/mccain-isis-ramadi -memorial-day/27933069/, accessed July 5, 2015.

37. Frederick W. Kagan and Kimberly Kagan, "The Fall of Ramadi Was Avoidable," *The Washington Post* (May 18, 2015).

38. "U.S. Policy in Iraq and Syria" (May 21, 2015), c-span.org/video/?326186-1 /hearing-us-policy-iraq-syria, accessed July 6, 2015.

39. Theodore Schleifer, "Lindsey Graham Calls for 10,000 U.S. Troops in Iraq," CNN.com (May 18, 2015).

40. Emmarie Huetteman, "U.S. Defense Secretary Blames Iraqi Forces for ISIS Victory in Ramadi," *The New York Times* (May 24, 2015).

41. Mark Thompson, "Pentagon Rhetoric About Ramadi's Fall Risks U.S. Credibility," *Time* (May 25, 2015).

42. Kristina Wong, "Pentagon Sending 2,000 Anti-Tank Weapons to Iraq," *The Hill* (May 21, 2015).

43. "Statement by the Press Secretary on Additional U.S. Steps in the Counter-ISIL Effort" (June 10, 2015).

44. For a cogent exploration of the potential benefits of rapprochement with Iran, see Flynt Leverett and Hillary Mann Leverett, *Going to Tehran* (New York, 2013). For an example of the anxieties induced by that very prospect, see the review of that book by Roya Hakakian appearing in *The Wall Street Journal* on March 1, 2013.

45. Ed O'Keefe and Joby Warrick, "Weapons Prove Iranian Role in Iraq, U.S. Says," *The Washington Post* (July 5, 2011).

46. David E. Sanger, "Obama Order Sped Up Wave of Cyberattacks Against Iran," *The New York Times* (June 1, 2012). For a book-length account, see Kim Zetter, *Countdown to Zero Day* (New York, 2014).

47. Tom LoBianco and Sophie Tatum, "GOP 2016 Hopefuls Slam Iran Deal," *CNN Politics* (July 14, 2015); Burgess Everett, "Ted Cruz's Iran Doomsday," *Politico* (July 21, 2015); Eric Bradner, "Huckabee: Obama Marching Israel to 'Door of the Oven,'" *CNN Politics* (July 26, 2015).

48. Isabel Kershner, "Iran Deal Denounced by Netanyahu as 'Historic Mistake,'" *The New York Times* (July 14, 2015).

49. Max Boot, "The Dawn of the Iranian Empire," *Commentary* (July 14, 2015).

50. For a concise description of Iran's response to ISIS, see Dina Esfandiary and Ariane Tabatabai, "Iran's ISIS Policy," *International Affairs* 91 (January 2015), 1–15.

51. "Joint Chief General Martin Dempsey Testimony to the Senate Armed Services Committee" (September 16, 2014), youtube.com/watch?v= Yp7XDLXGLGg, accessed July 12, 2015.

52. "Department of Defense Press Briefing by Secretary Hagel and General Dempsey in the Pentagon Briefing Room" (August 21, 2014).

18. Generational War

1. PPS 23, "Review of Current Trends, U.S. Foreign Policy" (February 24, 1948).

2. "World Population by Country," worldometers.info/world-population/; "List of Countries by Distribution of Wealth," en.wikipedia.org/wiki/List _of_countries_by_distribution_of_wealth, both accessed July 8, 2015.

3. Melvyn P. Leffler, *A Preponderance of Power* (Stanford, 1992).

4. "Defense Planning Guidance, FY 1994–1999" (February 29, 1992).

5. *The National Military Strategy of the United States, 2015* (June 2015), 3.

6. General Stanley McChrystal, who presided over Zarqawi's assassination via two 500-pound bombs in June 2006, later wrote that the killing had come "too late." More to the point, Zarqawi's elimination, however justified and psychologically satisfying, was largely beside the point. Much the same can be said of the others once occupying a place on America's most wanted list. McChrystal, *My Share of the Task*, 234.

INDEX

Page numbers in *italics* refer to maps.

PHOTO: © DALE ROBBINS / MOYERS & COMPANY

Andrew J. Bacevich grew up in Indiana, graduated from West Point and Princeton, served in the army, became an academic, and is now a writer. He is the author, coauthor, or editor of a dozen books, among them *American Empire, The New American Militarism, The Limits of Power, Washington Rules, Breach of Trust,* and *America's War for the Greater Middle East.* He lives in Walpole, Massachusetts.